The Influence of Air Power
upon History

The
Influence
of Air Power
upon History

Walter J. Boyne

Pen & Sword
AVIATION

This 2nd edition first published in Great Britain in 2005 by
PEN & SWORD AVIATION
an imprint of
Pen & Sword Books Limited
47 Church Street
Barnsley
South Yorkshire
S70 2AS

ISBN 1 84415 199 9

First edition published in 2003
by the Pelican Publishing Company, Inc, Louisiana, USA

Printed and bound in Great Britain by
CPI UK

Pen & Sword Books Ltd incorporates the imprints of
Pen & Sword Aviation, Pen & Sword Maritime, Pen & Sword Military,
Wharncliffe Local History, Pen & Sword Select,
Pen & Sword Military Classics and Leo Cooper.

For a complete list of Pen & Sword titles please contact:
PEN & SWORD BOOKS LIMITED
47 Church Street, Barnsley, South Yorkshire, S70 2AS, England.
E-mail: enquiries@pen-and-sword.co.uk
Website: www.pen-and-sword.co.uk

This book is dedicated to the airmen and airwomen of all nations.

Contents

Acknowledgments

Writing this book has been a great pleasure, and I am indebted to the many people who made it possible. It is only fitting that the first persons to be acknowledged are Kenneth S. Giniger, who suggested that the book be written, and Dr. Milburn Calhoun, of Pelican Publishing, who undertook to publish it. My fine agent, Jacques de Spoelberch, collaborated with these two men to work out the contractual details.

In the research and writing, I turned to many colleagues for information, analysis, and ideas. I am grateful for the many valuable suggestions made by Dr. William F. Trimble in his thorough review of the manuscript; he gamely endured my many writing gaffes with patience and good humor. Auburn University doctoral candidate Bert Frandsen also reviewed the entire manuscript and gave me many insightful tips. Dr. Phillip Meilinger sent me much valuable material, for which I am most grateful. Dr. W. David Lewis also pointed me to some excellent resources. Dr. William M. Leary was very helpful.

I sent many of the chapters to specialists in the field, and to authors and experts such as Gregory Alegi, August Blume, Warren Bodie, Peter Bowers, Donald Caldwell, Howard Fisher, George Mellinger, Stéphane Nicolaou, Lon Nordeen, Lee Payne, James Streckfuss, Guillaume de Syon, Spencer Tucker, George Watson, and Mark Witzel. All were most responsive, providing many excellent suggestions for correcting my sins of omission and commission. Philip Handleman took time from his busy schedule to review the manuscript; his insight, as always, was invaluable. Wally Meeks not only made his usual good suggestions, he also provided some of the most valuable research material. Richard de Angelis, Susan Fischer, and David Rezelman all contributed material via *Air Warfare: An International Encyclopedia.*

To everyone, my thanks; if I have forgotten anyone, please forgive me, and know that I am grateful, if forgetful.

Introduction

It was with no little trepidation that I chose to use a title so closely matching that of one of the most important military books of its time, Alfred Thayer Mahan's *Influence of Sea Power upon History, 1660-1783*. As the following pages will reveal, it is not my intent directly to compare Mahan's ideas on sea power with ideas on air power, nor to make obvious every parallel that could be inferred from reading both books.

Instead, the present work is intended to look into the development of air-power philosophy over its history by examining the theory and practice of air power as demonstrated not only in war, but also in politics, diplomacy, technology, and mass culture. To do so necessarily involves recounting the history of air power on a selective basis, choosing as examples historic events that demonstrate the influence of air power—or in some instances, the failure of air power—to influence events.

There is a considerable body of literature on air power, much of which is centered on arguments as to whether air power is or is not *decisive* in warfare. These arguments will be examined on their merit, but the principal thrust of the book is implicit in its title, that is, the *influence* of air power on history. From a surprisingly well organized if comparatively small beginning in the early days when balloons defined air power, this influence has grown from being considerable in World War I to tremendously important in World War II and thereafter. The concept of whether or not air power was or was not decisive in any particular situation will be dealt with as required, but it is important to repeat that the *influence* of air power extends far beyond war or the threat of war. I believe the reader will find that the influence of air power has in many instances been far more important than any question of its decisiveness in battle, for it has affected the direction of national policies, the growth of industries, and perhaps most important, the rapid advance of technology, even in times of peace.

This is fortunate, for questions about both the influence and the decisiveness of air power were never more important than today, when the world is faced with an entirely new kind of terrorist-driven war-making, with new kinds of enemies, shadowy groups of warped individuals who murder in the guise of religion. These new enemies have converted their weakness in numbers and arms into the terror of an especially depraved concept of "asymmetric warfare" in which the killing of innocents of any nation is substituted for meeting the warriors of an enemy state in battle. Neither air power advocates nor naysayers ever anticipated the sheer perversity of the terrorists' attacks, from bombing kindergartens to crashing highjacked airliners into buildings to the threat of using weapons of mass destruction in cities around the world.

These challenges will be met in the future, just as other new challenges of conventional or unconventional threats were met in the past. As a single example, the British responded to the totally new threat presented by Zeppelins and bomber aircraft during World War I, which, as we will see, brought terror to the populace and changes in force disposition to the military. Then, one war later, the British used many of the ideas developed in that early response to ward off what time and usage had converted to the conventional German bombing attack during World War II. These ideas included the use of early warning systems, a ground observer corps, audio direction finding (that was replaced by radar direction finding), and a centralized command and control of defensive air power.

Turning for the time being from this ultimate horror, it should be noted that this book also focuses extensively on the influence of personalities on air power, and thus their influence on history. There were marvelously gifted leaders in sea warfare, from before Nelson until after Nimitz, but there have been relatively few evangelists of sea power. The reason, perhaps, was that sea power was so much a given that it took a Mahan to reveal the full measure of its importance. Advocates of air power, in contrast, had to struggle to get their ideas across, often choosing a message so stridently optimistic that their credibility was inevitably lost. There emerged many forceful, articulate, and, it must be said, widely divergent personalities, attempting both to define and direct air power. This came about in part because practitioners of air power by their very nature are forceful individuals and in part because the technology of air power changed so swiftly over time.

These personalities received widespread notice because there was a powerful factor abetting the influence of air power on history. This was the chronological coincidence of aviation, motion pictures, radio, and the growth in the influence of the press—the media as it is called today. Fictional concepts of air power predated the Wright brothers' first flights in 1903, but more serious expressions on the use of air power began to be heard after Louis Blériot's famous 1909 flight across the English Channel, a flight that told the world England was no longer an island. Over the course of the next half-century, ideas on air power and its use received a wide reception because people in general were vastly more informed about air power than their predecessors had been about sea power.

Indeed, they were often "too well informed" because air power became a tool and a target of intensive propaganda efforts. It was the case after World War I that people of democratic nations were conditioned to believe in the efficacy of the enemy air forces and to depreciate the effectiveness of their own air services. In contrast, people in totalitarian countries were led to believe that their air forces were invincible, while those of potential enemies were inferior. Fortunately, during World War II, both sets of beliefs proved to be incorrect.

Another factor in the greater influence of air power was that for many nations, particularly those in Europe, air power was endowed with an urgency that differed from the time-honored concepts of sea power. For the most part, the influence of sea power was perceived directly only by the sailors engaged in battle. The effects of the exercise of sea power might be felt later (and even disastrously, as in the case of the blockade of Germany in World War I), but they were rarely immediate, and usually experienced only if shells actually rained down on a coastal city in a raid or in some gunboat diplomatic action. In contrast, air power from the very earliest days presented an immediate, perceivable, and intimidating personal threat to individual citizens in their homes, beginning with the tentative but indiscriminate bombing of Venice as early as 1849. The citizens of London, Paris, and German frontier cities experienced aerial bombardment during World War I. The terrible bombing raids of

World War II gave the term "home front" a new and terrible meaning for much of the world. The continental United States did not face these threats until the advent of the Cold War, and (except for trivial Japanese pinpricks from submarine-borne aircraft and balloon-borne bombs) was spared an actual attack until the September 11, 2001, terrorist assaults on the World Trade Center and the Pentagon. America's previous freedom from attack heightened the horror of September 11. It, and subsequent acts of terrorism, impinged on the consciousness of the American public in an unprecedented way.

The measurably greater influence of air power on public opinion, as compared to sea power, was in large part the result of the coincidence of new media technologies with the dawn of aviation. The first commercial film projector appeared in England in 1896 at London's Alhambra Theatre, the start of a burgeoning interest in film as entertainment. This was just four years before the Wright brothers began their aerial experiments, and seven years before their first successful flight on December 17, 1903. By 1909, the two inventions, flight and motion pictures, had coincided at Centocelle, near Rome. There, on April 24, Wilbur Wright carried a Universal newsreel cameraman to make the first motion picture footage ever recorded in flight. There were no such things as "residuals" in those days, a misfortune for the photographer, for the film has been shown thousands of times since, often being represented as the first flight at Kitty Hawk.

For the next several decades, the importance of film to air power— and vice versa—grew rapidly, especially after the introduction of sound newsreels in 1927. The sight and sound of Lindbergh's Ryan NYP *Spirit of St. Louis* bumping along the ground in its takeoff from Long Island's Roosevelt Field electrified the world and helped start an explosive expansion in aviation. The newsreel became the medium by which the horrors of aerial warfare would become universally known as it recorded the tragic effect of bombing upon Guernica, Rotterdam, London, Hamburg, Tokyo, and hundreds of other cities.

Nor were newsreels the only place in which air power and film were mixed. Their mutual ties were demonstrated artistically in the same year as Lindbergh's flight in the first motion picture to win an Oscar, William Wellman's *Wings*. All over the world, the feature motion picture became a medium for advancing the cause of air power—or warning of its effects. Among these films, the 1935 British epic *Things to Come,* based on the H. G. Wells novel, warned of the effects of air power and of weapons of mass destruction. In contrast, the 1941 American film *I Wanted Wings,* a rendition of Beirne Lay's book, was one of the most effective recruiting films of all time.

Newspapers were, for most of the century, of primary importance in forming public opinion. The grip of newspapers on the public imagination was enhanced by the aggressive editorializing typified by the Hearst publications and a combination of technical advances such as halftone photographs and typesetting machines. Flying was still a new and dangerous occupation, and almost any flight—and certainly every crash—received full coverage. Newspapers also adopted flying as a statement, with competing publishers using aircraft to transport reporters or to bring back the first photographs of a major event, such as a heavyweight championship fight.

In a relatively brief time, radio equaled then surpassed the importance of newspapers in the expansion of airpower's influence. While the existence of electromagnetic radio waves was first known in 1860, it was not until 1904 that voice transmission was demonstrated. By 1925, however, there were six hundred broadcast stations, and a booming industry in radios. Like the newsreel, radio fastened on each new aviation event with unbridled enthusiasm. By the 1930s, the voices of such stars as Charles Lindbergh or Amelia Earhart were as familiar (and as similar) as their faces. Perhaps the best-remembered single incident combining an aviation subject, newsreel film, and radio occurred on May 6, 1937, when the famed German Zeppelin *Hindenburg* exploded and crashed at Lakehurst, New Jersey, its death throes recorded indelibly in the broadcast words of reporter Herb Morrison. More ominously, Joseph Goebbels used the airwaves with remarkable skill to foster the impression of a mighty German Luftwaffe.

And while television came relatively late in the history of aviation, it has had a greater effect than all the other media combined for it was soon able to present events in real time. The whole world witnessed the arrival of Neil Armstrong on the moon and the return of the *Voyager* from its round-the-world flight. The world was able to watch tragic events as well, such as the bombing in Vietnam, the crash of the Concorde, or the terrorists' attacks on the World Trade Center. Television reinforces the greater power of its color images with the endless repetition of the events being covered. A radio message, once broadcast, was gone forever; a newspaper, once read, was discarded. But the public's demand for twenty-four hours of news, seven days a week meant that the television screen became a bottomless maw demanding to be continually filled with images. As a result, channels must now relentlessly repeat the material they have gathered, particularly the horror-du-jour. A curious phenomenon of this endless repetition on television is that when people can no longer stand the current rehash, they often turn to documentary channels to review the history of past achievements or past horrors.

This confluence of very diverse technologies—mass newspaper coverage, film, radio, and television—provided individual advocates of air power with the mechanisms needed to reach out to the general public, and they seized them early on. The new media bestowed a degree of prominence and influence upon these aviation proponents that was unavailable to their counterparts in the early days of naval and other military developments. While there were of course many famous military heroes throughout history who received widespread fame, the work of the comparatively few military philosophers was appreciated almost exclusively by professionals. They had little or no effect upon public opinion, and this may be said to be true of Mahan himself. As influential as he was in the services and even the governments of many nations, and despite the fact that his writings did appear in contemporary magazines and newspapers, he was not widely read or appreciated by the general public. In marked contrast, many of the most influential practitioners of air power had powerful personalities that resonated in the media, none more so than the United States' famous brigadier general William ("Billy") Mitchell, of whom much more will be discussed later.

Mahan's book dealt with a relatively short 123-year period of naval warfare, one that was not characterized by great change in technology or tactics. The ships, as complex and difficult to handle as they were, remained wooden and wind-driven over the period, equipped with muzzle-loading cannons of much the same range and firepower. The tactics used by the Dutch fleet against the French and English at the battle of Southwold Bay on June 7, 1672, were not substantially different from those used by the Spanish against the English almost 125 years later at the Battle of St. Vincent—they were just better executed.

In the less than a hundred years of heavier-than-air warfare, however, technology and tactics have changed continuously and drastically, generating a constant flow of new equipment used in new ways.

The rapid advance of technology has made it difficult for the philosophers of air power to keep up with the practitioners.

Nowhere has this phenomenon been more evident than in the campaign against terrorists in Afghanistan. Western air-power practitioners were confronted with a perverse demonstration of asymmetric warfare. Small bands of terrorists, hiding in unmarked caves in the Afghan wilderness, were still able to conduct their own offensive operations through sleeper surrogates in the Western homelands.

The direct response exercised in so many past conflicts was suddenly no longer applicable, for there were no substantial enemy concentrations to target. Air-power leaders had to devise new tactics on the spot, without the advantage of a philosopher's foresight and with the logistician's nightmare: war conducted without proper bases. New responses had to be developed, and air power had to be applied in new ways, including the incongruous execution of compassionate missions simultaneously with a systematic air assault.

No such incongruity had ever occurred in sea warfare, even though sea power antedates air power by many centuries. Despite this difference, this book will cover a longer period of time than Mahan's choice of 1660 to 1783. For editorial purposes, the beginning of air power in 1783, the last year that Mahan covers, is covered in an appendix. That was the year that gave the balloon to the world, and while there is a general awareness that balloons were used in battle as early as 1792, few people realize how well organized and how effective the early balloon services were. In a similar way, the use of balloons in the American Civil War is well known, but the extent of that use, and the systematic way in which it was developed, is often overlooked.

Before examining the history and effect of balloons and other subsequent instruments of air power, it is necessary to define air power, and its modern equivalent "aerospace" power. First of all, air power must be understood to be different from (although a part of) the concepts of air superiority and air supremacy. Air superiority means the ability to deny the enemy the use of its own air space, while allowing the "friendly" force the ability to use that space to accomplish its tasks. If air superiority is absolute, and extends over all of the enemy's territory at all times, it can be redefined as "air supremacy." This is the sought-after condition, for with it the military operations of other vital land and sea forces can proceed without impediment from the air.

In contrast, air power is the ability to conduct military, commercial, or humanitarian operations at a chosen place, but not necessarily at all places nor at all times. This distinction recognizes that while two nations' air forces may be vastly different in power, the less powerful nation may still be able to conduct meaningful air operations at certain times and places and thus still possess air power, even if to a limited degree. This was demonstrated on several occasions during World War II, as when Jimmy Doolittle was able to deliver a surprise raid on Tokyo in 1942, or when the battered German Luftwaffe was able to conduct a strong (if futile) attack on January 1, 1945, against Allied airfields in Holland, Belgium, and France. (There were many parallels to this situation in sea power, as in the War of 1812, when the presence of the modest United States Navy was perceived as a tremendous threat because of its proximity to Britain's New World markets.) As a result, the end goal in most modern conflict is the complete eradication of enemy air power and the establishment of air supremacy, permitting the free use of air power, as in the Persian Gulf War, the Balkans, and Afghanistan.

Air power might be termed "aerospace power" when (as is most often the case currently) it is exercised in or through space by means of intercontinental ballistic missiles, or via the medium of space assets, such as navigation, communication, meteorological, or intelligence satellites. In this book, the term air power is intended to mean both air and aerospace power.

Both air power and aerospace power are made up of military and civil components. The military and uniformed components of the aerospace power of the United States, for example, include the United States Air Force, and the aircraft and missile-operating components of the Army, Navy, Marine Corps, and Coast Guard. The civil components include all of the elements of the entire nation, including its leadership, industry, natural resources, and general population.

Modern air power is so replete with the most advanced technology that the average citizen is amazed at the degree of expertise and achievement associated with it. Yet this has been a fundamental condition of air power all through history, from balloons to the remarkable use of air power in the very first days of World War I.

The Influence of Air Power
upon History

Chapter One

Fledgling Wings

The world which rocked with excitement at the invention of the balloon in 1783 would find the nineteenth and twentieth centuries filled with far more sophisticated lighter-than-air (LTA) and heavier-than-air (HTA) craft vehicles, each one successively more capable.

The latter would soon prove to have far more military potential than balloons (of which a concise history can be found in the appendix) or airships, but would face similar problems in development and in gaining acceptance by military leaders. Progress in aeroplanes, as they were known in the early days of heavier-than-air flight, was far more rapid than that of LTA types, thanks to their inherent greater utility. Aircraft, as they became known, revolutionized warfare, although the fact was not fully accepted at first. The first instances in which air power had influence on history were direct and decisive military intervention on the battlefield. The second, less obvious effect was that aviation revolutionized industry with its demand for precision production and with the continual introduction of new and complex systems to make aircraft more effective. This industrial revolution would have profound effects upon the world's economy by increasing productivity even as it increased quality of manufacture.

The aircraft revolution from the beginning carried the seed of a problem that was not recognized for decades, and that was the heavy support the employment of aircraft required, both in the military and in industry. No previous weapon, not even the dreadnoughts that precipitated the naval shipbuilding race before World War I, had required such a large ratio of support to combatant personnel, nor such a huge industry to support it.

Continued Lighter-Than-Air Progress

While the basic systems of the hydrogen balloon had been provided in the very earliest days of ballooning by Professor Jacques Alexandre César Charles, the necessary components to create a balloon that could be flown under power against the wind and steered in a desired course came much later, as did the term to describe such a conveyance, "dirigible." Dirigibles were subject to continuous improvement, a process that goes on to this day.

The first practical airship was conceived of in 1785 by General Jean-Baptiste Marie Meusnier, but was not built because there was no adequate power plant. Several people pursued the basic Meusnier idea, but Henri Giffard was the most successful, flying his airship from the Paris Hippodrome on September 24, 1852. Essentially a 144-foot-long, football-shaped envelope filled with hydrogen, Giffard's dirigible was powered by a three-horsepower steam engine that enabled it to achieve a speed of six miles per hour. Giffard, who at the age of twenty-four had invented the injector used in all steam engines of the time, piloted his craft from a small open basket suspended beneath the envelope. After a second dirigible of his design crashed, he turned to ballooning again, creating an 883,000-cubic-foot monster that was the largest hydrogen balloon ever built and a great success at the 1878 Paris World's Fair.[1]

The dangerous combination of a coal-burning steam engine and a hydrogen-filled envelope was evident to all, and alternatives were sought. Things were somewhat simplified when coal gas for inflating the envelope became more generally available, and later, when the internal combustion engine came into general use.

These two innovations were first exploited by Paul Haenlein. In 1872, Haenlein's large 1872 airship cleverly ran an early internal combustion engine on gas from the envelope rather than carrying a separate fuel supply. The 164-foot-long envelope held 85,000 cubic feet of coal gas, which had only about one-half the lifting power of hydrogen. Haenlein's dirigible was not completely successful, but it pointed the way to the future.

The next notable attempt was made by a veteran of balloon flights during the siege of Paris, Gaston Tissandier, and his brother, Albert. Their airship was only ninety-two feet long, but was filled with hydrogen, giving it ample lift. Their choice of electric power was a mistake, however, for the Siemens electric motor they selected had only one-and-one-half horsepower, and could drive the dirigible at only three miles per hour.

It was fitting that the first successful dirigible would come from the old Aérostier's headquarters at Châlais-Meudon near Paris, where, in 1877, the Central Military Installation for Ballooning had been created, the first of the great government-sponsored aeronautical laboratories, like those at Farnborough in England and McCook Field in the United States. Created by the portly Lieutenant Colonel Charles Renard and Captain Arthur Krebs, the dirigible *La France* lifted off from Châlais-Meudon on August 9, 1884. It flew for twenty-three minutes in a great circle, averaging about fourteen miles per hour. It was the first time that an airship had been able to make a controlled flight with a return to its starting point. The 165-foot-long *La France* was inflated with 66,000 cubic feet of hydrogen, and was powered by an eight-horsepower electric motor weighing 220 pounds. These were energized by a special installation of 1,500 pounds of chlorochromic batteries designed by Renard. Krebs had designed the motor, which delivered one horsepower for each 215 pounds of power plant.

The great breakthrough for airships came with the introduction of Gottlieb Daimler's internal combustion engine, which had a much better power-to-weight ratio, producing one horsepower for each eighty-eight pounds of power plant. Unfortunately, imprudent engineering started German airship development off with the same sort of bang with which it ended when the *Hindenburg* exploded in 1937.

No less a personage than Kaiser Wilhelm had taken an interest in the development of airships, and he ordered the Royal Prussian Aerial Navigation Department to assist Dr. Karl Woelfert in testing his Daimler-powered dirigible, the *Deutschland*. Unfortunately, Woelfert had installed the engine too close to the envelope. He and his mechanic, Robert Knabe, had made three flights before taking off from Tempelhof Field in Berlin on June 14, 1897. As the dirigible reached about 2,500 feet, vented hydrogen was ignited by the engine's open-flame ignition system. The *Deutschland* blew up, killing both crew members. This tragedy—and many subsequent ones—did not diminish German interest in the airship, however.

Airships: Popular and Professional

Two aristocrats now emerged upon the scene. One, Alberto Santos-Dumont, was to popularize dirigible flight in a series of personal vehicles. The other, Count Ferdinand von Zeppelin, was to create gigantic airships which would win the heart of his people, establish the first commercial air service in the world, and create a fleet of combat-capable Zeppelins which would conduct the world's first strategic bombing campaign.

Santos-Dumont was a wealthy Brazilian whose indulgent father sent him at the age of eighteen to Paris to be educated, providing $500,000 to ensure that it was a liberal education. Although small in stature and somewhat reserved in personality, Santos-Dumont became a popular figure in French society. He had a serious side, however, and was dedicated to the idea of flight. No dilettante, he learned the lighter-than-air business in more than a hundred balloon flights.

The young Brazilian designed and had built a series of airships tailored to his size and taste. His first was eighty-two and one-half feet long, and was capable of lifting only 450 pounds with its 6,345 cubic feet of hydrogen. But that was enough to get the 110-pound Santos-Dumont and his two-cylinder De Dion three-and-one-half-horsepower internal combustion engine airborne, albeit briefly.

Santos-Dumont went on to construct nine more dirigibles, and flew them himself, above, and on one occasion, into, the rooftops of Paris. The crash took place with his No. 5, and left the gallant Santos-Dumont to be rescued from a lightwell of the Trocadero Hotel, to the joy of his adoring Parisian audience. It was his No. 9 that gained him the most fame, however, for it was a personal runabout that he used to cruise the boulevards, dropping in on his favorite spots for a drink or dinner and parking his airship on the sidewalks as casually as modern Parisians do their Citroëns.

Increasingly fascinated with heavier-than-air flight, however, Santos-Dumont would soon lead Europe in that field as well.

There were others who advanced the idea of the dirigible, including: Paul and Pierre Lebaudy, who created the first semi-rigid aircraft; Thomas Baldwin, who followed Santos-Dumont's design lead; and Walter Wellman, whose adventures in the large dirigible *America* were thrilling but never quite successful.

In marked contrast, Count von Zeppelin never contemplated using his dirigibles as a personal vehicle or for adventurous stunts. He intended them from the start to be used commercially for profit and militarily as a weapon.

The first Zeppelin was far grander than any previous dirigible, for it was 416 feet long and carried 399,000 cubic feet of hydrogen. The hydrogen did not fill the envelope of the *Luftschiff Zeppelin* (Airship Zeppelin) LZ-1, as he called it, but instead was retained in seventeen gas bags within the aluminum, fabric-covered framework. Two sixteen-horsepower Daimler internal combustion engines drove four propellers. Horizontal control was provided by rudders, while vertical control was provided by a sliding weight.

First flown on July 2, 1900, the LZ-1 had a top speed of about seventeen miles per hour. Unfortunately, the LZ-1 encountered difficulties on all of its three flights, and no one offered to purchase it. The Zeppelin firm was out of funds, and the LZ-1 was broken up and sold for scrap.

Zeppelin persevered, and by 1905, a second aircraft, the LZ-2, was ready, only to be damaged when it was launched. Repaired, it flew again on January 17, 1906, crashing in a violent storm. With government backing, Zeppelin created the LZ-3, which met with some initial success, and attracted widespread popular backing.

The Count and his company were learning with each new Zeppelin, and by LZ-4 they had created a 446-foot-long airship with 530,000 cubic feet of gas, and capable of lifting more than 10,000 pounds of crew, passengers, fuel, and cargo. This was, at last, a practical airship, and Germany began to become very partial to Zeppelins, so much so that when a storm wrecked LZ-4, there was a spontaneous outpouring of sympathy and six million marks in contributions. More important, the German Army agreed to acquire two airships, for an additional 2.5 million marks. This began a long and ill-fated relationship between the German military and the Zeppelin, one which sustained the Zeppelin factory, but which cost Germany a great deal of resources that it could ill afford.

The Zeppelin firm was well and truly launched, and despite a continuing series of crashes, in the coming years it would operate a highly successful passenger airship line, Deutsche Luftschiffahrts-Aktien-Gesellschaft (German Airship Transport Company). Usually called Delag for short, the company began operations on November 16, 1909, only to encounter difficulty with three more crashes. It was sustained by German Army financing, in return for which the company trained military airship crews. This military/industrial support enabled Zeppelin to persevere. He retained the admiration and affection of the German public so that by 1911 he could put LZ-10 in service as the *Schwaben*. The following year, three more Zeppelins joined the Delag fleet, including the *Viktoria Luise, Hansa,* and *Sachsen*. The airline flew more than 100,000 miles, carrying 37,500 passengers, and despite several crashes, had no fatalities.

In the meantime, both the Imperial German Army and Navy were acquiring Zeppelins that were presumed to have a formidable military air-power capability, and these would have a definite influence on history.

The Heavier-Than-Air Flying Machine

The internal combustion engine also paved the way for the first flying machine. Unlike the dirigible, the heavier-than-air flying machine proved to be an insoluble problem to everyone but the inimitable Wright brothers of Dayton, Ohio. Orville and Wilbur Wright were self-taught engineers who did not approach flying as scientists seeking basic principles, but as practical men intent on solving the problems of flight. The two men, acting almost as if their personalities were fused, systematically went from an interest in the possibility of flight in 1899 to the successful first flight on December 17, 1903. At that moment in time, they were at least ten years ahead of all possible competitors in the world, including some who had been working on the problem for decades.

There were people who would hotly dispute this fact in 1903, and some people today would still dispute the claim. There are societies that in all honest belief carry the banner for many of these individuals, claiming that this one or that one flew before the Wright brothers did. As a result, the following straightforward paragraphs will perhaps offend those who wish to believe that others had achieved powered, man-carrying flight, or were very close to doing so, prior to the Wrights' success on December 17, 1903.

The hard facts are, however, that no one, not Clement Ader, Alexander Graham Bell, Octave Chanute, Captain Ferdinand Ferber, Lawrence Hargrave, Augustus Herring, Samuel Pierpont Langley, Otto Lilienthal, Hiram Maxim, John Montgomery, Gustave Whitehead, or anyone else had a development line going which approached that of the Wrights, or which could have led in a reasonable time to a controllable, man-carrying aircraft.

This statement seems harsh, but detailed examination of each of these would-be first-flighters reveals just how deficient their approach and their apparatus were. Ader's machines, which had received more than 500,000 francs ($100,000) in government financing, were immensely complicated and uncontrollable, and worse, shrouded in fraudulent claims that were later exposed. Bell believed that a flying machine should have the inherent stability to be found in kites, and specialized in intricate tetrahedral multi-cell kites that flew well on a cable, but led nowhere. Chanute acted as information central, gathering information from all over the world, and trying different ideas as they came to him on an almost random basis. He did well in recording and disseminating the actions of others, and created a successful biplane glider. However, he failed to develop a systematic program of his own. Perhaps his greatest failure was his inability to understand what the Wrights were doing, even though he visited them often and observed their activities. Chanute, for all his engineering background and immense knowledge of the aeronautical scene, never grasped that the Wrights had seen and solved the problem of flight in three dimensions. The French enthusiast Ferber was at best an inept copycat, also unable to see the heart of the Wright idea even after studying it, and strangely and sadly incapable of quality craftsmanship. His finished machines looked like a schoolboy's drawing of the Wright glider. The Australian Hargrave might have been the best of the lot, but he was a kite-flyer, tied to antiquated ideas. Herring was bright and ambitious, perhaps the most able of all except for Lilienthal and the Wrights. Unfortunately he was a schemer, claiming ideas that were not his own, more prone to borrow ideas than to create them, and given to achieving his business goals by fraudulent claims to patents he did not own. Langley was the most culpable of all, a man of science who systematically ignored the scientific approach, and was content to scale up what was essentially a model airplane into a design that had no provision for control, was not stressed for either its catapult launch or flight, had a bizarre launch mechanism, and made no provision for landing. Langley topped himself by entrusting this impossible concatenation of anomalies to a Charles Manly who had created a brilliant engine for him. The problem was that Manly had never flown before, not even a single gliding flight. Manly had no means of controlling the Aerodrome, as Langley called it, and because there was no provision for alighting, was condemned to be submerged immediately upon landing. Fortunately, two crashes yielded no manslaughter charges.

Lilienthal was the most important of this group, and did contribute the concept of a hang glider, controllable by shifting the weight of the pilot. Yet this method placed an inherent limitation on the size and weight of his craft, and ultimately resulted in the crash that killed him. Lilienthal also contributed a great deal of data, not all of it accurate, but a starting point.

It does not get any better. Hiram Maxim, father of the famous machine gun that bore his name and an immensely wealthy industrialist, built a huge machine with a powerful engine and absolutely no means of controlling it if it happened to get airborne. San Jose's favorite son, John Montgomery, made very dubious and unsubstantiated claims about gliding flight, then sent another man and himself to their deaths in gliders that were demonstrably not airworthy. Gustave Whitehead made fanciful claims that could never be corroborated about an aircraft of dubious strength and lift that had one mysterious engine for ground run, and another mysterious engine for flight.

Other than Lilienthal's efforts, with their useful, if flawed data tables, only one lasting contribution to aviation was made by all of these experimenters, the two-surface (biplane) glider of Chanute. Nothing useful to aviation was ever developed from any of the other efforts of these experimenters who, despite all claims, were never in any way meaningful competitors to the Wright brothers. And it must be remembered that these were the most credible of the Wrights' competitors. There were many others who were simply laughable poseurs who wished to sell stock to a gullible public. Still others were sincere eccentrics, totally incapable of creating a flying machine, but still able to garner publicity.

Yet having said this, it should be stated emphatically that all of these men, from Ader to Whitehead and including the poseurs and eccentrics, should be applauded for the attempts they made, for they contributed to the spirit of the age, and made the world conscious of the possibility of flight.

The two brothers from Dayton were smart enough to recognize just how far ahead of the pack they were. They knew how difficult were the problems that they had solved, and how often that a solution came by a chance insight that might under other circumstances never have occurred, and would probably never occur again. Their experience told them that others, less systematic than they, and perhaps less gifted as well, would take years to cover the same ground.

The Wrights' approach was simple. They believed that previous experimenters had proved that a fixed-wing flying machine could glide, just as birds soar without beating their wings. They also believed that lightweight engines of sufficient power would be available to power the flying machine. They differed from all other experimenters in two basic beliefs, however, and these were crucial to their success. The first of these was that flying was a three-dimensional problem, and that the flying machine should not be inherently stable, but should be controlled about all three of its axes by the movement of control surfaces—not by shifting the center of gravity. They also understood that the pilot of a flying machine would have to learn to fly by moving control surfaces to direct his course and altitude, and that this would take much practice.

Many inventors moved from one configuration to another. Chanute, for example, was equally interested in experimenting with his multiple-wing *Katydid*, his two-surface hang glider, his Lilienthal-type machine or, Edward Huffaker's bizarre cardboard glider. In contrast, the Wrights preferred to solve one problem at a time, building upon past successes. All of their machines had a deep family resemblance. As a result, they moved swiftly from a kite in 1899 to a fairly successful glider in 1900. Their 1901 glider was less successful, and drove them almost to despair, even as it led them to the solutions that would create the highly successful 1902 glider. From there it was but two giant steps—the design and creation of an engine and the propellers—to powered flight in 1903.

The 1903 Wright Flyer is a classic example of designing to a point with economy and finesse. The Wright brothers calculated exactly how much lift would be required to raise the machine and a pilot into the air, and then designed and built wings that would provide that lift—plus a little more as a margin for error. The wings had a span of forty feet four inches and a chord (width) of six feet six inches, providing 510 square feet of wing area. They calculated that they would require an engine of at least eight horsepower to propel the aircraft forward against the wind, and were delighted when the one they themselves designed and built (with the assistance of Charles Taylor) delivered twelve, giving them another very measured margin of safety. The biggest engineering challenge was the propellers, for there was no existing data from which to work. They had presumed that there would be a great deal of information on the design of marine propellers from which they could extrapolate data. There was not. Then, intuitively seeing the propeller as a rotating wing, they created a marvelously efficient design that delivered, within 1 percent, the thrust they calculated they needed. The finished aircraft weighed 605 pounds, to which had to be added the 140-pound weight of the pilot, both Orville and Wilbur weighing about the same.

The Wrights were also extremely practical and economic in their approach, having spent only about $1,000 on their experimentation by the time of their successful first flights. Professor Langley had spent about $73,000 on his Great Aerodrome, of which a large percentage, perhaps as much as $20,000, had gone into the houseboat and catapult system he had devised to sling it into the air. The launching system did not work properly, or at least Langley claimed that it did not. The Wrights' launching mechanism consisted of some two-by-four boards laid end-to-end and three bicycle wheel hubs, with a total cost of four dollars. It worked beautifully. The difference in approach really sums up the difference between the Wrights and Langley as aircraft designers, i.e., a successful launch system for four dollars, versus an unsuccessful one for $20,000.

Designing and building a machine to their own remarkably exact specifications was not enough; it was also necessary to be able to fly it. Fortunately, both Orville and Wilbur had made hundreds of glider flights in the essentially similar glider of 1902 and had taught themselves how to fly. It was an unimaginably important asset that, surprisingly, none of their competitors had considered necessary.

The degree of the Wrights' skill was evident in the fact that they did in fact make four successful flights in the face of high winds on December 17, 1903, the first of 120 feet and the last of 852 feet. No one else in the world could have actually flown the skittish Wright Flyer, for no one else had practiced so much nor knew it so well. Ironically, there is considerable question whether a well-trained modern pilot could fly an exact replica of the Flyer, so demanding are its control requirements. (The question may be answered by the time this book is published, for exacting reproductions of the Kitty Hawk Flyer are being built, and a comprehensive attempt is being made to learn to fly it via the use of gliders and simulators.)

The Wright brothers' conviction that they were ten years ahead of all competitors would prove ultimately to be their undoing, for things change. They would continue to improve their product and extend their lead over everyone through 1905, when they created the first practical airplane in history. Incredibly, the Wrights themselves elected not to fly again from October 1905 to May 1908, concerned that someone might see the flights and steal their secrets from them.

But time, personality, and events would work against them, and as word of their achievements leaked out to a largely disbelieving public, competitors began to gain on them.

The Wrights were extremely, perhaps obsessively, secretive, but Wilbur had published two articles and given two important lectures on their work. The Wrights had discussed their project extensively with Octave Chanute, who also published articles that included material on the Wrights, and had, with colleagues, visited the Wrights at Kitty Hawk. Their 1904 and 1905 aircraft had been seen in flight at Huffman Prairie, the flying field near Dayton that they used after 1903. A sketch of the 1905 Wright Flyer was published in *L'Auto* in Paris on December 24, 1905.[2] The sketch clearly showed the front biplane elevator, the hip cradle in which the pilot lay, the skid undercarriage, the yoke and rail system for launching, the shape and placement of the two pusher propellers, and the double rear rudder.

This body of knowledge allowed European imitators to expand on their own efforts, buoyed by the knowledge that flight was indeed possible, aware of the general configuration of the Wright Flyer, and relieved that pursuing flight could no longer be considered a foolish, impossible endeavor—the Wrights had flown! There were some, of course, who insisted that the Wrights were poseurs who had never really flown at all.

Rivals sprang up both in Europe and in the United States and Canada. France, which had been first with the balloon and the dirigible, had long demanded that it must be first with a flying machine, and the voluble patriots of the Aéro-Club de France as well as the editor of *L'Aérophile* cried for action. In response, Henri Deutsch de la Meurthe and Ernest Archdeacon established prizes so that the "homeland of Montgolfier" (the father of ballooning, see the appendix) would not be disgraced by having a foreigner be the first to create a flying machine.

Paradoxically, the French copied the ideas implicit in the Wright Flyer with the same zeal with which they condemned the Wrights as "liars not flyers," insisting that the Wrights had never actually flown. But it was not until October 23, 1906, after months of testing, that the redoubtable balloonist, Santos-Dumont, hopped his strange-looking No. 14-bis into the air in Paris to win the Archdeacon Cup for a flight of more than twenty-five meters. The actual distance was about sixty meters, and it was no more than a powered leap into the air. The little Brazilian did better on November 12, 1906, however, making a flight of 772 feet—substantially more than a hop, and an effort that sent shock waves of enthusiasm throughout France.

The greatest threat to the Wright brothers' primacy came from Canada, however, where the great Alexander Graham Bell had gathered four young men of talent into a consortium called the Aerial Experiment Association (AEA), whose stated purpose was "To Get Into The Air." Founded on September 30, 1907, the organization was funded by $20,000 put up by Mrs. Bell. The four men included John Alexander Douglas McCurdy, who would become the first man to fly in Canada; Frederic W. ("Casey") Baldwin, who would always be confused with the balloonist Tom Baldwin; First Lieutenant Thomas Selfridge, a man who knew the ways of the military bureaucracy sufficiently well to get himself posted to the AEA; and Glenn Hammond Curtiss, who, like the Wrights, had owned a bicycle shop, but had moved on to building lightweight engines for motorcycles and then began building his own brand of motorcycle. His capability with powerful lightweight engines and his manufacturing experience more than compensated for the fact that he was the only one of the four without a college degree.

It was a powerful group, handicapped only slightly by Bell's persistence in pursuing the tetrahedral kite as a flying machine. With some chutzpah, members of the AEA wrote to the Wright brothers for information on their flying experience. The Wrights replied with general information on their patents and the papers they had published. The Wrights did not consider the AEA a commercial threat, believing it to be a research agency, as it was under the auspices of

Alexander Graham Bell. Nothing could have been further from the truth.

By early 1908, the AEA had developed its first aircraft, the *Red Wing,* which closely followed Wright practice in that it was a pusher (propeller facing the rear) biplane with a "horizontal rudder" in front and a vertical rudder in the rear. The *Red Wing* had no means of roll control and crashed on its first flight, which covered almost 320 feet. The *White Wing* that followed (the name deriving from the color of the cloth with which the wings were covered) was almost identical to the *Red Wing,* but had two small ailerons mounted on the upper wings, the first attempt made to sidestep the Wright patent for three-axes control. The *White Wing* flew on May 17, and while not up to the Wright standard of design or construction, was flyable, nonetheless, and the AEA was "in the air."

Glenn Hammond Curtiss altered the picture forever on June 21, 1908, at his namesake hometown in Hammondsport, New York, with three successful flights in his *June Bug.* (The name was whimsically selected to acknowledge the myriad "June bugs" that infested Hammondsport and its vineyards that year.) His aircraft still echoed the Wright formula but was powered by an engine of his own design, directly driving the pusher propeller. It also was equipped with a wheeled tricycle undercarriage, and wing-tip ailerons. In it, Curtiss would win the prestigious Scientific American Trophy on July 4, generating tremendous publicity and serving notice to the Wrights that they had a formidable competitor. The AEA, making free use of the knowledge gained from observing the Wright efforts, had caught up, not in ten years but in less than one.

Curtiss traded on his success by offering aircraft for sale commercially. The Wrights responded with the first of many lawsuits, a process of litigation that would drain them of creative effort.

The two brothers from Dayton had always hoped to sell their aircraft to the United States government, naively hoping that as a weapon it would make war impossible because there could no longer be surprises on the battlefield. However, when the U.S. government persisted in refusing to buy, they were forced to attempt to sell it to a foreign government.

Several factors worked against such a sale. The first was the uncompromising standards of the Wrights, who for reasons of secrecy, would not agree to show, much less demonstrate, their aircraft prior to having a signed contract in hand. They did not demand any money prior to such a demonstration, but they expected potential buyers, including such notoriously difficult clients as the British and French armies, to sign a contract for purchase, sight unseen. In the United States, the War Department was still smarting over the bad publicity it had received for the $50,000 it had advanced Langley. In Europe, no minister wished to go to his government and explain that he was buying an American product sight unseen, when it seemed probable that a native product would be developed soon.

The impasse was not resolved until Congressional pressure and common sense intervened, and the Wrights (and forty others!) accepted an invitation to compete for a Signal Corps requirement for an aircraft that would be "capable of carrying two men and sufficient fuel supplies for a flight of 125 miles, with a speed of at least 40 miles per hour. It must remain aloft for at least one hour and land without damage." The request for proposal also stipulated that the flying machine be designed so that an intelligent man could become proficient in its use in a reasonable length of time, and that it be so constructed as to be able to be transported on a standard Army wagon.

In the event, none of the other competitors actually appeared, and Orville had the parade ground at Fort Myer, Virginia, to himself. The demonstration of the 1908 Wright Military Flyer was a success up to the point that a crash occurred on September 17, injuring Orville severely, and killing First Lieutenant Thomas Selfridge. The first man to die in the crash of a powered aircraft, Selfridge was a member of the team evaluating the aircraft. His presence had irritated Orville, for as a founding member of the AEA, he was a rival to the Wrights. Fortunately, Orville had demonstrated the aircraft so well that there was no doubt that the Army wished to buy it, and the terms of the contract were extended so that the Wrights could rebuild the aircraft and demonstrate it the following year.

Industrial competition and espionage began early in the aviation business, and perhaps could be said to have commenced on September 23, when AEA members Bell, McCurdy, and Baldwin came to serve as Selfridge's pallbearers, and paid a courtesy call on Orville, in the Fort Myer hospital. They were turned away, but then took the time to pay another courtesy call, this one on the balloon hangar where the wrecked Military Flyer was awaiting shipment back to Dayton. There they persuaded the sergeant on guard to admit them, and Bell was seen to make a measurement of the wings.

While Orville was meeting first success and then disaster at Fort Myer, Wilbur was dazzling Europe with his remarkable, record-setting flights in France. The aviation world was now well aware of the general outline of the Wright design, and could infer from observation how the controls operated. Some, as with Louis Blériot, simply adopted the Wright method of control without a by-your-leave. Others, including Curtiss, sought alternate means of lateral control, such as ailerons, to avoid the Wright patent.

An important by-product of the Wrights' convincing demonstrations that the aircraft had indeed arrived was the establishment of associations that lobbied for air power. In 1908, there sprang up the Air Fleet League in Germany and the National Air League in France, while the Aerial League of the British Empire was formed in 1909.[3] Similar organizations blossomed in Italy and Russia. These organizations corresponded to very popular institutions which promoted the respective interests of their national navies, and which had both political and economic influence. The new organizations were better funded, and far more active, than the typical national "aero clubs." The formation of such groups, linked to the large numbers of young military officers who were intrigued by flying, would help explain why the governments of those nations should spend so much money on the development of air power before the First World War. Further, it became the common practice for members of these organizations to pledge their services and their aircraft to the military, if war came. In return, they were given a stipend for maintaining their aircraft, and were paid a per diem for every day they served in practice maneuvers.

Orville returned to Fort Myer to complete the tests in 1909, resulting in the sale of the first military aircraft in the world, the Wright Military Flyer to the U.S. government. (The Wright Military Flyer still exists, and may be seen in Washington, D.C., at the National Air and Space Museum of the Smithsonian Institution.)

But it was now obvious that the Wright brothers' once unassailable lead had begun to evaporate in 1908 when their brilliant performances served to inspire competitors. By 1909 it was badly eroded, although the Wrights were still sufficiently ahead of all competition to conclude a series of business deals that would make them rich. It should be noted that the progress in aviation was so rapid, and governments were so nationalistic, that had the Wrights waited another year they probably would not have been able to reach the profitable arrangements they had made in Great Britain, France, and Germany.

Unfortunately for the Wrights, many of their competitors would draw on much of what they had done and significantly improve upon it. The great air shows at Rheims, Los Angeles, and elsewhere provided prizes as additional incentive. The Wright brothers' aerodynamic lead began to fade, and by 1911 their aircraft were not just obsolete compared to some foreign and domestic products, they were coming (correctly) to be regarded as inherently unsafe because of the large number of fatal accidents in which they were involved.

First Military Uses of the Airplane

In almost every country there were adventuresome military personnel who wanted to demonstrate the utility of the aircraft in warfare. As soon as aircraft performance would permit carrying a few more pounds than just those of the pilot and his observer, attempts were made to install and use weapons. On January 19, 1910, the famous Louis Paulhan flew an airplane over a field in Los Angeles, and U.S. Army Lieutenant Paul Beck dropped dummy bombs. On June 9, the French lieutenant (later general) Philippe Féquant made the first photo-reconnaissance flight. On August 20, Lieutenant Jacob E. Fickel, U.S. Army, fired a rifle from his Curtiss biplane at a target in Sheepshead Bay, New York. On November 14, Eugene Ely launched naval aviation with a flight in his Curtiss pusher from the USS *Birmingham*. He would make the first landing on January 18, 1911, on the USS *Pennsylvania*. On March 3, the famed Wright exhibition pilot, Phil O. Parmelee, and his passenger, the future Chief of the United States Army Air Corps, Lieutenant Benjamin ("Bennie") Foulois, used both radio and carrier pigeons to communicate with the ground from their Curtiss biplane. On June 2, 1912, Lieutenant Thomas DeWitt Milling flew a Wright Model B biplane, with Captain Charles de Forest Chandler firing a machine gun from the air. Both men became famous U.S. Air Service aviators. Similar indications of progress, not so well reported, took place in the military services of other countries.

Yet long before Chandler and Milling had fired a shot, the aircraft had gone to war, and in a significant way. On September 28, 1911, Lieutenant Colonel Vittorio Cordero di Montezemolo ordered the Aviation Unit of the Italian Specialist Battalion Headquarters to send an "air fleet" to Libya (then a part of the Ottoman Empire) as a part of a Special Army Corps "to protect Italian commercial interests." It was, in fact, essentially an invasion of Turkish territory. Five pilots, under the command of Captain Carlo Piazza of the Eighth Field Artillery, were assigned to the task. They brought with them nine aircraft, including two Blériots, three Nieuports, two Farmans, and two of the dove-like Etrichs. All of these aircraft were equipped with fifty-horsepower Gnome rotary engines, and each one was provided its own hangar. More aircraft were dispatched later, along with a lighter-than-air unit consisting of four observation balloons and two airships.

The Italian invasion of Libya began on October 2, 1911, and had gone off relatively smoothly, but the transportation of the air fleet could not be undertaken until after the fall of Tripoli. Thus it was not until October 21 that Captain Piazza could report that his aircraft was ready for action.

The world's first combat flight took place on October 23, when the Commander of the Air Fleet, Captain Piazza, took off at 6:19 A.M. to reconnoiter Turkish positions. In a sixty-one minute flight, he discovered several enemy encampments. While he was airborne, Captain Riccardo Moizo also took off to observe enemy dispositions. By this time, military observations from balloons had been conducted for many years, but this was the first military observation from an aircraft. The difference was enormous, for while the balloon was tethered (normally), the aircraft was free to fly wherever the pilot wished, allowing him to observe many more hundreds of square miles than the balloon observer could do.

There followed a yearlong series of sorties under extremely dangerous conditions. The French Military Air Force had signaled the Italian headquarters that it had found daytime flights over the desert to be particularly hazardous because of the air currents and the possibility of sandstorms. Nonetheless, the Italian air fleet carried on with surprising effectiveness for an initial effort at full-scale warfare.

On October 26, Captain Moizo's Nieuport became the first aircraft ever to sustain combat damage. He had discovered a large encampment of some six thousand men, and came under rifle fire, suffering three hits in the wing, but no major damage.

It fell to Second Lieutenant Giulio Gavotti to make the world's first combat bombing sortie, flying an Etrich Taube. He carried four of the grenade-like "Cipelli" bombs, each weighing about four pounds and roughly the size of a grapefruit. He dropped one on a Turkish position at Ain Zara, and three on the Oasis of Jagiura. Gavotti's raid was widely reported, and had great effect upon the thinking of airmen in other armies. Another raid, this time by Captain Moizo, resulted in the Turkish government issuing what would become a familiar protest. They stated that bombs had been dropped on a hospital, a claim the Italians investigated and denied.

The tempo of the air campaign was accelerated, with heavier bombs being brought into play. Reconnaissance flights took place every day until weather conditions during December and January made regular sorties difficult.

During the long campaign, there were many other notable firsts, including the first dropping of propaganda leaflets, spotting for artillery, night-bombing and reconnaissance missions, and radio communications that involved no less a person than Guglielmo Marconi himself. The first pilot to be wounded in combat was Captain Carlo Montu, who was struck by a rifle bullet on January 31, 1912, over Tobruk. Sadly, the first pilot to die in combat was Second Lieutenant Piero Manzini, who crashed on August 25, 1912, shortly after takeoff for a photographic reconnaissance mission. The valiant Captain Moizo was forced to land behind enemy lines on September 10, when his Nieuport developed engine trouble. He was the first airplane pilot ever to be taken prisoner, and was not liberated until after the armistice was signed in November 1913.

The successful Italian air campaign received worldwide notice. On August 12, 1912, the *London Times* stated that "no one can have observed the work accomplished by the Italian airplanes at Tripoli without being deeply impressed by the courage and the ability of the Italian pilots and without being convinced of the valuable use of aviation in wartime."[4]

On September 10, 1912, the *Berliner Tageblatt* took a slightly different view, reporting "for now at least, airplanes and airships are not practical used as offensive weapons: they have, however been shown to be very useful for reconnaissance. The Italian Command is always, thanks to aircraft, informed of every displacement of Turkish troops, and knows the exact positions of them. Moreover, following the photographs and relief maps made by the airships and airplanes, it has been possible to compile a map with which to conduct the war."[5]

The Italian air campaign had great effect upon the Italian people, who rejoiced when the principals were showered with decorations, and responded with a flood of poetry, songs, and even a board game celebrating it.

Perhaps the most influential aspect of the Italian campaign was philosophical rather than military, for it fell to Major (General Staff) Giulio Douhet, provisionary battalion commander, to make the full report on the campaign. Douhet had for years been an advocate of air power, writing articles in the service journal *La Preparazione,* but the campaign in Tripoli gave him his first chance to report facts rather than theories, and he made the most of it. His extensive report analyzed the technical and professional considerations that had affected the use of aircraft, and he drew interesting inferences on the preparation of flying personnel, their recruitment and training, as well as the types of aircraft to be procured. He concluded with an organizational proposal that became the structural framework for Italian aviation and industry during the 1914-18 war in Europe.

His experience and his report prepared him to write one of the most influential documents in the development of air power, *Command of the Air.*

Other Conflicts

The First Balkan War of 1912-13 saw Turkey in conflict once again, this time with the Balkan League consisting of Bulgaria, Greece, and Serbia. This was the first international war during which all combatants deployed operational aircraft. While the air war was not integrated as tightly into the ground war as it had been in the Italian campaign in Libya, it was nonetheless influential, coming as it did on the heels of the Italian successes. One of the major contributions, to become so significant in later years, was the export of military aircraft, a business that would come to have significant importance, not only in the balance of payments but also in the political alignment of nations.

Greece had sent six officers to France in 1911, and there purchased aircraft to equip its newly formed air units in the Greek Army and Navy. The Army Aviation Unit was ready for action on October 12, 1912, conducting reconnaissance operations.

Serbia had purchased two German observation balloons in 1909, and in 1912 had sent six people to France for pilot training and to purchase eleven aircraft. Major (later General) Joseph Barès sent two additional French aircraft to Serbia as a goodwill gesture. The Serbia Aviation Command was formed on December 24, 1912, and began conducting operations in March 1913.

The third member of the Balkan League, Bulgaria, had not made formal efforts to obtain training, but instead used French aircraft and French and Russian pilots as mercenaries to do reconnaissance and bombing.

Turkey had established a balloon unit by 1911, and also sent officers to France in 1911 for training. With greater resources than the other three combatant nations, Turkey purchased more than a score of aircraft from France, Great Britain, and Germany, using them, as the others did, primarily for reconnaissance, but also for bombing. The reconnaissance mission was by far the most fruitful, for there were as yet no bomb sights, and few targets that were bombed were hit. Those that were suffered only minor damage because the bombs were so small.

Although the air efforts in the first Balkan War were relatively small, they accurately forecast what might develop on a larger scale in a conflict between major countries, and had a strong effect on the thinking of military leaders in the great European powers and in Russia. This influence was reflected in military budgets and in the surprising growth in the aviation industry in the years prior to 1914.

The Western Hemisphere also saw the application of air power. In 1911, a Native-American pilot, Hector Worden, a Cherokee Indian, was commissioned a captain in the Mexican Army to fly reconnaissance and bombing missions in Blériot XIs against revolutionaries. The following year, the world's first dogfight took place in Mexican skies when two mercenary airmen, Dean Ivan Lamb, flying a Curtiss pusher, engaged Phil Rader in a Christofferson biplane. The men exchanged pistol shots, without doing serious damage, but setting a pattern that would become all too familiar during World War I.

The General Situation in Europe

Each of the major European powers found itself in similar situations, in respect to air power. On the one hand, national governments and the top military leaders did not wish to expend large sums on a new and as yet unproven weapon. The existing competitive demand for battleships, artillery, horses, and so on by their respective arms—and their civil and industrial backers—already strained defense budgets. On the other hand, the growing evidence of the usefulness of aviation, and the growing influence of aviation proponents, including the slowly emerging aviation industry, called for appropriations at some level.

The division in opinion was easier to handle within the military than within the government. The relatively few pro-aviation officers were often regarded as eccentrics who had no idea about career progression. To many professional military officers it was self-evident that only someone who had given up all hope of promotion, or who had a death wish, would sacrifice a comfortable assignment in a crack cavalry or artillery unit for the unknown and extremely hazardous world of aviation. It was more difficult at the political level, for even in the early days, the promise of a large aviation industry was attractive for the very reason that it is today—profits, jobs, and the assignment of contracts to specific areas of the country.

Yet the eccentrics who wanted to be in aviation had a driving passion that could not be denied, and the industry that aviation was giving birth to was attractive to many businessmen and politicians. And there was the matter of national pride. No government wanted to admit to its people that another nation was making faster progress in a new branch of service than it was. When Germany perceived that France had seized the advantage in heavier-than-air craft, and that there was little chance of matching it in the near future, the Germans decided to move forward in the lighter-than-air field as rapidly as possible. Despite many wise protests, the Germans seized upon dirigibles as a primary weapon, one in which Germany already had clear superiority. This lead in lighter-than-air craft was then used for propaganda purposes to counter the French claims, and to satisfy the *amour propre* of the military leaders.

The general popular appreciation of the use of air power in Libya and the Balkans exerted influence on both democratic and totalitarian governments in Europe, and always in the same way. When people with influence and an interest in aviation understood that the general public was aware of the effects of air power, they reached out with programs that enlisted the public's interest and gave it a voice with which to express its opinion to the government.

This created the previously mentioned phenomenon peculiar to Europe—and totally foreign to the United States—the formation of civil associations designed to promote interest in, and more important, raise money for, the air services. The model was the German Flottenverein (Navy League) that was founded in 1898 and grew to have 1.1 million members by 1914. The Navy League's push for German naval equality with Great Britain was an extremely important factor in the great naval rearmament race prior to the First World War, and may be said to have been an important causal issue for that war. Besides raising money to buy dreadnoughts, its jingoistic-anglophobic publications conditioned the German public, not just to the inevitability of war with Great Britain but the desirability of it.[6]

The German Navy League was far larger than any of its aviation counterparts. The corresponding German Air Fleet League had 3,000 members by 1909 and 12,500 by 1912. But aviation was new, and the Air Fleet League often recruited important industrial and political figures and attracted some extremely important people, including Hermann von der Lieth-Thomsen, the architect of Germany's Army Air Service, and his superior, the redoubtable General Erich Ludendorff. The latter, with Field Marshal Paul von Hindenburg, would virtually rule Germany from 1916 on, all the while giving tremendous support to the German Air Force.

In many countries, activist political organizations, such as the German Air Fleet League, were supplemented by more popular movements, e.g., the German National Aviation Fund. Other countries had similar sets of organizations, and these spurred both popular and governmental interest in aviation, doing it with the hard cash of the time. These groundswells of enthusiasm for aviation were led by powerful personalities who focused popular opinion on practical results such as the purchase of aircraft or the training of pilots. Thus in Germany, Prince Heinrich of Prussia was the well-liked figure who led a drive in 1912 that netted the National Aviation Fund 7.2 million marks. These were used to purchase 62 aircraft and trained no less than 162 pilots. In Russia, the Grand Duke Aleksandr Mikhailovich became the royal patron of aviation. (The grand duke, after failing in his attempts to establish a reasonable government in Russia, would in 1916 predict the revolution.[7]) With the

Imperial All-Russian Aero Club he worked both inside the government and with the public to raise funds, buy aircraft, establish flying fields, and train pilots.[8] Similar, if smaller, organizations would be found in Austro-Hungary, Great Britain, and Italy, doing much the same work in much the same way.

Another factor in common among the great nations that would soon be tearing at each other's vitals was the basic similarity of the equipment available to them. While aviation progress had been rapid since 1903, and especially since 1909, it was still quite early in the history of aeronautics, and all nations were more than content just to have their air forces equipped with two-place aircraft for use in reconnaissance. They were stable, slow, and while often unreliable, nonetheless provided that crucial look at "the other side of the hill." There were, in all countries, air-power advocates and prophets who saw the future and knew that it consisted also of bombing aircraft and fighters whose task it was to prevent the enemy from observing and bombing. But, correct in their ideas as they may have been, they were in the minority, for aviation technology had not yet reached a point where their claims could be justified. Indeed, some of the more extravagant claims could not be justified for another thirty years, but the reasonable claims were within only a few years of being proven.

The soon-to-be combatant nations were similar in another way. While all wished to see a strong civilian aircraft industry in their homeland, their military services were determined to control that industry, but beset by conflicting ideas. In each country the military services were concerned that the industry would not build aircraft to meet its requirements, that a few large companies might be in a monopoly position, able to dictate price and schedules, and that many smaller companies would not have the skill or productive capacity to meet demand. Each country established centralized controls, which tended to distort, rather than regularize, industry. It was not until the pressures of war forced wholesale changes that a rationalized industry came into being in France, Germany, and Great Britain. In Russia, not even the pressures of war could overcome the intricate bureaucracy, and despite having excellent designers and builders, including Igor Sikorsky, the Russians were unable to establish an aviation industry comparable to the Western European powers.

One factor was very different among the countries in question, and that was in the capability to produce large numbers of high-quality aircraft engines. It was not yet fully realized that engines were a more difficult engineering challenge than airframes, and developing an engine from concept to production took many years and much investment.

France led the way. Its Gnome, Renault, Clerget, Salmson, and Anzani engines gave it a range of types (rotary, in-line, and radial) and horsepower that no other nation could match. Indeed, France supplied engines, particularly the Gnome, to many nations, including those with which it would soon be at war. Germany was a poor second, with a capability to produce a limited number of good, if heavy, Daimler in-line, water-cooled engines. England, Italy, and Russia relied on France for engines, although all three countries were trying hard to establish an indigenous engine industry.

The aviation engine industry is in fact a metaphor for the early effects of air power on history, for the demands of that industry are many. The entire culture and economy of a country has to bend to accommodate the creation of an engine industry, for it requires a new kind of engineer, new kinds of plants, new standards of machine tools, and new manufacturing, inspection, and testing methods. It also calls forth new materials, new instruments, new standards of quality, new education programs in schools, new sub-contractors—the list goes on and on. If this metaphor is expanded to include aircraft, airfields, flying training, the training of mechanics, and such sciences as meteorology, it quickly becomes obvious how great an effect establishing an aviation industry will have on culture and economy. Deeper analysis will reveal that the effects go further, intruding on agriculture, mining, forestry, transportation, manpower requirements, raw material use, priorities—in short upon almost every aspect of national life.

Nonetheless, in the years prior to 1914, the old order held sway, with aviation receiving a very small percentage of each nation's defense budget. That portion allocated to aviation did grow over the years 1910 to 1913, probably at as great a pace as the infant industry could absorb.

In several countries, there were two important manifestations of the increased regard for military aviation indicated by the growth in spending. The first of these was the formal establishment of an air arm, while the second was the establishment of formal trials to obtain aircraft designed for military use.

Naturally, given its great interest in aviation, France was a leader, establishing on October 22, 1910, a Permanent Inspector of Military Aeronautics to oversee all aspects of aeronautics. A long battle for control of military aeronautics ensued between the artillery and the engineering branches, the former advocating the close control of aircraft by ground units, the latter wishing to establish a more autonomous air arm. The issue was resolved in favor of the artillery, and there was no formal French Air Force established until 1934. The French held a Military Aeroplane Competition in October and November 1911, which attracted thirty-one contenders, of which only nine passed the trial elimination tests.[9]

In Great Britain, the first step was the creation of the Air Battalion of the Royal Engineers on February 28, 1911. This was followed by the establishment of the Royal Flying Corps on April 13, 1912. It had a Naval Wing, a Military Wing and a Central Flying School (ultimately, perhaps the most important constituent.) A Military Airplane Competition was held in August 1912, attracting a wide variety of "aeroplanes" to be evaluated.[10]

Germany's preoccupation with large airships and a bureaucratic standoff had dampened aircraft development. Most of the available funds went for Zeppelins, and when German aircraft manufacturers sought funds for development of aircraft, they were told that the government was interested only in buying already developed aircraft, which hampered formal military trials. In November 1910, the Chief of the Central Staff, Helmuth von Moltke, established an Inspectorate for Aviation and Motor Vehicles to procure aircraft. A Fliegertruppe (Flying Force) was established in October 1912, and its units were completely subservient to the German Army, actually coming under the Railways and Transport Communications Department.[11] Exactly one year later to the day, an Inspectorate of the Flying Force and an Inspectorate of the Airship Service were formed.

When the First World War began on August 3, 1914, the great powers had not yet embraced aviation as an essential part of their armed forces, but nonetheless each had surprising aerial strength.

Chapter Two

Air Power in World War I

The general question of the influence of air power upon history was settled in the first thirty days of World War I. This is a bold statement, given the nature of the subject and the relatively inaccurate reporting made of air power during World War I, but nevertheless, the influence of air power was enormous and rapidly demonstrated for both the Allied and the Central Powers.

Unfortunately, only a few people were perceptive enough to be aware of this influence at the time, for by a curious coincidence the initial effects of air power's influence were muted when Allied and German successes essentially cancelled each other out. As we will see below, the major Allied success occurred on the Western Front. The Germans had some generally unheralded air-power successes also on the Western Front, but scored a tremendous triumph on the Eastern Front, one directly attributed to air power by the architect of the victory, then-General Paul von Hindenburg.

If these first air-power successes had occurred on only one front or the other, the nature of the war and its final outcome might have been very different, and air power might have been seen in a very different light. The successes alluded to were the result of aerial reconnaissance, and struck directly at the heart of the notorious Schlieffen plan (see below) upon which not only German strategy, but in fact, Germany's willingness to go to war, was based.

Before investigating these undeniable aerial achievements, it is necessary to see just how the opposing forces were equipped in those early August days of 1914, for they reflected years of planning and the best hopes of prominent individuals on both sides. Success in the use of air power would, from the very start, depend on a combination of two circumstances: visionary leadership at the top, and capable men at the operational level. Not all nations were equally blessed with these two states of affairs.

By 1914, Germany and France had each expended the equivalent of $26 million on their respective air services. Russia had spent $12 million, while Britain is estimated to have spent about $9 million. The United States was not yet engaged in war, and had spent only about $400,000. (All amounts measured in 1914 dollars.[1]) American spending exceeded only Austria-Hungary, which had expended a little more than $318,000.

The immediate result of these expenditures could be seen in the forces ready to be placed into the field, with the necessary pilots and mechanics to operate them. France began the war with about 140 aircraft apportioned among twenty-one squadrons. There was a general reserve of slightly smaller size, made up in part of civilian aircraft attached for duty. Approximately 220 pilots were on hand.[2]

Britain's Royal Flying Corps had about 180 aircraft of which approximately one-half were unfit for service. There were just over one hundred pilots available to fly the aircraft that were fit. The Royal Naval Air Service had fifty aircraft and about forty pilots.[3]

In the East, Imperial Russia had almost 250 aircraft spread across that great country, along with fourteen dirigibles. Unfortunately, almost all of the aircraft were of foreign manufacture and were well worn, for the Russian system of maintenance was primitive in the extreme. There were two hundred trained pilots (including thirty-six non-commissioned officers) and a hundred observers.[4]

In marked contrast to Russia, Germany had gone to aerial war with the efficiency that characterized its army. Out of a total of perhaps 500 aircraft, it could put 250 first-line machines in the field, with a pilot for each one, along with no less than nine dirigibles. Germany's Austro-Hungarian ally could field just under forty aircraft, but had eighty-five pilots.[5]

In the next few months, each of these countries would learn just how valuable aircraft and trained crews could be, and each would double and redouble its efforts to increase its aerial strength. Unfortunately, none of these countries had any idea of the extraordinary wastage that would be involved, not just in warfare, but in the routine day-to-day operation of their air forces. (The Royal Flying Corps would lose two-thirds of its aircraft in the first eight weeks of the war.) It would take months before the wastage factor would be recognized by the respective governments, and many months after that recognition before provision would be made to resupply aircraft and crews at the necessary rate. Some countries— notably France, Germany, and Britain—would rise to the challenge, and create the mammoth industries and training programs necessary for modern air war. Some would not, lacking either the material resources or the organizational skills to do so.

There were in most countries individuals whose outstanding interest and ability were used to overcome all the obstacles of conventional thinking to put the most effective air force possible into the field. They would be, for the most part, little known and ill rewarded by their countries and usually highly controversial within their own service, but their efforts were essential.

In Britain, there were several leaders of note. Sheer deference must place Winston Churchill's name at the top of the list for his early and consistent support of aviation, which exerted the same strange fascination upon him as did the sound of bullets missing him. Captain Henry Robert Moore Brooke-Popham, among his many achievements, foresaw the future of aerial combat, and procured the Hispano Suiza engine for British aircraft, filling a vital gap.[6] A flamboyant, witty Irishman, Mervyn O'Gorman, founded Great Britain's scientific approach to aeronautics by his brilliant leadership of the Royal Aircraft Factory at Farnborough. His naval counterpart was Captain Murray Sueter, who did for the Royal Naval Air Service what O'Gorman was doing for the Royal Flying Corps. Both men had the great advantage of a small but growing aviation industry in which were to be found such giants as Frank Barnwell, Geoffrey de Havilland, Richard Fairey, Henry Folland, Frederick Handley Page, Frederick W. Lanchester, A. V. Roe, the Short brothers, and young T. O. M. Sopwith, to name but a few. The combination of government leadership in research (although it was often castigated for failed designs and its tendency to keep obsolete aircraft in production) and a vibrant private industry enabled the Royal Flying Corps to grow from its opening strength of some sixty-three aircraft deployed on the continent in August 1914 to become the Royal Air Force with a worldwide strength of 22,650 aircraft by 1918.[7] As an index of just how massive the growth had been, in Britain, the total production for the first ten months of 1918 was 26,685 aircraft and 29,561 engines.[8]

France's preoccupation with the glory of flight, fostered by brilliant airmen and remarkable air shows at Reims and Issy-les-Moulineau, made it receptive to the strong leadership provided by Captain Ferdinand Ferber; General Pierre Roques, future commander of the First Army; Colonel Jean-Baptiste Estienne, who would also be an early advocate for tanks; Eduoard Barres (who organized similar aircraft into squadrons for specific tasks); and Colonel Charles Duval, who masterminded a reorganization of the French aviation industry at a time when such seemed impossible.[9] Like their British counterparts, they could call upon a strong and diversified industry that was not yet rationalized for mass production. These factories were founded and led in large part by the great early French flyers, including Henry Farman, Louis Blériot, Louis Breguet, Alfred de Nieuport, Robert Esnault-Pelterie, and Gabriel Voisin. A silk merchant, financier, and sometime rascal, Armand Deperdussin founded the Société Pour les Appareils Deperdussin, and built record-setting aircraft. After he was arrested for embezzlement, his company's name was changed to the more famous SPAD (Société Anonyme Pour l'Aviation et ses Dérivés). With this foundation, and supported by a magnificent engine industry, the French Air Force would grow from its 140 aircraft in 1914 to more than 13,000 by 1918. French production for the first ten months of 1918 was about 22,000 aircraft and more than 44,000 engines.[10]

German interest in military aviation ran from the very top, from the man who would ultimately be blamed for the failure of the Schlieffen plan, the Chief of the German General Staff, General der Infantrie Helmuth Graf von Moltke himself. (There is some irony in this situation, given that aviation played a great part in the Schlieffen plan's failure.) Von Moltke erred, however, in his belief that the dirigible would be a lethal, first-strike weapon. Despite strong internal resistance to von Moltke's ideas on aviation, the German General Staff nonetheless set about a sensible, systematic approach to establishing an air force, with consideration given for training, supplies, procurement, and all the other elements necessary for any arm of the service. In time, as the war changed from the scheduled six-week victory in France followed by a six-week victory in Russia to the harsh reality of trench warfare on two fronts, von Moltke was succeeded as Chief of the German General Staff first by Field Marshal Erich von Falkenhayn, who would stub his toe at

Verdun. Field Marshal von Hindenburg, with his Quartermaster General, Erich von Ludendorf, next followed Falkenhayn on August 29, 1917. The latter two men had seen air power in action, and in part owed their promotions to it, so they were also strong backers.

Farther down the command chain, three major leaders emerged. Hermann von der Lieth-Thomsen was assigned to oversee developments in military aviation in 1908, and became a champion of German air power. As Chief of Field Aviation he worked toward unification of all of the diverse agencies responsible for training, aircraft procurement, and deployment of flyers into an independent branch of the service. In October 1916, the Air Service (Luftstreitkräfte) was established—as part of the Army—under the command of General Ernst Wilhelm von Hoeppner, with Thomsen as Chief of Staff. The gratitude of Kaiser Wilhelm was so great that both Hoeppner and Thomsen were awarded the Orden Pour le Mérite (the "Blue Max") on April 8, 1917, the only two non-combat airmen to be so honored.[11] Another important figure was Major Wilhelm Siegert, who was the bomber chief at the German High Command. He was a combat pilot who put into action principles he had learned at the front, and, at war's end would provide, in his resignation, a poignant paean to the German air service, predicting the rise of the Luftwaffe in the future.

Germany (as usual) had planned on a short war, and its aircraft industry was not yet mature. Unlike France, where airmen had seemed to spring like dragons' teeth from the ground, the aircraft industry had a labored beginning. The Wright brothers had formed a company in Germany with strong backing from the giants of German industry. Unfortunately, the Wright design was obsolete, and only a few aircraft were sold. When war broke out, there were about a dozen aircraft manufacturers in Germany, including many that would soon become well known, such as Albatros, Aviatik, Fokker, Gotha, Pfalz, Roland, and Rumpler. Other firms shared the German predilection for long, intricate names, so that there were Allgemeine Elektrizitats-Gesellschaft (A.E.G), Lufthfarzeug Gesellschaft (L.F.G), Luft Verkehrs Gesellschaft m.b.H. (L.V.G.), and Deutsche Flugzeug-Werke (D.F.W). These companies did not become as well known outside of Germany, but produced large numbers of excellent observation and training aircraft.

In the course of the war, Germany was hampered by a lack of natural resources and the Allied blockade from expanding its aircraft industry to the extent that the Allies did. It compensated in part for this lack by shaping its strategy and tactics to accommodate the disparity in numbers. This compensation not only affected the outcome of World War I, it also influenced political and military events during both the postwar period and in World War II. Nonetheless, the Germans were able to increase production steadily during the war, so that the Luftstreitkräfte remained a formidable opponent until the last day of the war, when there were more than 11,000 serviceable aircraft in Germany. Production for the first ten months of 1918 was small by Allied standards, with 14,356 aircraft and 16,412 engines delivered.[12]

The level of effort for the Imperial Russian Air Service (IRAS) was much lower, with only about 5,000 aircraft being produced by the time power passed from the Romanovs to the Bolsheviks in 1917, and of these, no more than 1,000 were at the front. There simply had not been the leadership nor the industrial base to compete with German efforts.[13] However, the IRAS did pioneer strategic bombardment with the first four-engine bombers, all variants of the Igor Sikorsky's Il'ya Muromets.

The plight of Germany's ally, the Austro-Hungarian empire, was captured by the brilliant scientist Theodore von Karman, when he said, "Aircraft were not valued as highly as a horse. As a cavalry officer expressed it, an aircraft required too many troops for maintenance and one could not use it in poor weather."[14] The Austro-Hungarian aviation industry supplied about 5,200 aircraft and 4,900 engines during World War I, with the remainder of its forces being supplied by Germany.[15]

To recapitulate, as war broke out in Europe in 1914, the air armies of the contending sides were approximately equal in size and capability. Neither the United States nor Italy were belligerents as yet, so their forces (or lack of them) can be discounted.

The First Major Instances of Air Power's Significant Influence

In the summer of 1914, the great nations of Europe were prosperous, enjoying a host of new scientific and engineering discoveries, and their people, for the most part, were able to enjoy life as never before. The imbecilic manner in which they stumbled from this relative state of grace into the horrible killing of what they termed "the Great War" has been told many times, most notably in Barbara Tuchman's *The Guns of August.*

There were tensions, of course. Germany believed itself to be denied the rights of other great nations and feared that it was being surrounded by its enemies. France still suffered from the humiliation of 1870 and longed for revenge. Britain felt that its industrial, trade, and naval supremacy was threatened by Germany. Austria-Hungary was subject to rebellious calls for independence from many of its member-states, a situation exacerbated by Russia's diplomatic efforts in its own interests. Italy was just beginning to develop a sense of itself as a nation and wished to reassert its power in the Mediterranean world. The years of repression combined with its defeat at the hands of Japan had brought Russia nearer to revolution than ever, and the management of both the state and the armed forces was conducted in a haphazard manner.

Tradition, treaties, and misunderstandings had resulted in an alliance that bound France and Russia together, with Great Britain closely aligned. Germany and the Austro-Hungarian Empire were allied, and believed that they were supported both by Italy and the Ottoman Empire.

Each of the nations maintained large military forces, best suited to their needs, with Great Britain depending upon its navy, and a very small army. The French Army was large, well trained, and bursting with *élan,* that joyous insanity which caused young men in bright uniforms to fling themselves forward time and again against murderous machine-gun fire. Having learned from Trafalgar onward that it could never compete with the British fleet, France maintained a navy adequate only to protect its interests in the Mediterranean and to show the flag elsewhere. Italy had a relatively small army but enjoyed an extensive reserve system. Its navy was intended to be a match for Austro-Hungarian forces. Germany had a huge army, and its navy had been built up in the costly naval arms race with Great Britain. The Austro-Hungarian Army was relatively large, but, like the rest of the empire, lacked cohesion. Its member states were more concerned about their own ethnic and religious interests than the welfare of the empire. The Austro-Hungarian Army was forced to depend upon two hundred common military words and phrases as the central communication bridge among the many languages in use. Its navy, in contrast, was more homogeneous, surprisingly large and relatively well equipped. Imperial Russia had a huge army and a navy humbled by its bitter experience in the war with Japan.

Germany's fear of encirclement had led it to what became infamous in history, the Schlieffen plan. Created by General Albert von Schlieffen, Chief of the German General Staff from 1891 to 1905, the plan was predicated upon the absolute necessity of avoiding a two-front war by swiftly defeating France, and then turning the German forces eastward against Russia. The key to this swift reversal of fronts lay in the superb German railroad network. Unfortunately, the intricacy of the railroad system, and its susceptibility to gross disorganization if its schedules were interfered with, meant to the German General Staff that once the order for mobilization was given, the process could not be halted for any reason. They believed that if the mobilization was halted, the resulting sheer chaos in the railroads would render Germany vulnerable to enemy attack.

The Schlieffen plan called for sending no fewer than forty-one German army corps in four lines against France, with ten divisions left in the east as a holding force against the Russians. The principal attack was to sweep through Belgium, Holland, and Luxembourg in a wide arc that would break through French lines and sweep to the Swiss frontier, ending the war in six weeks. The German railroad system would then move the victorious troops across Germany to meet and defeat the Russians. Little resistance was expected from either the Dutch or the Belgians. Inexplicably, Great Britain was not expected to intervene, and the Russians were supposed to take at least six weeks, and perhaps longer, to mobilize.

Von Schlieffen continued to modify the plan even after his retirement, bringing it to (in his judgment) "perfection" by 1912. Unfortunately for the plan, he was succeeded as Chief of Staff by Helmuth von Moltke. The new chief lacked the stomach to carry out the plan as devised, particularly when, in the very first days of the war, things began to go awry. In fairness, it should be noted that von Moltke was facing a different military and political situation than von Schlieffen had counted on. That von Moltke, the German General Staff, and Germany itself continued to rely on the Schlieffen plan despite those changes is one of the great mysteries of history.

Von Moltke has received blame for the failure of the Schlieffen plan because he excluded Holland from the invasion, weakened the right wing of the German Army before the battle began, and then took further strength from it when the Russians mobilized quickly and invaded East Prussia. Where Count von Schlieffen had called for 90 percent of German strength to be placed in the right wing, even if this meant that Alsace-Lorraine would be temporarily lost, von Moltke allocated only 60 percent.

Yet it is fair to say that the ultimate reason for the failure of the Schlieffen plan was the reconnaissance reports made by both British and French aviators, and which, almost miraculously, were not only believed but acted upon by Allied commanders. They came about in the following manner.

The first step in the long chain of events leading to the stalemate on the Western Front took place on August 4, 1914, when five of the eight squadrons of the Royal Flying Corps (RFC) were mobilized. The other three squadrons existed on paper only.

Of the five mobilized, No. 2, 3, 4, and 5 Squadrons were to go to France with forty aircraft, to be followed by the Aircraft Park. This was a reserve made up of twenty-four aircraft in packing cases and the attendant equipment. The mobilization orders allowed three days to get ready, a fourth day to fly to Dover, and then two more days to fly to France. All the equipment of the squadrons was to follow the aircraft by sea. A great deal of planning had been done, so that the date and time that each aircraft, each train, and each ship would depart was already scheduled. The exact equipment to be brought along was specified, from the number of spanners (wrenches) per squadron to the pilot's personal equipment, which included a revolver, field glasses, a spare pair of goggles, a water bottle, a small stove, biscuits, cold meat, a piece of chocolate, and soup cubes.[16]

Tragedy struck immediately, when an aircraft of No. 3 Squadron crashed on takeoff on its way to Dover. On August 13, the remainder of the force—thirty-nine aircraft—left for France. The aircraft making this cross-Channel journey into combat were broadly representative of Allied aircraft in the first months of the war. At the time, only the French had begun to recognize the logistical importance of having aircraft of a similar type assigned to one unit. The British mixed their aircraft types freely within a squadron, often at the preference of the pilots, many of whom had paid for their own flight training and thus had a particular interest in a certain type of air-craft. In regard to their training, a pilot with twenty-five hours would have been considered an experienced veteran.

The British took 63 aircraft to France (including the 24 in the packing crates) and left 116 behind, of which only about 20 were fly-able. The 63 included Blériots, Henry Farmans, Avros, and B.E.8s.

The RFC Blériot XI-2s were very similar to the aircraft that Louis Blériot had flown across the English Channel in 1909, and which had served the Italians in Libya. Most were two-seat aircraft powered by the eighty-horsepower Gnome rotary engine. All had the basic Blériot monoplane configuration, with the uncovered aft fuselage and large "knee-action" undercarriage. The Blériots used wing-warping just as the Wrights had used on their Flyers, and fully loaded, weighed just over nine hundred pounds. There was no fixed armament, but the pilot and/or observer could carry a revolver or a rifle. Top speed was about seventy-five miles per hour, and endurance was from two to three hours.[17]

The designs of Henry Farman were a perfect example of how the French had seized (stolen is perhaps too harsh a word) upon the basic Wright formula, and then proceeded to improve upon it. The Farman F.20s that went to France were two-seat pusher biplanes, equipped with ailerons and powered by the ubiquitous eighty-horse-power Gnome rotary. They mustered a top speed of about sixty-five miles per hour. The great beauty of the Farman was that it lent itself to experimentation, and when fitted with machine guns or bombs, it promptly engaged the enemy.

The first aircraft of British design to be deployed to France was the Royal Aircraft Factory's B.E.8. (The use of "B.E." as a designa-tion was an anomaly that went back to the early days of the Royal Aircraft Factory, when an aircraft designed by Geoffrey de Havilland was designated Blériot Experimental No. 1 [B.E.1] in honor of Louis Blériot. The designation was continued through the B.E.12). Called the Bloater by the RFC, B.E.8 was a rather large two-seat biplane, weighing about two thousand pounds, and capable of a sev-enty-mile-per-hour speed. It could carry up to a hundred pounds of bombs and was used on several early bombing raids. All of the early aircraft were difficult to fly, but the B.E.8 was described as "a nasty contraption" by one of its pilots.[18]

The final type which made the first great journey to France, the

Avro Type E, was similar in most respects to the B.E.8, but had the great honor of being the ancestor of one of the greatest training planes of all time, the Avro 504. The Type E had a maximum speed of only sixty miles per hour and was never employed operationally.

These were hardly formidable machines, and it was fortunate indeed that the enemy aircraft of the period were of about the same size, shape, and capability. Besides not having a sparkling performance, all of these machines were temperamental, difficult to fly, and ill suited for a campaign in the field. It is thus all the more remarkable that the men who flew them were able to achieve so much.

As happened in most of its wars, the British Army began World War I with a long, arduous retreat. The British Expeditionary Force (BEF) consisted of four infantry divisions and one cavalry division. It was positioned near Mons on the left of the seventy-two French divisions that waited for the German onslaught, which had been delayed by the unexpectedly stiff resistance of the Belgian Army—the next part of the Schlieffen plan to go wrong.

On August 19, Captain Philip B. Joubert de la Ferté of No. 3 Squadron and Lieutenant G. W. Mappelbeck of No. 4 Squadron took off on the first aerial reconnaissance of the war, flying a Blériot and a B.E.8, respectively. Nothing was discovered on this flight, or on flights on the next two days. On the twenty-second, however, No. 3 Squadron's Captain L. E. O. Charlton and Lieutenant V. H. N. Wadham discovered that a huge column of the German First Army was passing through Grammont. It was the beginning of a movement by General Alexander von Kluck to initiate the right wheel of the Schlieffen plan. This was the first in a series of key observations that would permit the British and French armies to survive.

Armed with this knowledge, Field Marshal Sir John French, the commander of the BEF, undertook to make a stand at Mons, determined to hold for twenty-four hours to give the French Army, under General Charles Lanrezac, time to avoid Kluck's enveloping maneuver.

There followed the famous series of battles in which the British retreated, day by day, their accurate rifle fire inflicting grievous losses on the Germans and immortalized in the famous book by Captain Walter Bloem, *The Advance from Mons*. During the retreat, the British were hard pressed, lacking food, water, ammunition, and hope; in contrast, the Germans were surprised at the level of

British resistance, but more concerned about their inability to supply sufficient black bread to the troops who hungered for it.[19]

During the British retreat, the Royal Flying Corps flew continuous sorties, reporting the position of the Germans, and suffering several losses. The great coup of the RFC came on August 31. General von Kluck had been ordered to stop his eastward advance that would have carried his First Army north of Paris. Instead, he was ordered to turn in two columns, one to the south and one to the southeast, a route that would, if successful, envelop Paris. This fateful error was immediately observed by Lieutenant A. E. Borton and Captain E. W. Furse of No. 5 Squadron. Two other crews confirmed the sighting. Von Kluck was marching into a cul-de-sac formed by the Ninth French Army on the left, the Sixth French Army on the right, with the French Fifth Army and the British Expeditionary Force at the bottom of the trap.

These were the general dispositions for the initiation of the Battle of the Marne on September 6. That it occurred was due to the fact that Allied airmen had observed the enemy and divined his intentions, and to the more amazing fact that these observations were believed and acted upon by the British and French High Commands. Sir John French wrote in his dispatch of September 7, "I wish particularly to bring to your lordship's notice the admirable work done by the Royal Flying Corps under Sir David Henderson. Their skill, energy and perseverance have been beyond all praise. They have furnished me with the most complete and accurate information which has been of incalculable value in the conduct of operations."[20]

France knew of the Schlieffen plan, but did not believe the Germans had the forces necessary to make it work. The French immediately implemented their notorious Plan XVII, which played directly into the hands of the Germans by thrusting forward into Alsace and Lorraine, giving the German right wing the best possible chance to cut them off. (It was an eerie forecast of Allied efforts in May 1940.) The French had mobilized almost four million men in sixteen days formed into the five French armies in the line. There were thirty-one units, each of six aircraft, and these were apportioned evenly among the five armies, an unfortunate dispersion of forces that would foreshadow problems for the French in World War II when they made the same faulty dispositions with both planes and tanks.

On September 2, none other than Corporal Louis Breguet—scion of the famous watch-making family, engineer, and a prominent aircraft manufacturer—flew a prototype Breguet 13 aircraft on a reconnaissance mission. (Photos of the spindly Breguet 13 reveal that one would have to be a brave man to attempt to fly it at all.) He too discovered the change in movement of von Kluck's forces and relayed this news directly to General Joseph Gallieni, the military governor of Paris. Breguet's report was reinforced by similar information from Lieutenants Prot and Hugel. Gallieni urged the French Commander in Chief, Marshal Joseph Joffre, to join General French in making a stand on the Marne. Gallieni then made the famous (if over-ballyhooed) decision to use Parisian taxicabs to carry troops to the front, reinforcing the newly created French Sixth Army.

As a result of the Battle of the Marne, Paris was saved, and the war was shifted from the swift thrust of the Schlieffen plan to the bloody trench warfare that would scar Europe for the next four years. All German hopes of a quick victory over France disappeared, and it was saddled with its longtime nightmare, a war on two fronts. Air power thus influenced the gigantic conflict that ensued and which would, in turn, influence the shape and substance of air power for all time.

An Air-Power Offset

The results of the early Allied exercise of air power in the form of telling reconnaissance might have had an even greater effect on the outcome of the war if the Germans had not benefited from aerial reconnaissance to the same or greater degree on the Eastern Front. The details of this exercise in air power will be given below, but the point is that if the Germans had not won a large victory on the Russian front, they would have been compelled to draw back even more resources from the already depleted Western Front. This might well have led not to trench warfare but instead to an Allied offensive that might have won the war in 1915.

The Germans had planned to deal with the French in six weeks, and depended upon the Russians to take six weeks or more to mobilize. To Berlin's dismay, the Russian forces were mobilized far more rapidly. The long-planned Russian offensive against Austria was begun on schedule, and on August 9, Grand Duke Nikolai

Nikolaevich decided to move the First and Second Armies in an improvised twin-pronged offensive into East Prussia. In the east, General Pavel Karlovich Rennenkampf's First Army attacked with the objective of overwhelming the weak German Eighth Army left as a blocking force there. Rennenkampf intended to advance to the Vistula River, from which point the route to Berlin would be opened. From the south, the relatively inexperienced General Alexander Samsonov ordered his Second Army, despite its inadequate equipment, to attack the Germans from the rear. Samsonov's ambitious goal was to cross East Prussia all the way to the Baltic and thus isolate and destroy the German Eighth Army. As it happened, Rennenkampf and Samsonov were bitter personal enemies, and this strained relationship may have contributed to their ultimate debacle.

The weight of the attacks panicked the German General Max von Prittwitz, who called for and received reinforcements from von Moltke, thus further weakening the "strong right wing" of the Schlieffen plan. When Prittwitz announced his intention to retreat to the Vistula, however, von Moltke sacked him, replacing him with sixty-seven-year-old General Hindenburg, who was recalled from retirement. His Chief of Staff was the forty-nine-year-old General Erich Ludendorf, who had distinguished himself on the Western Front with the capture of the fortress city of Liège.

German intelligence was greatly assisted by the Russian practice of broadcasting their orders in the clear (i.e., not in code), and information thus gathered was often quickly confirmed by aerial reconnaissance. Between August 29 and 31, aerial reconnaissance discovered the unexpected Russian buildup to the south. On the twenty-ninth, Lieutenants Gottfried Mertens and Ernst Canter were flying a Taube, the birdlike observation aircraft widely used in German service. They landed to report to their Army Corps headquarters, where telephone lines were knocked out. The two flyers were then dispatched on a dream assignment for ambitious young officers. They were to carry their important news directly to Eighth Army headquarters with instructions to report directly to Hindenburg and Ludendorf. The news they brought avoided a German surprise and enabled troops to be moved to exploit a weakness about to be discovered in the Russian dispositions. On the thirtieth, observer Oberleutnant Martin Korner and pilot Leutnant

Hans Hesse noted the isolation of the Russian VI Army Corps, which permitted the encirclement of the Russian Second Army.[21] Airmen also kept close tabs on the slow advance of the Russian First Army so that the Germans could use their forces against the Second Army without undue concern.

The combined result of German radio intelligence and reconnaissance by both aircraft and the Zeppelin L IV enabled General von Hindenburg to win the Battle of Tannenburg, in which Samsonov's Second Army was crushed with a loss of 140,000 men, its commander committing suicide. This victory immediately relieved the pressure for recalling troops from the Western Front, and in fact, allowed troops to be sent from the east to the west as reinforcements. It also catapulted Hindenburg to the forefront of German military leadership, positioning him to become the revered president of Germany during the postwar years and the man who would acquiesce to Adolf Hitler's accession to power as chancellor of Germany.

Hindenburg was quickly promoted to Generaloberst (equivalent of the U.S. four-star general rank). He was lavish in his praise of the aircrews who performed the reconnaissance, telling Major Siegert to tell his airmen "Without airmen, no Tannenberg!" In an interview with an Italian newspaper reporter, Hindenburg expanded on this situation saying, "However, the most remarkable people are my airmen. I cannot begin to tell you the remarkable things they have done on their reconnaissance missions."[22]

It should be noted here that in German crews, the observer was what today would be called the "aircraft commander," while the pilot was essentially a chauffeur. German pilots were often enlisted men, and there are tales of an autocratic Prussian officer dragging his pilot out of the cockpit, throwing him to the ground, and beating him after the pilot was forced to land behind enemy lines. The usual case, however, was that a close bond developed between "Franz and Emil," the comic-strip names adopted for observer and pilot respectively, regardless of rank.

Aircraft were far too primitive to be decisive in battle, but they were extremely influential on both fronts. In both the battles of the Marne and Tannenberg, the High Commands on both sides were aware that a significant new dimension had been added to warfare. Over the next four years, the Germans would become acutely aware of the importance of air power, because it was needed to redress the ever-growing overall advantages in Allied strength. Germany, however, would be increasingly short of the resources required and so would never be able to build an air force equal to the combined strength of those of the Allies. The Allied leaders also appreciated air power, and so much did they foster its growth that their air forces spilled over into other theaters of war, including Italy and Mesopotamia.

The leaders of the Allies and the Central Powers had anticipated neither trench warfare nor the size and complexity of the air forces that trench warfare would require. Within a few months of the outbreak of the war, the fledgling air arms had demonstrated a wide variety of air-power missions, including air-to-air combat, artillery spotting, close air support, covert special operations, mapmaking, night bombing and reconnaissance, photoreconnaissance, propaganda efforts, strategic bombing, tactical bombing, and visual reconnaissance. These efforts were made almost entirely by unspecialized aircraft that had been in service as the war began. By 1918, almost every element of modern air power would be demonstrated or experimented with, including cruise missiles but excluding nuclear warfare and true precision-guided munitions. And by 1918, highly specialized aircraft, developed specifically for one or two distinct missions, would be the rule rather than the exception.

This rapid growth and specialization was necessary to meet and match the developing capabilities of the air forces of each side. Another factor, less obvious, but almost equally important, was that German aircraft had to be even more specialized, to offset the general German shortage of resources. As a single example of this factor, to be further reported on below, the Germans developed close air support aircraft and tactics to a far greater degree than the Allies, to assist their outnumbered ground forces. Their success with these tactics would have profound effect upon German military equipment, training, tactics, strategy, and even diplomacy before and during World War II. The mental set deriving from the successful use of these tactics had a tremendously influential effect upon German expansion in the 1930s.

It will be shown later that almost every one of the wide variety of missions which will be examined here would, at some later date, have profound influence on world history.

Mission Specialization

The most important function of air power during World War I was the gathering of intelligence by visual and photographic means. Ironically, by 1915, just 132 years after the Montgolfier brothers' first flight, trench warfare brought balloons back into prominence despite the invention of the aircraft.

The spherical balloon used for many years was difficult to manage in high winds, its constant movement often nauseating observers to the point of helplessness. In 1896, a German dirigible enthusiast, August von Parseval, introduced the so-called kite balloon, which had an elongated sausage shape and inflated vertical surfaces.[23] The kite balloon was more stable, as it would, like an airborne wind gauge, turn into the wind and remain positioned in that direction.

Initially, the German High Command was so unhappy with the performance of observation balloons that serious consideration was given to discontinuing their use. However, two factors intervened. The first was trench warfare, and the second was the steady growth in the supply of artillery munitions on both sides of the front, which meant that firing became almost constant, especially before an attack. Coincident with these events, the information from the balloon observers began going directly to artillery commanders, who appreciated and used it on the spot. Formerly it had gone to the High Command as "balloon intelligence," and by the time it was transmitted back down to the operators in the field, it was out of date. (The problem has been partially overcome only in recent years with information proceeding from observation platforms to satellites to field commanders in real time. The requirement for security processing still poses delays.)

Balloon strength grew rapidly thereafter from the nine on the Western Front in January 1915 to as many as three hundred on the front by 1918. The Germans continued to improve their balloon designs, using ideas from captured French balloons (see below). The later models were called "Drachens." With up to 35,000 cubic feet of hydrogen, they were able to ascend to 4,000 feet, an altitude from which the observer could see as far as fifteen miles behind enemy lines.[24]

The French had abandoned their tradition of balloons in 1911, but quickly reconstituted their balloon corps with the advent of trench warfare. By October 1914, they had ten balloon companies fielding thirty balloons in service, and from that point on the French balloon industry would grow by leaps and bounds.

Captain Albert Caquot, who was always at the forefront of new developments and would become one of the most important engineers in the history of the French Air Force, made his mark first by improving on the German balloon design with larger vertical surfaces. He also designed a better two-motor winch mounted on a four-wheel-drive truck chassis to haul the balloon up and down. Some four thousand of the Caquot balloons were built during the war, and they were also used by the British and Americans. When some Caquot balloons were torn from their moorings by a storm and drifted over German lines, their features were studied and adopted by the Germans.[25]

Both sides found the balloons to be invaluable for artillery spotting, maintaining contact with advancing troops, and general reconnaissance. They would continue to be used throughout the First World War, and in many smaller conflicts thereafter. The Germans were even able to employ them on quiet sections of the Eastern Front during World War II. Balloons were vulnerable to attack by fighter aircraft, and the advent of accurate long-range artillery made it generally impossible to position balloons at a point from which they could see beyond enemy lines.[26]

The balloon had certain advantages over early reconnaissance aircraft. It could be maintained in one position for long periods of time, and the observers had direct telephone contact with the ground. Balloon observers became expert in their field, knowing the battlefield so well that they could immediately detect a newly dug line of trenches or the shift in the position of a battery. The aircraft moved swiftly over a larger area, but its pilot or observer could not have the same intimate knowledge of the balloon observer. Initially, reports by aircraft were either made verbally at the end of a mission, or written on a message pad and dropped near a headquarters. It was not long, however, until radios became generally available, and then the greater area that the aircraft could cover became important.

The Growth of Aerial Reconnaissance

Airborne radios had been used in limited numbers almost from the start of the war. The sets were primitive in the extreme, and could be used for sending only, as the noise of the aircraft made reception impossible. Communication from the ground was by means of prearranged signals, such as the British Popham panels that used a black cloth as backdrop for white cloths laid out in specified patterns.

On September 24, 1914, at the Battle of the Aisne, Royal Flying Corps crews used wireless telegraphy to direct artillery shoots. Using B.E.2 aircraft, Lieutenants D. S. Lewis and B. T. James directed artillery fire in what became a classic manner. Following is a record of one of their "shoots" on September 24 as recounted in *Per Ardua* by Hillary St. George Saunders:

> 4:02 p.m. A very little short. Fire Fire.
> 4:04 p.m. Fire Again. Fire Again.
> 4:12 p.m. A little short; line o.k.
> 4:15 p.m. Short. Over, over and a little left.
> 4:20 p.m. You were just between two batteries.
> Search two hundred yards each side of your last
> Shot. Range O.K.
> 4:22 p.m. You have them.
> 4:26 p.m. Hit. Hit. Hit.
> 4:32 p.m. About 50 yards short and to the right.
> 4:37 p.m. Your last shot in the middle of three batteries
> in action; search all round within 300 yards of
> your last shot and you have them.
> 4:42 p.m. I am coming home now.[27]

Within six months, the RFC had evolved a new system. It placed the target in the center of an imaginary clock face, with true north at twelve o'clock. A ring of imaginary concentric circles was drawn around the target at intervals of 10, 25, 50, 100, 200, 300, 400, and 500 yards, the circles being lettered Y, Z, A, B, C, D, E, and F, respectively. The pilot conducting the operation would note where incoming shells burst according to the clock and ring position, as in "C3" (i.e., 200 yards from the target and directly east from it). The French continued to use a much simpler system, recording "over," "under," "right," and "left," with the estimate of the distances involved.[28]

The Germans depended upon their superiority in artillery to enable them to maintain a defensive line on the Western Front with relatively few troops. This had been forced upon them by their inability to defeat Russia in the East, and exacerbated by the almost continual requirement to reinforce the Austro-Hungarian forces. Artillery spotting was therefore extremely important to them, and they developed a sophisticated grid system that systematically broke the target area into smaller and smaller squares that permitted target areas to be identified down to the nearest thirty meters.

This brief snapshot of early artillery spotting is important because it contains the nucleus of what became the most important aspect of air activity during World War I, directing artillery fire. The essence of the technique is simple: The observer sees the target, he sees the shells fall, and he "walks" the shells to the target.

The Battle of the Aisne that began on September 13, 1914, was followed by the "race to the sea" in which trenches were constructed on both sides all the way from Switzerland to the coast. During this period, and for several weeks thereafter, the aerial activities on both sides declined sharply because of the heavy losses caused in part by combat, but in the main by accidents and simple wear and tear. Every combatant was forced to realize how few aircraft were available (at one point, the Royal Flying Corps had fewer than ten aircraft ready to fly) and how many more were needed, which began the great industrial buildup of what had been a cottage industry.

As invaluable as the airman's eyes were, it was obvious that aerial cameras were required. Germany, with its fabled optics industry was the best prepared, the Germans possessing more than a hundred aerial cameras when the war began. In France, success once again depended upon an individual in the field. Major Paul Louis Weiller was an observer in a Maurice Farman, and used his own private camera to take pictures. He was immediately distressed when he found that the official French Army maps, prepared by the Army Geographical Service, differed vastly from his photographs.

Weiller created a camera of his own design, with a focal length of 1.3 meters, so, it was said, that his boss, General Charles E. M. ("The Butcher") Mangin could "see some Boches." (Mangin earned his nickname because of his indifference to casualties inflicted on his troops.) The camera provided such extraordinary photographic results that Weiller, over time, was able to sell the idea of a special unit of long-range reconnaissance Breguet XIV aircraft which would photograph the entire front to a depth of one hundred kilometers behind enemy lines every day.

A crew of twenty in a photographic lab developed the photos in a few hours, then submitted them to thirty photo interpreters, each one an expert in his own section of the front, who compared them to the photos of the previous day. They were then submitted directly to General Maxime Weygand, Marshal Ferdinand Foch's Chief of Staff. At war's end, Foch personally decorated Weiller with the Legion of Honor, but urged that his methods remain secret.[29]

All of the opposing armies had similar requirements for long-range reconnaissance. It was a relative term, as in practice it meant flights of no more than thirty-six to sixty miles behind enemy lines, conducted at altitudes up to 20,000 feet or so, and flown at ninety to a hundred miles per hour. On the German side, long-range reconnaissance aircraft came to be highly specialized, as with the German Rumpler C VII Rubilt which appeared late in the war. It employed a 240-horsepower Maybach engine, using an extra high-compression ratio as a crude form of supercharging. The Maybach's full-throttle horsepower could not be used at lower altitudes without causing damage. As altitude increased, however, the reserve horsepower could be called upon to improve performance. The C VII Rubilt could fly at a hundred miles per hour at altitudes as high as 24,000 feet. It routinely operated at 20,000 feet, well above the ceiling of most Allied fighters and out of the range of most antiaircraft fire.[30]

No one could have imagined that fifty years later, with the Lockheed SR-71, "long-range reconnaissance" would mean missions several thousand miles long conducted at three times the speed of sound and at altitudes of 60,000 feet and more.

The Royal Flying Corps had not anticipated the need for cameras, and its airmen often provided their own equipment until the spring of 1915 when a specially designed camera developed by J. T. C. Moore-Brabazon (later Lord Brabazon of Tara) and Lieutenant C. D. M. Campbell was placed into general use. It was a simple box camera, with a five-inch-by-four-inch glass plate, affixed to the side of the aircraft and operated by the observer.[31]

The provision of these cameras made possible the first great exercise in reconnaissance, which took place before the British attack on the German salient at Neuve Chapelle on March 10, 1915.

During the preceding month, Royal Flying Corps crews of No. 2 and No. 3 Squadrons, flying primarily B.E.2s, prepared for the forthcoming attack by photographing the entire German trench system.

The photos were used to make an amazingly detailed map, of which fifteen hundred copies were made and distributed to the British Army units scheduled to go over the top.

In addition to their value in mapping the intricacies of the German defenses, the photos were also used for another military first, the determination of strategic targets to be bombed in conjunction with the attack. German railroad junctions were identified and targeted on the basis of the February photographs. The object of the bombing was to prevent German reinforcements being brought up.

By the end of the Battle of Neuve Chapelle, the capability of observation aircraft had been fully demonstrated. From that point on, there were no radical changes in the exercise of the observation function except that equipment and tactics became increasingly sophisticated.

Both sides began to allocate more and more assets to the reconnaissance function. The Germans began 1915 with a paper strength of 432 observation-type aircraft distributed among seventy-two units. Actual strength was about 215. By March 1918, there were 300 reconnaissance aircraft and 741 artillery observation aircraft in the field, and this despite the extensive buildup of fighter and ground-attack units. Other air forces built up their reconnaissance capability in a similar manner.[32]

It became the practice of both the Allied and the Central powers to separate their reconnaissance units into two distinct groups. Typically fewer aircraft were designated to do long-range reconnaissance, while the bulk of the force was assigned the task of short-range reconnaissance. This included patrolling and photographing the front lines and providing artillery-spotting services.

A third type of observation duty was perhaps the most hazardous, the "contact patrol" initiated by the RFC at Neuve Chapelle, but subsequently used by all the air forces, with the Germans becoming particularly adept at the task. In this work, the aircraft had to fly low enough to identify the front lines (fluid during an attack) and communicate the new positions back to the headquarters staff by dropping message packs. Aircraft on contact patrols were particularly vulnerable to attack from enemy fighters, which had the advantage of altitude. In addition, the pilot was to observe the enemy positions and bring down artillery fire upon targets of opportunity.

Losses were high in this work, because it immediately gave the advantage of height to enemy fighters, and aircraft operating low over the front were subject to everything from rifle fire to antiaircraft guns ("archie" in British parlance) to chance obliteration by passing artillery shells—which, despite their speed, were often observed in flight by the pilots if their relative alignment was correct.

Reconnaissance pilots were also tasked for special operations that included landing and picking up agents behind enemy lines at night. Given that the aircraft of the period lacked instruments and interior lighting and that the landings were made without lights on unprepared fields, it was extremely hazardous duty whether or not the enemy was waiting.

It was obvious that military return from reconnaissance was great, but so was its demand for resources, particularly fuel. In addition to the aircraft and their crews, reconnaissance units had to have the usual staff for armament and aircraft maintenance. There also had to be facilities for developing the photographs, analyzing them, and seeing to their proper distribution. The photographic staff was relatively large because time was critical; the photos could be worse than useless if they did not arrive at headquarters promptly. An entire science of processing photographs and analyzing them grew up, and it became customary for new photographs to be distributed so widely and so rapidly that they reached down past divisional level to the troops in the field.

Given that the value of reconnaissance became immediately understood at all levels, it is unfathomable that in the peacetime military budgeting process, reconnaissance funds were always among the first to be cut. So it was that much that was learned about reconnaissance had to be relearned not only for World War II, and relearned again for subsequent wars, including Korea. After that point, however, the developments in aircraft and camera were so startling that reconnaissance began to receive more adequate resources even in peacetime.

The Growth of Naval Air Power

The need for reconnaissance was felt even more keenly by naval officers. Eugene Ely had demonstrated flights from a stationary ship in 1910 and to a stationary ship in 1911, the same year that Glenn

Curtiss sold the first military seaplane to the Navy. Curtiss next volunteered to train Navy personnel to fly at no cost—a brilliant first expression of the aeronautic military-industrial complex.

Great Britain and Germany were equally desirous of adding an aviation scouting arm to their fleets, and on May 9, 1912, that great pioneer of English aviation, Commander Charles Rumney Samson, made a takeoff in an amphibious Short S. 38 from the HMS *Hibernia,* moving at fifteen knots.[33] (Some sources credit Lieutenant R. Gregory in a Short S. 27. Both men were among the first four selected for pilot training by the Royal Navy.)[34]

With its massive fleet, the largest in the world, Great Britain began a rapid expansion of its naval air power. On May 13, 1912, the Naval Wing of the Royal Flying Corps was formed; it soon adopted the title of Royal Naval Air Service (RNAS), which was granted recognition as a separate service on July 1, 1914, by which time it had more than a hundred trained pilots and seventy-eight aircraft, including forty land planes, thirty-one seaplanes, and seven airships.

When on April 1, 1918, the Royal Naval Air Service and the Royal Flying Corps (RFC) were combined into the Royal Air Force (RAF), the RNAS had grown to a force of 67,000 officers and men, with 2,949 airplanes and 103 airships.[35] It had among its many responsibilities the air defense of Britain and anti-Zeppelin and anti-submarine patrols over vast reaches of the sea.

Because flight from the sea is much more demanding in terms of the aircraft's performance, its maintenance, and the flying abilities of its crews, tremendous ingenuity was required to meet all of the many missions expected of naval aircraft. Initially, of course, there were no aircraft carriers in the modern sense, but vessels were quickly adapted to carry seaplanes, which were raised and lowered from the ship by massive cranes. Seaplanes could land and take off only in the calmest of seas, and the process of loading and unloading them was hazardous. Planners realized from the start that an aircraft carrier that could launch and retrieve aircraft with conventional landing gear would be preferable.

While the idea of the aircraft carrier was gestating, seaplane carriers and seaplanes were used in a wide variety of raids, from those on Zeppelin sheds to the first successful use of an aerial torpedo. On August 12, 1915, the seaplane carrier *Ben-My-Chree* (a converted Isle of Man packet) launched a Short Type 184 seaplane flown by

Lieutenant Commander C. H. K. Edmonds, who promptly torpedoed a Turkish transport ship off Gallipoli. Five days later, he torpedoed another ship, setting off a train of weapon development that would reach a peak in World War II.

Seaplanes were widely used throughout the British Empire, but experimentation with the aircraft carrier concept continued, and on August 2, 1917, Squadron Commander E. H. Dunning landed a Sopwith Pup on the forecastle deck of the *Furious,* becoming the first British pilot to alight on a ship. (Dunning was killed in another attempt captured in unforgettable photographs just five days later.)

The RNAS responded to the German declaration of unrestricted submarine warfare with further growth, including the acquisition of two unique classes of aircraft. The first of these was lovingly called "battle bags." It was a hybrid craft that consisted of the body of a B.E.2c aircraft slung beneath the bag of a Willows airship, thus creating the S.S. (submarine scout) airship. This was succeeded in service by the larger C airships. The crews of these craft conducted long and lonely vigils far out to sea, with submarine sightings occurring about once in every 2,416 hours of flight.

The second type was America's most significant contribution to the air war in World War I, the Curtiss H.4 "Small America," and its improved successor, the H.12 "Large America." The latter resulted from the practical improvements conceived by Lieutenant Colonel John C. Porte, whose recommendations overcame the rather poor seaworthiness of the H.4.[36]

The Curtiss flying boats became an important component of RNAS craft involved in "The Spider Web," a special patrol designed to hunt German submarines. The Spider Web was sixty miles in diameter, with the North Hinder light vessel as the central point. It was an octagonal figure with eight radial arms each thirty-eight nautical miles in length. Circumferential lines at ten, twenty, and thirty miles from the center crossed each of the arms. The pattern allowed searching four thousand square miles of the sea. Four aircraft could search the entire area in less than five hours. German U-boats passing through the area stood a good chance of being sighted.

Curtiss H.12s claimed to have sunk at least four German submarines, and shot down the airship L 22. Yet as incredibly valuable as they and the other patrol aircraft of the RNAS proved to be, their use was overlooked by both the British and the German military in their planning for World War II. Great Britain began World War II with a severely limited Coastal Command, and it was not until 1943 when the American Consolidated B-24 became available in quantity that it was able to establish patrol patterns that could control the vital areas of the North Atlantic. Germany not only began the war with a small number of submarines, it never established the proper degree of cooperation between the Luftwaffe and the U-boat service, nor did it anticipate the Allies being able to use aircraft so effectively. Of all the lessons not learned in World War I, the effectiveness of aircraft against submarine was perhaps the most important.

In Germany, prewar emphasis had been on the airships that were intended for use as reconnaissance over the North Sea. Seaplanes were obtained by the simple means of installing floats on existing landplane types. When war came, the need became obvious, and a great number of naval air bases were created; these became home to both seaplanes and the relatively few flying boats that were acquired. The lightning-like raids of British aircraft against the Zeppelin sheds led to the establishment of defense units. The German Naval Air Service was also quick to undertake air raids against Great Britain.

In time the Germans developed excellent seaplanes that could be used for reconnaissance and air combat. One of these, the Hansa-Brandenburg W 12, designed by Ernst Heinkel of World War II fame, was particularly effective against the British flying boats, wreaking havoc on them wherever they were found. One of the units using the W 12 flew out of Zeebrugge, and was led by First Lieutenant Friedrich Christiansen. Christiansen, who had twenty-one victories and had won the Pour le Mérite, also shot down a British airship and sank a British submarine. Between the wars, he captained the gigantic Dornier Do-X, then went on to become a general in the Luftwaffe.

Germany, perhaps more than any other nation, forgot its hard-earned naval air-warfare experience learned in World War I, and suffered for it greatly during World War II. This probably came about because Hermann Goering, the Luftwaffe Commander in Chief, was so jealous of his own prerogatives that he eschewed cooperation with his naval counterparts, and refused to allocate the necessary assets to naval requirements.

One of the totally unintended consequences of the success of reconnaissance aircraft on both land and sea was the extension of its mission to drop bombs, with the result that specially designed bomber aircraft came into being. Both reconnaissance aircraft and bombers required counter measures, and the best one developed was the fighter—another new and specialized aircraft type.

Chapter Three

Fighters and Bombers

The military potential of enemy observation aircraft was so great that an entire new combat arm, fighter aviation, grew up to defeat them. It can be said of fighters that they are at once the least useful and most important of aircraft types. They are least useful in the sense that they (as a pure fighter) do not drop bombs nor gather information, and their dogfights, while colorful, do not gain anything for either side except the possibility of air superiority. And that one fact is the reason that they are the most important type, for the obtaining of air superiority dictates the operation of other types of aircraft, including the bombers and reconnaissance types.

Once both sides created fighters, a seesaw battle for air supremacy immediately ensued, for to defeat the observation planes, one had first to defeat the fighter planes protecting them. As each side introduced a new fighter, the other side would attempt to counter; this competition led to a rapid improvement in the quality not only of fighter aircraft, but of all aircraft, as the natural engineering spinoffs accrued. The gradual introduction of fighters, and the ensuing fighter-versus-fighter combat, saw a rapid increase in attrition among pilots, already great because of accidents.

There was a curious reverse Darwinism that has persisted down through the present time. The very best pilots are usually selected to fly fighters, and this is the job they usually want. Unfortunately, fighter pilots are the first killed off in a conflict, so that the best pilots are often dead before they have a chance to prove themselves. There is another curious, very human factor at work in this equation. The best pilots want to be, and are assigned to be, fighter pilots. Yet only 1 percent of all the fighter pilots ever trained entered combat, and of those few who did, only 5 percent ever became aces, a title given those who shot down five enemy aircraft. Thus of all the

75

thousands of pilots selected to be fighter pilots over time, only .0005 (five ten-thousandths of a percent) became aces.[1] The aces, because they were among the few who actually engaged in combat, suffered by far the greater percentage of casualties. This makes the ace a true elite—but a product of a vast misallocation of resources.

During World War I, the goal of both sets of combatants was to establish air superiority over a limited sector of the front so that observation and bombing planes could accomplish their missions. By World War II, the goal became to establish air superiority in specific fronts or theaters. Implicit in this goal was the hope eventually to acquire command of the air so that enemy air forces were not allowed to operate anywhere at any time, while friendly air forces were permitted to carry out their missions with little interference. In more recent conflicts, the strategic sights were raised again so that the aim is to establish not just command of the air, but air dominance, in which all of the enemy air and land defenses are completely destroyed and offensive missions can be conducted with impunity.

The pilots and observers of early World War I reconnaissance aircraft had sought to destroy each other from the start. There were instances in which passing enemy aircraft waved courteously enough, but it was war, and duty called for damage to be done to the foe. The limited power of early reconnaissance aircraft made it difficult to equip them with an effective weapon. Some combats ensued with the opponents using side arms or rifles and some aircraft were shot down, but for the most part, the correct combination of aircraft and armament was not reached until the advent of the Fokker E I. It was not the first to use a machine gun mounted on the center-line of the airplane and firing forward, through the propeller, but it soon became recognized as the most effective and efficient.

To Roland Garros and the French go the honors for creating the first fighter mounting a machine gun firing through the propeller. Previously, some pusher-types (propeller in the rear) had been fitted with a forward-firing machine gun, and some tractor types (propeller in the front) had guns mounted on top of the wing, or at bizarre angles that required double deflection shooting. These types were generally so slow that they could not engage in combat at will, and the installations were awkward to use. Many early aircraft had the pilot in the rear, and the observer in the front seat, under the wing, from where it was almost impossible to shoot.

Air combat is difficult under all circumstances, as it is conducted in three dimensions at relatively high combined speeds, and shooting requires great skill to anticipate where the always-moving target will be. With the machine gun firing through the propeller, the pilot merely had to align the flight of his machine with that of the enemy and fire, making a very complicated task much easier. (This is an oversimplification, but it illustrates the advantage of a synchronized machine gun.)

Garros, who won fame with the first flight across the Mediterranean before the war, had a specially modified aircraft that had been fitted with deflectors on the propeller and, some sources say, also with a crude form of synchronizing gear with which a pioneer aircraft firm, Morane-Saulnier, had been experimenting. It was a brave effort, for 10 percent of the bullets being fired would strike the steel wedges, and as delicate as the thin wooden whirling propeller was, it was quite likely that a few hits could destroy it. Garros used his Morane-Saulnier Parasol Type L (a high-wing monoplane, not the shoulder-wing Type N example in which he is usually pictured) to shoot down three aircraft before he himself was brought down and captured on April 18, 1915, by a chance shot from an infantry rifle. (Garros escaped in early 1918, returning to fly a SPAD in a much more complex period of air combat. He was killed one month before the November 11 armistice. The great tennis stadium in Paris is named for him.) The engine and machine gun from Garros's aircraft were given to the Dutch plane-builder, Tony Fokker, for analysis. Fokker's engineers were evidently familiar with the pre-war patents of Franz Schneider for a synchronizing mechanism, and soon came up with an interrupter gear that permitted firing the gun through the propeller. The device was placed in a few Fokker F. I "Eindeckers" (single wingers) to begin the history of fighter aviation.

Even after creating the Eindecker, the Germans were not entirely sure how to use the aircraft. They were at their most successful in the defense of the homeland against long-range French bombing attacks, inflicting no less than nine casualties on one French formation in August 1915. The Eindeckers were originally parceled out to various two-seater units, but elements of public relations and vainglory came into play when two young German pilots, Lieutenants

Oswald Boelcke and Max Immelmann, of Feld Fleieger Abteilung (Field Flying Section) 62 received Fokker E Is for their own use and promptly began to shoot down Allied aircraft with skill and precision.

The public relations of their victories was exploited primarily because the rest of the story of war in the trenches was so horrible that governments and the press both looked for anything that could be presented as good news. Vainglory arrived when it became known that medals, fame, and more awaited those who shot down enemy aircraft in great numbers.

While nominally friends, the two young pilots had very different personalities, with Immelmann being self-centered and intent only on his success. The likeable Boelcke, though eight months younger than his twenty-four-year-old colleague, was more mature and already beginning to develop the aerial tactics (the "Boelcke Dicta") for which he would be famed.

The two men initially flew independently, but soon found that they had better success operating as a unit. They sought out enemy observation aircraft and dispatched them with a surprising head-on attack. Their scores mounted rapidly. Both men were awarded the coveted Pour le Mérite on January 12, 1916, after they had achieved their eighth victories.

Immelmann was shot down by a British two-seater after his fifteenth victory, while Boelcke scored forty victories before perishing in a mid-air collision with one of his own men.[2] The net effect of the two young aces was to focus attention on the purely imaginary glamour of air combat, and to hasten in all air forces the formation of specialized units composed entirely of fighters. The term "imaginary glamour" is used deliberately, for death in the air was as final and as appalling as death on the ground, and the image of chivalry given by the press was mostly a false one. In the realistic and informed words of the American "Ace of Aces," Captain Eddie Rickenbacker, air combat was "scientific murder."

Immelmann and Boelcke also had an effect on the reaction in the press, in the British Parliament, and in the French Chamber of Deputies. One English Parliamentarian, the irrepressible Noel Pemberton-Billing, referred to the gallant British airmen as "Fokker fodder," while the press painted the E I as being overwhelming in both numbers and performance. The E I actually had at most a mediocre performance with a top speed of only eighty miles per hour. By December 1915, there were no more than forty on duty on a front that stretched 475 miles from Switzerland to the sea.[3]

The degree that the press and the politicians distorted the importance of the Fokker E I threat is revealed in a simple statistical comparison. During the month, January 16, 1916, when the Fokker furor was at its height, the British suffered only ten losses in the air. During 1915, Great Britain and its Commonwealth partners had suffered 11,652 casualties in four days of March at Neuve Chapelle, 60,000 casualties in thirty-five days at the second Battle of Ypres, and more than 225,000 in the long agonizing campaign at Gallipoli. Later in 1916, they would lose 60,000 in the first day of the Battle of the Somme. "Ordinary Wastage" along the front amounted to as many as 2,500 killed and wounded every day. Yet somehow, ten air casualties in a month caused a near panic. It was a classic example of the effect of air power upon the political and press psyche, one that would be repeated many times in the years to come.[4]

An antidote to the Fokker was found in the French Nieuport 11, which mounted a forward-firing Hotchkiss machine gun over its top wing, and in the British de Havilland D.H. 2, a pusher mounting a forward-firing gun in its nacelle. This was the second stage of the seesaw race for air superiority that continues to this day. The Germans introduced the Albatros D I in 1916. Equipped with two forward-firing machine guns, it rapidly became the dominant fighter on the front, and was succeeded by a series of improved models. The Allies would not wrest air superiority back from the Germans until the introduction of the Sopwith Camel and SPAD VII in 1917.

As new aircraft were introduced, new air tactics were developed. These would be extremely influential until the first years of World War II. The lessons learned in World War I would be applied to training, organization, and procurement for the next two decades, albeit almost invariably incorrectly. Their effect was, ironically much more deadly when former aces assumed positions of power in later air forces, and applied their knowledge of World War I tactics to World War II conditions. Two primary examples are Hermann Goering and Ernst Udet. Goering, a twenty-two victory ace (although many of his victory claims are suspect), became head of the new German Luftwaffe. His influence declined after 1940, but whenever he intervened, he did so on the basis of his World War I experience. Udet, with sixty-two victories, was the leading German ace to survive the war, and he too attempted to apply World War I ideas (preferring maneuverability over speed), to the detriment of the Luftwaffe.

Far more important, the tactics developed during World War I directly affected the decision processes of the major powers in the series of diplomatic crises precipitated by Germany from 1935 on.

Initially, fighter tactics were slow to evolve, primarily because so few aircraft of the type were available. The first major confrontation of fighter forces came in February 1916, at the notorious Battle of Verdun. As a part of their gigantic preparation which General Falkenhayn predicted would cause the "forces of France to bleed to death," the Germans stationed most of the aircraft opposite Verdun. Two-seat "C" type aircraft were intended to maintain a "barrage patrol" to prevent French aircraft from operating over the front. These were reinforced by 180 aircraft, mostly Fokker E Is and some of the very similar Pfalz E Is, that were to intercept any French aircraft that eluded the aerial barrier. It was the intent of General Erich von Falkenhayn, who had replaced von Moltke as Chief of Staff, that these aircraft would dominate the skies over Verdun.

At first the German tactics worked well, and French forces were overwhelmed. The French were led by General Henri Philippe Pétain, to whom was attributed the battle cry "They Shall Not Pass." Pétain reorganized the French system of supplying munitions and personnel, and, in passing, appointed Major Tricornot de Rose to defeat the Germans in the air. Pétain reportedly told the major, "Rose, sweep the skies clear for me because I am blinded. If they chase us out of the sky, its quite simple—Verdun will be lost."

The mustachioed Major de Rose called upon the best pilots in the area to form a provisional Groupe de Chasse—with Morane N and Nieuport 11 aircraft. Among the pilots were such aces as Albert Deullin, Georges Guynemer, Charles Nungesser, Georges Boillot, and Raoul Lufberry. The valiant group of American volunteers in the Lafayette Escadrille earned their spurs over Verdun. The provisional Groupe de Chasse eventually grew into thirteen permanent Groupes de Chasse, and among them the famous Cigones (Storks.)[5]

General Pétain issued explicit orders that would serve as a template for Allied air action. He called for offensive patrols to be carried out on a regular basis at times fixed by the commander of the groupe. Pétain explicitly stated that the mission of the escadrilles was to seek out the enemy, to fight him, and to destroy him.[6] By late March, France had attained air superiority over Verdun. When the hideous bloodbath of 700,000 casualties dribbled to an end in June, the French had won complete control of the air, a situation that had great and perhaps decisive influence on the outcome of the battle, for if the Germans had been able to concentrate their air power on the famous Voie Sacrée (Sacred Road), the famous single route from the southeast into Verdun, they might have choked off the supply of artillery munitions that dominated the battle. They failed to do so because they were not yet sufficiently aware of the value of ground attack. Had Verdun occurred in 1918 rather than 1916, they would not have made the same mistake.

The general pattern of air combat by increasingly larger formations of fighter aircraft was established at Verdun. Both the Allies and the Central Powers had found that it made logistic sense to have specialized units operating the same type of aircraft, a practice the French had inaugurated. Circumstances sometimes forced the Germans to deviate from this policy more often than not, operating two or three different types of aircraft.

Germany, stretched thin by its war on two major and two minor fronts and increasingly hampered by the rigorous British naval blockade, recognized that it could not match the Allies on a plane-for-plane basis, and therefore had to reorganize its air force to obtain the maximum results. A decision was made to form special units dedicated to air combat, using the latest single-seat fighters available. These were known as Jagdstaffeln (fighter units), with a strength of about a dozen aircraft. The German goal was to have thirty-seven such units in action by April 1917. The youngest captain in the German Army, Hauptman Boelcke was appointed to command the Royal Prussian Jagdstaffel 2, among the first and ultimately one of the most famous of them all.

The Jastas (as they were abbreviated) proved to be a fertile training ground for future aces and commanders, none more so than Jasta 2. They were opposed by French escadrilles and British squadrons, which differed somewhat in strength, and most decidedly in methods of operation.[7]

In attempting to establish air superiority, fighter-versus-fighter combat became the order of the day, with the imbalance between Allied and Central Powers resources dictating the tactics that would be used. In general, the British pursued a relentless offensive policy that did not take into consideration numbers of aircraft, numbers of trained pilots, or the suitability of aircraft for the mission. Major General (later Marshal of the Royal Air Force) Hugh ("Boom") Trenchard insisted that his pilots and crews always be on the attack, regardless of casualties and ignoring the fact that RFC/RAF equipment was for long periods of time totally inadequate for the task. Trenchard claimed that his policy established a moral ascendancy over the enemy. This was in fact true, and indeed was a factor extending through World War II, but it was obtained at an unconscionable cost in the lives of the pilots and crews. At one point in 1917, pilots were arriving with as little as twenty hours flying time; by 1918, a squadron could lose as much as one-fourth of its strength in a day, and a fighter pilot's lifespan at the front was very short, with some estimates as low as eight days.

The Germans adopted the opposite policy, preferring a basically defensive posture that allowed "the customer to come to the store." An initial attempt was made to maintain the Luftsperre (barrage patrol), with the intention to prevent any enemy aircraft from crossing the front lines. This soon proved to be impossible—there were far too many cubic miles of airspace to defend, and far too few aircraft with which to do it. The Germans then became much more selective. They flew some standard patrols, but for the most part relied on a good early warning system, using observers at the front to relay messages on the nature and presumed intent of enemy activity. Fighters were then dispatched as needed to contest specific missions. It was an economical and sensible way to fight the war, conserving aircraft usage as well as fuel and supplies. It had several great advantages. First, the prevailing winds came from the west, which worked against the return flight of Allied aircraft, and second, while the crewmen of shot-down Allied aircraft were either killed or captured, German crewmen who survived were able to return to combat. A minor plus was the yield in materials that captured Allied aircraft provided, as engines, rare metals, and fuel became in ever shorter supply in Germany.

The French fighter philosophy fell midway between the British and the German, being not as aggressive as the RAF, but more venturesome than the German Air Force. It also varied from unit to unit and from one period of the war to another, reflecting the general state of French morale at that moment. The French made the same mistake with flying personnel that the Germans did, tending to group the best pilots in "star" units. This resulted in some very outstanding escadrilles and Jastas, indeed. Unfortunately, it meant that the bulk of the other units not only were staffed with mediocre personnel, but were forced to recognize the fact, a psychological hazard that had terrible effect upon both morale and performance.

Later, when the American forces began to appear, those who were trained by the British naturally followed British philosophy. While there are not many nonfiction books on these American pilots, their exploits were rendered vividly in the barely disguised "fiction" of Elliot White Springs. (A wealthy Southerner, Springs was a twelve-victory ace who introduced the mint julep to London society.) Those American pilots who were trained by the French tended to go beyond French policy of moderation toward the more aggressive pattern of the British.

The first Jastas were initially equipped with Fokker Eindeckers and a few of the more modern Fokker and Halberstadt biplane fighters, but they came into their own when the Albatros D I became the standard fighter in the fall of 1916, with the first units forming in October. The Germans took some time to learn to use their new aircraft, but the superiority of the Albatros over its Allied opponents was so great that April 1917 became known as "Bloody April" in the RAF. In that single month, 245 British aircraft and 316 British aviators were lost, at a time when the RFC's strength consisted of an average of about 500 operational aircraft and 850 pilots and observers. During the same period, the French lost fifty-five aircraft and sixty-three airmen.[8]

These figures are all the more remarkable, because during the period of execution, there were only about an average of forty-seven German fighter planes available at any one time. Four of the Jastas—2, 5, 11, and 12—scored 55 percent of the victories. In the same month, seventy-six German aircraft were destroyed, although 196 had been claimed by Allied pilots. (Overclaiming victories is endemic in air combat, never more so than in the claims of bomber gunners in World War II.)

There were many reasons for the margin of German victory. The Albatros was inherently superior to most of the aircraft it faced, particularly two products of the Royal Aircraft Factory, the B.E.2 and F.E.2.

The B.E.2 was a two-seat tractor biplane with a top speed of seventy-five miles per hour, and armed with an almost useless machine gun operated by the observer, who sat in the front seat, directly under the wing. The B.E.2 was designed to be inherently stable, and hence was inherently unmaneuverable. The F.E.2 was a two-seater pusher with a single forward-firing machine gun and a top speed of ninety-one miles per hour. Both were cold meat for the 103-miles-per-hour Albatros, which, in comparison to these two "crates" was delightfully maneuverable. It would prove to be less maneuverable than the Allied fighter aircraft that opposed it, for its two-machine-gun armament increased its wing loading.

Just as the Eindecker had called forth remedies in the form of the Nieuport and the de Havilland, so the Albatros elicited opposition in the Sopwith Camel, Royal Aircraft Factory S.E.5a, and French SPAD VII. Such was the rapidly accelerating nature of Allied aircraft engineering and manufacture, and such was the advantage in Allied engines and fuels, that these aircraft remained superior to every German offering until the appearance of the Fokker D VII in May 1918.

The D VII is generally regarded as the best fighter aircraft of World War I, and it presaged the design of the next decade of fighters with its thick, near-cantilever biplane wings and steel-tube fuselage construction. The Allies continued to introduce improved fighters, such as the Sopwith Dolphin and Snipe and the SPAD XIII. These often had elements of performance superior to that of the D VII, but the latter had two characteristics that earned its "best-fighter" accolades. The first was its generally pleasant flying qualities that were said to make good pilots out of bad ones, and aces out of good ones. The second was its combat capability at high angles of attack, being able to "hang on its propeller" to shoot at an opponent.

The Germans believed that mass served them in the air as on the ground. Sometimes a large formation was able to dominate an area over the front without ever engaging in combat. As a result, larger organizational units were created to control the larger number of aircraft being employed at a single time. The first of these of a permanent nature was the Royal Prussian Jagdgeschwader Nr. 1, formed on June 26, 1917, and commanded by none other than Rittmeister Manfred von Richthofen, the leading—and most celebrated—ace of World War

I. It was composed of four Jastas, numbers 4, 6, 10, and 11. Four additional Jagdgeschwadern were formed by September 1918.[9]

The German sense of discipline allowed them to use another method of grouping squadrons together, on a less formal basis, the Jagdgruppe. These were more or less special purpose units, which had various Jastas assigned to them, and which were in existence for fairly limited periods of time. They were often given a designation featuring their commander's name, as in Jagdgruppe "von Greim" or Jagdgruppe "von Braun," or their location, as in Jagdgruppe "Lille."

The new, larger organizations were often supported by trains, for the Germans continued to rely on railroads operating on their internal lines of communication to offset the superior strength of the Allies. The trains provided transport for the pilots and ground crew, and could carry the aircraft, equipment, and armament as well. The use of these trains, and the brightly colored aircraft, gave rise to the term "Flying Circus" to describe, for example, the Jagdgeschwader Nr. 1.

Strangely, the Allies did not respond immediately to the larger German formations. There were a number of reasons for this lack of response, including the difficulty in managing large formations during their assembly, flight to the combat area, and maneuvers in combat. Without any form of communication other than the waggle of wings and hand signals, controlling a large formation was difficult. Eventually, however, it became obvious that the only sane way to bring the German formations to battle was to meet them in something approaching equal numbers. The result was the employment of larger Allied units, two or more squadrons at a time, often flown at the altitudes best suited for the type, Sopwith Camels down low, S.E.5as at the middle levels, and a top cover of Sopwith Dolphins. This change in tactics brought about the relatively few "dogfights" in which large numbers of fighters were involved.

While films and fiction have led to the impression that the Western Front was always a whirling wheel of lead-spitting fighters, in actual practice most combat patrols were barren of action and relatively few large-scale dogfights occurred. When there was combat, it was usually between small numbers of aircraft and took place in an extraordinarily brief period of time. Post-mission reports from the pilots are filled with comments indicating that the sky was full of aircraft at one moment and empty the next. And it became the practice of the leading aces to make their attacks in such a manner that their victim was usually unaware that he was in combat until the bullets began hitting his aircraft.

By 1918, the full weight of Allied superiority in resources and industrial capacity was being brought to bear, and the Germans were badly outnumbered. While some individual units, staffed with less able pilots and inadequate equipment, suffered a crisis in morale, the fighting spirit of the German Air Force as a whole was never diminished. There were terrible shortages in fuel and lubricating oil, and the Jastas were forced to take such economy measures as rolling their aircraft around on the ground on wooden wheels, sparing the scarce rubber wheels for actual combat sorties.

The Germans responded to their shortages in a very practical and sensible way by designing aircraft for the most important specialized tasks. One manifestation of this tendency had a significant influence on the course of World War II. This was the creation of a new type of unit, the Schlachstaffeln (Battle Flights) and later the Schlachtgeschwadern (Battle Wings.) These new units did not employ conventional fighters, but specially designed close air support aircraft that could be employed far more offensively than were the more famous fighter squadrons. The latter retained a defensive role until the end of the war.

These new types proved to be among the most successful German aircraft of the war. They included the Halberstadt CL II and CL IV, the Hannover CL III, and the Junkers J-1. The compact and strongly built Halberstadts were as fast as the Albatros fighters of the period, but featured a two-man crew placed in a single cockpit. The Hannover was of the same size and speed, and had a distinctive biplane tail that gave its gunner a better field of fire. The Junkers J-1 was also a biplane, but of all-metal construction, and well armored, with the crew and engine completely enclosed by five-millimeter chrome nickel sheet steel.[10] Almost twice as heavy as the Halberstadts, it nonetheless had a top speed of ninety-six miles per hour. It carried three machine guns, a radio, and small bombs and grenades, and sometimes was used to reprovision small units that were cut off by the enemy. It was not very maneuverable, but the armor provided welcome protection from small arms fire.

The German Army became very proficient in the employment of these close support aircraft, and a captured German document published by the Department of War on February 26, 1918, reveals how sophisticated they had become. The document, entitled "The Infantry Aeroplane and the Infantry Balloon," states, "The infantry aeroplane (contact patrol) is, if there is proper cooperation with the troops, the most reliable and rapid means of reconnaissance and of obtaining information on the battlefield."

The document goes on to outline the duties and employment of the infantry aircraft, with flights arriving over the lines before dawn, using its own machine guns to suppress enemy ground fire. Flights made during the day were to make approaches by indirect methods, making sure not to compromise the direction or position of a German infantry assault. The Schlachstaffeln aircraft were urged to fly as low as possible, for "assembly of troops in trenches can be overlooked by even a trained eye if the flight is made at a height of over 300 meters."

The instructions were specific that all crews in a Schlachstaffel be well trained in the mission. Coordination with the infantry was emphasized, and some offensive battles were planned which required split-second arrival of the attack aircraft to support German storm troops assaulting a position.[11] All of these ideas found expression in the German Luftwaffe of World War II.

After the failure of the great German offensives in the spring and early summer of 1918, the Schlachstaffeln had to be used more and more in a defensive role where they proved themselves to be equally invaluable.

The British also recognized the importance of close air support, which they conducted for the most part with Sopwith Camels, S.E.5s, and Bristol F.2B fighters. The de Havilland D.H. 5 was introduced in 1917 as a ground attack plane, but was unpopular for a number of reasons, not least of which was the pilot's vulnerability to ground fire, and his almost certain death in case the aircraft turned over on landing. In May 1918, the Sopwith Salamander, an armored ground attack aircraft, was tested in France, but no operational units were outfitted with them by the end of the war.

The losses with the Camel and the D.H. 5 were utterly appalling, averaging 30 percent per day every day they were used in close air support.[12] The effect upon the RFC/RAF's morale was so devastating that the ground attack mission was virtually expunged from practice during the postwar years. It was for this reason that the RAF was so deficient in ground assault aircraft and tactics in World War II, not developing either specialized aircraft or tactics until late in the Desert War with the appearance of the Hawker Hurricane modification, the "Hurribomber." Ironically, emphasis was placed on "light bombers" such as the Fairey Battle and Bristol Blenheim, which were slaughtered when they engaged in combat in France in 1940. It is not an exaggeration to say that the adverse British experience in ground support work during World War I severely affected RAF performance in the early years of World War II.

The success of the cooperation between the Schlachstaffeln and the infantry had a profound effect both upon German military thinking and upon history. The Versailles Treaty reduced the size of German armed forces of all kinds to a miniscule level. Germany was allowed no air force, a tiny navy with no modern capital ships or submarines, and a 100,000-man army intended only to maintain internal order. Although the treaty did render Germany impotent for years, it did not stop surreptitious research and development in aircraft, tanks, and submarines. It also had several unintended consequences. The 100,000-man internal security force became an army of the elite, with only the ablest officers and noncommissioned officers being retained, and with provisions for cycling through good candidates to form a superb reserve. When Germany began to rearm (secretly under the Weimar Republic, more openly after Adolf Hitler became chancellor), it was forced to rearm with modern weapons. And, most important to all, the Army leaders were determined to use these weapons in ways never seen during World War I. The Schlachstaffeln and storm trooper combination of World War I was the direct ancestor of the dive-bomber and panzer combination of World War II upon which Germany had made its plans and with which it achieved its greatest victories.

The Allies were faced with the reverse situation. France maintained a huge army, staffed by senior officers of increasingly advanced age as the years passed; when World War II broke out, its Commander in Chief, General Maurice Georges Gamelin, was sixty-seven years old. It retained all of its World War I equipment, and most of all, it retained its World War I mentality. It was much the same in Great Britain, which continued to rely upon a battleship navy while operating under the notorious "ten year rule" for military appropriations. This concept, which surprisingly was first enunciated by Winston

Churchill, stipulated that planners should look ten years into the future to see if a war was probable. If no war seemed probable in the next ten years, defense expenditures could be cut.

As a result, the Royal Air Force was hopelessly obsolete by 1938, when it became apparent that war was perhaps only one—and not ten—years away. The fact was recognized by the Royal Air Force and the British military in general. As a result, they intensely lobbied Prime Minister Neville Chamberlain to appease Hitler, to gain time to rearm. This was in accord with Chamberlain's own thinking, of course, but it was he who forever bore the stigma of the Munich agreement that dismembered Czechoslovakia. In the matchless way that war has of reversing expectations, the British failure to modernize ultimately worked to their advantage. Having survived the Nazi onslaught in 1940, Britain was able to introduce a whole series of new aircraft to combat, while Germany was forced to rely for most of the war on the aircraft types with which it had started in 1939.

For the United States, the experience gained so quickly and at such great expense in World War I became irrelevant after 1918 as military budgets were slashed for the next twenty years. The statistics on the budgets for the period are at once amazing, revealing, and depressing as the following table shows:

Year	Direct Cash Appropriation
1916	$ 801,000
1917	18,681,666
1918	735,000,000
1919	952,304,758
1920	26,124,300
1921	35,124,300
1922	25,648,333
1923	13,060,000
1924	12,626,000

Source: *USAF Statistical Digest,* 2000[13]

Spending did not rise again to the 1918 level until 1941, and of the small budget available, the great majority went for personnel costs. Of the pitifully small amounts of the budget remaining for aircraft, the majority was spent on the purchase of observation types for reconnaissance.

The failure of the Allied Powers of World War I to spend adequately upon air power in the years after the war was the reason that a Germany prostrate in 1932 could become intimidating by 1935, and brilliantly effective by 1939 in Poland. In the 1930s, however, there was an even more important factor driving world politics, and that was the specter of strategic bombardment. It was initiated in World War I by both Great Britain and Germany, brought to an amazingly sophisticated level by both countries, and became the basis upon which the first air-power philosophers built their theories. It also became the pattern for how Germany and Great Britain would fight in the air during World War II, and in another brilliant example of unintended consequences, we will see that both countries adopted measures opposite to those they had used in the First World War.

Bombing in World War I

Bombing is so morally offensive to those being bombed that it has always been used as a propaganda device. The Turks complained that the Italians had bombed a hospital in the very first bombing raids in Libya in 1911. The Germans went a step further, introducing the preemptive bombing lie by claiming in their formal (if belated) August 3, 1914, declaration of war on France that French bombers had without provocation bombed Nuremberg the preceding day.

Yet bombing appears not to be morally offensive to those intending to bomb, and each of the nations involved in the Great War developed a strategy for its bombing as it gathered practical experience. It is instructive to look at them nation by nation to see how that experience influenced their subsequent development, and, in particular, how it affected the theory of air power as enunciated by the air-power philosophers of the postwar period.

France

Marshal Joseph Joffre, the "Hero of the Marne," saw the advantages of aviation early on, being particularly impressed by the military maneuvers of 1912, in which sixty aircraft had participated, the greatest number ever in France to that time. Many innovations were introduced, including the concept of the "flight" of six aircraft each, the recognition of the hazard involved by the institution of "flight pay," a dashing new uniform for aviators (dark black, with an ill-advised but handsome close-fitting collar), and the use of a tricolor roundel under each lower wing. It was Joffre who authorized the formation on September 27, 1914, of the first bomber group in history, Groupe de Bombardement No. 1 (GB 1), composed of three flights of Voisin LA 5 pusher biplanes. The fiery, articulate Gabriel Voisin himself went to the French flying fields to supervise the bomb racks being installed on his aircraft. Initially ninety-millimeter artillery shells equipped with Salmson fin assemblies were used, but these were quickly replaced by the Swedish Aasen bombs that had been developed for use by French dirigibles. Later 155-millimeter artillery shells were adapted for use.[14]

By 1915, under the leadership of Major Louis Marie de Goÿs de Mezerac, the French began to organize a deliberate bombing policy, one that acknowledged the principle that to be effective, bombing had to be done on a massive scale. (The problem was that the correct definition of "massive" continued to elude planners for the next thirty years.) The eighteen aircraft of GB 1 were stationed near Nancy, with an adequate supply center. Crews were carefully trained, in part, by the use of a "simulator," not unlike those used in World War II. The trainee bombardier was placed in a tower over a "moving carpet" which contained the usual images of a landscape, and would use his simulated altitude, air speed, and winds to determine when to release his "bombs." Other experimentation was done to determine which was the best type of bomb to use on which structures: demolition bombs on brick buildings and railroads, incendiaries on barracks, and so forth.

In war, one weapon calls forth the use of another. On April 22, 1915, the Germans introduced gas warfare by discharging 168 tons of chlorine from four thousand cylinders in the Ypres salient. Two French divisions and one Canadian division were the target of this devastating attack and those that followed. Had the Germans thought to have adequate forces in hand to exploit the gap they created in the lines, the course of the war might have changed. As it happened, the battle ground to a halt in a series of bloody attacks and counterattacks, as most did on the Western Front, with nothing to show for it but casualties on both sides.

Yet the French were prompt to take action in response. On May 27, 1915, all eighteen aircraft of GB-1 took off in fifteen-second intervals at 3:00 A.M. to bomb the Badische Anilin und Soda factories at Ludwigshafen, where the chlorine gas was presumed to have been produced. All aircraft but the one flown by Major de Goÿs returned, and the factory reportedly suffered damage. (De Goys survived and later became a general in the French Air Force.)

The Germans soon reacted to further French attacks on industrial targets, and the inferior performance of the Voisin showed up immediately. When taxed to the utmost, the Voisin bombers cruised at seventy-five miles per hour and had a range of about three hundred miles. On the outbound journey, with a tail wind of twenty-five miles per hour, they could cover a hundred-mile bombing raid in one hour. On the return flight, however, the ground speed dropped to fifty miles per hour, and the Germans had two hours in which to attack them. On August 9, the Germans took advantage of this agonizingly slow egress speed to shoot down nine of the eighteen aircraft attacking Saarburg. By the following year, France confined almost all such raids to the night hours. Geography played a part in this decision, for the German incursion into France and Belgium had enabled it to deploy forces with the range necessary to attack France and England. At the same time, the invaded territories provided a buffer that shielded all but the German border towns from French or British attack.

It was not until late in 1917 that suitable equipment began to arrive in the form of the successful Breguet XIV B 2. The French resumed daylight raids with the Breguets, striking enemy targets beyond the reach of conventional artillery, and concentrating on railroad stations, factories, and airfields; but results here were not entirely successful, and losses were heavy. The French bombing tactics foreshadowed World War II, for the Breguet formations dropped their bombs when the leader dropped, in an attempt to secure a greater mass of explosives in a given area. Another taste of World War II came with the Caudron R-11 multi-place escort fighter, capable of 111 miles per hour, and carrying five machine guns. In 1918, the R-11 would clear the way through opposing enemy formations for the Breguets to follow.

The war ended with France focused on the task of day bombing, with strategic bombing relegated to a much lower priority. The post-World War I era saw the French military mired in the past, believing that it would win the next war by fighting it in the same manner. The emphasis France placed on the cooperation of air and land forces in defensive operations during World War I would also be replicated in World War II, which would prove to be a fatal error, playing directly into the hands of German strategists.

Italy

The Italian Military Aeronautics Corps was formed on January 7, 1915. When Italy entered World War I with its May 23, 1915, declaration of war against Austria-Hungary, its army possessed about 150 aircraft, 91 pilots, 20 observers, and 20 student pilots. The Navy had an additional thirty-four seaplanes and six semi-rigid dirigibles. The Italian aviation industry was still in a primitive state, with the total production of its five aircraft firms amounting to no more than fifty planes annually.[15] Foreign planes, mostly French, were procured to meet the growing requirements, but the intensely nationalistic Italians wanted their own industry and their own aircraft.

Operationally, the Italians were at the same relative disadvantage as the French, for while the Austro-Hungarian air forces could bomb Italian targets (primarily Venice), the Italian Air Force did not have the range to reach Austria-Hungary. Many of the targets it could reach were in areas that Italy hoped to acquire as a result of the peace treaty, and it thus made little political or economic sense to bomb them. The requirement for long-range bombing led the Italians to build up a large fleet of airships, deploying more than seventy-five of them. The Italian airships did not achieve even the limited success of their German counterparts.

The first prophet of air power, Giulio Douhet, made one of the most important contributions to military aviation by allowing, without proper authority, Gianni Caproni to proceed with the construction of the first of his trimotor bombers for the Italian Air Force. Douhet had already angered his superiors by his pronouncements that bombing campaigns should be directed against the morale of an enemy's population. In December 1914, they used his relationship with Caproni as a pretext to demote him from his position as Commander of the Aviation Battalion, sending him to serve with an Army division. Then, in 1916, when he inadvertently left behind material criticizing the Italian war effort, he was court-martialed and sentenced to a year in prison. (The American air-power advocate Billy Mitchell would suffer a similar if less draconian fate a decade later.) Douhet used the prison time to good advantage to formulate his thoughts on air power, and returned to active duty in January 1918.

Thanks to Douhet, the Italians eventually possessed a small but efficient bomber force composed of three-engine Caproni bombers; upon this force would turn a number of powerful events in air-power history. Caproni began an Italian trend when he created his first three-engine bomber in 1913, for trimotors continued to be used by the Regia Aeronautica through World War II—and for the same reason, a lack of higher power engines. While the initial designs had three 100-horsepower engines, Caproni used larger engines as they became available, and his last World War I designs had engines of 200 hundred horsepower at a time when Great Britain was building the 360-horsepower Rolls-Royce Eagle engine.

The Capronis were used with good effect on the Italian front in two roles, serving as short-range tactical bombers to strike Austrian targets in mountainous areas, and as long-range attack aircraft to hit the Austrian naval base at Pola. The Capronis were also pressed into service in France, and a later model was selected for manufacture in the United States. Many consider them to be the best performing Allied bomber of World War II.

The Italians' attacks were pinpricks to begin with, but subsequently built up into relatively large raids of as many as fifty aircraft—a huge number for large bomber attacks at the time and more than twice as large as any the Germans would make over England during World War I.

Production increased every year until, by 1918, Caproni built no less than 420 of its giant bombers. Italian aviation production had undergone a revolution, with 6,488 aircraft and 14,840 engines being turned out in 1918.[16]

The success of these attacks seemed to validate Douhet's claims, and provided the basis for his seminal book *Command of the Air*. The essence of Italy was embodied in one of the foremost—and perhaps least likely—proponents of air power, the poet Gabriele D'Annunzio, who also had close ties to Caproni. In 1915, at the age of fifty-two, he obtained permission from the Italian prime minister to fight the war as an individual on a personal crusade. Customarily called *Il Poeta*, and beloved by the Italian people (if not by many Italian husbands), D'Annunzio found in flight the perfect amalgam of romantic love and death that permeated his poetry. He began an inspirational series of spectacular long-range flights over enemy cities to drop propaganda leaflets of his own creation. Not a pilot himself, he flew as observer and leaflet dropper. His first poetic bombing raid was on Trieste, and his last on August 9, 1918, by leading eight single-engine Ansaldo reconnaissance planes all the way to Vienna to drop his leaflets, which he signed "Gabriele D'Annunzio, in the sky of Vienna." While the physical damage to the enemy of D'Annunzio's attacks was minimal, he had a tonic effect upon Italian morale, and he became an influential supporter of Douhet. And it should be noted to his credit that he also flew unromantic but vital reconnaissance missions over the Adriatic.

The most fateful effect of this Italian renaissance in aviation was upon Benito Mussolini, who assumed power in Italy in 1922. Mussolini, envisioning Italy as a gigantic aircraft carrier dominating the Mediterranean, embraced both Douhet's theories and D'Annunzio's romantic call for Italian glory in the sky. Mussolini greatly expanded the Regia Aeronautica, and learned to fly himself so that he could be seen as an *avant garde* dictator, at the controls of modern Italian aircraft as he was at the control of Italy. His son Bruno became a military pilot, fought in Ethiopia and in the Spanish Civil War, and was killed in 1941 flying one of Italy's four-engine bombers, the Piaggio P.108. Unfortunately for Italy and the world, Mussolini's unfounded belief in the myth of Italian air power helped persuade him to embark on military adventures that included the easy conquest of Ethiopia and disaster in Greece and North Africa. Italy was never able to implement Douhet's ideas, but contrary to anecdotal history, its air crews were skilled and brave, and its torpedo pilots were among the best in the world.

Russia

Although, as has been noted, Russia entered the 1914–18 war with a significant number of aircraft and airships, its real problem was its industrial infrastructure, which could not design, build, or maintain warplanes of adequate quality. The aircraft it bought from the Allies were usually obsolete and often well worn. The most significant contribution was the Sikorsky four-engine bomber, of which ninety-three were produced during the war. The big Sikorskys flew four hundred sorties and dropped sixty-five tons of bombs. They were unique in their ruggedness, none being lost to German fighters, and one returned to land safely after two engines on one side had been shot out—a remarkable feat for both the aircraft and its pilot, for "engine-out" flight remained a difficult and hazardous feat for many years.

Despite recruiting problems, the Imperial Russian Air Service grew to 135 detachments by the time Russia ended the war, and included a notable first by allowing Princess Evgeniyua Shakovskaya to become the world's first female combat pilot in 1914. There were twenty-six Russian pilots who became aces. The most important of these was the six-victory ace Aleksandr Nicolaevich Prokofiev de Severskii, who became a prominent aircraft manufacturer and air-power philosopher in the United States. With his name anglicized to Alexander P. de Seversky, he took up Douhet's mantle and advocated a strong air force in his influential book *Victory through Air Power.*

When Russia withdrew from World War I after the Communist takeover and the 1917 treaty of Brest-Litovsk, the Air Fleet of the Workers and Peasants Red Army emerged from the battered remnants of the former Imperial Air Service. This, the Red Air Force, almost totally ignored the lessons learned from operating the four-engine Sikorskys. Instead, the Red Air Force was dedicated to the support of the Red Army, and functioned superbly in this role in the later years of World War II. Lip service was paid to Douhet's ideas, and some significant large bombers were built, but strategic bombing did not loom large in Soviet strategy until the advent of the Cold War.

The United States

Not unlike an eager puppy with a new toy, the United States plunged into World War I aeronautics with enthusiasm, money, and willing vendors—but not much else. (The notable exception to this situation had been the creation in March 1915 of the National Advisory Committee for Aeronautics (NACA), an organization which would have profound influence not only on the United States, but also international aviation, and which would lead ultimately in 1968 to the National Aeronautics and Space Administration.)

In spite of the almost zero base from which it started, however, the United States was represented by the Lafayette Escadrille beginning in May 1916. The Escadrille (and later the expanded Lafayette

Flying Corps, along with volunteers in the RAF) provided the foundation for the first U.S. pursuit squadrons, with the 103rd Pursuit Squadron becoming operational on February 18, 1918. The 96th Bombardment Squadron arrived at the front by June 1918, operating well-worn Breguet XIVs. On September 14, just after the Battle of St. Mihiel commenced, the 96th was incorporated into the First Day Bombardment Group, along with the 11th and 20th Bombardment Squadrons, flying the British-designed but American-built de Havilland D.H. 4s.

Given its later arrival upon the scene, it is somewhat surprising that the most important demonstration of air power during World War I was provided by the United States at the Battle of St. Mihiel. The United States was admittedly using borrowed aircraft designs and even borrowed squadrons of foreign aircraft, but the concept was uniquely American in terms of scale and execution. It would be the pattern for the future.

The architect of the St. Mihiel aerial offensive was Colonel Billy Mitchell, who assembled the largest air force ever committed to battle and drew up plans for its employment.

Mitchell was regarded as a maverick by the regular United States Army establishment, but his talent and his contacts could not be denied, and he became Chief of the Air Service, First Army, the American Expeditionary Forces. In that capacity, he commanded no less than 1,481 aircraft and twenty balloons assembled from 101 British, French, and Italian squadrons, to be used in an offensive designed to pinch off a German salient at St. Mihiel. Among the aircraft were thirty Caproni "450s" and forty-eight Handley Page 0/400s.[17] His planning was grandiose for the time, calling for simultaneous strikes by as many as five hundred aircraft at the enemy troops.

Bad weather and a preemptive German withdrawal blunted some of Mitchell's planning efforts, but by the end of the battle, the Americans had flown 2,469 sorties, engaged in 135 aerial combats, and claimed 52 victories. Forty Allied crew members died in the action, and sixteen more were taken prisoner.

The battle set the tone for future American air operations, beginning the tradition that, whatever the odds and whatever the opposition, no mission would ever be turned back. St. Mihiel also established Mitchell as one of the foremost air-power philosophers to emerge from World War I, and would be the platform from which he influenced the strategy and planning not only of the United States, but of Japan, in the years to come.[18] He was already originating a bombing philosophy that would parallel but not duplicate that of Douhet's, and that would be realized in the 1920s with profound effect upon the world's politics and weaponry.

The majority of American bombing was largely confined to support of the armies in the field, although a covetous eye was cast on both the British Handley Page 0/400 and three types of Caproni bombers, all of which were ordered into production in the United States. By August 16, 1917, wild-eyed plans to procure as many as nine thousand Capronis were in effect. This enthusiasm was enhanced by reports from Foggia, Italy, where some seventy American airmen of those trained (among them the future mayor of New York, Fiorello H. LaGuardia) went to fly Caproni bombers in Italian *squadriglia.*

Unfortunately, difficulties with the Italian bureaucracy, including Gianni Caproni himself, made production almost impossible, and only five were ultimately delivered by the Fisher Body Company. The first of these did not reach the Air Service until January 16, 1919, and they served until 1921, with one example participating in a mock attack on New York City on July 29 of that year.

The Handley Page effort was both less ambitious and more successful. Plans called for building parts for five hundred Handley Page 0/400s and shipping them to Britain for assembly. As things worked out, seven were assembled and flown in the United States, while a hundred sets of parts were sent to Britain. They were not assembled there but were instead returned to the United States, where they became lost to history. One can only hope that some abandoned warehouse still contains a hundred sets of Handley Page parts waiting for some earnest aircraft restorer to discover them.

The wartime aviation production record of the United States is usually dismissed as having been wasteful and inefficient, but this is not the entire story. The United States went from virtually no industry at all to one that produced several thousand aircraft and fourteen thousand engines in seventeen months. Moreover, had the war lasted for another year, that same industry would have produced thousands of aircraft and engines of indigenous design capable of fighting on the Western Front. Balloon production had soared, and the United States could have supplied all balloon requirements for the Allies in 1919.

There was waste, and there was also some questionable networking, but on the whole, despite the furor and the allegations, the funds appropriated so belatedly by Congress were well spent. Unfortunately, the same Congress that waited so long to fund the American aviation industry before the war wasted no time in cutting off its funding when the war ended, setting in motion a replay of events for World War II.

Great Britain and Germany

It is both convenient and instructive to tell the story of the bombing and defensive efforts of Great Britain and Germany in a single passage, for they were interactive and reactive for the length of the war. Further, the results of these intertwined efforts influenced the national military policies of both nations over the next thirty years, although in quite the opposite way than might have been expected.

Air crews and commanders on both sides were panting to start bombing, and bombs began to fall soon after the start of the Great War. The German naval Zeppelin L 6 raided Liège, Belgium, as early as August 6, 1914; the bombs intended for the fortresses there missed, but killed nine civilians, the first in a long series of "collateral damage" incidents.[19] A German Taube, piloted by Leutnant Ernst von Hiddesen (sometimes rendered "Hindelsen") dropped four small (about five-pound) bombs on Paris, along with a cheeky note stating that "The German Army is at the gates of Paris. You have nothing left but to surrender. Lieutenant von Hiddesen."[20] (As has been so often the case, the observer's name is lost to history. Observers, navigators, and bombardiers, though perhaps the most vital members of any air crew, have most often been treated shabbily by their pilots, their service, and the general public.)

The dark side of von Hiddesen's bombing was that an innocent woman was killed, the first of five hundred to die during World War I from either aerial bombardment or the shells of (the erroneously named) "Big Bertha," the huge long-range cannons used to harass Paris. Other aircraft followed von Hiddesen (who was shot down over Verdun the following year), and a few dozen more small bombs were dropped on the City of Lights by what became termed "the five-o'clock Taube."

This off-hand and ironic reference is more important than it looks, for it was an indicator that urban populations could adapt to the threat of aerial bombardment. What should have been a welcome, if grisly, fact of life, the ability of civilian populations to endure bombing, was ignored as a matter of policy by air-power advocates and by political leaders in the post-World War I period. As a result, the threat of bombing would assume ridiculous proportions in relation to the danger it really represented.

It should be mentioned here that while the original Taube was built by the Etrich firm, it was also built under license by Rumpler and others. In addition, there were other aircraft of roughly similar birdlike configuration that were called "Taube" so that it became a generic term for German aircraft early in the war. The average British citizen reportedly pronounced it "Torb."

Bombing and the National Psyches

The bombing campaigns of World War I were limited compared to those of one war later, yet so much happened during both the British and the German campaigns that it is worthwhile to examine them in considerable detail.

Anyone standing in the shattered ruins of Berlin in the summer of 1945 would have been amazed and disheartened to know that the massive destruction had its start with the reports (not confirmed in England) of a raid by Lieutenants Karl Caspar and Roos (first name unknown) in one of the ubiquitous Taubes on October 25, 1914. The first confirmed report of a raid on England came on December 21, when Kapitänleutnant zur See Stephan von Prandzynski, flying a German Friedrichshafen FF 29, dropped two small bombs in the sea near Dover's Admiralty Pier. A second raid on December 24 by the same type of twin-float, two-seat biplane caused an estimated forty (English) pounds in damage when it struck in a resident's garden near the Castle at Dover. Thus sewn were truly minor winds that would reap inconceivably massive whirlwinds across Europe and Asia only thirty years later.

These first German raids were correctly regarded as mere pinpricks, for the English public had been firmly fixated on the possibility of Zeppelin raids, so much so that before the war "phantom airships" had been seen over England on much the same basis that UFOs were seen half a century later. This mass apprehension was due in part to literary works such as H. G. Wells' famous *The War in the Air* and in part to Germany's boasting about the effectiveness of the Zeppelin.

The boasting sprang from the almost hysterical adulation of Count Zeppelin and his creations in Germany. This national enthusiasm reached to the very highest levels, including the Kaiser and the Chief of Staff, von Moltke, and the German airship fleet (which included both Zeppelins and the Schütte-Lanz dirigibles that used plywood rather than aluminum for their framework) was touted as being a supreme weapon that no other nation could match. This was partly correct, for while not so fast as aircraft, the airships had unmatched range and bomb-carrying capacity. But neither the British nor the Germans foresaw that the ability of the rigid airship to navigate and bomb accurately was very limited nor that it was so adversely affected by wind and weather. The failure to see these facts is hard to explain, for the short history of dirigibles had been repeatedly punctuated by disasters from these elements.

Nonetheless, the fear of Zeppelin (the term became generic; few in England were even aware of the Schütte-Lanz, which built only twenty-two dirigibles) raids led to the first true strategic bombardment raids in history, as Great Britain sought to slay the dragons in their lairs. The longtime aviation advocate, then First Lord of the Admiralty, Winston S. Churchill, launched Royal Naval Air Service aircraft in a series of daring raids on airship bases.

The first of these raids took place on September 22, when four Avro 504s of the RNAS took off to bomb airship sheds at Cologne and Düsseldorf. The raids were not successful. Commodore Murray Sueter, the inspirational leader of the Admiralty's Air Department, proposed another such raid. On October 8, 1914, Squadron Commander D. A. Spenser Grey and Flight Lieutenant R. L. G. Marix executed his plan, flying Sopwith Tabloid biplanes from Antwerp, to repeat the attack. The shapely little Tabloid biplanes were descended from the 1914 Schneider Trophy winner, and carried a pilot and some twenty-pound bombs at ninety-three miles per hour. Grey could not find his target and bombed the Cologne railway station instead. Marix demonstrated the qualities that later led him to become an air vice marshal by not only finding Düsseldorf, but from six hundred feet making a direct hit on the shed housing the Zeppelin L 9, destroying both. His aircraft was damaged by ground fire, and he had to force land thirty miles from Antwerp.

After extensive planning by no less a personality than Noel Pemberton Billing, on November 21, 1914, three Avro 504s flew from Belfort, France (where the factory had shipped them, still in packing crates), to the Zeppelin sheds at Friedrichshafen, each one carrying four twenty-pound Cooper bombs. Led by Squadron Commander E. F. Briggs, the tiny biplanes flew 125 miles—an extreme distance in those days—to drop their bombs on the sheds and factory with great success. Briggs was shot down over the target and roughly handled by the local population, another glimpse into the sad future.

On Christmas Day, 1914, a fourth raid, by seven Short seaplanes against the Zeppelin sheds at Cuxhaven, failed when the target was not found. Their raid had totally unexpected results, however, for it enabled the guiding spirit of the German Zeppelin fleet, Peter Strasser, to prevail upon the Chief of the Naval Staff, Admiral Hugo von Pohl, to obtain permission from the Kaiser to allow the British Isles to be bombed.

These beginning raids were the start of strategic bombing, but not the start of strategic bombing campaigns, which would fall to Germany to begin. They have been described in some detail not so much because of their intrinsic importance, but because they reveal the basic problem that has always confounded advocates of air power. Throughout most of its history the expectation of results from the application of air power has been vastly out of proportion to the resources used to obtain those results. This was because the people who decided the objectives for air power to achieve were in most cases not experienced in aviation, and their expectations were sometimes heightened by unusual achievements such as Marix's raid on Düsseldorf, such achievements being seen as the norm rather than the exception.

Ironically, the people deciding what an aircraft could do were in fact often the very same people who previously had refused to allocate a sufficient portion of the budget to the creation of the instruments of air power. There are many examples of this fact, from Moltke's belief in dirigibles to Hitler's hope that Nazi air power could achieve air superiority over Great Britain to the Japanese Imperial belief that its highly skilled but small air forces could, if not defeat the United States, at least force it to accept a favorable peace agreement. Only in rare instances have the resources necessary to achieve what has been expected of air power been allocated. The examples are fewer here, but the buildup of United States and Soviet air forces during World War II and the creation of the Strategic Air Command in the post-World War II period are perhaps the best.

Germany was so convinced of the potential of dirigibles as far-ranging ships in the Mahan tradition that it allowed the Army and the Navy to develop their own airship fleets, a very costly duplication of production, construction, and training efforts. Both the Army and the Navy hoped to use the airship to carry the war to Britain, but the Navy also had a genuine scouting requirement, to guard against the approach of the British fleet. This scouting role was probably the best use to which dirigibles could be put, for they could range over long distances in relative safety and relay their information back by radio. But such work was not glamorous, nor did it fill what seemed to be an instinctive desire: dropping bombs on the enemy.

The Army had used the airship for reconnaissance on the Eastern Front, but soon found that it was too vulnerable to gunfire for similar use on the Western Front. At a joint meeting in September 1914, representatives of the Army and Navy decided that there were as yet too few airships to bomb England, and further, that they were inhibited by Kaiser Wilhelm's reluctance to bomb the homes of many of his royal relatives. This represented one of the few times that the respective airship divisions had a true meeting of the minds.

It is a characteristic of air power that no matter how monumental the weapon—be it a Zeppelin or a B-52 or an intercontinental range ballistic missile—there is almost always a single individual who acts as its champion and who sparks its use. With the B-52 it was General Curtis E. LeMay, while with the ICBM it was General Bernard A. Schriever. With the Zeppelin, that individual was Fregattenkapitän (Frigate Captain) Peter Strasser, whose combination of determination, bravery, and technical skills led him to become Chief of the German Naval Airship Division.

The thirty-eight-year-old Strasser was the very image of the German naval officer, who, with mustache and dagger-shaped goatee, combined a crisp official manner and a rare but engaging grin. He used his personal charm to get to know his air and ground crew members as well as he knew the officers who commanded the airships. Yet he could be stern if the situation demanded it, and, like all warriors, his personality—and possibly his judgment—

changed over time under the stress of command in battle. Strasser was himself a protégé of the great airship commander Hugo Eckener, and his businesslike manner imparted discipline and purpose both to the few hundred sailors in his unit and, remarkably, also to his superior officers.

The first attack took place on January 19-20, 1915, with two out of three Zeppelins—L 3 and L 4—successfully reaching England. The L 3 was commanded by Kapitänleutnant Hans Fritz, an almost comic-book name for a German Zeppelin commander. Flying in rain at five thousand feet, Fritz dropped six 110-pound bombs and seven incendiaries on Greater Yarmouth, then dropped four more 110-pounders as he exited. The L 3 returned, weary and worn, after more than twenty-two hours in the air. The damage it had done to England was slight: two killed and several wounded. The L 4, commanded by Kapitänleutant Magnus Graf von Platen Hallermund, missed a chance for infamy when he attempted to bomb Sandringham, the British royal estate, unaware that King George IV was visiting there. Fortunately for Great Britain, von Platen hit another target, and the damage was slight even there.

With these raids, the die was cast. German Zeppelins were going to strike at the heart of Great Britain, and in doing so, would (the German High Command hoped) sow confusion into British ranks, forcing them to divert resources from the Western Front, and, most of all, to degrade British morale to the point that the British government would be forced to sue for peace. The Zeppelins certainly had a negative effect on British morale, a predisposition derived from the pre-war concerns about them. All of the fears seemed to be realized on the night of October 13-14, when five Zeppelins slashed across England, dropping almost two hundred bombs and killing seventy-one people and injuring another 128. Although British newspapers and politicians would have had the public believe that the Germans were deliberately placing the crosshairs of their diabolical bombsights on schools, hospitals, churches, and ladies' sewing circles, the truth was that in this war, as for most of the next, the bombs were being dropped indiscriminately. The Zeppelin crews hoped to hit military targets, and they tried to drop at least in the general area of those targets, but when time, weather, or emergencies dictated, they dropped them on whatever happened to be below.

The Germans attempted to learn the art of aerial navigation and bombing from the air, but the wind and the weather made it far more difficult than contemplated. However, Zeppelin crews, like the bomber crews who followed them for the next eight decades, almost always claimed hits on legitimate military targets, and most often truly believed what they claimed.

Despite the difficulties, the expense, and the losses, the Germans persisted, with a total of forty-nine airships embarking on twenty raids in 1915. A more concentrated effort was made in 1916, when 164 airships embarked upon twenty-three raids. The term "embarked" is used because weather, wind, and mechanical difficulties sometimes kept airships from reaching their targets. On October 8, 1916, Ernst von Hoeppner became Kommandierende General der Luftsreitkrafte (Commanding General of the Air Force). He had already decided that airship attacks were nonproductive, and that the task of carrying the war to England should be given to bombers as soon as possible. Thus the number of airship attacks dropped sharply in 1917, with only seven raids and forty-six attacking airships. In 1918, the game was up, with only four raids, on which eighteen airships started.

The recognition that not much damage was being done to the enemy, and the rise in British defense measures, caused a decline in German effort. Field Marshal Lord John French, a cavalryman at heart, was appointed Commander in Chief of Home Forces on February 16, 1916. (It was a demotion, one he bitterly resented, for he had been replaced as commander of the British Expeditionary Force in France by the indomitably inept Field Marshal Douglas Haig.) One of French's first actions was to prohibit the firing of anti-aircraft guns at any aircraft, even those known to be hostile. His concern was that mistakes might be made in identification, and that the debris from the exploding antiaircraft shells might injure civilians on the ground. Later he had to rescind his ruling.

A series of airfields was set up, and night-flying training became a priority for the RFC and RNAS. By June 1916, 271 antiaircraft guns and 258 searchlights were available—about half of those required. Eight squadrons were deployed at twenty-five airfields, with a strength of 134 aircraft, again about half the number estimated to be needed. By the end of 1916, there were twelve squadrons, and the defense network was served by more than seven thousand officers and men. The German hopes about diversion of resources were being fulfilled to some degree.

Of the 134 aircraft, twenty were Royal Aircraft Factory B.E.12s, while most of the remainder were B.E.2cs, supplemented by a handful of Bristol Scouts. The B.E.12 had the "best" performance, but it was pitifully inadequate as a Zeppelin interceptor. Essentially an upgraded B.E.2c with a more powerful 140-horsepower engine, it had a top speed of 102 miles per hour, a service ceiling of 12,500 feet, and an endurance of three hours. It was very stable, however, which made it especially suitable for night flying on Home Defense work, an important feature given its lack of instruments and the fact that cockpit and airfield lighting were completely improvised. The B.E.12 was heavily armed for the time, with up to four Lewis machine guns or ten unguided Le Prieur rockets.

There was a tremendous discrepancy between the capabilities of the Home Defense aircraft and the intruding Zeppelins. Yet somehow the defenses worked, for on June 17, 1917, a B.E.12 piloted by Second Lieutenant Loudon Pierce Watkins shot down the Zeppelin L 48 on its first mission over England.

The L 48 was one of the new generation of "height climber" Zeppelins, especially designed to operate at altitudes as high as twenty thousand feet. These altitudes, while rendering the Zeppelin safe from attack, made navigation and bombing accuracy virtually impossible. It was, in addition, extremely difficult for the crew to endure the bitterly cold temperatures and the lack of oxygen. Primitive oxygen systems were available, but they themselves induced illness among the crew, who, in general, preferred a shot of brandy as an alternative to oxygen.

The L 48 was commanded by Kapitänleutnant der Reserve Franz George Eichler, on his thirteenth raid, leading four other Zeppelins, L 42, L 44, L 45, and L 47. His orders had been succinct: "Attack South England—if possible, London." The L 48 encountered some difficulty with its engines on the inbound leg of its mission, but pressed on. After dropping a dozen bombs in open fields near Kirton, Eichler elected to gain the advantage of a tail wind and descended to 11,500 feet—just about the maximum height that Watkins could reach in his B.E.12.

The British Home Defense system had worked perfectly, picking up the L 48 on its way in, and tracking it through its mission. As it passed over England, several aircraft were dispatched to intercept it. Watkins, a Canadian, was among the last of these sent aloft, along with Captain (later Air Marshal) Robert Saundby and Second Lieutenant Frank Holder. All three attacked the L 48, but Watkins was subsequently given credit for the victory. In his account, he tells of firing three drums of incendiary ammunition into the Zeppelin before it caught fire. The L 48 then exploded and sank stern first to the ground at Theberton, Suffolk. Surprisingly, three of the twenty-two-man crew survived the crash—a rare occurrence, for most crews were burned to death before they hit the ground.

More German Zeppelins fell victim to weather and accidents than to enemy action, and it was soon apparent to the German High Command that Zeppelin warfare cost more than it was worth. Yet the Leader of Airships, Peter Strasser, had lost none of his enthusiasm, and on August 5, 1918, led five Zeppelins in an attack on England. It was to be the last Zeppelin raid of the war.

Strasser commanded the raid from L 70, a massive dirigible, 693 feet long and with a volume of 2,195,800 cubic feet. It had a lifting capacity of 97,100 pounds and a top speed of eighty-one miles per hour. For some unknown reason, Strasser's usually excellent judgment failed him, and he launched the raid so that it would arrive over Great Britain before nightfall.

The British defense system seized the opportunity, sending thirty-five aircraft to intercept the Zeppelins. Major Egbert Cadbury and Captain Robert Leckie took off in a de Havilland D.H. 4, an aircraft with a performance adequate for its task. Both men were experienced, with Cadbury having been credited in part with the destruction of the L 21 the previous November, and Leckie credited with shooting down the L 22 in May 1917. They attacked the L 70 head on at about seven thousand feet, and their controversial Pomeroy explosive bullets tore a tremendous hole in the airship's envelope, igniting the hydrogen-filled lifting cells. Strasser died in the ensuing crash, and with him died all hopes of further use of the Zeppelin over England.[21]

After the war it was possible to assess the material and personnel costs of the Zeppelin campaign. The Germans dropped an estimated 220 tons of bombs from Zeppelins, killing 557 and injuring 1,358. The bombs also caused about $7.5 million in damages. Seventeen Zeppelins were destroyed by aircraft, with almost three hundred crew members perishing, and another sixty-six were destroyed by bombing raids, weather, or accidents. The average 1918 dollar cost of a Zeppelin was about $100,000, so that the cost of lost airships was roughly $8.3 million, far more than the material damage inflicted on Great Britain. If one includes the cost of the total of 122 Zeppelins built, their expensive bases with huge rotating hangars and hydrogen-generating equipment, the air and ground crew training, and so on, it is evident that airship bombing campaigns were not cost effective. (All figures are in then-year values and based on contemporary exchange ratios, i.e. the pound being about five dollars and the dollar being about five marks.)

There is no question that the Zeppelin raids had an adverse effect upon British morale, although they did not crack, much less break the British spirit. The Zeppelin operations also diverted some British effort from the Western Front, and caused money to be expended on a system of home defense against air raids. The home defense system was one of the best investments of the time, for it would not only prove itself in the second phase of Germany's World War I strategic bombing campaign, it would form the basis (with the addition of radar) for Great Britain's aerial defenses during World War II.

The Second Phase of the First Strategic Bombing Campaign

Germany had committed itself to aerial warfare over England, and, for reasons of prestige, it was unwilling to give up on the idea. The Germans had determined to use aircraft to bomb England from the start of the war, and, just as the Zeppelin force had its Peter Strasser, so did the bomber proponents have an energetic leader, Major Wilhelm Siegert. Age seemed to do nothing to dim a German officer's belligerence, and, at forty, Siegert was determined to create a bombing unit that reported directly to the German High Command for operations against England. He was given command of this Englandgeschwader (roughly England Wing) unit, which was officially titled Fliegerkorps der Obersten Heeresleitung (Flying Corps of the High Command) but operated under the code name Brieftauben-Abteilung Ostende (BAO), the Carrier Pigeon Section at Ostende. The code name was hardly opaque. Many German units operated Taube (Dove) flying machines, so that an able British cryptographer should have been able to make the connection.

Siegert gathered about twenty-four aircraft into the BAO, and began assembling pilots into what became first an elite outfit, and then an incubator for future leaders of German aviation. His plans for bombing England fell through when the German advance through Belgium and France was held up, and the necessary bases were not acquired. Instead, the BAO began bombing operations against targets in Belgium and France, and was later transferred to the Eastern Front, where it operated from a railway train, just as the fighter "Flying Circus" would do later. The BAO was so successful in its operations that it rapidly became overworked. Calls from ground commanders for its services resulted in heavy casualties, and almost 20 percent of its original sixty officers were lost to enemy action. Thirty additional officers were transferred to provide command and leadership in other units, vitiating the BAO for all practical purposes.[22]

Technical and tactical developments offset the decline of the original BAO. Two new groups were formed to be deployed at the discretion of the German High Command, Kampfgeschwader der Obersten Heeresleitung Nr. 1 und Nr. 2 (roughly, General Headquarters Battle Groups 1 and 2). They were equipped with a second generation of bomber aircraft, the so-called Kampfflugzeug (Battle Aircraft). The first of these was the A.E.G. series of twin-engine bombers, which in their most produced form, the A.E.G. G II, were powered by two 220-horsepower Mercedes engines, had a top speed of ninety-nine miles per hour, and could carry up to 660 pounds of bombs. (Manfred von Richthofen flew as an observer/gunner in an A.E.G. G II early in his career, and suffered his first wound when he accidentally stuck his hand into the propeller.[23])

At about the same time that General von Hoeppner had decreed that the Zeppelin offensive was counterproductive, a new aircraft emerged on the scene, the famed Gotha bomber. After considerable development, the Gotha G. IV. (G for Grossflugzeuge or large aircraft) appeared in the fall of 1916. With a wingspan of almost seventy-eight feet, two 260-horsepower Mercedes D IV engines, the Gotha had a top speed of eighty-eight miles per hour and a range of five hundred miles. It carried a crew of three and a bomb load of up to a thousand pounds. This was a remarkable performance, especially when one realizes that this aircraft appeared only thirteen years after the Wrights' first flight at Kitty Hawk.

The German High Command realized that the Gotha was the instrument that could replace the Zeppelin in the British bombing campaign. It also anticipated using even larger aircraft, the Riesenflugzeuge (Giant) bomber, in the near future. Some early types of these R-planes, as they were called, had been introduced on the Eastern Front as early as 1915, as a counter to the Russian Il'ya Muromets bombers. They had undergone the long process of development to be expected in so large and complex an aircraft.

Thirty Gotha aircraft were assigned to Kampfgeschwader 3 at Ghistelles in Belgium, but stationed at a number of flying fields farther inland. The new unit was under the command of Hauptmann Ernst Brandenburg, in an operation code-named Turkenkreuz (Turk's Cross). Many of the members of KG 3 were former members of the original BAO.

Brandenburg might have been played by Erich von Stroheim in a film, for his large, bald head seemed to brim with Prussian vigor and intelligence. Severely wounded in 1914, he did as so many others did in World War I when they were no longer physically able to fight in the trenches—he turned to flying as an observer. General Hoeppner personally selected the thirty-four-year-old Brandenburg to lead KG 3, giving him a crushing assignment in the process. With the thirty Gotha bombers, Brandenburg was expected to provide a basis for peace by intimidating the morale of the English people and crushing their will to fight. Further, he was to disrupt the British war industry, disorganize communications between coastal ports and London, attack the supply dumps of the coastal ports, and hinder the transport of war materials across the Channel.[24] Then, just incidentally, KG 3 was to cause the transfer of aircraft and guns from the Western Front to England.

These naïve instructions illustrate just how far removed from reality even the strong supporters of aviation were at the time. They were in fact misleading, for General Ludendorff believed that the primary reason for the Gotha raids was their propaganda value. Unfortunately, military and political leaders of all countries would continue to have the same blind, misplaced trust in air power for many decades to come—trust that the knowledgeable practitioners of air power did not share, but which was nonetheless encouraged by them for political reasons. If they, the practitioners, did not spread the belief in the efficacy of air power, they would not receive the budget necessary to develop an air force that might someday become as efficient as they claimed.

On May 25, 1917, twenty-three Gothas embarked on their first mission over England, taking off from two airfields near Ghent. So critical was the Gothas' fuel supply that they landed at Nieuwmunster, only forty miles away, to top off their tanks. Two aircraft dropped out, and twenty-one proceeded at twelve thousand feet hoping to reach London. Bad weather intervened, and they instead bombed Folkestone and the nearby Shorncliffe army camp as targets of opportunity, dropping their bombs at about 6:00 P.M.

In a single raid, the Gothas did more damage than the Zeppelins. Ninety-five people were killed and 185 injured, with about $100,000 damage being done. But even more troubling to the British than the casualties was the insolent manner in which the twenty Gothas paraded over England, disregarding antiaircraft artillery (AAA) and the seventy-seven aircraft that were dispatched to intercept them. (Field Marshal Lord French had long since withdrawn his sanction against the use of AAA.) Interception was just about impossible, as the B.E.2 and B.E.12 aircraft had such low rates of climb that they could not reach the intruders by the time they had finished their business and departed—a problem that would persist until the advent of radar. Three aircraft which happened to be at altitude when the raid took place did engage the enemy, and all three claimed victories. The Germans admitted to one loss in combat, and to another crash.

The morale of the British public, just beginning to recover from the Zeppelin attacks, was now assaulted by what was obviously a vastly more efficient weapon. People were incensed at what they considered a barbarous intrusion on civilian life, and inquests of the victims often returned the verdict of "willful murder," indicting the Kaiser and the Crown Prince.

Although concerned that he might have lost the advantage of surprise, Brandenburg returned on June 5, leading twenty-two Gothas to the attack. There were two targets, the munitions factories at Shoeburyness on the north shore of the Thames, and the Admiralty docks five miles to the south at Sheerness. Brandenburg was unaware that despite the haze, crowds of pleasure seekers were at the beach, enthusiastically soaking up the unaccustomed sixty-degree temperature.

Both targets were protected by antiaircraft guns, which began sporadic firing. Either a coincidental engine malfunction or a lucky shot out of the 329 fired caused a Gotha to crash into the sea two miles off

Barton's Point, where dozens of small boats soon surrounded its wreckage. Neither the pilot nor the observer survived, but the gunner, Unterofizer Georg Schumacher, escaped with just a broken leg.[25]

In this attack, the Gothas killed thirteen, injured thirty-four, and did about twenty-five thousand dollars in damage. (As a convention for this work, all figures are in then values, based on contemporary exchange ratios, the pound then being about five dollars and the dollar about five marks.) Sixty-two fighter sorties launched against the attackers revealed all that was wrong with the British defense system. The fighters included everything from a Farman F.40 to a Bristol fighter among the sixteen types of aircraft used in the defense, but they had insufficient warning, no means of communication among the aircraft, and no contact with the ground. No tactics had been worked out—each pilot was on an individual chase.[26] Defending pilots claimed a total of three victories and four "driven down out of control," and the *Daily Express* newspaper translated this into ten victories out of twenty attackers. In fact, only one aircraft was lost on the raid, but two others crashed near the home base.

The Gotha, while actually quite agile when carrying one-half to a full load of fuel and bombs, became difficult to handle at lighter weights as the center of gravity moved aft. A pilot, exhausted by the strain of the long flight and combat, had to deal with a fractious tail-heavy aircraft at the most critical part of the flight, a night landing at home base. Later models of the Gotha had their wings swept back in an effort to cure the instability problem at lighter weights.

In looking at the influence of air power on history, one despairs at noting the many instances when the same general error was repeated. The Germans erred in committing the Gothas to combat over England without sufficient testing. In the next war, they would do exactly the same thing with their largest bomber, the Heinkel He 177. Both aircraft would suffer more losses to accidents than to enemy action.

Eight days later, Brandenburg struck with his Englandgeschwader again, this time against the target dearest to German hearts, London. Eighteen of twenty Gothas succeeded in attacking, killing 162, injuring 432, and inflicting almost $650,000 in damages. Ninety-four British aircraft rose in defense, but none reached the bombers before they had dropped their bombs. A few aircraft harassed the bombers briefly on their return journey, but none was damaged.

The Kaiser was delighted with Brandenburg's efforts, personally decorating him with the Pour le Mérite, Prussia's highest decoration for valor. Ironically, he was killed on his return flight to the base when the Albatros two-seat aircraft in which he was being carried crashed on takeoff.

He was replaced in late June by Hauptmann Rudolph Kleine, a highly decorated officer who had learned to fly in 1913, and had been wounded twice in air battles. Observers normally commanded German bomber units, just as it was their practice for observers to command the aircraft in which they flew. Kleine's experience was invaluable for he was an original member of the Ostende Carrier Pigeon group.

He took the Englandgeschwader into action shortly after he arrived, bombing Harwich and Felixstowe on July 4. It was not until July 7 that twenty-one Gothas infuriated all of Great Britain by a "parade march" over London. Parliamentarians and newspaper editors were absolutely outraged by the insolence of the Germans, and the apparent inability of the British defenses to prevent raids. This time the force of twenty-two Gothas killed 57, injured 193, and caused more than $1,025,000 in damage.

Yet despite the furor in the newspapers, British defenses were improving, and 108 sorties were mounted. The Gothas were engaged both on their inbound and outbound routes, and one was shot down, by an Armstrong Whitworth F.K.8 flown by Lieutenants Frederick Grace and George Murray. Gothas shot down two Royal Flying Corps aircraft.

At this point both sides had begun to achieve their goals. The British were forced to recall two squadrons from the Western Front, including the crack No. 56 Squadron, home to many leading British aces. The raids had so unsettled the British public that a subsequent raid on the coastal town of Felixstowe caused a panic in London. Yet the British warning system was falling into place, and both antiaircraft and interceptor aircraft efforts were improving.

This was not enough for the press or the government, and the clamor continued. On the German side, the basic flaw of the Gotha—extreme tail-heaviness at lighter weights—was working against it, for four Gothas crashed on landing. The total of five losses represented a loss rate of 24 percent, which was clearly unsustainable.

Just as the Luftwaffe was forced to do in the waning days of the Battle of Britain, in September 1940, the Imperial German Air Force turned (temporarily, it was thought) from day bombing to night bombing in September 1917.

The reason was simple: British defenses had improved remarkably, but the performance of a later version of the Gotha, the G.V., had not. Flying at night permitted flight at lower altitudes, saving both time and fuel, and increased the problem of the British defenses by an order of magnitude. Finding a great behemoth of a Zeppelin at night was not easy; finding a much smaller aircraft was almost impossible. Navigation was somewhat more difficult for the Germans, but given that the bombs were to be dropped indiscriminately, there was not much difference in the bombing accuracy.

Four Gothas made the first night raid on September 3, against Chatham, killing 132 naval recruits and injuring another 96, but causing only about $20,000 in damage. This was the most effective use of a Gotha against a military target to date. The next night, nine Gothas raided London, dropping 6,000 pounds of bombs, killing nineteen, injuring seventy-one, and causing about $230,000 in damage. One Gotha was lost.

The entrance of the United States into the war on April 6, 1917, had galvanized the German High Command, which realized that it must win the war before millions of American troops arrived to make that goal impossible. The optimistic predictions that the United States would "darken the skies with aircraft" would prove to be totally unfounded, but in 1917 the German High Command took it seriously, and launched the Amerikaprogramm. Undertaken at the request of General Hoeppner, the Amerikaprogramm called for an increase of forty pursuit units and seventeen training units. Aircraft production was to be increased to 2,000 per month, with aircraft engine production set at 2,500 per month. They were to have a priority second only to U-boats, which were needed to implement the unrestricted submarine warfare policy upon which Germany now rested its hopes.

Such a program also meant a vast increase in the production of machine guns, instruments, bombs, and all other elements of equipment. The massive requirements of the previous production acceleration, the Hindenburg program, had exhausted stocks of many critical materials, including rubber, aluminum, copper, zinc, gasoline, and coal. This increase meant that materials for the new aircraft program had somehow to be squeezed out of the supplies previously destined for other industries supplying the Army with cannons and other munitions, and by wholesale substitutions of one material for another.

Despite the many difficulties, the Amerikaprogramm was generally successful, while, as has been noted, the American production program was not. The net effect of the Amerikaprogramm was to make life much more difficult for English and French units during late 1917 and for most of 1918.[27]

Among the materials that suddenly came into short supply was seasoned wood. This was before the era of kiln-dried wood, and there was no ready way to accelerate the process. The use of unseasoned lumber, along with new equipment requirements, adversely affected the weight of both the later model Gothas and the new and formidable Riesenflugzeuge (giant aircraft.)

The Riesenflugzeuge—the "R-planes"—were large aircraft, with several designs being built by several companies. The most produced and best known was the Staaken R.VI, the largest aircraft to fly in World War I, with a wingspan of 138 feet, five and one-half inches, and loaded weight of 25,269 pounds. Four Mercedes D. IVa engines were installed in tandem pairs, relatively close to the fuselage center line. It might be noted that the Heinkel He 177, the largest German bomber to fly over England in World War II, had a wingspan of only 103 feet.

The Staaken R.VI had a top speed of a little over eighty miles per hour, but it could reach almost ten thousand feet in altitude in a little less than an hour, and had a flight duration of seven to ten hours, depending upon engine installation.

The R-planes were not just simply a bigger Gotha. Instead they were the product of a well thought out plan to have a versatile aircraft that could carry a reasonable amount of bombs over a long distance, or a large amount of bombs over shorter distances. The German specifications called for the R-plane to have the capability to remain in the air for several hours, with large loads. To assure that it could so, it was to be equipped with multiple engines, navigation and bombing equipment, and guns for defense. Where necessary fuel tanks could be substituted for bombs. Two pilots, with duplicate controls, were called for along with a radioman and an engineer to attend to the engines. These, in some designs, were to be accessible so that minor in-flight repairs could be conducted. Considerable thought was given to ease of maintenance and the time required for engine changes and loading and unloading bombs.[28]

In general, had the same degree of thought and planning that went into the design, development, and employment of the R-planes been duplicated by Luftwaffe planners in the 1930s, Germany would undoubtedly have had better bombers with which to fight the Battle of Britain.

The maturity of the R-plane design and the general disposition of its engines and bomb loads made it easier to fly than the Gothas. This fact was evident in the results obtained in operations on the Eastern and Western Fronts, and against England, where their effect was the greatest.

The R-planes were well equipped for night flying, employing a gyro-compass and a turn and bank indictor, which, with an altimeter and an airspeed indicator, was just enough to permit safe flight at night or in moderate weather. The R-planes' first raid over England came in conjunction with twenty-five Gothas on the night of September 28-29, 1917. The R-planes made ten more raids before the bombing of Great Britain was halted in July 1918, dropping a total of about 60,000 pounds of bombs, including the largest bomb dropped on England, a 2,200-pounder. They proved to be exceptionally reliable and battleworthy, and, in the raids over Great Britain, suffered no losses in aircraft or personnel to enemy action. The R-planes in fact pointed the way to the future: large aircraft with sufficient range to strike the enemy heartland with an adequate supply of bombs. Unfortunately for Germany, but fortunately for the rest of the world, Luftwaffe planners did not understand what the R-planes had taught.

The last great German raid of the war took place on May 19-20, when no less than thirty-eight Gothas, two single-engine aircraft, and three R-planes raided Essex, Southend, Kent, and London. By dropping about 24,000 pounds of bombs, they killed 49, injured 177, and caused $886,585 in property damage.[29]

Three more daylight reconnaissance raids were made, and then the German bombing ended for another twenty-one years. In all, fifty-two aircraft raids were made against Great Britain. Some 2,772 bombs were dropped, with a weight of 164,821 pounds of explosives.

There were 857 killed, and 2,058 injured, and total property damage reached $7,172,630.[30]

The Germans would assess the combined effects of their airship and bombing campaigns against Great Britain, and come to the conclusion that the results obtained were not worth the cost expended in obtaining them. This conclusion would have a profound effect upon a military mind-set that already was predisposed to using air power as an extension of its army ground forces.

It would have the reverse effect upon Great Britain, which would undertake a massive—many say disproportionate—strategic bombing effort in World War II, and which had a military mind-set already prejudiced against the use of air power with its army ground forces.

Great Britain's Bombing Efforts

Mention has already been made of Great Britain's early preemptive strikes against Zeppelin sheds. Additional strikes were made at intervals, including one flown from the modified cruiser *Furious* on the airship sheds at Tondern, Germany, on July 19, 1918. (Aircraft could take off from the *Furious,* but could not land on it.) Seven were flown off the *Furious,* six reached Tondern, and their fifty-pound bombs destroyed the L 54 and L 60 in their sheds. The Camels were supposed to fly back and land by waiting destroyers, but only two pilots accomplished this rather difficult feat. Three became lost and landed in Denmark, while a fourth was drowned at sea.[31]

In general, however, British bombing was confined to daylight raids behind enemy lines, with small numbers of aircraft attacking a variety of targets. Given that the bombers were such obsolete types as the Royal Aircraft Factory B.E.2c and R.E.8 aircraft, and that the bombs usually weighed either 20 or 112 pounds, it is not surprising that little damage was caused. In early 1916, tactics changed so that a large number of bombers would attack single targets in what were termed "mass raids," even though the largest number in any single raid was thirty-one, on March 9, 1916. Further, formal bombing instructions issued in February 1916 stated that no bombing should be done at a distance greater than a few miles from the front lines. The bombing of railway stations and bridges was not to take place unless in conjunction with "definite operations of an important nature."[32]

The wisdom of this directive was borne out in the surprisingly satisfactory bombing operations conducted during the Battle of the Somme, in which some 185 aircraft were deployed against railways, airfields, and ammunition depots with much success but with heavy losses. The losses derived in part from the fact that when the B.E.2c aircraft carried bombs, they were obliged to leave the observer/gunner behind, and were thus virtually defenseless against German fighter attack. The greatest effect of the British effort was perhaps on German morale, which was highlighted in a blistering memorandum issued by General Fritz von Bulow, commander of the First German Army. In it he noted that "the first weeks of the Somme battle were marked by a complete inferiority of our own air forces" and that "heavy losses in personnel and material were inflicted on our artillery by the enemy's guns, assisted by excellent air observation, without our being able to have recourse to the same methods."[33]

Yet the proportion of bombing sorties to all other aerial activities of the Royal Flying Corps remained low. The Battle of the Somme lasted from July 1 to November 17, 1916. At the beginning of the battle, there were 426 pilots available; during the battle, 576 were killed, wounded, or missing; new recruits brought pilot strength up to 585 by the end of the battle. During that time there were 164 enemy aircraft claimed destroyed. A total of 298 bombing raids had been conducted, with 292 tons of bombs dropped. In the same period, there were 19,000 photographs taken and 8,612 enemy targets registered by aerial observation. Clearly, bombing had not yet come to the fore in the RFC, primarily because the equipment was inadequate both in numbers and in capability.

The initial German daylight Gotha raids, combined with a recent change in the political climate, altered British thinking in many ways. On December 7, 1916, the combative Lloyd George succeeded H. H. Asquith as prime minister. Lloyd George set up a War Cabinet that, after January 3, 1917, featured Lord Cowdray as President of the Air Board (essentially, an Air Ministry) overseeing RFC and RNAS operations. An Air Organization Committee was formed under the leadership of General Jan C. Smuts, who had led the Boer enemy forces in South Africa. One recommendation of the Air Organization Committee was the formation of the Royal Air Force by amalgamating the Royal Flying Corps and the Royal Naval Air Service, to take effect on April 1, 1918.[34]

On October 1, 1917, Major General Hugh Trenchard was instructed to create a force that could strike Germany from bases in France. Officially called the Inter-Allied Independent Air Force, it was usually referred to simply as the Independent Force. Trenchard immediately formed a special unit, the Forty-First Wing, which, composed of three squadrons, was set up at Ochey and placed under the command of Lieutenant Colonel Cyril L. N. Newall, later to become Chief of the Air Staff, RAF. Despite vicious winter weather, the new unit added two more squadrons and became the VIII Brigade. It made 142 bombing attacks, with fifty-seven of them on German military targets in Cologne, Stuttgart, Mannheim, Mainz, and Coblenz between October 11, 1917, and June 5, 1918.[35]

A second and far more significant result of the change in politics was a decision to relieve Trenchard of his command, replacing him with Sir Frederick Sykes, a longtime enemy of Trenchard.

Trenchard, while tremendously popular with his troops, was difficult to deal with. One of his greatest admirers, Marshal of the Royal Air Force Sir John Slessor, describes him as inarticulate, a bad pilot, absentminded, and always mixing up people's names.[36] He was regarded with cold hostility by many of his superiors for the infuriating way in which he responded to orders and suggestions. Nonetheless, he was a great wartime leader who would, in the ten years after the war, keep the Royal Air Force in being.

Trenchard's demotion had led, after immense political backbiting, to his assignment as commander of the newly created Independent Force, which was intended to carry out a bombing offensive against Germany without being subject to the current demands of the battlefield. Trenchard was bitterly hurt by his dismissal, and did not believe that the Independent Force was a good idea for several reasons, including the fact that there were not yet bombers with the capability to do an adequate amount of damage to German cities. Yet Trenchard's appointment, his creation of the Independent Force as of June 6, 1918, and his use of that force would precondition Great Britain's military strategy in World War II by establishing a tradition of courage and proficiency that would be echoed in Bomber Command.

Initially the Independent Force was the VIII Brigade renamed, including a day wing (the Forty-First) with three squadrons and a night wing (the Eighty-Third) with three squadrons. This force would grow over time, and less suitable aircraft (such as the very obsolete F.E.2b and the unsatisfactory D.H. 9a) would be replaced with more efficient aircraft.

Trenchard dedicated the force to attack as many industrial centers as he could reach with the equipment at hand. As a part of his plan he intended to gain air superiority by attacking German airfields. He chose railways as the target of first importance, followed by steel mills.

A third decision was made to increase the number of squadrons from 108 to 200, with the majority of the new units being equipped with new bombing aircraft. No less than seven hundred de Havilland D.H. 4s were ordered. The D.H. 4 was a two-seat aircraft with a superb performance. When powered by the 250-horsepower Rolls-Royce Eagle, its 119-miles-per-hour top speed was faster than all German fighters. It had a ceiling of 16,000 feet, a range of 300 miles or better, and could carry up to 460 pounds of bombs. With a fixed forward-firing machine gun and flexibly mounted twin guns in the rear cockpit, the D.H. 4 was formidable. It did have some flaws—the pilot and observer were separated by a fuel tank, making communication difficult and fires easy. Unfortunately, many of the D.H. 4s were cancelled in favor of an "improved" model, the D.H. 9, which had development problems that were not solved until late 1918. With these (and other) aircraft, British bombing efforts would skyrocket in 1918. In Sir Douglas Haig's triumphant dispatch, "The Advance to Victory," he notes that the Royal Air Force dropped 5,500 tons of bombs between January 1 and November 11, 1918.[37]

The initial relatively modest British bombing efforts did not derive from any shortage of combativeness, for as early as 1914, Murray Sueter had gone to the thirty-year-old Frederick Handley Page asking for a "bloody paralyzer" of an aircraft, one that could wreak havoc on German cities. It was not the most specific expression of requirements, but the young aircraft manufacturer had long believed in the inherent advantages of large aircraft and responded with the Handley Page 0/100, a twin-engine biplane that was slightly larger than the German Gotha, and had a better performance, thanks to its 250-horsepower Rolls-Royce Eagle II engines. In an event which would reoccur with some frequency during World War II, the third 0/100 built landed in error behind German lines, providing the enemy with a glimpse of the latest British technology. Approximately fifty-six 0/100s were built for the RNAS. They were used for night raids, usually one aircraft at a time. More important, however, the 0/100 had been sufficiently developed to serve as a basis for a night bomber that the Royal Flying Corps could use to match the raids by the Gothas and the R-planes.

With a minor redesign and the installation of new, more powerful Rolls-Royce engines, the 0/400 emerged. This four-place heavy bomber had a wingspan of 100 feet, weighed 13,360 pounds fully loaded, had a top speed of 97.5 miles per hour at sea level, and could carry up to 2,000 pounds of bombs. While quite a handful to fly, it was far more pleasant in the landing regime than the Gotha.

The German night raids of September 7, 1917, convinced the British that night bombing was an effective way to wage war, and the number of 0/400s ordered was increased to four hundred. Production 0/400s did not reach Trenchard's Independent Force until the spring of 1918. The British were at the same disadvantage as the French in terms of reaching German targets. There was no hope of retaliating by bombing Berlin with the 0/400, but there was in the works an even larger aircraft, the V/1500, intended to do exactly that.

It was possible to bomb German cities, however, and two 0/400s of No. 215 squadron attacked Mannheim on the night of August 25-26, 1918, with the Badische chemical works as the target. With immense daring, the lead 0/400, piloted by Captain W. B. Lawson, glided through searchlights and antiaircraft fire, dropping down from five thousand feet to only two hundred feet in order to bomb and strafe. The low attack had a unique advantage. the searchlights were so depressed that they illuminated the target area. In the meantime, Lieutenant M. C. Purvis attacked from five hundred feet.[38] Their daring would be recaptured in such World War II attacks as the Dam Buster raid.

The majority of attacks on Germany took place after the formation of the Independent Force, so the following statistics are relevant: in a total of 675 raids, of which 446 were at night, 14,208 bombs were dropped on German targets. There were 746 killed, 1,843 injured, and $6,000,000 damage done.

It is interesting to compare these totals with the combined totals of German airship and bomber raids on Great Britain. Taken together, the Germans made 103 raids, dropped 7,776 bombs, killed 1,414, and injured another 3,416. Property damage amounted to $14,675,000.

Before noting the conclusions that were drawn by the respective sides, there are two situations that must be mentioned. The first is that Germany made its best effort in both the Zeppelin and the aircraft bombing campaigns, and elected to stop those efforts when losses and costs became prohibitive for the results being obtained. It was also the German assessment that the British air raids did not achieve results commensurate with the effort required for them, and that the fall-off in German production and the effect upon German morale was too slight to be taken seriously.[39]

In contrast, Great Britain had not yet made its best effort in bombing Germany, and would not have been able to do so until 1919 at the earliest. Thus while it discounted the effects of the German air raids on Great Britain, it had a great, if unfulfilled, belief in the long-term efficacy of British air raids on Germany.

Both nations, of course, were making judgments on far too little evidence, and this fact should have been evident to them. If, on an ordinary "quiet" day on the Western Front, 2,500 could die, and if, on a "busy" day, there could be as many as 80,000 casualties, the combined total of 2,160 killed in almost five years of bombing should have obviously been discounted as militarily insignificant. In terms of material costs, both nations spent every day more than the total damages caused by bombing of both sides, so this fact too should have been seen in its proper light.

Yet it was not. Instead, this situation, in which Germany did not believe in the value of strategic bombing, and Great Britain did, would have profound influence on the political events of the next twenty years, as well as upon the military events of World War II. In Chapter Four we will find perhaps the strangest aspect of this remarkable misunderstanding in which German politicians would use the British perception of the effectiveness of bombing against both Great Britain and France—and French and British politicians would help them do it.

Chapter Four

Growth of Air-Power Theory

As rapid as the buildup of the air forces of the combatant countries had been, and as pervasive and important as their newly created aviation industries were, the end of the war brought about a rapid demobilization that literally erased air power from the grasp of England, the United States, Russia, and Italy. France did not demobilize quite so rapidly, and remained for many years the premier air power in Europe. Germany was not allowed an air force under the terms of the Versailles Treaty, and Austria-Hungary was no more, broken up into a number of smaller states.

The precipitous demobilization was both a psychological and a budgetary reaction. All nations were sick of the slaughter of the Great War, and all nations, with the exception of the United States, were virtually bankrupt because of the vast expenditures of the previous five years. There were internal factors within the services operating as well. When an army is reduced in size, fewer general officers are needed. Those that remain are naturally jealous of their position and their prerogatives, and stay fiercely loyal to their original branch of service. The officers of a junior branch, as the air force was in every country, do not have the bargaining power to affect intraservice events, especially the apportioning of the budget. This was true in all countries with the curious exception of Germany, where the strictures of the Versailles Treaty were so comprehensive that the ordinary rules of military bureaucracy no longer applied. Germany benefited from the fact that its severely limited armed forces were under the control of a man with exceptional vision, Generaloberst Hans von Seeckt. Though not an airman, he knew that air power might be fallen Germany's saving grace.

During World War I the combatant nations expanded their air forces from a tentative gathering of nondescript aircraft flown by amateur sportsmen to huge numbers of highly specialized aircraft, filled with special equipment and flown by highly skilled airmen. A mirror image of this change occurred in the increasingly sophisticated aviation industry, where plants grew by orders of magnitude, became more specialized, and produced highly skilled designers and managers.

From this titanic effort there also emerged several people who became identified as exponents of air power, the thinkers whose experience and insight led them to define separate philosophies of air power. The most famous of these were Guilio Douhet, Hugh Trenchard, and William ("Billy") Mitchell. Their philosophies would be debated for the rest of the century, and would be influential with those studying and creating air-power doctrine.

Of these three men, Mitchell was the most important in shaping air-power doctrine as it emerged in World War II. In spite of the intense way in which their writings have been analyzed for the past eighty years, those of Douhet and Trenchard for the most part had little real effect upon events. (Only about half of *Command of the Air* has ever been translated into English, and the first general edition in English did not appear until 1942.) It must be noted that it was not Mitchell himself who effected doctrine so much as a handful of his devoted followers. This was an essential difference. As time progressed, Douhet had no such core of former subordinates who assumed positions of influence, and while Trenchard had many loyal supporters in the RAF, events dictated against their fulfilling his not very explicit doctrine as he had conceived it.

Mahan, in his *Influence of Sea Power upon History,* identifies six conditions affecting the sea power of nations. They include the following:

1. *Geographical Position.* This is far more important as a condition for sea power than for air power, because air refueling now gives intercontinental range.

2. *Physical Conformation.* Again, this is far more important for sea power than air power. To Mahan, physical conformation included the seaboard of a country, with its harbors and other facilities for naval power. Because air power takes place in the third dimension and cannot be "landlocked," such things are less important.

3. *Extent of Territory.* This was much more applicable to air power in its early days; Germany had a much better position in World War I because of the extent of its empire. In more modern times, pre-1967

Israel was a remarkable contradiction. Its tiny amount of territory, surrounded by enemies, was difficult for its ground forces to defend. Curiously, Israel's small area was an advantage to its air force, which could attack enemy territory in an almost 360-degree sweep, losing no time over its own territory.

4. *National Character.* While a more sensitive issue in today's politically correct world, national character plays the same role in air power that it does in sea power.

5. *Character of Government.* This factor is applicable to air power as it is to sea power.

Mahan was not the only philosopher of sea power, and more recently, the works of Sir Julian Corbett (1854-1923) have been raised as a standard of comparison. In essence, Corbett concurred with Mahan's views on these points:

—Command of the sea is vital.

—Weaker powers must depend upon commerce raiding.

—Lines of communication are vital.

Corbett disagreed with Mahan on the following points:

—While the command of the sea is vital, the sea is not normally commanded, and it is often sufficient to have just the control of the seas.

—Joint operations of land and sea forces are essential to success.

Corbett imputed more importance to advances in technology than did Mahan, feeling that they could dictate not only tactics but also strategy. And according to Corbett, there were cases where the navy might have more important tasks than the defeat of the enemy's main fleet, as important as that was.

To determine the influence of the ideas of air-power theorists on the development and employment of air power, we can state that there is an analogous set of factors that molds air-power theory and determines its success or failure. For later identification, let us call these the Five Factors that measure the effect of air-power theory. These Five Factors operated to the mid-1950s, when they were succeeded by first the concept of massive retaliation as enunciated by President Dwight D. Eisenhower, and subsequently by the concept of mutually assured destruction (MAD). This concept assumed that both the Soviet Union and the United States had the capability to accept a first strike and still be able to inflict unacceptable damage in a retaliatory strike. As insane as this sounds on the face of it, the theory worked for all of the Cold War, and it is working still. The Five

Factors include:

1. the size of the military budget, and the air force's relative share of that budget;

2. each nation's contemporary political perception of the major threat to its security;

3. the level of aviation technology, expressed often in the early years by the emergence of a type of aircraft, such as a new bomber;

4. the national politics of the rulers of each nation (for example, Chamberlain's policy of appeasement versus Hitler's policy of aggression, the confused turmoil in France, and the isolationism of the United States, essentially, Mahan's Character of Government);

5. and, most important of all, the relatively small number of people who are most influential in the command structure of an air force at various key periods.

The last item is perhaps the least obvious, despite its importance. It is interesting to note that these influential people are rarely aces, and are even more rarely well known. They are usually bright individuals whose love of the service committed them to a career where financial rewards were nonexistent and chances of promotion were rare. Those careers, however, were filled with challenges that brought out the best in them, including opportunities to be responsible for innovations in weaponry that called for huge investments, and upon which their nation's life would someday depend.

The list of five major factors is iconoclastic in that it runs counter to most analyses of past air-power events. These, in book or lecture form, are usually discussions of a war or a campaign and how they relate to a particular theory of air power. It is worthwhile to spend some time elaborating on the five major factors and note their relationship to the development of air power in each of the countries in which we are interested. Doing so will reveal how the world arrived at the air-power position it held upon the outbreak of war in 1939. It will also show the relatively small degree of influence exerted by most of the leading air-power theorists over this air-power position.

Great Britain

No matter how rational the economic reasons for the rapid downsizing of the Royal Air Force, it is amazing, from a purely logistics standpoint, that so much could have been accomplished in just six months. The October 1918 returns indicated a force of 22,271 aircraft of all types, sustained by almost a quarter of a million personnel, of whom 22,000 were officers. By March 1919, the reduced budget directed that the number of aircraft be cut to about 200 aircraft, with 3,280 officers and 25,000 enlisted personnel.[1] These forces were scattered throughout the Empire, with only two squadrons to defend Great Britain.

Demobilization of personnel proceeded at an astounding rate, as did the disposition of surplus war matériel. Part of this vast disposal effort was done through the usual government surplus sales, in which individual aircraft or engines were sold to civilian customers. In order to preserve some sort of a market for the civilian manufacture of new engines, it was sometimes stipulated that only "damaged" engines be sold. Often the "damage" was that inflicted by a man with a sledgehammer before sale, and it was said that a well-placed pound note could drastically reduce the damage by affecting his aim and power.

In one instance, the British government made a sound business deal with a syndicate backed by Handley Page, Ltd. In this transaction, the entire stock of the Aircraft Disposal Board (worth some $28,500,000) was purchased from the Ministry of Munitions for a solid $5,000,000—probably the best return on investment any government has ever made on surplus sales (with the notable exception of the Aerospace Maintenance and Regeneration Center at Davis-Monthan Air Force Base, Arizona). The Handley Page syndicate, operating as the Aircraft Disposal Company, Ltd., received ten thousand aircraft of all types and thirty-five thousand engines, along with thousands of tons of parts. The deal effectively gave Handley Page almost a monopoly on the sale of surplus aircraft and spare parts, but the firm never recovered the initial investment. The market was far smaller than anyone believed possible, and surplus aircraft tended to deteriorate rapidly. Engines did not, but they were often not compatible with new aircraft types.

The vast reduction in forces also called for a reorganization in the top leadership. In a move that was intended to presage the end of the Royal Air Force as an independent service, British Prime Minister Lloyd George on January 9, 1919, combined the Ministry of War and the Ministry of Air into a single unit. Fortunately, he chose Winston S. Churchill, that old friend of aviation, to head the combined ministry.

Churchill's most urgent tasks were to deal with the fight against Bolshevism in Russia and to supervise the demobilization of forces. The latter had reached such a critical state that the Horse Guards and the Household Cavalry had to be used to arrest mutineers refusing to return to France or go to Russia.[2]

Yet, the Royal Air Force was close to Churchill's heart, and he sought to preserve it if he could. He resumed his personal flying instruction only to have two crashes within a month that forced him to give it up. Both crashes were while flying with his personal instructor, the thirteen-victory war ace Captain Robert Scott who was Commandant of the Central Flying School, and who suffered so badly from war injuries that he had to be lifted in and out of the cockpit.

There is an immutable saying in the military that what goes around comes around, and it proved true in the case of Sir Frederick Sykes, the man who had eased Trenchard out of his position as Chief of the Air Staff. It happened that Churchill did not care for Sykes, and when the latter submitted a postwar budget proposal calling for 154 squadrons that would cost 75 million pounds annually, he was "promoted" to the position of "Controller of Civil Aviation." To replace him, Churchill turned to a man of his own fighting stripe whom he had known from his days in India, Major General Hugh Trenchard. He requested Trenchard to prepare a plan showing his vision of the peacetime RAF.

Trenchard did not come willingly. He had been offended when Sykes had displaced him as CAS, effectively demoting him from commanding all of the Royal Flying Corps to commanding only a small percentage of it, the Independent Force. Yet he did not feel it honorable to participate in replacing Sykes in the same manner that Sykes had participated in replacing him. Nonetheless, Churchill liked the short, eight-hundred-word plan that Trenchard presented, and insisted that he take the position.[3] In doing so, Churchill saved the Royal Air Force from being reintegrated into the Army and the Navy, which would otherwise almost certainly have been the case if anyone but Trenchard had commanded the truncated RAF.

The best available biography of Trenchard is by Andrew Boyle, who paints a wonderful picture of this powerful leader who admitted he could not say or write what he wanted done, but expected his subordinates to understand him and do it anyway. Yet Trenchard's very ineptness gave him an advantage in negotiation, where he was patronized by his opposite numbers. In the Army it was the conspiratorial, verbose Sir Henry Wilson, while in the Navy it was the handsome, popular hero of Jutland, First Sea Lord Admiral David Beatty. Beatty was a particular problem, for he wanted the Royal Naval Air Service restored safely under Navy control. In a three-man meeting, Trenchard acknowledged that the fledgling RAF did not have the political influence to oppose the Army and the Navy in its quest for independence. But, knowing his audience, he asked for a sporting chance, pleading, "Give me twelve month's grace to get started." Wilson was indifferent—after all, he was not doing the talking—but the request triggered Beatty's sense of fair play, and he acquiesced.[4]

Now one would think that if the premier British architect of air-power philosophy, Trenchard, were given command of the RAF for ten of its most critical years, from 1919 to 1929, the RAF of World War II would certainly have reflected his air-power philosophy. Such was not to be the case. To understand why it was not, we need to examine first just what Trenchard's philosophy of air power was.

It is characteristic of most philosophers of air power, as, indeed, it is with most philosophers in general, that their positions change over time and with changes in circumstance. So it was with Trenchard, who had a great ability to adjust his vision to the resources he had to work with. Before the war, he had breathed life and substance into an as yet unorganized Central Flying School. In 1914, Trenchard replaced his *bête noire*, Sykes, as commandant of the Military Wing, when the latter was promoted. He found the Military Wing greatly depleted, and worked hard to restore it. Then in 1915, he became commander of the Royal Flying Corps, and somehow breathed the spirit of aggression into a badly equipped and often ill-trained service.

Trenchard was a hands-on manager, all too aware that his philosophy of having the RFC always on a "relentless and incessant" offensive was costly in lives and aircraft. Yet he persisted because he felt that it was a winning strategy in the long run. He shared with all air-power philosophers the idea that air superiority must be obtained, and it seemed to him that an offensive policy was the key to obtaining it.

When the RFC began to receive more capable equipment, Trenchard expanded his views on bombing. He believed for a time in the value of attacking German airfields, but the results changed his opinion on this subject. He articulated what would later be called "panacea bombing" by attacking transport networks and supply facilities. Looking ahead, Trenchard thought that strategic bombing might be useful in striking the enemy production centers for steel, chemicals, armament, and similar essential war industries.

When elbowed aside by Sykes from his position as CAS and made commander of the Independent Force, Trenchard understood that he was to conduct "a sustained and continuous attack on one large center after another until each center was destroyed and the industrial population largely dispersed to other towns." In other words, he was to create a mirror image, doing to Germany what Germany had wished to do to Great Britain. If possible, he was in particular to destroy Berlin.

Trenchard was a realist, and he knew what might be done with the relative handful of Handley Page 0/400 and de Havilland D.H. 4 and D.H. 9 equipment available. He chose the second of the two alternatives available to him, to attack "as many large industrial centers as it was possible to reach with the machines at my disposal."[5] Trenchard believed that the moral effect of bombing was to the physical effects of bombing as twenty is to one, so that widespread bombing of many industrial centers would have the greatest cumulative effect from the equipment and weapons he had in hand.

When Trenchard looked to the future, he saw that it might be possible to have aircraft capable of reaching long-distance targets in sufficient numbers to realize the first alternative. It was his belief, as it would be the belief of most air-power theorists, that the bombing could break the enemy's will by striking industrial targets. He did not believe in the indiscriminate bombing of civilian targets, but he accepted that civilians would die accidentally when industrial targets were bombed. He also made a subtle distinction among civilian deaths, holding that killing a worker in an armaments factory was essentially no different from killing an enemy soldier, while killing someone not engaged in actual armament work was to be avoided if possible.

During his peacetime tenure as CAS, Trenchard retained his belief in the essential requirement to obtain air superiority. He also continued to believe that bombing did more to hurt morale than to damage industry, and for that reason, a strategic bombing campaign had to break the will of the enemy population to resist. His arguments would be accepted by RAF leaders philosophically and be incorporated into written doctrine. If all things had been equal, they would have been implemented during World War II. Unfortunately, his philosophy could not be executed for the Five Factors mentioned above: reduced budgets, Great Britain's perception of the threat to its security, advances in aviation technology, its political leaders, and a few of the top leaders in the RAF who followed him. Let us address each of these in turn.

The size of the military budget is absolutely critical to decision making. No matter how cogent and persuasive a philosophy of air power may be, if the air force's share of the military budget is too small to buy the necessary equipment to execute the philosophy, there is nothing that can be done. During most of the prewar years, the Royal Air Force received about 15 percent of the quite small total military budget.

It is important to note that Trenchard saw to it that the majority of the RAF funds were spent not on a fleet of long range strategic bombers, but instead on air bases, on training, and on maintaining a logistics base, the latter done primarily by somehow keeping no less than sixteen aircraft manufacturers in business with small contracts. The decision to spend the limited funds in such a manner ruled out fulfilling his philosophy of air power—but it kept the RAF alive. Trenchard was forced to be content to have the RAF equipped with a few squadrons of open-cockpit biplane fighters with fixed landing gear and fixed pitch propellers—in short, slightly improved versions of World War I fighters. His stated view was that fighter defense had to be kept to the smallest possible number.[6] Similarly, he retained slow, cumbersome bombers such as the Vickers Virginia, which differed little in appearance or performance from the Handley Page V/1500, one of which had bombed Kabul in May 1919.

Great Britain underwent a significant revision to its perception of the threats to its security during the latter part of Trenchard's term, and in the following five years. While it is difficult to believe in retrospect, France was considered to be the prospective enemy for many years after World War I. The feeling was based in part on the absence of Germany as a threat, in part on the many years of warfare between France and England over the previous two centuries, and in part because France had voted to double the size of its air force.

Trenchard and his staff knew just how limited the capability of the French Air Force was for conducting a powerful surprise attack. Yet he did nothing to quiet fears, for those fears were his only hope of expanding his budget. This same phenomenon would recur in every country: knowledgeable airmen would encourage reckless claims about an enemy's potential ability to inflict damage, not because they believed them, but because they knew those claims were necessary to obtain a larger budget. Mitchell did this repeatedly in the United States.

One fortunate result of the misapprehension about the French threat was the establishment of the RAF fighter bases in the south-eastern part of England. These became vital during World War II against another enemy.

By 1934, Germany had replaced France as the prospective enemy, but the world was gripped in a global depression that kept budgets limited in the democracies. Great Britain was hampered by the "Ten Year Rule," initiated by the Committee of Imperial Defense in 1919, and renewed each of the following years. Churchill advocated the Ten Year Rule, which called for defense spending in any one year to be reviewed on the assumption that there would be no European war for the next ten years.[7]

No such rule restrained Hitler, who since the Enabling Act of March 24, 1933, had dictatorial powers. Thus it was that while Great Britain fought the depression by cutting back on defense spending, Germany fought the depression by spending billions of marks rearming.[8] Great Britain would be almost fatally weakened by not ending the Ten Year Rule until 1933, when it was already in error by a margin of four years.

The restrictions on Great Britain's budget would dominate the structure and the doctrine of the Royal Air Force through 1937. Even when the threat became clear, and funds were budgeted, the British economy was so weak that the manufacturers could not gear up for the production rates already established in Germany. After 1937, the disposition of the budget, and hence the structure of the RAF and its war-making capability, would be favorably influenced by the national policies and by advances in technology that had been fostered by a few farsighted individuals.

Fortunately for the RAF, when Stanley Baldwin became Prime Minister again on June 7, 1935, he had appointed Philip Cunliffe-Lister (later Viscount Swinton) to be Secretary of State for Air, with the charge to modernize and expand the RAF. Swinton selected top-notch personnel to assist him.

Great Britain was at a psychological disadvantage, for it had the memories of German bombing in World War I combined with the oft-cited 1932 admonition of Prime Minister Baldwin that "the bomber would always get through." Two phrases, "a bolt from the blue" and "the knockout blow," also gained currency. These referred to the prospect that a sudden surprise attack by air might "knock out" London and/or Paris.

RAF exercises during the mid-1930s, using the incredibly slow Handley Page Heyford, an ungainly biplane with a cruising speed of 115 miles per hour, proved Baldwin's point conclusively. The interceptors that failed to intercept were also biplanes, armed with small-caliber machine guns. In stark contrast, Germany was fielding one modern aircraft after another, replacing its biplane fighters with the Messerschmitt Bf 109, and its Junkers Ju 52/3m bomber fleet with more modern Junkers Ju 86s and Heinkel He 111s. As late as September 3, 1937, the future Marshal of the Air Force, Sir John Slessor, estimated that Germany had eight hundred long-range bombers and Italy four hundred, contrasted to Great Britain's ninety-six. The RAF's bombers were sorry examples as well, consisting of thirty-six each single-engine Vickers Wellesley, and twin-engine Bristol Blenheims, along with twelve each of the pathetic single-engine Fairey Battles and the equally inadequate twin-engine Handley Page Harrows.[9]

What was not given sufficient consideration was that as modern as the German Luftwaffe was reputed to be, there was no way that it could have delivered a "knockout" blow even with repeated attacks. There were simply too few aircraft, too small bombs, and too many targets for this to happen.

Here the budget restrictions intersected with national politics and, most fortunately, with technology. Thomas Inskip, who had acceded to the reversion of the Fleet Air Arm to the Navy, was minister for coordination of defense with the customary charter to reduce spending. Inskip saw that he could procure three fighters for the cost of one bomber, and that there were on the horizon three significant technological advances that would augment defense. The first of these was the Rolls-Royce Merlin engine, which would power the new fighters and many other aircraft as well. The second was the advent of two new fighters, the Hawker Hurricane and the Supermarine Spitfire. These aircraft departed completely from the previous World War I biplane standard, being cantilever-wing monoplanes with enclosed cockpits and retractable landing gear.

With these new aircraft the effect of brilliant individuals is best shown. The Hurricane was the design of Sidney Camm, while the Spitfire was the product of the genius of Reginald J. Mitchell. The Merlin engine was the product of a large Rolls-Royce team, but was refined and improved by the ideas and leadership of J. E. Ellor and Stanley G. Hooker. The massive eight-gun armament packages were the result of the advocacy of Wing Commander A. T. Williams and Squadron Leader (and later Air Marshal) Ralph S. Sorley, who recognized that a speeding bomber would present a fleeting target and a large number of hits would have to be made in just a few seconds.

Let us focus on this one development for a moment to see just how difficult it was to sell. First it went against tradition—most aircraft in the past had employed two machine guns, and all the design specifications, not only for airframes, but for synchronizing gear, gunsights, structural load criteria, and so forth, would have to be revised to accommodate to the new concept. In addition it meant quadrupling the number of machine guns ordered, and doing the same for ammunition, machine gun belt-links, and all of the ancillary equipment required. Now each of these individual considerations represented what today is called a "rice bowl," that is, each one was monitored by people who had budgets, traditions, perks, etc., that were threatened by the change. To effect such a change was not a matter of mere suggestion; it meant intense politicking to get to the desired goal. And under the severely limited budget, success in getting these goals accomplished could be achieved only at the cost of the goals of another organization.

And so it was with all of the improvements, from cockpit armor to controllable-pitch propellers to training mechanics in the new systems. Each one represented a fight for budget, personnel, and prestige, and each one was hotly contested. Such narrow-vision parochialism was not confined to the RAF, of course; it existed and still exists in all bureaucracies.

The third and even more important new technology made its appearance at about the same time the Hurricane and Spitfire were taking form, and would become known as radar. Henry Tizard, who as a RFC test pilot during World War I had helped solve the critical problem of how to recover from a tailspin, was now Chairman of the Aeronautical Committee of the RAF, which met for the first time on January 28, 1935. Tizard consulted with R. A. Watson-Watt, who two weeks later submitted a paper on "Detection and Location of Aircraft by Radio Methods," which was the genesis of the British radar system.

Radar and the new interceptors made Baldwin's statement that the bombers would always get through far less certain. Moreover, it relegated to the same wastebasket Trenchard's ideas about keeping fighters to the minimum number possible.

The Royal Air Force was blessed with excellent leaders who could capitalize on the advances in technology, and after 1938, on the increased funding that was available. Among those leaders were the Chief of Staff and Marshal of the Royal Air Force, Sir Edward Ellington; his successor (and a former commander of the 41st Wing of the Independent Force), Air Chief Marshal and future CAS, Sir Cyril Newall; a dynamo and innovator, Air Chief Marshal Sir Wilfrid Freeman; the future hero of the Battle of Britain, Air Chief Marshal Hugh C. T. Dowding; Air Commodore Edgar Ludlow-Hewitt; Wing Commander (later Marshal of the Royal Air Force) Arthur Tedder; Slessor; and many others. These men had the vision to reverse a two-decade trend, and turn the RAF from a small force that was often and fairly characterized as a "gentleman's flying club" into the lethal instrument it became in World War II.

Despite increased funding and enlightened leadership, the Royal Air Force simply could not catch up with the Luftwaffe by the time of the Munich agreement in September 1938. The danger was so great that the Air Staff advised Prime Minister Neville Chamberlain that it would be better to fight in 1939 than 1938. The reasons given were that the Chain Home radar system was only 50 percent complete, that twenty-four out of the available twenty-nine fighter squadrons were equipped with obsolete aircraft, and that the five modern squadrons could not fire their guns above fifteen thousand feet because of freezing problems.[10] This advice enabled Chamberlain to feel comfortable with his policy of appeasement.

Despite tremendous effort, Trenchard's philosophy of breaking the will of the enemy by bombing industrial targets did not play a major role during World War II because it had not been prepared for adequately. The budget limitations had vitiated his philosophy by excluding all of the necessary requirements for a bombing campaign including the most obvious one of building bombers. It failed to take into consideration the number of bombers that would be required and the type of bombing and navigation equipment the bombers would have to have to be successful, the intensive training that bomber crews would require to deliver their bombs on target, and even the type and variety of bombs necessary to be effective. No real thought was given to the method of selecting targets, or the probable loss rate that would be encountered in operations.

Instead, the idea carried forward was simply to bomb Germany and to build bombers to do so. It was utterly simplistic, and it failed utterly for most of the war, yet it fit into prevailing circumstances. In 1940 Great Britain was driven off the continent by Germany, and bombing became the only means of attack available. After June 22, 1941, with Britain under great pressure from the Soviet Union to provide some assistance, bombing was the only weapon in its arsenal. The RAF was forced to resort to area bombing by heavy bombers in what eventually became a colossal effort that consumed a vast proportion of Great Britain's industrial capacity.

Heavy bombers gradually became available in the form of the four-engine Short Stirling, Handley Page Halifax, and the Avro Lancaster under the industrial push of Wilfrid Freeman. They would be deployed in Bomber Command under the leadership of Air Marshal Sir Arthur Harris, who had no illusions about targeting only industrial and military targets. His aim was to "de-house" Germany and force it to its knees by area bombing.

While Trenchard's bombing philosophy was not executed, he was nonetheless critical to the RAF's success in World War II. He kept it in existence, he nurtured it on very tight budgets, and he made it attractive to the highly qualified men who did direct its destiny from 1939 to 1945. That they did not insist on implementing his philosophy is a tribute to their pragmatism. They did what they had to do with what they had available.

Italy

Giulio Douhet (1869-1930) was perhaps the first of the true air-power philosophers, with his interest in military aviation beginning in 1905, when Count Almerigo da Schio built the airship *Italia I*. Douhet immediately established his career pattern by engaging in arguments with his superior, Colonel Maurizio Moris, about the relative importance of the airship and the airplane. Airships were supreme to Moris, and Douhet had to fume as he saw as much as three-quarters of Italy's Air Force budget spent on lighter-than-air craft as late as 1914.[11] Moris was appointed Director General of Aeronautics from December 1918 to July 1920, dates which coincide with a less than glorious period of Douhet's career.

Douhet started his military career as a twenty-three-year-old artillery officer in 1892. Early on he became convinced that an independent air force commanded by an airman was necessary. This could not be regarded as personal ambition, because Douhet himself was not a pilot. He was, however, a good friend of Gianni Caproni, and the two would meld their talents, with Caproni building large bombing aircraft, and Douhet rising to successively more important positions within the fledgling Italian air service. In 1912, Major Douhet commanded the Italian aviation battalion at Turin. He had just written a report on the extensive use of aircraft and airships in the Libyan war, and he next wrote "Rules for the Use of Aircraft in War," the first written manual for the employment of air power in any air force.[12]

The fiery, diminutive major now had a platform from which to preach his message. Unfortunately his message was not well received by his superiors, and he began to be perceived as a political crank. Unlike Trenchard, but like Mitchell, Douhet had no patience with standard military practice, and abused his position as commander of the aviation battalion by ordering his friend Caproni to build several of his three-engine bombers.[13]

There is no evidence to suggest that there was anything but military altruism in Douhet's action, but the incident was perceived as an opportunity to shut him up, and he was reassigned to a mundane position as Chief of Staff to an army division in 1914. The Italian military hierarchy of the time must have been of a forgiving nature, for his misbehavior did not affect his promotion path, and he became a colonel the same year.

For the next two years, Douhet continued to write and to upset military protocol, a not uncommon occurrence with air-power theorists who had what they believe was a pure glimpse of the future, and had difficulty making their superiors understand it.

In his early writings, Douhet postulated the one belief held by all philosophers and practitioners of air power, that command of the air must be secured. He later defined this belief as follows:

To have command of the air means to be in a position to wield offensive power so great it defies human imagination. It means to be able to cut an enemy's army and navy off from their bases of operation and nullify their chances of winning the war. It means complete protection of one's own country, the efficient operation of one's army and navy, and peace of mind to live and work in safety. In short, it means to be in a position to win. To be defeated in the air, on the other hand, is finally to be defeated and to be at the mercy of the enemy, with no chance at all of defending oneself, compelled to accept whatever terms he sees fit to dictate.

This is the meaning of the "command of the air."[14]

This is a remarkably prescient statement, one which was perhaps not completely validated until the Persian Gulf War, but which was the goal of most air campaigns. Unfortunately, it is not the lot of pioneers to have superiors who understand and support them, and Douhet continued to be contentious even when Italy was having disastrous results in its war with Austria. Instead of closing ranks, Douhet criticized his superiors while trumpeting his ideas for winning the war, which included such helpful advice as building five hundred bombers to drop 125 tons of bombs on enemy cities every day, a feat that eluded Bomber Harris, Jimmy Doolittle, and Curtis LeMay during World War II.

By September 1916, Douhet's criticism of the conduct of the war had become so offensive that he was court-martialed and confined to prison for a year, where, in true air-power-martyr fashion, he continued to write.

Unfortunately for Italy, most of Douhet's criticisms were on the mark, and when he was released from prison in 1917, he was given the position of Central Director of Aviation in the General Air Commissariat. Still dissatisfied, he retired from the Army in 1918. After the war he had two great triumphs. In 1920 he appealed his court-martial verdict. It was overturned, and he was promoted to the rank of brigadier general, although he did not choose to return to active duty. The following year, he published *Command of the Air*, upon which, for most, his reputation rests.

Douhet continued to write and to speak in the same vein. He confined his efforts to Italian journals, but he did have an early influence on American thinking through his meetings with Billy Mitchell, and via the industrial relations that Caproni had established in America. He was read by German officers, upon whom he also had an effect. Apparently he was not influential with the Royal Air Force or in the Soviet Union.

Like Trenchard, Douhet altered his opinions over time, but he was largely consistent with his earliest writings, adding to them as he gained a greater appreciation of technology, then sticking to them defiantly when criticism began to mount. In the most condensed form, it might be said that Douhet's philosophy consisted of the following:

1. Command of the air must be won.

2. Command of the air should be won not by confronting the enemy's air forces, but by destroying his means of resistance with bombing attacks. Air battles were to be avoided if possible.

3. Future wars, as with the 1914-18 war, were to be national contests, fought between the peoples of the nations involved.

4. The aircraft had succeeded old forms of weaponry; the next war would be fought and won in the air.

5. It was impossible to defend against a bombing attack, and therefore pointless to spend money on defensive weapons such as fighters and antiaircraft guns. Nor was it worthwhile to spend money on "auxiliary aviation" such as front-line reconnaissance, artillery spotting, and transport. Long-range reconnaissance to assess damage by the bombers was acceptable.

6. Five basic target systems—communications, government, industry, transportation, and (the most nebulous of all) the will of the people were to be assaulted in an initial and overwhelming attack.

7. Chemical weapons—such as poison gas—were essential to bring about the catastrophic attack that would break the enemy population's will so that it would force the enemy government to surrender.

8. The ideal airplane would be a multi-purpose "battle-plane" able to make long-distance bombing raids carrying a great weight of explosives, and able to defend itself against any enemy fighters that might attack.

In retrospect, it is obvious that much of his thinking was incorrect, as indeed it was proved to be over time. He may have known this himself, and may have taken extreme positions just to garner the maximum publicity possible for his basic theories. Further, he used incorrect data upon which to base his theories, having very optimistic ideas about the number of bombers that would be available; the number of bombs needed and the distance they could be carried; the accuracy of the navigation and bombing; the damage created by a bomb; the number of fatalities per bomb dropped; and, most of all, the fragility of the will of the people being bombed.

Italy was perhaps the best country to rely entirely upon Douhet's principles, given that it would possess an army that seemingly was doomed to lose most of its campaigns and a navy that preferred convoy duties to open battles with the Royal Navy. Italy's dictator, Benito Mussolini, was an advocate of aggression, if not specifically of Douhet's theories, and he embraced aviation as representing the best of Fascist Italy. He learned to fly, and was often pictured at the controls of a Regia Aeronautica aircraft, very much the modern dictator.

Italy lacked resources, but if it had taken Douhet at his word and reduced its conventional forces, it might well have been able to build up a strong strategic air force in the 1920s and 1930s.

Unfortunately, the Five Factors affected Douhet's theories even more than they did those of Trenchard's in Great Britain. Italy was desperately poor, and building a huge air force would have meant that the Italian Army and Navy would have been reduced almost to zero. This was politically impossible, particularly given the royalist backing of those services.

Douhet, unlike Trenchard or Mitchell, was further handicapped by not having a strong following of young officers who took his theories to heart, and were willing to risk their careers to do so. Instead he began and ended as an outsider, a one-man-band irritant whose arguments became more shrill and repetitive as time went on. General Amedeo Mecozzi, who advocated tactical aviation, with emphasis on the support of Army operations, vehemently opposed Douhet. Mecozzi had great influence on Field Marshal Italo Balbo, the charismatic leader of the Regia Aeronautica.[15]

In consequence, the Italian Air Force, far from becoming the instrument of Douhet's philosophy, instead became, essentially, a defensive arm subordinate to both the Army and the Navy. And for Italy, technology was not a spur but an anchor, because Italy was unable to develop a modern engine industry comparable to other major nations, and its aircraft designs suffered accordingly. While some Italian aircraft were undeniably handsome, and some had excellent performance, they were produced in laughably small numbers by the standards of other nations.

National politics was Italy's greatest disaster. It utterly failed to perceive its real threat, Germany, and instead embraced it, which required Italy to turn on France and Great Britain, and ultimately become involved in war with the Soviet Union and the United States. In terms of personalities, Italy and its ruler, Benito Mussolini, were deluded by the apparent strength of the Regia Aeronautica, at a time when any objective observer could see, by inspection, that it was an obsolete and ill-trained force.

Air Marshal Italo Balbo, a capable man, led the Regia Aeronautica until his death in 1940. Balbo was wedded to the concept of the air force supporting the ground and naval forces, and recognized that a strategic air force on a Douhetian scale was beyond Italy's capacity. Given the limitations on Italy's resources and its production facilities, a moderate air force of semi-obsolescent fighters and bombers was all that he could elicit from Italy's halting war machine.

Balbo had accomplished a great deal before, in the 1920s and 1930s, with his civilian mass flights and in the conduct of operations in Ethiopia. But when Mussolini involved Italy in a war against France and England, the Regia Aeronautica was doomed, and with it any possible Italian use of Douhet's theories. Mussolini also resented and feared Balbo's popularity, and was probably relieved when he was accidentally shot down by Italian antiaircraft fire in 1940.

In retrospect, Douhet should be honored for being the first to speak out in a methodical way about air power, and for inspiring others. The bare bones of his ideas still have some relevance today, but the more his theories developed, the more they departed from real world results, and the more vulnerable they were to the immutable Five Factors.

United States

In the United States, although the Air Service and then the Air Corps received small budgets, the emphasis was slightly different. Despite his demands for an independent service, Brigadier General William ("Billy") Mitchell and other leaders, including his archrival Brigadier General Benjamin ("Bennie") Foulois, were well aware that the Army was absorbing the greatest part of their housing and maintenance costs, so that a relatively greater percentage of the remaining air service budget could be applied to research and development. Aircraft procurement, however, was pitifully low, and would remain so until 1940. There were other factors, however, that helped offset the budget deficiencies.

Billy Mitchell was unquestionably the most charismatic of the three principal philosophers of air power under discussion here. Born in Nice, France, on December 28, 1879, Mitchell carved out a meteoric military career mostly on his own merits. He charted new paths, embraced new technologies, and created a core of able adherents who did their best to implement his philosophy of air power. Never the most tactful of men, Mitchell proved to be the brutal blocking back behind whose slashing efforts other men would act as quarterbacks to advance the concept of an independent air force.

When war with Spain came in 1898, Mitchell enlisted as a private in his father's old regiment. His wealthy father was now a United States senator, and his influence allowed young Billy to be commissioned—at the age of eighteen—in the Signal Corps. He immediately demonstrated his leadership and organizational ability in tours in the Philippines and Alaska, making some waves in military protocol in the process. Nonetheless, he was the youngest captain in the Army by the age of twenty-three, with the promotions earned by his own merit. Nine years later he became the youngest person to be appointed to the Army General Staff.[16] Intrigued by aviation, he paid for his own flying lessons at the Curtiss Flying School at Newport News, Virginia, paying $1,470 for twenty-four and one-half hours of training.[17] That he paid for his own training would allow his principal enemy in the Air Service, Bennie Foulois, to stigmatize him as not a "regular flyer" because he had not been to an Army training school. There was no little irony in this accusation, as far from attending a regular Army training school, Foulois had taught himself to fly, aided by correspondence with the Wright brothers.

Mitchell's flying catapulted him to prominence, and he became Deputy Chief of the Signal Corps Aviation Section in 1916, being promoted to major. This was his ticket to the top, for he found his way to France as a military observer, arriving in Paris on April 10, just four days after the United States had declared war on Germany. Mitchell seized the opportunity. He was soon recognized as the premier

United States aviation officer in France. Promotions followed quickly. He became a lieutenant colonel in May and a colonel in June, and was given the rating of Junior Military Aviator despite not having attended an Army flight training course.

Mitchell was an immediate success, not least because he was fluent in French and had a dashing style, dressing flamboyantly and living in a huge chateau. He raced about France in high-powered cars or flew himself to meetings as he became what today would be called a master networker, making friends, lining up resources for the United States, and promising what he could only hope to deliver in the form of aircraft and personnel. Mitchell also succeeded in making a friend of Hugh Trenchard—no easy task for that busy man did not suffer fools lightly—whom he selected as a mentor, and whose ideas he eagerly absorbed. Many of these ideas—but not all—shaped his own views on air power. Mitchell also met with Douhet after the war, and found many things with which to agree.

Mitchell immediately embraced Trenchard's concept of aircraft as offensive weapons, and of the absolute need for air supremacy, ideas he had demonstrated in the Battle of Saint Mihiel.

He began to publish his ideas while in the various command positions he held in France. Like Trenchard and Douhet, he would modify them over time. Unlike them, he was susceptible to the suggestions of both his mentor, Trenchard, and to those of his staff, especially of the relatively unsung Major Edgar Gorrell, who was in the invidious position of being friends both of Mitchell and his archrival, Foulois.

Gorrell, at age twenty-six, became Chief of the Technical Section, Air Services, AEF, and as such was responsible for anticipating and purchasing the supplies and equipment the infant Air Service would need in the years to come. A veteran, with Foulois, of the First Aero Squadron during its Mexican expedition against Pancho Villa, Gorrell had a master's degree in aeronautical engineering from the Massachusetts Institute of Technology at a time when such degrees were rare indeed. Employed as a member of the Bolling Commission that was tasked to review European aircraft for production in the United States, he stayed on to run the Technical Section. One of his many achievements there was the formulation of a plan for both tactical and strategic bombardment that contained many of the ideas Mitchell later espoused.

As a young lieutenant colonel, Gorrell worked directly with Trenchard and French General Maurice Duvall, and laid the groundwork for United States cooperation in the Independent Force that Trenchard would command. Gorrell was named Officer in Charge of Strategical (sic) Aviation, a position he held until January 1918.[18]

Mitchell's first recorded comments emphasized strategic bombardment in mass formations. He then switched to tactical bombing, with the concept of first obtaining air supremacy so that the Army could subsequently be given support in its offensive operations. Later he began to emphasize strategic operations again, and influenced by Gorrell's detailed planning, was firmly convinced that had the war lasted into 1919, it would have been decided by a strategic air assault on Germany's heartland.

Most American Army officers were rapidly promoted during the war, and demoted just as rapidly when peace came in November 1918. By a mixture of chance and his undeniable charisma, Mitchell retained his rank. However, what some saw as charisma, others saw as insubordination, and Mitchell was denied his real goal, to be Chief of the Air Service. That position went to Major General Charles Menoher, who never learned the knack of managing Mitchell, who became Third Assistant Executive and Chief, Training and Operations Group. The latter position gave him effective control over Air Service operations, and enabled him to generate sufficient turbulence to discommode both his Army superiors and his Navy rivals.

Mitchell was, in truth, a difficult subordinate, but he knew how to play to the press and to the Congress, and, conscious of the support of his family, he was willing to place his job on the line more readily than others were able to do. It was not by chance that Mitchell was sent on long "inspection trips" abroad, to Europe and to the Pacific, for they kept him out of Washington—and out of the Army's hair. The trips were fruitful, however, for Mitchell returned from the European tour with a host of ideas on aircraft construction and procurement, and from the Pacific tour with a clear presentiment that Japan was the future enemy.

Mitchell knew that he could never prevail over the top leadership in either the Army or the Navy, so he laid out a path that led him to his greatest heights—and ultimately to his court-martial. He became a popular figure as a witness at Congressional hearings, made fiery speeches, and wrote inflammatory articles on his ideas of air power.

By telling an economy-minded congressional committee that "1,000 bombardment airplanes can be built and operated for about the price of one battleship," he forced the United States Navy into agreeing to the famous bombing tests off the Virginia Capes, upon which Mitchell's reputation would rest, and which would provide him the platform to speak out on other issues later.[19] The Navy was not averse to bombing tests, having suggested them as early as 1919, but it did not wish to have Mitchell dictate how the tests would be conducted.

Mitchell knew that his theories were being tested by the bombing tests, and he supervised both the preparation and the execution of the tests with his customary intensity. It may well have been that this dedicated effort that won Mitchell the fierce loyalty of his subordinates helped insure the execution of his philosophy during World War II.

Mitchell organized a task force of Martin, Handley Page, and Caproni bombers, and assembled and trained the air and ground crews who maintained them. He saw to the development of new bombs, including a 2,000-pound "ship-buster," and assumed command of the 1st Provisional Air Brigade, as the bombing unit was termed.

Even in the midst of these preparations, Mitchell provoked a controversy that foreshadowed his future. One of his pilots, Lieutenant Stanley M. Ames, crashed in a storm, killing himself and six men flying with him in a Curtiss Eagle. Mitchell blamed the crash on the general lack of meteorological, radio, and navigational facilities, and was almost court-martialed for doing so.

Mitchell trained his crews in bombing and directed operations from the air at the tests, which began on June 21, 1921, and used obsolete American vessels and captured German ships as targets. It should be noted that like politicians arranging a debate, both the Navy and Mitchell attempted to tilt the rules in their respective favor as much as possible. After a series of successful but unspectacular tests on a German submarine and destroyer, Mitchell's Martin bombers made history on July 18 by sinking a German cruiser, literally lifting the *Frankfurt* out of the water with their bombs.

The big event came sixty miles off the Virginia Capes with the attacks of July 20 and 21 on the German dreadnought *Ostfriesland*.

The *Ostfriesland* was built in the style of the Imperial German Navy, whose leader, Admiral Alfred von Tirpitz, demanded "unsinkable gun platforms." He saw to it that his capital ships had heavy armor and many watertight compartments, and *Ostfriesland* had survived the British shells and mines at Jutland. A war prize, it was commissioned in the United States Navy as the USS *Ostfriesland*.

Mitchell had a powerful audience, for watching the tests were Secretary of War John W. Weeks, Secretary of the Navy Edwin Denby, General of the Army John ("Black Jack") Pershing, and Major General Charles T. Menoher, who would have been delighted to court-martial Mitchell for any number of reasons. Also watching were the military attachés of many foreign countries; for some of them, the bombing would have deep meaning for the future of their own navies.

The attacks of July 20 did not do much damage, but on July 21, Mitchell sent in his Martin MB-2 bombers with 1,100-pound bombs, two of which struck the battleship. Later in the day, eight Martins and three Handley Page 0/400s attacked, with the 2,000-pound bombs that Mitchell had personally monitored as they were being built. Mitchell ordered that the bombers try for near-misses, believing this to be the most damaging method of attack. Two bombs were dropped, one striking the side of the *Ostfriesland* to explode about twenty-five feet away, as near a miss as could be desired.[20] The ship sank within twenty-one minutes, and Mitchell now had a lifetime platform from which to trumpet his ideas. The tests would also have a profound effect on the development of both land-based and naval aviation, and these in turn would have profound effect upon the histories of nations.

The Joint Army and Navy Board analyzing Mitchell's success found that aircraft added to the dangers the Navy faced, but did not make battleships obsolete. It noted, almost as an aside, that the test proved the need for aircraft carriers and effective antiaircraft equipment.[21] This might well have been the most important result of the tests, for the Navy became even more air minded than it had been. It established the Bureau of Aeronautics in 1921 under Admiral William A. Moffett, who would become one of Mitchell's canniest opponents. The tests also help convince "battleship admirals" to accept the conversion of two battle cruiser hulls (both slated for the scrap pile under the terms of the Washington Naval Treaty) into the magnificent aircraft carriers *Lexington* and *Saratoga*.

(American naval air power would enjoy a similar serendipitous situation with the advent of the intercontinental nuclear bomber, which at first seemed to render aircraft carriers obsolete. It soon developed, however, that many large, nuclear-armed carrier groups were a vital part of American strategy.)

Mitchell drew quite different conclusions from those of the Joint Army and Navy Board, and submitted a report that called for an independent and equal air force to provide frontier and coastal defense. The ensuing bureaucratic battles saw Mitchell's boss, General Menoher, replaced by Major General Mason M. Patrick, who knew how to keep Mitchell in line when, as was his habit, he threatened to resign. Patrick let Mitchell know that any offer to resign would be accepted, and Mitchell had to back down.

Another bombing test was conducted in 1923. Mitchell made the most of the successes he achieved, violating military protocol by taking his argument directly to the people through speeches, articles, and interviews—which rankled his colleagues and superiors, including President Calvin Coolidge.

This act was a critical mistake, for Mitchell was clearly no match for Coolidge in rank or in political acumen. Coolidge determined to wait until an issue arose upon which Mitchell made a significant error, and then nail him.

As Mitchell expected, his position as Assistant Chief of the Air Service was not renewed in March 1925. He reverted to his permanent rank of colonel and was assigned to be Air Officer, Eighth Corps Area, in San Antonio, a dead-end job.

Then Mitchell capitalized on two incidents—the apparent loss of the Naval Aircraft Factory PN-9 patrol plane on a flight to Hawaii on September 1, 1925, and the very real crash of the airship *Shenandoah* on September 3. (The PN-9 was lost at sea for ten days but eventually was rescued.) He openly charged that the accidents were "the direct result of the incompetence, criminal negligence and almost treasonable administration of our national defense by the Navy and War Departments."

It was, at last, too much, and President Coolidge himself preferred charges. To prevent Mitchell from becoming a martyr at his court-martial, Coolidge asked his good friend Dwight Morrow to convene a board to examine American aviation, and at which Mitchell would be invited to testify.

The Morrow Board began its sessions on September 21, and Mitchell made a very poor impression, confining himself for the most part to reading passages from his book *Winged Defense* into the record.

Mitchell was court-martialed in Washington, with the trial beginning on October 28. During seven weeks of the trial he once again tried to make his case to the public on air power and national defense, but his usual eloquence and charisma wilted under expert cross-examination. On December 17, he was found guilty of insubordinate conduct and making statements that were prejudicial to good order and military discipline. The sentence was suspension from duty and forfeiture of pay and allowances for five years. Coolidge gracefully eased this sentence, allowing Mitchell half-pay. The president was content with the way things had played out, for on December 3, the Morrow Board had made a report that curiously undercut Mitchell's personal position but advanced many of his ideas. The Morrow Board said, among other things, that the United States was still protected by its geographical position from attack by air, and that there should not be a Department of National Defense with co-equal Army, Navy, and Air Force elements. Instead, it stated that the Army and the Navy should retain control over their own air forces. It was, therefore, a vindication of the status quo, just as Coolidge and the Navy wished. Despite this decision, legislators drew inferences from the Morrow Board that led to the establishment of the United States Army Air Corps in 1926, a major first step on the way to an independent air arm.

Mitchell resigned from the service on February 1, 1926, and continued to campaign for air power, but was progressively less influential. Lacking a staff for stimulus and ideas, his statements became repetitive. Speaking as a civilian, he lacked the necessary forum from which to operate, and his magazine articles and books were less and less well received by editors. He died in 1936, uncertain that his great crusade would have any lasting effect. Yet by the end of World War II, it was apparent that many of Mitchell's ideas on air power had proved correct, and that he had laid the foundation for the independent United States Air Force that came into being in 1947. Many subsequent events restored his reputation, especially the Japanese fulfilling his prediction that they would attack Pearl Harbor early one Sunday morning. The United States Congress recognized his achievements in 1948 by awarding him a special medal, and promotion to the rank of Major General.

From the start, Mitchell's ideas were centered always on the requirement to win air supremacy, which would make the time-honored task of destroying enemy army and navy forces easier. In time, budget considerations and the battleship-bombing triumph made him switch to emphasizing the bomber as a war-winning weapon. In this aspect, his advocacy drove his philosophy; because if he wanted the Air Force to be an independent arm, equal to the Army and the Navy, he had to place the bomber role first. Eventually he would claim that air power alone could defeat an enemy by destroying its vital centers. His followers ardently believed this claim, and developed aircraft such as the Boeing B-17 and equipment such as the Norden bombsight to give them a chance to execute Mitchell's ideas when war came.

While many of Mitchell's ideas derived from Trenchard and Douhet originally, and later also from his staff, he was able to do more than just articulate those ideas. He successfully campaigned them, even at the ultimate cost of his own career. Mitchell was unique among air-power philosophers in two ways. First, he was able publicly to demonstrate his ideas by means of the battleship-bombing experiments. Second, he so inspired his able subordinates that they were able to survive the black marks of their association with Mitchell to rise to the top ranks of leadership. Once established, they made Mitchell's ideas their doctrine and did their best to implement them during World War II. Circumstances did not allow a complete success in these efforts until the necessary technology arrived in 1944 and 1945 in the form of the B-29 and the atom bomb, respectively.

The Five Factors also applied to Mitchell and his philosophy, but some outside events influenced them. While budgets were small, Mitchell still chose to devote a great deal of money to research and development at McCook Field, and later, the Wright Field laboratories. The scope of this effort was remarkable, for it included advanced airframes, engines, cabin pressurization, flight instruments, self-sealing tanks, new methods of construction, in-flight refueling, navigation instruments, improved radios, improved fuels, autopilots, and, perhaps most important of all, the supercharger, which was to be the key to American fighter and bomber success in World War II. Moreover, Mitchell's dedication in research was passed on to General Henry H. ("Hap") Arnold, who fostered it in both the United States Army Air Forces and, by his legacy, in the United States Air Force.

Both the United States and Great Britain were fortunate to have established organizations fostering aeronautical research and development. The previously mentioned NACA and the Royal Aircraft Establishment (including the British Advisory Committee for Aeronautics) undertook systematic research and invested in expensive capital equipment, such as wind tunnels.

Foreign sales somewhat ameliorated the severe Air Corps budget crunch in the late 1930s. The French and British Purchasing Commissions buoyed the American aviation industry by ordering American aircraft and by providing the funds to build the factories to produce them. Almost all American airframe manufacturers benefited from this support, and from smaller sales to China, the Netherlands, Sweden, Thailand, and elsewhere. The aircraft used by foreign nations included the Boeing B-17, Brewster Buffalo, Consolidated Catalina, Curtiss P-36 and P-40, Douglas Havoc, Grumman Martlet, Lockheed Hudson, Martin Maryland and Baltimore, Seversky P-35, Vultee Vanguard and Vindicator, and many more.

These sales were vital, for the United States was the political victim of isolationism, which regarded the Atlantic and the Pacific as ample bars to any threat from overseas. Perhaps even more important, these sales were vital to technology, for they showed just how far behind American requirements were for the standards of a European war. As a result, armor, self-sealing tanks, heavier armament, and increased power were soon factored into American designs.

The national politics of the United States were ostensibly neutral, but in fact President Franklin D. Roosevelt had correctly assessed the Nazi and Japanese threats and realized that war was inevitable. After his unprecedented election to a third term in 1940, he had a freer hand in moving the United States closer in alignment with Great Britain. There followed a series of events that included the pronouncements of the Atlantic Charter, the institution of Lend-Lease, the assumption of convoy duties in the Atlantic, and the embargo of oil and steel shipments to Japan, all of which moved the United States closer to war. His calls for rearmament were startling for a nation locked into a depression, for they included the building of a two-ocean navy and the production of 50,000 aircraft. While insisting that he had no intention of going to war, Roosevelt nonetheless took the steps that allowed the United States to enter the war better prepared than it had been in 1917.

Mitchell's saving grace was the number of able officers who believed in him and who made the bomber the United States' weapon of choice. Perhaps the most surprising aspect of his court-martial was the manner in which his subordinates supported him during the trial and even after his conviction, even though they knew they were putting their own careers at risk. His advocates included such luminaries as the future Commanding General of the Army Air Forces and later the first and only General of the Air Force, Henry H. Arnold; the first Commander of the Eighth Air Force, General Ira Eaker; the Commander of Air Transport Command, Lieutenant Harold Lee George; the first Chief of Staff of the United States Air Force, General Carl A. ("Tooey") Spaatz; Medal of Honor-winner Brigadier General Kenneth Walker; and many others.

The remarkable thing about the loyalty of these men is that they did indeed suffer from Mitchell's court-martial. After he was convicted, their next assignments induced many to think that their own careers were over. But they persisted, and they kept Mitchell's ideas alive, the most important of which was the consistent, unwavering pressure for an independent air force. They were able to present his ideas as doctrine at the Air Corps Tactical School (ACTS), and in doing so created several generations of leaders who believed that the bomber and not the fighter—as important as it was—was the primary weapon. Unfortunately they did not perceive that this belief was a near-catastrophic error, one that brought the United States Army Air Force perilously close to defeat in 1943.

Offsetting this error, these same ACTS graduates were in the fortunate position of being leaders at a time when budget, production capacity, and technology all came together in a manner never seen before. The United States was producing about 3,000 aircraft per year in 1939; by 1944, it was producing larger and more complex aircraft at the rate of 100,000 per year. Pilot training increased from a few hundred pilots a year in 1939 to hundreds of thousands by 1944. And the nation that lagged technologically behind almost all major powers in 1939 had, by 1944, leaped to a position where it would secure air supremacy in all theaters of war.

Mitchell was not highly regarded as a pilot by some, even though he established a world's absolute speed record of 222.93 miles per hour in 1922 in a hot Curtiss R-6 single-seat racer—not a task for an amateur. And he was pilot enough to realize that his Martin MB-2 bombers lacked the range, speed, and instruments to be as effective as he claimed they would be. Yet he also knew that other bombers with the necessary capability would follow if the time and money necessary were devoted to creating them. Mitchell was well aware that he could not deliver what he claimed while he was claiming it— and this awareness made him despicable in the eyes of his opponents. But he was also aware that if his claims paved the way for an independent air force, and if that air force was allowed to develop his ideas of bombing, he would make the United States the most powerful nation in the world. As controversial as he was, he succeeded in this objective in a way that no other philosopher of air power would approach for almost sixty years.

Germany

Germany did not produce a philosopher of air power comparable to Douhet, Trenchard, or Mitchell. Instead it looked carefully at the past, analyzed the statements of Douhet and others, then committed itself to a course of action that in time led to the mighty German Luftwaffe of World War II. The land of von Richthofen would have remarkable good fortune in the selection of its air force leaders from 1919 through 1936, and remarkably bad fortune in the years that followed. The Five Factors came into play, but because of circumstances, they operated in a different, sometimes completely opposite, manner from the way they operated in other countries.

Germany ended World War I with only its air service still capable of putting up an effective defense, a fact the Allies recognized in the Versailles Treaty by absolutely denying Germany any air force at all and severely restricting its capability to build civilian aircraft. Thus, while Great Britain and the United States demolished their air services voluntarily through a helter-skelter demobilization, Germany's air service was forcibly demobilized.

The treaty also limited Germany to an army of 100,000 men, designed for internal security and a moderate frontier defense capability. Its navy was similarly limited to 15,000 men, with submarines forbidden, and no modern capital ships allowed.

What the Versailles Treaty could not prohibit, however, was the clever planning of Generaloberst Hans von Seeckt, who was the last

Chief of the General Staff of the former Imperial German Army, and, after October 11, 1919, the first Chief of Staff of the new and severely limited Reichswehr. The fifty-three-year-old von Seeckt, known as "the Sphinx" within the Army because of his arrogant secretiveness, seemed to have a hopeless task, with his country surrounded by enemies and still suffering from the rigors of the Allied blockade and the ravages of influenza, disrupted industries, rampant Communism, a broken economy, and immense reparation payments. Yet in his memoirs, *Thoughts of a Soldier,* Seeckt wrote, "Fear was always a bad counselor, and fear is no position from which to view the world. Against a technical means of attack, the same technical concept has always found a defense."[22] This concept would be his philosophy in laying the foundation for what the world in just sixteen short years would come to fear as the Luftwaffe.

An ardent royalist who despised the new government of the German Weimar Republic, Seeckt was determined that Germany would have a new and independent air force. A majority of former officers, faced with the dismal German economy, sought to become part of the new 100,000-man army. Seeckt was thus in a position to be both selective and reflective. He picked the best people, including 180 specially selected to analyze the lessons to be learned from the 1914-18 war. Of these, no fewer than 130 were assigned under the leadership of Lieutenant Colonel Helmuth Wilberg to study air power, and how it might be employed in the future German Air Force. Wilberg would be of great influence, for he was essentially Chief of the Secret Air Staff from 1919 to 1927.[23]

In another move that revealed Seeckt's consciousness of the value of air power and his hope for Germany's future, he saw to it that 180 of the 3,800 officers allowed to his 100,000-man force had experience useful to the future Air Force. It is interesting to note that Seeckt did not bring any of the top aces into the new Reichswehr. The reason was simple: There were no aircraft for them to fly, and he needed planners and builders, not aces.

What emerged from the intensive study was an understanding that while the strategic air campaign against Great Britain had not been successful, it was still necessary to have a strategic bombardment arm. The studies also showed how successful the cooperation of air force and army units had been, and that this combined effort could be even more important in the future.

Finally, it was recognized that "letting the customer come to the door," fighting a defensive air war, was ultimately a losing proposition. This was a difficult decision to reach, for the 1914-18 defensive policy had been successful, with the Germans shooting down 7,425 Allied aircraft during the war. Even in 1918, when Germany was so hard pressed, its airmen shot down 3,732 Allied aircraft while losing only 1,099 during the period January to September 1918.[24] The strategy allowed the German Air Force to be a viable service to the end, when it was still operating more than 2,700 aircraft on the Western Front.

The acknowledgement that aircraft were essentially an offensive weapon, and the decision that their primary function should be in support of the Army, were two important factors for the future Luftwaffe, which had already begun to take shape in shadow form in several arenas under the Weimar Republic.

It should be noted that under the Weimar Republic and under Hitler, Germany had unique perceptions of the threats to its security. Before Hitler, Germany had a well-founded fear that either or both France and Poland would initiate a war. France did use its military might to occupy the Ruhr in 1923, and there were so many disputes at the Baltic and Polish frontiers that the so-called Freikorps, essentially private armies serving the helpless German state, were formed to resist them. Under Hitler, the perception of the threat was the same, with the added specter of the might of the Soviet Union added to the equation. The character of his government, however, was to use bullying diplomacy to obtain whatever was possible to obtain, and then to use preemptive aggression to obtain *lebensraum* (living room) in the territories all the way to the Ural mountains to the east. Hitler, and his able colleague, Joseph Goebbels, used an essentially phantom threat of air power to leverage Germany's capacity for bullying.

One of the arenas in which the future Luftwaffe would be shaped was the air-mindedness that Germany had fostered in its population. Germany was particularly attentive to its youth, creating in 1920 the Deutsche Luftfahrt-Verband as a sort of national flying club for building models and flying gliders. A second arena was the early development of German airlines that culminated in their combination into Deutsche Luft Hansa (DHL) in January 1926. DHL would dominate European traffic until World War II, at least in part because it was led by the future Field Marshal Erhard Milch. It became the training ground not only for pilots, but also for mechanics and other ground crewmen, as well as a laboratory for instrument flying, navigation, and radio equipment. Specially selected pilot candidates obtained licenses at the German Commercial Flying School, and the best of them went on to receive fighter training at a secret base in the Soviet Union.

A third factor in shaping the Luftwaffe was Seeckt's prescience in 1922 in establishing secret relations with the Soviet Union by which Germany obtained airfields and labor at which to create training bases, while the Russians gained access to the technical advances the Germans would demonstrate. The retired Colonel Herman von der Leith-Thomsen, a monarchist who had not rejoined the service, headed the mission. By 1924 a training field was established at Lipetsk, about 180 miles to the southeast of Moscow. At the same time, Germany contributed 100,000,000 Reichsmarks to build a Junkers aircraft factory at Fili, near Moscow.[25] Unlike Lipetsk, where everything expected and more was achieved, the Junkers factory was a relative failure. With a capacity of 600 aircraft a year, it built only 142 in the four years it existed before being taken over by Tupolev.

The Luftwaffe prepared its industrial foundation with the establishment of German companies manufacturing aircraft in foreign countries, including Albatros in Lithuania, Dornier in Switzerland and Italy, and Junkers and Heinkel in Sweden. This dispersion allowed German firms to maintain an engineering force, keep up with foreign developments, and even make a profit on sales to other countries.

The man who had led the bomber offensive against England during World War I, Captain Ernst Brandenburg, became key to revitalizing Germany's aviation industry. As a Ministerial Director in the German Transport Ministry, Brandenburg diligently sought the relaxation of Versailles Treaty restrictions on building aircraft, and ultimately succeeded in his task by the fall of 1926.

Thus the creation of a new German Air Force was well under way by the time Adolf Hitler came to power on January 30, 1933, with his commitment to spend billions of marks to build an air arm for future conquests.

Hitler had a natural liking for aviation, for his political successes were partly because he used aircraft in his election campaigns. With his future personal pilot, Hans Bauer, usually at the controls, Hitler flew in three separate campaigns in the critical 1932 elections, visiting at least sixty-five cities on each one, sometimes as many as six in a day.[26] The flights were sheer theater for the enthusiastic crowds waiting at the airport for their leader to arrive, sometimes descending majestically through an overcast, for Bauer was an accomplished instrument pilot. So novel was this approach that "Hitler Over Germany" came to be an accurate (and portentous) campaign slogan. Hitler flew in Rohrbach, Messerschmitt, and Junkers transports, with a Junkers F-13 carrying the soon to be infamous Sepp Dietrich ahead of him as an "advance man" in today's parlance.

On January 30, 1933, the day that he assumed power as Germany's chancellor, Hitler appointed his comrade and World War I ace, Herman Goering, who had just turned forty, to be the Reich's Commissioner of Aviation, in charge both of German civil aviation and its still secret air force. At the time, Goering was a good choice, for World War I technology had not been totally superseded, and he was well connected both with the officer corps and the aviation industry. The former fighter pilot was then quite energetic and could be as ruthless as required with businessmen who did not wish to take the risks he saw were necessary to build up the industry to the scale and at the speed that Hitler demanded.

Goering was actually too occupied with his many other tasks (including heading the Four Year Plan to reconstitute German industry) and allowed others to supervise the Luftwaffe's rapid growth. Hitler fostered this growth by seeing to it that the Luftwaffe's share of the defense budget rose from 10 percent in 1933 to 38 percent in 1936.

This seemingly disproportionate share of the budget stemmed from a canny, crucial decision that Hitler had made on the basis of advice from Erhard Milch and Goering. They in turn had obtained their concept from Dr. Robert Knauss, a former combat pilot and Lufthansa colleague of Milch. Knauss's theory was that the most effective way to defend Germany in the early days of the Hitler government was to build up a fleet of heavy bombers as a Risiko Flotte, the term used by Admiral Tirpitz to describe the "risk fleet" he had built up as a deterrent to Great Britain's Royal Navy. The scheme was attractive for several reasons, the most important of which was the psychological effect that the threat of bombing had upon Great Britain and France. Almost equally important, it could be done relatively inexpensively, costing about 80 million Reichsmarks, or the equivalent of outfitting five army divisions.

As it happened, Knauss's plan could not be adopted at the time of its proposal in 1933 because the German aircraft industry was not up to building such a strategic fleet. Yet Hitler, a consummate bluffer, was quick to see the potential for the threat to use such force, even if the force did not exist.

Before the public announcement of its existence on March 9, 1935, the Luftwaffe had been a "secret" air force, although every major intelligence service knew that pilots were being trained and new aircraft being produced for Germany's use. With Goering busy, running the air force was left to a succession of competent deputies, including Wilberg, whose Jewish background soon disqualified him. He was succeeded by the head of Deutsch Lufthansa, Erhard Milch. Ironically, Milch's father also was Jewish, but Milch managed to redefine himself as an Aryan by having his mother and father swear that he and all his siblings were the natural children of his mother's Christian lover, Baron Hermann von Bier.[27] Milch became Secretary of State for Aviation, which infuriated some regular Army members, for his highest previous military rank was that of captain.

Yet Milch's experience with Lufthansa proved to be immensely valuable, for he knew that the German Air Force would need far more than just planes and pilots. He established an extensive building program for air bases, and used his airline experience to acquire sophisticated navigation and communication gear that would have been the envy of every air force in the world.[28]

It was a time of intoxicating expansion for the German armed services, and it speaks to the fairness of the Minister of War, General Werner von Blomberg, that the new service was provided with a number of excellent officers. They included Colonel Hans-Jurgen Stumpf; Lieutenant Colonel Walter Wever; Colonel Wilhelm Wimmer; Captain Baron Wolfram von Richthofen, a cousin of Manfred, a nine-victory ace in World War I, and the very best Luftwaffe field commander in World War II. Another great asset was Colonel Albert Kesselring, who would become the German field marshal best able to conduct a tough ground defense in the absence of any German air power.

When he was appointed to a position of Chief of the Air Command Office (effectively Chief of the General Staff of the

Luftwaffe) in September 1933, Walter Wever had much to learn, and he rapidly set about doing it. First of all he learned to fly (at the age of forty-six), and he learned to recant all that he had said about not having an independent air force. Wever had a pleasant personality despite being a workaholic who drove himself harder than anyone. Although he is best known for his advocacy of strategic bombing, Wever had a well-rounded view toward air power and understood the value of close air support to the German Army.

As a staff officer during the 1914-18 war, Wever had argued for the use of an elastic defense to minimize casualties. The same desire, to minimize casualties, led him to believe, like Trenchard and Douhet, that the way to win wars was to destroy the enemy's industrial heartland. For this reason he backed the development of the four-engine bomber, and two advanced prototypes, the Junkers Ju 89 and the Dornier Do-19, were built for the task. Unfortunately for Wever, no available German engine had adequate power to give the two aircraft the performance they needed, a situation reflecting the general state of the engine industry.

Wever was killed in an aircraft accident on June 3, 1936, when, in his usual tearing hurry, he skipped the aircraft preflight and took off in a relatively hot Heinkel He 70 Blitz with the aileron controls locked. With his death, the impetus behind the four-engine bomber program was lost.

Kesselring succeeded Wever, and on the whole did his usual excellent job. His biggest mistake was recommending that development of the four-engine bomber be canceled on the grounds that it required too many resources and would use too much fuel on operations. Goering issued the cancellation on April 29, 1937. As has been noted many times, Goering was glad to acquiesce, for many more twin-engine bombers could be built than four-engine bombers, and, as he noted, the Führer "asked him how many bombers he had, not what kind."

The still young Luftwaffe was going through a period of organizational confusion. Goering's personality would not tolerate Milch's increased prestige and responsibility as he orchestrated the swift expansion. As a result Goering insisted on a number of personnel changes to place in positions of power people he believed would be loyal to him, personally. The most disastrous of these was the appointment of the highest-scoring surviving German World War I ace, Ernst Udet, as head of the Technical Office, and soon there-after, head of the Office of Supply and Procurement.

Udet had a checkered postwar career as stunt pilot, filmmaker, aircraft manufacturer, and hard-drinking *bon vivant*. He was consti-tutionally unsuitable for his new responsibilities, and he knew it. While he had the expert pilot's intuitive understanding of aircraft, he had no scientific or technical bent. Further, he had absolutely no understanding of how to manage a bureaucratic organization, and no wish to learn. In short order, he had more than twenty depart-ment heads reporting directly to him, personally, with no interme-diate layer of management to make decisions in his absence. This lack of organizational skill was particularly unfortunate, as it was his habit to absent himself from his place of work for days at a time, and upon returning to make important decisions on a spur-of-the moment basis. Despite his obvious unsuitability, Goering regarded him as "his man" and continued to promote him so that the one-time captain was a Generaloberst by July 19, 1940.

Udet's influence was disastrous for the Luftwaffe, but the effect was not perceived until after 1942. In effect, the adverse effect of the Fifth Factor, the influential people in the command structure, was tem-porarily offset by the Fourth Factor, national politics. Germany, as an aggressor, had the great advantage of choosing when it would go to war. Hitler was conscious in 1939 that his armed forces were more modern than those of England and France, and that in two or three years, his enemies would have closed both the qualitative and quantitative gap that existed in 1939. The harm of Udet's mismanagement came with his disruption of the second wave of German aircraft, which should have begun coming on line in 1942. A few new types were introduced, but only one, the Focke Wulf Fw 190, served in meaningful numbers. Others such as the Messerschmitt Me 209, 309, 210, 410, and 163 were either bad designs or did not reach production. Udet's backing of dive-bombers, and Goering's acquiescence in his demands, resulted in requirements for two- and even four-engine bombers to have a dive-bombing capability. This was sheer lunacy, and the manufacturers did not hesitate to say so, but the demand caused additional delays for the already change-plagued Junkers Ju 88 and the ill-fated Heinkel He 177.

Timing and technology are everything for air forces, and the Luftwaffe's initial technology was excellent, resulting in Germany's going to war in 1939 with the most modern and efficient air force in the world. (German technology was lacking only in engine development, and it compensated for this lack in part by building larger displacement engines, which, although heavier, generated adequate horsepower.) The mismanagement by Goering, Udet, and a later Chief of Staff, Generaloberst Hans Jeschonnek, forced the Luftwaffe to fight till the end equipped for the most part with its first generation of war planes—and far too few of them.

France

Traumatized by World War I, France could draw few inferences about air power from its victory. Instead it attempted to respond to all challenges in what one author has called a "reactive doctrine"[29] even as it remained totally subordinate to its Army. France had attempted some strategic bombing during the war, but had deemed it to be a failure. Air power was seen as an integral part of the doctrine of defensive warfare to which French generals, almost without exception, clung. The Five Factors of air power have unusual application when considering France

Like that of all nations, the French military budget was severely reduced, and its air forces had shrunk from almost four thousand front-line aircraft in 1918 to about eight hundred in 1920. The effect of the reduced budget was amplified because France was beset by bureaucratic and political problems that inhibited any focus on a French doctrine of air power. One of the great difficulties was that a French Air Ministry did not exist until 1928, and that the French Air Force—the Armée de l'Air—was not formed until 1934.[30]

French airmen were aware of Douhet's *Command of the Air* and used it to campaign for an independent air force, but did not otherwise attempt to embrace his theories. Some claim that the French Bombing, Combat, Reconnaissance (B.C.R.) series of aircraft derived from Douhet's call for a "battle-plane." French historians believe that these large, awkward, ugly, and vulnerable aircraft such as the Amiot 143 and Potez 540 came about instead from budgetary problems and the success experienced during World War I with the multi-mission Caudron R XI. The French defense budget was so small that the Army could not afford to buy bombers and close support aircraft, so it bought aircraft intended for both functions—almost always an inherent handicap to developing aviation technology.[31]

France had a real perception of the major threat to its security, and that was Germany's population of seventy million and a rising birth rate, and France's population of forty million and a declining birth rate. It was concerned, to a far lesser extent, about Italy, and even Spain, but the primary threat was always seen to be Germany even immediately after the war when that nation was prostrate in defeat.

As a result of its heavy casualties in World War I, and of its eventual success with its defensive methods, the French national politics dictated a defensive posture, one that was ultimately expressed in the short-sighted folly of the Maginot Line. And it was France's misfortune to be beset by feuding political parties that kept its defense budgets low even as the German threat became ever greater. France's national politics spelled failure for its armed forces.

Given the grievous losses suffered in World War I, it is not surprising that France's political leaders might have been reluctant to take steps that might be construed as warlike. What is surprising is that the French military high command advised them to take this stance. When Hitler ordered the reoccupation of the demilitarized Rhineland in March 1936, the French government, under Premier Albert Sarraut, was inclined to take military action against the Germans, despite having been given no support by Great Britain.[32] General Maurice Gamelin, Chief of the General Staff, informed the government that it was not prepared to oppose the Germans unless a general mobilization was ordered. Sarraut was astounded to learn that the French Army could only fight static defensive battles, and had no expeditionary force that could be moved into the Rhineland. General Gamelin stated further that "our going into the Rhineland can bring in response a German attack on us through Belgium, as in 1914, and aerial bombing of Paris, of our bases and assembly points, of London, Brussels, Liège, etc."[33] In essence, Gamelin said that to eject three German regiments, France would have to mobilize a million men and spend thirty million francs per day—and that it would take more than eight days before it could even begin operations.

Unlike the nations previously mentioned, the outstanding personality in French aviation during this period was not a military man, but a left-wing, Radical-Socialist politician, Pierre Cot. Cot was a pilot during the war, and served twice as Minister of Air, from January 1933 to February 1934 and again from January 1936 to December 1938.

Cot had a vision in which France would depend upon air power for its deterrent effect, with the formidable French Army consigned to a defensive role. The fiery air minister campaigned for a larger air force, and in 1933 pushed through a production plan that envisaged 1,010 aircraft, consisting of 350 bombers, 350 fighters, and 310 reconnaissance planes.[34] Unfortunately, the stagnant French bureaucratic system meant that the plan would not be accomplished until 1937, by which time the aircraft would be obsolete.

When back in power in 1936, Cot again attempted to accelerate French aircraft procurement. This time he was handicapped by a series of bitter strikes that brought production to a halt. The French Air Force was bankrupt in terms of aircraft, personnel, and production facilities. Cot brought about the nationalization of the French aircraft industry. By January 1937, 80 percent of the previously cottage-style French industry was nationalized, with the state acquiring two-thirds of the stock. Only a few firms, including Breguet, Amiot, Morane-Saulnier, Latecore, Caudron-Renault, Gourdou, and Levasseur were permitted to remain in private hands.[35] Only 10 percent of the aero engine industry was nationalized, even though France lagged behind other nations in the production of high-powered engines. A decision to disperse aircraft manufacturers, formerly concentrated around Paris, to other parts of the country also contributed to the general low quantity of aircraft manufactured.

Cot called for France to produce the aircraft that would permit it to obtain control of the air, and to carry out strategic bombardment. Despite his best efforts, France's confused procurement system could not initiate the procurement of fairly modern designs until 1938, when the first Morane-Saulnier M.S. 406 fighters and Potez 630 multipurpose aircraft were ordered. Under his successor, Guy LeChambre, the concept of a strategic air arm was dropped, and emphasis was placed on fighters for defense. France was forced to purchase aircraft from the United States, with the result that the outmoded Curtiss P-36 Mohawk was one of France's first-line fighters when World War II began.

It was perhaps Cot's misfortune that no French airmen of equivalent stature and vision emerged to work with him and second his ideas. The Air Force Chief of Staff from 1938 to 1940, General Joseph Vuillemin, typified the French officers. Vuillemin was a brave and very experienced officer, but his chief contribution was to be thoroughly duped by the Germans. On a courtesy visit to Germany in August 1938, he was shown a Potemkin air force that completely destroyed his belief in the possibility of France resisting Germany in a war.

Thus French aviation struggled fitfully in the short twenty-one years between the wars. No coherent theory of air power emerged, and French aircraft, like French tanks, were assigned to support army units in their strictly defensive role. Individual French pilots fought bravely when the German attack came in the spring of 1940, but they had no chance to influence the outcome.

Soviet Union

The totally inadequate efforts of Imperial Russia to establish an effective air service disappeared in the flames of the October Revolution. Experience of a sort was gained in the civil war that followed, and in the simultaneous war with Poland from 1918 to 1920.

During the 1920s, the Soviet Union attempted to establish an aviation industry and an air force. It was fortunate to have some excellent leaders, but development was always limited by the paranoid cruelty of dictator Joseph Stalin. Stalin called forth the very best efforts from people under his command, and, initially, rewarded those who did well with promotions and privilege. Doing well, however, carried with it the hazard of being seen as a popular figure. Stalin did not tolerate any popular figures other than himself, and unhesitatingly removed them by assassination or by trials in which coerced confessions of treason would earn a death penalty.

This was the fate of many men who might have made a difference in the history of World War II had they been allowed to live and carry out their ideas. The Soviet Union possessed some first-rate thinkers who were also doers, men who would have been outstanding in any air force in the world. They included, among others, Generals Yakov Alksnis, Yakov Smushkevich, Mikhail Frunze, and Marshal Mikhail Tukhachevski, all of whom merit mention here, for had their ideas been followed, a German invasion of the Soviet Union might well have been avoided, or if begun, immediately defeated.

General Frunze was Chief of Staff of the Red Army and became a commissar for national defense. He argued that a massive industrial base was the first step in acquiring an air force, and that the armed forces should be mobile, fast, and powerful. After Frunze was assassinated on Stalin's orders in 1925, he was succeeded by Marshal Tukachevski, who was the author of the concept of "deep battle" in which mobile forces were to break through enemy lines in the manner adopted by the Germans. Tukachevski developed the world's first airborne forces,[36] whose often filmed operations inspired imitators in Germany and the United States. A versatile man, he also created the Red Army's first mechanized units. Stalin deeply distrusted him because of his previous association with the Czarist army, and readily accepted intelligence planted by the Germans that Tukachevski was a spy. He was arrested, tried for espionage, and executed in 1937, setting off the great purge that would slash through the Red military like a plague. About 75 percent of the Red Air Force's senior officers were imprisoned or executed, and about 40 percent of the entire officer corps were eliminated. The survivors, as might be imagined, were terrified, and morale collapsed.

Alksnis became commander of the Red Air Forces in June 1931, and created a semi-independent military service that spread from European Russia to the Far East. He sponsored the introduction of the truly remarkable Tupolev TB-3, the world's first four-engine monoplane bomber in squadron service. Although a force of several hundred aircraft was built up, it was not intended as a classical strategic bombing force in the manner advocated by Douhet, who actually had little influence on Soviet thinking. Alksnis simply saw the need for heavy bombers to complement the other Soviet forces. He was, unfortunately, a friend of Tukachevski, and was arrested on a false charge of treason in December 1937 but not executed until 1940.

Yet another leading light, Smushkevich, had perhaps the most remarkable career of all, including commanding the Soviet air units in Spain under the pseudonym "General Douglas." This was a considerable force, amounting to more than 1,500 aircraft and 750 pilots. Smushkevich was responsible for defeating the Italians in March 1937 at Guadalajara during the Spanish Civil War with his ground attack operations. He then went on to take command of Soviet air units engaged in conflict with Japan in China and Manchuria. There with some 450 aircraft, in May 1939 he inflicted a sharp defeat upon the Japanese. (Here that air power had a tremendous influence on history, for the Japanese Army switched its support for imperial expansion from the north to the southwest.)

In November of that year, he became Chief of the Air Forces of the Red Army. All of his past achievements did not protect him from responsibility for the debacle attending the German invasion of June 22, 1941, and he was shot on October 28, 1941.[37] Stalin's memory was long, but his gratitude was short.

The brutal dictator's ire was not confined to military personnel, for Stalin jailed such prominent designers as Andrei Tupolev and Nikolai Polikarpov, whom he allowed to continue to work while incarcerated.

Stalin's bloody policies created such havoc that the Five Factors used to evaluate air-power philosophy in other countries simply do not apply. The Red Air Force had always received a reasonable share of the Soviet military budget. The Soviet Union, after some wistful attempts at an agreement with Germany before Hitler, understood that Germany was a primary threat, with Japan also a likely candidate. Under Stalin, the national policy was one of gradual acquisition of territory by threat or war, and he succeeded in taking parts of Finland, Poland, and Rumania plus all of Estonia, Latvia, and Lithuania before the German invasion. And perhaps saddest of all, Stalin destroyed his command structure by his ruthless elimination of the talented, patriotic men who tried to serve him well.

Somewhat surprisingly, and a tribute to Soviet engineers and designers, Soviet technology was not too far behind either the Germans or the Allies at the start of World War II. The deployed forces had not been modernized, but a series of fine aircraft were in the works. No coherent policy of long-range strategic bombardment had evolved, but the concept of using aircraft as an essential part of army ground forces was firmly implanted, which would be enough to defeat Germany in the long run.

Japan

The Japanese did not develop a unified theory of air power for a number of reasons, but by far the most important was the intractable division between the Imperial Japanese Army and the Imperial Japanese Navy. The bitter hostility of these two services, which continued until the very last day of World War II, completely ruled out the thought of an independent Japanese Air Force with a strategic mission. Instead there grew up a Japanese Army Air Force and a

Japanese Navy Air Force, each one subordinate to the service to which it belonged.

The Five Factors of air-power theory have different applications here. Japan was an impoverished country, and its large military budget was an onerous burden for its population to bear. Both the Army and the Navy viewed air power as a supporting arm, and each provided as much of the budget to its air arm as it thought necessary. Japan's major—or at least, most radical—air theorist, Admiral Shigeyoshi Inoue opposed this viewpoint, calling for an independent air force much in the manner of Billy Mitchell. For a Navy man, this was heresy, for he even advocated a naval air force that did not depend upon aircraft carriers, but depended instead on long-range, land-based bombers and flying boats. An admiral much more familiar to Americans, Isoruku Yamamoto, also believed that the Navy spent far too much on building big battleships. (Note: Japanese usage calls for the family name to be given first, Yamamoto Isoruku, but the English usage will be applied to Japanese names here.) Yamamoto was politically much more influential than Inoue, and was able to see to it that Japan had a powerful carrier force.

Japan was acutely aware of its lack of raw materials and perceived that first the United States, and then Great Britain, were the greatest threats to its security. This threat materialized fully in July 1941 when, after Japan had seized French Indo-China, the United States embargoed the sale of high-octane gasoline to the Japanese, ordered that petroleum sales be kept to normal levels, and froze Japanese assets. War became inevitable.

The Third Factor, the level of aviation technology, was to the surprise of all, in Japan's favor. After having followed its traditional process of calling on foreign firms for industrial assistance, Japan had created an able indigenous aircraft industry, and was producing first-rate aircraft for both the Army and the Navy. These aircraft were carefully tailored to their required missions, and while they did not meet current European standards for armor, self-sealing tanks, and firepower, they were very well suited for the tasks expected of them.

Where Japan suffered most, however, was in the paucity of people who were influential in the command structure of the services, and who were air minded. Only a few men stand out as outspoken air-power advocates, including Inoue and Yamamoto and also Admirals Jisaboro Ozawa, Takijiro Onishi, and a latecomer, Matome Ugaki.

Ozawa believed that carriers should not be spread about in separate fleets, but, instead, should be concentrated to maximize their offensive power.[38] With a courage rare in the Japanese naval bureaucracy, Ozawa went over Yamamoto's head in promoting his idea with the Navy minister himself. Yet, Yamamoto, with typical grace, agreed to Ozawa's ideas, and saw to it that the Japanese naval air service was reorganized into air fleets with corresponding land-based air flotillas. Vice Admiral Chuichi Nagumo commanded the first of these, the First Air Fleet, which in April 1941 was the most powerful organization of naval air power in history. Five months later it would be tested at Pearl Harbor.

Onishi was an ace in the air war against China, and was rabid in his condemnation of battleships. When the American fleet had effectively eliminated Japan's aircraft carriers from the war, Onishi had his naval aircraft fly off island air bases. Ultimately, and reluctantly, he embraced the idea of the Kamikaze attack, and organized the first Special Attack Units in October 1944. Dismayed at Japan's defeat, he committed suicide on April 15, 1945.

Ugaki had become an air-power advocate only after Japanese aircraft had sunk the *Prince of Wales* and the *Repulse* in December 1941. From that point on, he became an ardent supporter of Yamamoto, and was in fact shot down in the same flight with him on April 18, 1943. He survived to command Kamikaze attacks all through 1945, electing to die himself in the last such attack of the war on August 15, the day of Japan's surrender.

The man who might be considered Japan's greatest air-power practitioner, Yamamoto, had been particularly fortunate in the timing and the progress of his career. Commissioned in 1905 at the age of twenty-one, he had been wounded in the Battle of Tsushima. He became the naval attaché to Washington. He learned enough about flying to solo a training plane. His sea duty went well, as he commanded first the cruiser *Isuzu* and then the carrier *Akagi*. He ruffled feathers by openly championing the aircraft carrier over the battleship. From 1930-33, he was Chief of the Technical Division of Naval Aviation, and was there able to put his beliefs into practice, causing a program to be implemented that increased the buildup of carriers at the expense of battleships.

Yamamoto opposed war with the United States because he knew it could not be won. Nonetheless, when war was decided upon,

Yamamoto conceived the plan for the attack on Pearl Harbor and lobbied hard for its adoption. Thanks to his campaign for an adequate carrier fleet, his plan was successful, at least in part. He was also an avid proponent of the development of indigenous aircraft designs, pushing hard for the Type 96 bomber, the Mitsubishi G3M, which amazed the world with its long-range bombing attacks on China, and later, with its role in the sinking of the *Repulse* and *Prince of Wales*.

Yamamoto, however, lost face with his colossal defeat at the Battle of Midway in June 1942, and then presided ineffectively over the declining Japanese Navy until his death in combat on April 18, 1943, when he was shot down by a daring long-range attack by USAAF Lockheed P-38s.

Although Japan may not have produced a war-winning air-power theorist, it did have many able tacticians, such as Captain Kuroshima Kameto, who suggested Yamamoto's Pearl Harbor attack; Commander Minoru Genda, who drafted the plan; and Lieutenant Commander Mitsuo Fuchida, who led the raid. There were also many superb Japanese carrier captains, but in general both the Japanese Army and Navy lacked high-quality leaders who believed strongly in air power.

Chapter Five

Air Power and Its Influence Between the Wars

Timing and technology are incredibly important to the employment of air power in a war, but equally important is a nation's will to defend itself by spending a sufficient amount on armament during times of relative peace. In the 1918-39 period, the air-power world was divided into two camps. On the one hand were Great Britain, France, and the United States, whose politicians were afraid that they would lose their elected positions if they had to raise taxes to increase the defense budget. On the other hand, the autocracies in Germany, Italy, and Japan were rearming so that they could pursue a course of aggression of their own time and choosing.

Less susceptible to adverse public reaction to spending money on armament, these autocracies nonetheless systematically educated their people on the presumed threats to their nation while glorifying the ability of their military to defend them. In Italy, Benito Mussolini played on Italian nationalist feelings by telling the populace that they were a nation of warriors and promising to create an Italian empire worthy of their Roman heritage.

In Japan, the military had so firmly seized control of political sentiment that assassination became a way of life. Any politician who seemed to be less than avidly nationalistic might be assassinated by any junior officer—and the young assassin would not have to fear prosecution. In a propaganda scam greater than even Mussolini's, the Japanese leaders fostered the idea that the citizens of the still essentially peasant population were all potential Samurai. The vast majority of the Japanese were terribly impoverished. Hunger was their constant companion, and the opportunity for any job other than tilling the fields was remote. The Japanese public subsisted at a level far below that of the worst of the American Depression, so that for almost all the young men the prospect of a cruelly hard military life and possibly dying for the emperor seemed to be a good career choice. Those who died in battle were glorified.

In Germany, defeat, inflation, and depression had brought about an explosive situation in which gunfire in the streets was a constant reminder of the struggle between the Left and the Right. When Hitler came to power, his policy of rearmament was seen not only as restoring the nation's dignity, but also as the first and best means to escape from the Great Depression.

Rearmament and public works projects such as the building of the Autobahnen were certainly short-term solutions to the problem of unemployment. Unfortunately, the expense of rearmament carried with it an implicit requirement to use the newly armed German forces to obtain new assets from other countries, including land, industries, gold reserves, and natural resources. Ironically, the size and pace of the German rearmament was a primary factor in impelling Adolph Hitler to go to war in 1939, rather than in 1943 as he had so often promised his military leadership. In 1939, Germany's rearmament was incomplete, and its equipment was far from perfect, but it still had a great relative advantage over its primary potential enemies, France and Poland. (Britain, until late 1939, had wishfully and mistakenly not been considered a potential opponent by Hitler.) After 1939 that advantage would have been steadily eroded as France and Great Britain's own tardily begun rearmament programs matured. By 1943, the situation would have been reversed. French and British production would have reached or surpassed German levels, and the equipment, particularly the aircraft, being produced would have been more modern than that of the Luftwaffe.

The Soviet Union was the exception to this general scheme. It too was a dictatorship, intent on pursuing Russia's traditional policy of expansion by long-term methods. It maintained an enormous military force, one that was viewed with great pride but greater suspicion by dictator Joseph Stalin. But Stalin was aware of the deficiencies with the Soviet economy and its industry, and did not, for the time being, wish to provoke a war with any of the Western powers or with Japan. He particularly wished to avoid a situation in which he might have a war on both the European and Asian fronts. To avoid this possibility, Stalin played a skillful diplomatic game until Germany invaded the Soviet Union on June 22, 1941, absorbing vast areas of land in Estonia, Finland, Latvia, Lithuania, Poland, and Rumania at relatively little risk and less cost. These lands served a double purpose for they expanded the Soviet Union to include some former Russian territories and provided a buffer against German invasion.

German Peace-time Use of Air Power

It is more than a little strange that three distinctly different and very odd personalities should have combined to give air power its greatest influence upon history during the interwar period. The first and most important of these three was the Führer, Adolph Hitler, a cruel, ascetic megalomaniac who had already determined that he would use force to obtain territory in the east for Germany.

The second was the future Reichsmarshall, Hermann Goering, a voluptuary who earned Hitler's respect by the way he brought the Luftwaffe into being, and who gloried in showing it off. One result of this effort benefited the Luftwaffe in an unusual way. Hitler rewarded Goering's early efforts to build an air force by giving him control of the German economy in the first Four Year Plan. The Luftwaffe benefited because Goering had less time for it, and his second-in-command, Milch, was able to rationalize its expansion effort.

The third was perhaps the least likely of the lot, Minister of Propaganda Joseph Goebbels. Resentful of his physical handicap, a lame foot, Goebbels compensated for it with a brilliant, sardonic mind. Far more intelligent than almost all of his Nazi compatriots, he was totally dedicated to the casting couch technique of making films. Goebbels had no experience with aviation or with warfare, but was a master propagandist who saw in the Luftwaffe a banner that could be waved by the German media, the content of which was closely controlled.

As previously noted, Hitler had appreciated aviation in his election campaigns and had understood the value in the "risk fleet" of bombers proposed by Dr. Knauss as an interim step toward rearming Germany. More important, he understood the psychology of the French and British leaders, and knew of their fear of the bombers that "always got through." His decision, taken against the advice of his generals, to reoccupy the Rhineland on March 7, 1936, was a turning point. Hitler would later say, "The forty-eight hours after the march into the Rhineland were the most nerve-racking of my life. If the French had then marched into the Rhineland, we would have had to withdraw with our tails between our legs, for the military resources at our disposal would have been wholly inadequate for even a moderate resistance."[1]

"Wholly inadequate" did not begin to describe the state of the Luftwaffe at the time, for it was able to put up only three fighter units, all equipped with obsolete Arado Ar 65, Ar 68, and Heinkel He 51 biplanes. Of these, only one unit was fitted with machine guns, and these had not been bore-sighted for use. The three units were flown from airfield to airfield, and reportedly painted with different insignia to give any foreign observers the impression of much greater strength.[2] Luftwaffe bombers, primarily the Junkers Ju 52/3m that had started life as airliners, were incapable of striking the knockout blow. They might have reached London from German bases, but not if they carried bombs. The latter point was moot, however, for there were precious few bombs—some estimate less than two hundred total—in German arsenals.

The Germans were successful in their first use of air power as diplomatic propaganda, and the Rhineland occupation taught Hitler several things. First, he took his measure of the enemy powers and found that, as powerful as they were, they were not willing to fight. Second, it put him in a position of power over his generals, who had protested against the idea, which had secured for Germany the protection of the Ruhr and a springboard to attack France. Finally, it showed him the full potential of the threat of bombing as a means of blackmail and extortion, and not just as an instrument of destruction.

Later in the year, the spectacle of the Olympics played out in Berlin, and selected visiting dignitaries were shown fly-bys of new Luftwaffe aircraft. This show of force soon took on a more elaborate form, with especially favored guests being taken on impressive tours through German factories, testing stations, and even frontline units. Two prominent Americans, Charles Lindbergh and Alford Williams, were given this deluxe treatment, even though the Germans were well aware that the two men were experts on fact-finding missions for their government.

Lindbergh's visits are especially interesting, because the intelligence benefits they provided to the United States were later overshadowed by the public furor over the Lone Eagle's political naiveté. The American military attaché, Major Truman Smith, obtained an invitation for Colonel and Mrs. Lindbergh, who were received with open arms on July 22, 1936. During their eleven-day stay they met with Goering, Milch, Udet, and others. Lindbergh visited the Heinkel and Junkers aircraft factories, which impressed him not only with their current work, but their apparent suitability for vastly increasing their rates of production. He visited a first-line fighter unit, flew two German planes, and made a hands-on inspection of many others.

Lindbergh made careful reports on what he saw, and accurately depicted the comparative level of German design and manufacture compared to that of the United States. Unfortunately, he was not as astute in assessing the German leaders, considering Goering to be a unique combination of diplomacy and force, and Hitler to be "undoubtedly a great man" who had done much for the German people.[3]

Lindbergh made a second trip in October 1937, and this time visited the Focke Wulf and Henschel factories, Rechlin, the test facility, and the Daimler-Benz factory, where he correctly noted that German engine development was not yet up to American or British standards.

The Lindberghs returned to Germany in October 1938 for a nineteen-day trip in which all propaganda stops were pulled out. Lindbergh was allowed to inspect the top-secret Junkers Ju 88 and to fly the Messerschmitt Bf 109 fighter. Both airplanes impressed him greatly.

Permitting Lindbergh to fly the 109 was an extraordinary gesture at a time when first-line fighters were veiled in secrecy in all countries. In addition, flying a foreign high-performance aircraft carried with it the possibility of an accident with its consequent diplomatic problems. Yet allowing Lindbergh to fly was a psychological masterstroke, for it conveyed the message that the Germans were willing to back up their extensive propaganda campaign on the Luftwaffe with proof.

As important as Lindbergh's intelligence reports were to the United States, the informal reports he made to his many friends in France and England were perhaps even more influential. Intending to spur those nations to a greater effort in building new and better aircraft for defense, he discouraged them when he communicated his beliefs that the German Air Force was greatly superior to the combined British and French air forces. Further, it was his assessment that German bombers had the capability to deliver the proverbial great blow that could destroy London, Paris, or Prague. While it is impossible to measure the exact effect of these statements, his expert testimony did much to undermine the already softening Anglo-French resistance to Hitler's demands.

The great racing and stunt pilot, Al Williams, had a slightly different experience. He brought his famous orange Grumman Gulfhawk biplane to Europe, where it was flown by the incomparable aerobatic pilot, Ernst Udet. Williams was given excellent treatment, although not to the degree provided Lindbergh. He made a very detailed analysis of the German manufacturing process, and also flew the Messerschmitt Bf 109 fighter, which he proclaimed to be the finest he had ever flown.[4] Williams's analysis was important primarily to professionals in the aviation business. Politically, he was not much more sophisticated than Lindbergh, maintaining isolationist views right up to the time of his book's publication in the fall of 1940.

The German propaganda effort was not confined to the United States. In 1936, an RAF delegation, led by Air Vice Marshals Christopher Courtney and Douglas C. S. Evill, visited the usual round of factories and airfields, and was even shown details of the actual Luftwaffe construction program for the time. In October 1937 the RAF reciprocated, and a party of Luftwaffe leaders, including Udet and Milch, were treated to a tour of British airfields. They met with Air Chief Marshals Sir Edgar Ludlow-Hewitt and Sir Hugh Dowding, who were at the time the respective chiefs of RAF Bomber and Fighter Commands. The Germans did not regard the British equipment highly, and missed the implication of the "shadow factory" which, somewhat inexplicably, they were shown. The shadow factory system had been set up to permit manufacturers of automobiles and other similar high-volume equipment to engage in the manufacture of aircraft under license. The Rootes Group was the first to enter the system, and others followed. The shadow system dispersed production, with some of the shadow factories growing into principal suppliers of the Spitfire and other high-volume aircraft.

However, the real coup came in August 1938, when Milch staged a dramatic five-day trip for the French Air Force Chief of Staff, General Joseph Vuillemin. The short, stocky Vuillemin flew to Germany in the best aircraft France had to offer, a shiny silver prototype Amiot 340.

There he was dazed by the production of the Messerschmitt, Junkers, and Heinkel factories. On one occasion, Milch arranged for every flyable German fighter to be flown to one airfield where Vuillemin was making a routine and quick stop. The visitor was allowed to assume that it was just an ordinary airfield filled with the usual number of aircraft. Other, more elaborate, hoaxes were perpetrated, and the general went back to France convinced that France could not withstand a German assault for as long as a week.[5] (Some French historians minimize the effect of Milch's tricks on Vuillemin, but the essential fact remains that even without any propaganda, Vuillemin could only have concluded that France's air force was totally inadequate when compared to the Luftwaffe.[6])

Hitler was determined to play upon these successes, and, under his guidance, Goering and Goebbels systematically inflated the apparent strength of the Luftwaffe. The German Air Force was blooded in Spain, as we shall see, and had acquired a truly menacing reputation by 1938, enabling it to serve as a decisive instrument in the peacetime acquisition of new territories for Germany.

Germany used the threat of air power in three major political events, each one having a unique personal touch by either Hitler or Goering, and which more than any other depict the influence of air power upon history. In March 1938 Hitler delegated the diplomatic coercion of Austria to Goering, who promptly put the Luftwaffe on war footing. Its first task was implicit: to deliver, if required, "a bolt from the blue" to Vienna, and to threaten the same to London and Paris. Units were mobilized, new airfields were prepared, and there was an obvious increase in Luftwaffe activity. Its second and much more achievable task was to shower Austria with leaflets calling for its populace to resist its own government, which was headed by Chancellor Kurt von Schuschnigg. In the event, only the second effort was required, for Goering managed to manipulate both Austrian leaders and his own Nazi followers by telephone. Schuschnigg resigned, succeeded by Wilhelm Miklas who was able to put up only a limited resistance before caving in to the German demands. At first light on March 12, some three hundred Luftwaffe transports flew troops to key airfields; by that afternoon, Hitler was standing in his now-famous open Mercedes, receiving a tumultuous welcome from the Austrians in his home town of Linz. On March 15, there was what was to become the customary Nazi victory parade in

Vienna, where Hitler was greeted enthusiastically by most, if not all, the Austrian people present. The highlight of the parade—in case anyone in Great Britain or France had missed the point—was a fly-over of no less than 720 aircraft, one that combined both German and Austrian units.

Czechoslovakia was next on Hitler's list. He intended to go to war, using the alleged mistreatment of German minorities in the Czech Sudetenland as his *casus belli*. The British Prime Minister, Neville Chamberlain, who had never flown before, twice flew to Germany to appease Hitler and avoid the possibility of war, then returned again on September 29 to attend what became infamous as the Munich peace conference initiated by Mussolini. The principal attendees were Chamberlain, French Premier Édouard Daladier, Mussolini, and Hitler. No Czech representatives were permitted to attend the meeting.[7] Both Chamberlain and Daladier were conscious of the inferiority of their air forces and the concomitant threat of the "bolt from the blue." The two leaders acquiesced to the cession to Germany of the Sudetenland (which contained almost all of the formidable Czech fortifications). The agreement had been composed for the most part by Goering, and with a few minor quibbles, was signed as written.

The third and most brutal instance of Hitler's use of air power to influence events came the following spring. On March 14, Hitler summoned to Berlin the president of the rump Czech state, Dr. Emil Hacha. Hacha, who suffered from a heart condition, was forced to go through lengthy and tiring ceremonies before finally being ushered in to see Hitler at 1:00 A.M. on March 15. Hitler and Goering then played bad cop and bad cop, with Hitler threatening to unleash his armies while Goering promised to destroy Prague at dawn with his Luftwaffe. Hacha fainted, only to be revived by an injection from Hitler's notoriously incompetent personal physician, Dr. Theodor Morrell. By 4:00 A.M. on March 16, Hacha had agreed to Hitler's demands. He signed an agreement that made Czechoslovakia a German protectorate, and phoned his aides to insure that the Czech troops did not resist the invading Germans.[8]

Hitler marched troops in to establish the Protectorate of Bohemia and Moravia. On March 16, he occupied Slovakia, and one week later, in a manner so nonchalant that there was scarcely a protest from anyone, forced Lithuania to cede the port city of Memel to Germany.

Thus in little over a year, Hitler's implicit and explicit threats to use his air force had allowed him to acquire four additions to his territory that altered the map of Europe. Prior to 1938, the democracies, despite their lethargy and their fear of being bombed, had in combination been stronger than Germany. The loss of the Czech fortifications, manned by a determined Czech army of some thirty-four divisions and backed by a surprisingly strong if obsolescent air force, completely upset the balance of power. Poland was now isolated and was unquestionably Germany's next target, despite Hitler's protestations that he had no more territorial demands in Europe.

The threat of air power had been tellingly effective. Let us look now at the actual use of air power in four very different conflicts, where the actual use of air power was as effective as the threat of its use.

Great Britain and Air Control in the Middle East

One of the legacies of the Allied victory in World War I was the addition of entirely new and rarely profitable obligations in controlling areas of the former Ottoman Empire that were mandated by the new League of Nations to France and Great Britain. This artificial and unwelcome division of the lands of the Middle East stemmed from the Anglo/French secret 1916 Sykes-Picot Treaty in which the areas of Mesopotamia and Palestine were allocated to Great Britain, and those of Syria and Lebanon to France. These reflected both pre-war spheres of influence and the contemporary desire to protect the routes to existing colonial territories. There were also the first faint whiffs of interest in the potential petroleum resources of the region.

These areas represented a burdensome military expense to both countries, and both sought to find ways to fulfill their responsibilities to the League of Nations at a lower cost in money and blood.

The first experience with what became known as "air control" took place in Somaliland, where since 1899 the forces of Sayyid Muhammad Ibn Abdulla Hassan had been carrying on a jihad against British rule. Termed the "Mad Mullah of Somaliland," Hassan was the contemporary equivalent of modern terrorist leaders. A number of conventional land campaigns to rout him were unsuccessful, and the Great War in Europe in 1914 drew British attention from the area. In 1919, however, Great Britain was determined to restore its order and prestige—but did not wish to spend the millions of pounds necessary to do so. Air

Marshal Hugh Trenchard saw the occasion as a chance to find employment for the RAF, and offered a plan to use aircraft in concert with the more typical ground forces mounted on camels.

On January 20, 1920, in a style that would be followed subsequently by others, Trenchard's de Havillands dropped leaflets that delivered an ultimatum to the Mullah. He responded by making himself a target, bravely putting on new robes and sitting beneath a white canopy. The British responded to his defiant gesture by dropping a bomb that accidentally spared the Mullah, but killed his uncle. The Mullah fled with his troops, and a three-week campaign in which aircraft aided conventional forces ensued. Fortune then intervened, for the Mullah fled to Ethiopia where he very conveniently died the following year.

The RAF could claim that it had achieved success in a three-week campaign that cost an estimated 77,000 pounds. Contemporary estimates showed that a conventional campaign would have cost perhaps 5 million pounds. Not seen as important at the time, but of great importance only a few years later, was the fact that the de Havilland D.H. 9as and Bristol F.2Bs had killed relatively few of the tribesmen, and inflicted little of what today would be called "collateral damage."

Military jargon is constantly reinventing itself, and in the early 1920s the popular term was "substitution," meaning the substitution of air power for tasks previously assigned to ground forces. The concept was soon expanded. The RAF, still flying obsolescent and ill-maintained aircraft from World War I, became a fire brigade, attempting, and sometimes succeeding, in bringing resisting tribesmen to heel in the Middle East and in India. On October 22, 1921, the Air Ministry was given responsibility for Mesopotamia. It was allocated eight squadrons of bombers and a small contingent of mounted troops for the task. The technique was soon extended to Aden, Sudan (where anti-slavery patrols were flown), and Trans-Jordan, and to India's Northwest Frontier.

According to the RAF War Manual of the period, the object of air control was to interrupt the normal life of the enemy to such an extent that a continuance of the hostilities became impossible. In Sir John Slessor's words, air control was an "inverted blockade" in which the people were blocked out of their country instead of into it.[9] The success of the idea rested on the principle of communal responsibility, in which the various tribal communities were held responsible for the acts of their individual members. This concept was thoroughly in accord with local custom.

While the actual execution of air control often varied with the situation, under ideal circumstances it would begin with the tribe receiving a clear explanation of what was expected of it, and when it was expected. If the tribal leaders rejected or ignored the terms, they were advised to evacuate their territory by a specific date, and given the understanding that after that date, their territory was subject to being bombed without notice. They were also advised how to submit when they had been sufficiently bombed. Before the bombing began, the tribes were given twenty-four hours notice, and bombing was halted immediately when the tribes signaled submission.

This technique was followed in most but not all instances, and for the most part was an adequate formula. Using aircraft had many obvious advantages—the British could react more quickly over a larger area and with greater force than before. Yet there was another factor that was almost equally important. The tribesmen, whose lives revolved around fighting, found the aircraft frustrating, for not only could they not fight back, there were no spoils to be won. When conventional ground forces were used, there was always the possibility of an open battle with supply lines to be cut, depots to be raided, and spoils to be gained. In essence, aircraft took the sport out of traditional tribal warfare.

The success of air control varied from one situation to the next. It was extremely practical in large open areas where tribal movements could be followed and where RAF observers could obtain intimate knowledge of the personalities, terrain, and resources of the peoples they were trying to control. It was not possible to use air control in Palestine, which was too built up and where conventional means of control were still required. It has transpired that despite the fact that air control was not attempted in Palestine, it is sometimes described as an example of the concept.

It may be that the principal success of the air control idea was in keeping the Royal Air Force in being without any further reductions in size, and in furnishing realistic experience in the employment of air power that no training exercises could have provided.

Japan against China and the Soviet Union

The Japanese employed air power in a one-sided manner from

their first incursions into China in 1931 to the full-scale invasion in 1937. The Chinese were unable for many years to put up any meaningful sustained resistance to the Japanese Army and Navy air forces, even though they invested considerable sums in foreign equipment, and had the assistance of units of the Red Air Force equipped with first-line Polikarpov I-15, I-15bis, and I-16 fighters. In 1938, four squadrons of fighters and two of Tupolev SB-2 bombers were on hand, manned by 350 Russian "volunteers" commanded by Lieutenant Colonel Stepan P. Suprun. The thirty-one-year-old Suprun would score eight victories against the Japanese, and in 1941, four more against the Germans, before being shot down.[10] In addition, the Russians provided about 400 I-15s and I-16s for the Chinese to fly. Most of these were destroyed on the ground or in accidents.

Initially, the Soviets flew in all-Russian units; later, in the practice that they would follow in Spain, there were mixed Russian-Chinese units, and in the case of bombers, even mixed crews. About two hundred Soviet aviators were lost in China, although almost half of these losses were incurred while the aviators were passengers being flown to or from the combat area. The Russians claimed eighty-one aerial victories, although these have never been substantiated.

Things did not always go well between the two allies, for the Chinese resented what they considered meddling by the Russians, and the Russians took a dim view of Chinese stubbornness, poor training, and failure to care for valuable assets. The result was that in the summer of 1938 the Russians temporarily ceased to fight, withdrawing to their tents like Achilles. The same problem reoccurred in 1939, and the Soviet pilots were withdrawn in 1940, although some advisors remained to conduct training. The Soviets continued to deliver aircraft through April 1941, by which time they had supplied 1,250 aircraft of all sorts, including 347 I-15s and I-15bis and 216 I-16s.[11]

The Soviet Union would provide the only meaningful aerial resistance to the Japanese until the American Volunteer Group commanded by Claire L. Chennault went into action in December 1941. The standard of training of Chinese pilots in all-Chinese units was so low that the Japanese shot them out of the sky.[12]

The Japanese made efficient military use of air power, backing up the advances of their ground forces, engaging in extensive reconnaissance efforts, and enhancing their already vast superiority in artillery with spotting flights. They also used air power in a particularly brutal manner, bombing defenseless cities, apparently indifferent to the hostile reaction this practice provoked throughout the world.

This indifference to public reaction reached a critical height with the sinking of the USS *Panay* on December 12, 1937. The *Panay* was a 450-ton shallow-draft gunboat and was carrying American civilians, including members of the diplomatic staff, up the Yangtze river to escape the Japanese shelling of Nanking (Nanjing). Twenty-four Japanese Naval aircraft—fifteen bombers and nine fighters—bombed and strafed the *Panay,* dropping bombs of up to five hundred pounds, despite the fact that the American flag was clearly displayed. The attack began at 1:27 P.M. and ended at 2:25. The *Panay* sank at 3:54, with three passengers dead and twelve injured. Three small American oil company vessels were also sunk, and another sixty-two men injured.

Despite a United States naval court of inquiry that concluded that the attack was deliberate, Japan insisted that it was an accident, and offered an apology and an indemnity of $2,214,007.36, which was ultimately accepted. The *Panay* was the first United States Navy ship to be sunk by air action.[13] (There is an intriguing rumor that the reason the Japanese attacked—and the reason the Americans accepted the apology—was that the *Panay* was carrying salvaged pieces of a Japanese aircraft. The author cannot provide a source for the rumor, with its *Lusitania*-like connotations, but it would be interesting if it were so.)

Still, the sincerity of the Japanese might be called into question, given that in January 1942 a medal was awarded to Colonel Kingoro Hashimoto for his part in planning the attack. This action might be interpreted that the attack on the *Panay* was made with official government sanction and not by the private initiative of a hotheaded Japanese officer. Unfortunately for the Japanese people, Tokyo drew the conclusion that the United States was not willing to defend itself.

Japanese success in the air war over China came in part because of a series of indigenous designs that included bombers of very long-range and good load-carrying capacity, and fighters possessed of a high-speed and superb maneuverability. The quality of these modern aircraft was epitomized by the Mitsubishi firm, which built the G3M and G4M bombers and the A5M and A6M (Zero) fighters. The Western world, particularly the United States and Great Britain, discounted Japan's ability to build such excellent aircraft, which, for the Japanese mission, were fully up to world standards.

Unfortunately for the Japanese, they did not adopt modern mass production techniques, so that many of their aircraft were built on a "file to fit" basis. The result was that parts from one Zero (for example) would not fit another. Consequently, many aircraft in very good shape were written off in the field because they could not be repaired locally. Analysis of Japanese designs also indicates that there was an endemic tendency to over-engineer even some of the smaller assemblies. For example, the handholds on the sides of the Zero were complex spring-loaded mechanisms; the corresponding parts on an American fighter were simple folding pegs.

Ironically it was the very success of the Japanese air forces, particularly that of the Navy, which led to their ultimate failure in World War II. The Japanese concluded that a relatively small force of excellent aircraft flown by extremely proficient crews was the most economical and the most effective use of air power. They tailored their training and production programs accordingly.

Against an opponent like China, this conclusion was unquestionably true. Unfortunately for Japan, its future opponents would not always be poorly trained and ill-equipped Chinese. This was the fatal error, one that doomed any hope that Japan might have had for air superiority in a war against the United States. Japan's inability to draw the correct conclusions from its combat experience led it down two disastrous paths. In the first instance it permitted pilot training standards to be set so high that as few as a hundred pilots per year were graduated from flying schools. When it became necessary to vastly expand pilot training to meet the requirements of war against the United States, Japan was unable to do so. In a similar manner, Japanese aircraft had been optimized to certain design points—speed, range, and maneuverability. This meant that other critical areas were slighted, including armor, self-sealing tanks, and even structural strength. This design failure was not a handicap when it was the Japanese who were doing all the shooting, but when they encountered an enemy that shot back, Japanese aircraft were terribly vulnerable.

The Japanese persistence in drawing the wrong conclusions from their combat with China is all the more remarkable, given their experience fighting against the Soviet Union during the 1937-39 period. The first major battle took place in July 1938, near Lake Khasan. After a series of ground battles, the Russians made a major attack on August 6, 1938, using heavy Tupolev TB-3 bombers to assault Japanese positions in a manner that prefigured Allied carpet bombing in World War II. Closely coordinated tank and infantry attacks followed, involving more than 250 Soviet aircraft. The Japanese for some reason had decided to withhold their own air power, and as a result were forced to agree to an embarrassing cease-fire.

Seeking revenge the following year, the 23rd Division of the Japanese Kwantung Army (which deemed itself almost independent from orders of the Imperial General Staff) moved into a disputed section of the Mongolian/Manchukuo/Korean border referred to as the Khalkhin-Gol. Future Marshal of the Soviet Union, Lieutenant General Georgi Zhukov, was sent to take command of Soviet forces, which included five hundred tanks and six hundred aircraft.

A series of major air battles ensued, some with as many as two hundred aircraft involved. Initially the Japanese held an advantage, inflicting a three-to-one loss ratio on the enemy. The Soviets responded by bringing their most expert pilots, blooded in the Spanish Civil War (see below), and, over time, the Soviet Air Force seized command of the air and decisively defeated the Japanese Air Force. It also provided effective close air support for the Soviet ground forces. These extended battles were distinguished by the introduction of the RS-82 rockets for air-to-air work. These were used all during World War II, sometimes also for close air support. They prefigured the use of unguided R4M rockets on the Messerschmitt Me 262, and the hailstorm of 2.75-inch Mighty Mouse rockets fired in salvos of twenty-four by the Lockheed F-94 and North American F-86D interceptors. Later and far more sophisticated guided rockets owe a debt to the RS-82s as well.

Victory claims, as always, were exaggerated, but the scale of the fighting is indicated by the Soviet claim of 589 aircraft destroyed in the air and 87 on the ground, while admitting a loss of 207. The Japanese claimed 1,269 Soviet aircraft, while admitting a loss of 168 of their own.

The basic fact of the matter was that the Japanese were completely outsmarted by Zhukov, who used his intelligence resources to great effect. In the course of a series of battles, the Japanese lost some 25,000 killed.

The results of these Soviet/Japanese encounters were far-reaching. The Japanese were delighted to be able to disengage from battle, and their Army commanders came to two decisions. The first was that the Soviet Army would have to be defended against, meaning that large numbers of Japanese troops would be tied down in Manchuria. The second, and far more important decision, was that future expansion of the Japanese Empire should be to the south—and not to the north against the formidable Soviet Union. Thus the Japanese Army was reluctantly forced to sanction the course of action that had previously been recommended by its bitter rival, the Japanese Navy. (The same bitter rivalry had also resulted in the parallel development of Japanese Army and Navy aircraft, without any of the collaborative effort that would have helped both services in research, production, maintenance, and logistics.)

The full intercontinental political consequences of the Japanese decision to avoid conflict with the Soviet Union and instead move toward the resources of Southeast Asia would not be realized until December 1941. It was then that Stalin learned from the master spy, Richard Sorge, that the Japanese were not going to attack the Soviet Union with their strong Kwantung Army. The Soviet dictator then withdrew ten divisions from Asia, along with a thousand tanks and a thousand aircraft, enabling him to begin the counter-offensive that almost cost Germany the war that very winter.[14] Had the hotheads of the Japanese Kwantung Army won their air and land battles with the Soviet Union, there is almost no doubt that they would have taken advantage of the great German victories of the summer and fall of 1941 by attacking to the north. If they had done so, the Soviet Union would almost certainly have had to conclude peace in 1942, leaving Germany master of Europe and Japan still a threat to Southeast Asia.

Japan drew two vitally incorrect conclusions concerning its air forces from the battles with the Soviet Union. First, it did not recognize that it needed air forces organized on a vastly larger scale, with a tremendous increase in first-line strength, in production, and in training. The second was that with the current strength of its air forces, Japan was going to be able to fight the United States and Great Britain even though it had already decided that it could not fight the Soviet Union.

Part of this error in decision-making stemmed from the inter-service competition that permeated the Imperial General Staff, where the Japanese Navy now held the upper hand. The Japanese Army, already embarrassed by being unable to win the war in China, had suffered an intolerable loss of face in its battles against the Soviet Union. It therefore grudgingly acquiesced in the Navy's determination to secure petroleum resources by moving into Southeast Asia in force. The two services, for different reasons, thus agreed to go to war with the United States and Great Britain while still embroiled in China. The Western mind simply cannot fathom how the Japanese leadership could have entered this new war understanding that it had no chance of winning a prolonged conflict. Instead, Japan began a calamitous war based on the wistful hope that the Western democracies were soft and that a sharp opening blow would permit Japan to establish a defensive ring that the United States could not penetrate. The result was supposed to be a peace treaty giving Japan all that it requested.

In essence, the Japanese psychology of the time was such that incidents like the *Panay* and the acquiescence of French authorities in Indo-China promoted aggression, while incidents such as the defeat at Khalkin Gol promoted not just caution but denial.

Italy in Ethiopia

Italy had unsuccessfully attempted the conquest of Ethiopia in 1890, being defeated at Adowa in 1896, and was shamed by the memory of the failure. Italy had retained a precarious foothold there in territory next to Italian Somaliland and Eritrea. After months of careful preparation, a trumped-up border incident gave the Italians an excuse to invade Ethiopia on October 3, 1935. The citizens of France and England reacted in horror and disgust to the mismatch of a powerful European nation fighting Ethiopia, which, under Emperor Haile Selassie, was just beginning to emerge from its primitive past. However, the governments of the democratic nations took little or no action, for they hoped to secure Italian support against Hitler. In time, they merely registered disapproval through the League of Nations by ordering some minor sanctions against Italy. These were not carried out effectively, and in fact enabled Mussolini to proclaim to his people that he was bravely defying France and England in Italy's interest.

The situation was a joy for Hitler, who had kept Germany neutral throughout the war. The German leader stood to gain no matter what the outcome. If Mussolini became greatly involved in Africa, any objections Italy might make to German unification with Austria would be muted. On the other hand, if Mussolini won a decisive victory, the opposition of France and Great Britain might force him into an alliance with Germany.

The Italians attacked with overwhelming force, marshaling some 100,000 troops against an ill-trained enemy whose air force consisted of a few non-combat-worthy planes. The Ethiopians, under the inspirational leadership of Haile Selassie, often fought well, and their guerilla tactics inflicted continuing losses upon the Italian forces.

In many ways the Italo-Ethiopian war was similar to the war of the United States against the al-Qaeda and the Taliban in Afghanistan. The Italians were fighting hundreds of miles from home in a harsh environment against tribal chiefs who knew their territory intimately. The Italian leaders were astute enough to capitalize effectively upon the differences among the tribes, which in Marshal Emilio de Bono's estimate kept an additional 200,000 warriors from the battlefield.[15] In addition, the Italians made extensive use of modern equipment to develop their logistic base so that the troops in the field could be supported adequately.

The war permitted the Regia Aeronautica to distinguish itself, becoming a decisive factor in all operations. Although the Italian aircraft were generally obsolete by contemporary European standards, they were more than adequate for the reconnaissance, communications, and attack missions in which they engaged. The Italian forces were particularly adept in harassing fleeing enemy troops, but one of their most original actions was the aerial resupply of corps-size units, the first time this process had been accomplished.

Unfortunately, the Regia Aeronautica distinguished itself in another area, one that received worldwide condemnation: the use of poison gas against Ethiopian soldiers and civilians. Mussolini had authorized the use of gas prior to the invasion, and the Ethiopians claimed that mustard gas was employed on at least twenty occasions. In one of them, a battle in the Tigray area, the massive use of gas averted an imminent Ethiopian victory. The actual effectiveness of the gas has been the subject of great debate, but it undoubtedly destroyed Ethiopian morale and the will of poorly trained troops to resist. It also reinforced the general European dread of a mass air attack upon principal cities.

The image of Italian Air Force gallantry was not enhanced when Bruno Mussolini wrote a newspaper article in which he described Ethiopian cavalry units "bursting open like a rose" when bombed, events which he also described as "most amusing."

If the rest of the world was not impressed by the actions of the

Regia Aeronautica, given the lack of opposition, this was not the case with the Italians, and with Benito Mussolini in particular. The war in Ethiopia ended in victory on May 5, 1936, and Mussolini proclaimed King Victor Emmanuel III as emperor of Ethiopia. When the Spanish Civil War erupted on July 17, 1936, Mussolini was only too ready to intervene on the side of the Nationalists, who were led by General Francisco Franco.

Air Power in the Spanish Civil War

Yet as bellicose as his empire-building in Ethiopia had made him, Mussolini was not the first dictator to come to Franco's aid. Adolph Hitler rose to the occasion within hours of being asked. Hitler was riding the crest of a long series of triumphs that included an advantageous naval treaty with Great Britain and the highly successful 1936 Olympics in Berlin, at which the Germans won the most gold medals. The request for aid from Hitler came at a propitious time, the annual Bayreuth opera festival, a peculiarly personal indulgence of the Führer. At about 10:00 P.M. on the night of July 25, Hitler had just returned from a performance of *Siegfried* to his quarters in the Wagner family residence, Haus Wahnfried. He had been persuaded by his deputy, Rudolph Hess, to receive the two Germans who were acting as Franco's emissaries. Despite advice to the contrary from both the German Foreign Office and Hermann Goering, Hitler decided to help. The details were left to Erhard Milch to arrange, and ten Junkers Ju 52/3m transports were en route by July 29 to Cadiz (already in rebel hands) and Spanish Morocco. A further ten Ju 52s, equipped as bombers, followed a few weeks after. By July 31, eighty-five men and six Heinkel He 51 fighters were embarked on the SS *Usaramo,* also bound for Cadiz, along with bombs, bomb racks, and machine gun ammunition. The operation was given the code name "Operation Magic Fire," a tip of the Führer's hat to a musical passage in *Siegfried*.[16]

The influence of air power is often debated, but in the Spanish Civil War, it can be fairly stated that air power was strategically essential during the period July–October 1936, when German Junkers Ju 52/3m transports flew critically needed troops from Africa to join Nationalist forces in Spain. In that interval some 13,000 troops and 550,000 pounds of equipment were flown across the narrow Straits of Gibraltar, saving the Nationalist revolution from collapse.[17] This was the first time in history that a complete army had been airlifted into battle, and the scale of the effort was not exceeded until the German invasion of Crete in 1941.

The Germans also used the Ju 52 as a bomber. On August 14, two well-placed bombs were supposed to have put the Republican battleship *Jaime I* out of action for the rest of the war. (Later analysis indicated that the ship was sunk by a mine.)

The main body of German effort would come in November, when the No. 88 Volunteer Corps was formally recognized; it became known as the Kondor Legion. The term "Volunteer Corps" was camouflage, for these were standard German military units being blooded for future combat duties. The legion consisted of individual groups of fighters, bombers, reconnaissance, seaplane, and antiaircraft units, along with support personnel. A total of about 6,000 men and 100 aircraft were on hand at any one time, but at least 19,000 men and 350 planes served over the course of the war. Some 298 members of the Kondor Legion were killed, and another 1,000 were wounded by the time the war ended.

Although it took Mussolini longer to make up his mind about committing armed forces to Spain, when he did, he did so dramatically, sending three divisions totally 45,000 men, 2,000 artillery pieces, and 750 aircraft. Ultimately, more than 100,000 Italian troops and 6,000 Italian airmen would serve in Spain. More than 3,000 would die in the Spanish Civil War, including 174 airmen.[18]

The German/Italian intervention on behalf of the Nationalist forces was offset in part by the supply of aircraft and materials from France and the Soviet Union. The French government of Premier Leon Blum was sympathetic to the Loyalist cause, and sent a miscellaneous bag of about forty aircraft to Spain, under the nominal and idiosyncratic leadership of writer-philosopher André Malraux. Malraux was neither a pilot nor a soldier, but he had an international literary reputation and espoused the Loyalist cause. The value of the French equipment was much diminished because it arrived without armament, and supplies of spares were soon cut off when Britain and . France were pressured into an arms embargo of the conflict.

It was far different with the Soviet Union, which very much wanted to see the Loyalist government remain in power, and, in exchange for the Spanish gold reserves, sent about eight hundred aircraft to Spain during the course of the war. The aircraft included 155 I-15s, 62 I-15bis,

287 I-16s, and 96 SB-2 bombers, all first-line aircraft in the Soviet Union. Also sent were some 3,000 people, including 772 pilots, some of whom arrived before their equipment and warmed to the task by flying missions in obsolete French-built Breguet and Potez aircraft of the Spanish Air Force. The Soviet Union also licensed the production of another 229 fighters (I-15s and I-16s) in Spain.

The Western media was convinced that the Soviet aircraft would be inferior, to the ludicrous extent that they called the SB-2's "Martins" and indicated that the I-15 had been copied from a Curtiss fighter, while the I-16 had been copied from the Boeing P-26. To everyone's surprise, the Russian aircraft proved to be superb, far superior to any on the Nationalist side for many months after the German and Italian forces arrived, and much better than the aircraft from which they were supposed to have been copied.

These first-rate Russian aircraft enabled the Loyalists to gain an air superiority that was maintained through mid-1937, when German Messerschmitt Bf 109 fighters came into service. (Three prototype Bf 109s had been tested in Spain earlier.) The Russian planes allowed the Loyalist air force to gain one of the biggest victories of the war in March 1937. A Nationalist force composed of four Italian motorized units, including the elite Littorio division and eighty-one light tanks, had broken through the lines near Guadalajara, northeast of Madrid. The assault became bogged down in the mud caused by a week of torrential rainstorms. The Loyalist air force reacted promptly, shooting up the enemy vehicles and killing many soldiers. This was a seminal experience for the Red Air Force, which adopted the "conveyor" tactic in which a steady stream of attack aircraft, flying in successive relays, maintained a continuous pressure from the air. On March 18 the Loyalists counterattacked, and the Italian infantry broke and ran, to the disdain (and ultimately the amusement) of their Spanish Nationalist comrades-in-arms.

A second tactical event, the April 26, 1937, bombing of Guernica, would have even more profound repercussions. A Nationalist force of 40,000 troops led by General Emilio Mola attacked Guernica, backed up by a hundred planes of the Kondor Legion Bomber Group (K/88), Fighter Group (J/88), the "Experimental Squadron" (VB/88), and two Italian squadrons of Fiat fighters.

The German bombers conducted a three-hour attack, with bomb loads comprised of two-thirds 250-kilogram high-explosive bombs and one-third incendiaries. According to some reports, both fighters and bombers made strafing runs on the city. Somewhat less credible counterarguments have been advanced to the effect that the bombing was not as severe as claimed, and that much of the damage was caused by the Red forces systematically exploding and burning the center of the city as a part of a far-sighted propaganda effort.

The attack on Guernica was the most effective air assault to that date in terms of the destruction of a city. Its repercussions echoed throughout the world, its import highlighted in Pablo Picasso's starkly evocative painting *Guernica,* now housed, ironically enough, in the Reina Sofia Museum in Madrid.

It might be said that the net effect of the bombing of Guernica was negligible in terms of the outcome of the Spanish Civil War, which was already rapidly nearing its end with a Nationalist victory. However, the publicity and propaganda surrounding Guernica had far-reaching popular effect in the minds of the general public and of the leading politicians who would debate the fate of Europe until September 1, 1939. It seemed to corroborate the long-held fears of the "bolt-from-the-blue knockout blow," and while the numbers of casualties were magnified by rumor, it did portray the ugly future of aerial warfare.

A lesser-known but important attack took place during October 1937 on the Nationalist airfield of Garipinelos. The attacking Loyalist aircraft claimed forty aircraft destroyed on the ground, without any losses. Airfield attacks became a part of Soviet doctrine, making their terrible losses to such German attacks, in the first days of the June 1941 invasion, all the more inexplicable.

The contending major powers—Germany, Italy, and the Soviet Union—used the Spanish Civil War to test weapons and tactics. These tests produced both positive and negative results for all the parties.

For the Soviet Union, the experience in Spain provided invaluable combat training for later battles against the Japanese and Germans. For senior officers in those units, combat was, ironically, a relatively safe haven, for they were less likely to be consumed in the insane purges Stalin was visiting upon his officer corps. In terms of strategy and tactics, the Spanish Civil War confirmed the importance of air superiority, and spurred the development of a new series of fighters that would flow—just in time—from the Mikoyan-Gurevich, Lavochkin, and Yakovlev design bureaus.

Italy was slow to learn from its experience in the Spanish Civil

War. Its sturdy Fiat CR. 32 fighters were delightfully maneuverable dogfighters, the superb flying qualities of which suited the style and dash of Italian pilots, and were extremely valuable during the first year of the war. They acquitted themselves better against the Russian aircraft than did the German fighter biplanes, although they suffered heavily, some 159 being lost during the war.[19] The Italian government drew the conclusion that the biplane fighter was still viable in modern air combat (despite the evidence rendered by the German Bf 109) and entered a successor, the handsome Fiat CR. 42, into production, instead of concentrating its efforts on the more modern Fiat G. 50 and Macchi M.C. 200 monoplane fighters. The CR. 42 was a good aircraft, and indeed, served in operations until May 1945, but it was hopelessly outmoded from the start.

The Regia Aeronautica also failed to learn from its experience with the large losses incurred in combat, the high requirement for spare parts, and the need to have a sufficient weight of numbers. While it realized the backward state of its engine industry and its limited production capacity, it did not take the necessary steps to remedy the situation. Had Mussolini drawn the correct conclusions about his country's potential for combat, he would logically have stayed out of World War II entirely. He would have survived the war as a statesman, for Italy's absence from the conflict would have benefited both the Allies and Germany immensely.

Germany's learning experience in the Spanish Civil War provided mixed results. On the one hand, it was invaluable in revealing just how much effort had to go into maintenance, training, provision of spares, and many other workaday requirements of combat.

The performance of Luftwaffe bombers proved to be deceptive. Because the Heinkel He 111s were more than adequate in Spain, the Luftwaffe high command came away with the belief that they had adequate speed and armament to deal with any future opponent. This proved to be an almost fatal error in the Battle of Britain, where all of the German bombers, including the more modern Junkers Ju 88, were terribly vulnerable to the higher speed and the eight-gun armament of the British Spitfire and Hurricane fighters.

Even though the basic excellence of the Messerschmitt Bf 109 was validated in Spain, it was obvious that there was a need for improvement in power and armament as well. What was less obvious was that the Messerschmitt lacked the range for more demanding missions, such as air combat over England. This lack of insight proved to be fatal in the Battle of Britain. The Germans did know that an escort fighter was desirable, and thought until the fall of 1940 that the Messerschmitt Bf 110 twin-engine aircraft would fill the bill. It did not, primarily because the aerodynamic challenge of creating an airplane that could fly for a very long range and still be a formidable dogfighter was difficult to achieve. A true escort fighter would not be realized fully until 1943, with the advent of the North American P-51 fighter mated with the Rolls-Royce engine and long-range drop tanks.

In tactical terms, the Luftwaffe created a new formation for fighting units, with aircraft flying in a loose pair (*Rotte*) with two pairs composing the basic unit, a *Schwarm*. The *Schwarm* was flown in what was called the "finger four" formation, spread out so that a maximum flexibility was afforded the pilots for maneuver and visibility. The experience in Spain also enabled the Luftwaffe to develop effective ground attack techniques that would be invaluable in combination with armored units and confirmed the importance of dive-bombing.

In Spain, the Red pilots adopted the German-inspired "finger-four" formation, but were forced to give it up and revert to standard "V" formations when they returned to Russia. In the curious sort of "political correctness" reigning in the Soviet Union during the days of the purge, adopting a foreign combat formation was tantamount to treachery. In the United States, both the Army Air Corps and naval aviation adopted what was called the "fighting pair" during 1940 and 1941. Great Britain began using a spread-out formation in 1940, but as late as 1943 some units still used the old line-astern formation. Japan adopted the "finger-four" formation well into World War II.

Perhaps the most significant lesson that the Germans failed to learn was one of scale. Their most ambitious planning programs, already underway, envisioned a first-line air force of 11,732 aircraft, of which only 2,730 would be combat planes, with an annual production requirement for replacement purposes of about 300 per month. If war came, the production rate would be increased to 1,377 per month.[20] Germany could not achieve this target for many months after the outbreak of war, and would learn by 1942 that these numbers were totally inadequate. Despite having excess plant capacity and the undeniable managerial talents of Albert Speer, Germany would not be able to rectify the situation until late 1943, when it was already far too late.

Chapter Six

The Search for Air Power, World War II, 1939-41

We have seen how the threat of air power was used effectively to gain diplomatic ends during the interwar years even though it was rarely effective in achieving military ends. Air power also had profound economic effects during the 1930s, which were demonstrated in part by the makeup of the industrial infrastructure of the aviation industries and in the air forces of the nations that were about to take part in World War II. The political effects achieved by the threat of air power were themselves contributing factors for war.

What is absolutely amazing is that the outbreak of World War II did not see a single attempt at what politicians and the public had dreaded for so many years—the all-out surprise aerial assault on the capital cities. Not only did the combatants not launch the proverbial "bolt from the blue," they assiduously avoided any sign that they might do so.

The reason for this decision is obvious now. Although each of the combatant nations knew that it did not have the capability to launch such a blow, it could not be sure about the enemy. Therefore strategic aerial activity was confined to bombing purely military targets—and this on a limited basis—and to dropping propaganda leaflets, all to avoid possible retribution. Some even considered bombing military targets as "not quite cricket." A member of the English Parliament objected to attacks on the armament factories in the Ruhr on the sacred Tory grounds that they were private property.

There is a further anomaly, given the pervasive agreement among both the philosophers and the practitioners of air power in all countries that air superiority, that is, command of the air, was the *sine qua non* of modern warfare. Despite this general understanding, no nation except the United States went to the extraordinary lengths

193

necessary (and they were extraordinary in terms of time and money as well as aircraft quality and quantity) to achieve air superiority. Other nations merely balanced air superiority requirements with others for bombing, close air support, reconnaissance, and home defense, with the result that they were unable to sustain more than a temporary, and often just a local, air superiority in individual campaigns.

Germany, as we will see, established air superiority in its early campaigns against weaker opponents, but fell far short of doing so against its first major opponent, Britain. And while it obtained initial air superiority over the Soviet Union and sustained that air superiority for a considerable period of time, it ultimately lost out there as well. Failing to win air superiority over Britain cost Germany its best chance to win the war. Failure to sustain it against the Soviet Union brought Germany down to a catastrophic defeat.

Britain fell short in terms of air superiority throughout the war, including even the Battle of Britain, where it was fortunate to have just sufficient strength to deny air superiority to the Germans. Isolated from the continent, and with a tremendous reluctance to engage in another European land war with the German Army, Britain chose instead to create a huge night-bomber force that inflicted tremendous but indecisive harm while suffering terrible casualties.

The Soviet Union achieved air superiority at long last and only inadvertently, after a war on too many fronts had worn the Luftwaffe to the ground. Japan had maintained air superiority over a hapless China, but was unable to compete with the Soviet Union. It would establish air superiority over Britain and the United States in the Pacific in late 1941 and early 1942, but by 1943 would be in a hopeless position in the air.

Even with brilliant planning and exceptional production efforts, the United States did not achieve decisive air superiority until late in the war. The United States had to endure years of conflict in which it suffered humiliating defeats and suffered severe losses before reaching the state where it could exercise true air superiority. In the following analysis of the first two years of the air war, air power will be seen almost always to be influential, if not decisive, on the outcome of battle, if not necessarily always on history.

It is important to note that air power, as defined by its advocates, was exercised in every theater, but it was not until after 1943 that the bombing campaigns of the RAF and the USAAF combined at last to fight the air war on the apocalyptic scale envisioned by Douhet, Trenchard, and Mitchell.

The Early Battles

Historians now generally agree that the one-year reprieve from war provided by the infamous 1938 Munich conference was vital to Britain, enabling her to bring the Royal Air Force to greater strength with more modern aircraft. It is less generally noted that the same year enabled Germany to expand greatly the industrial base of the Luftwaffe, and allowed for the construction of many more airfields for use against possible campaigns in both the East and the West. The Luftwaffe was also able in the one-year interval to remedy some—but far from all—of the training problems that had saddled it with both a high accident rate and a relatively low in-commission rate (the number of aircraft actually available for operations).

Goering had announced on October 14, 1938, a plan for a five-fold increase in the Luftwaffe.[1] It is interesting to note the bureaucratic response in what most people considered a monolithic totalitarian German state, and compare it with the corresponding response to President Roosevelt's May 16, 1940, call for the production of 50,000 aircraft annually. In Hitler's dictatorship, the Technical Office responded that while nice in theory, increasing German aircraft production by a factor of five was too expensive, unfeasible in any case, and would demand far too much aviation fuel to be considered practical. The Technical Office submitted a program that called for the production, in four years time, of about 20,583 combat aircraft. In the democratic United States, not yet at war, the industrial response to Roosevelt's request was so enthusiastic that by 1944 aircraft were being produced at the rate of 100,000 per year. There was of course a substantial difference in American and German industrial capacity, but the fact that German production reached more than 40,000 aircraft annually by 1944, after years of bombing, shows that much more could have been done from 1938 on had Germany possessed a willing bureaucracy.

Contending forces wracked the German aircraft industry. Massive expansion and unprecedented funding were counteracted by a continual shifting of production programs. Worse was the interference from top leaders and, inevitably, shortages in skilled labor, key materials, and components. The result was that in August 1939, Germany had a monthly production of 427 combat aircraft—or an annual rate of just over 5,000. This rose slightly to about 700 per month after the war began. Part of this increase came from factories acquired in Czechoslovakia and Austria.[2]

In terms of first-line strength, Germany had increased its air-crew training and the number of aircraft available for combat in the year after Munich. The totals rose from 2,928 aircraft and 1,432 fully trained crews in October 1938 to 3,750 aircraft and a surplus of trained crews by September 1939. Pilot training had peaked at between 10,000 and 15,000 pilots per year, each of whom received from 200 to 250 hours of excellent flying training before being posted to an operational unit for further seasoning.[3]

In terms of equipment, at the outbreak of the war the Luftwaffe was in superb shape compared to other air forces in the world. It had adopted the Messerschmitt Bf 109 as the standard single-seat fighter and was introducing the E model of that aircraft into squadron service. Goering and the German High Command still considered the twin-engine Messerschmitt Bf 110 to be the premier fighter, and it would serve well in the first campaigns. Bomber units consisted of Heinkel He 111 and Dornier Do-17 aircraft, supplemented by the deadly Junkers Ju 87 Stuka. Even the obsolescent Henschel Hs 123 biplane was put to good use. This combination of aircraft, flown by enthusiastic and well-trained crews, overwhelmed the Polish Air Force when Germany invaded on September 1, 1939.

Working in combination with the panzer arm, the Luftwaffe established the pattern for *Blitzkrieg* (lightning war) operations upon which Germany depended for success. The Luftwaffe had matured into a perfect vehicle for continental air operations in wars of limited scope and duration. These were the only types of wars of which Germany at that time was capable, and they were the sort of wars that Hitler counted on to fulfill his plans of conquest. Unfortunately for him and the German people, World War II would prove to be of great scope and long duration.

By the practical end of the war in Poland on September 27, the Luftwaffe had learned much that would be of value in the months to come. The Polish campaign revealed some shortcomings in the German Air Force that needed to be addressed. The requirement for high production numbers had led to the reduced production of spare parts. There was a tendency by some of the Luftwaffe field commanders to regard aircraft as disposable, for it was often easier to obtain a replacement from the factory than to obtain the parts necessary to repair a damaged plane. One natural result of this was for the *Schwarze Männen* (Black Men), the black-overalled Luftwaffe mechanics, to hoard frequently needed parts, exacerbating the general shortage. Not until the dark days of the fall and winter of 1942 did the Luftwaffe, acting under procedures specified directly by Erhard Milch, begin to exercise the supply discipline that enabled damaged aircraft to be more rapidly returned to combat.

The Polish Air Force

In the early 1930s, the Polish Air Force had been one of the best armed in Europe, for it had been equipped with the series of gull-wing, all-metal monoplane fighters from its native Państwowe Zaklady Lotnicze (National Aviation Establishment). The P.Z.L. P.7 and P.11 fighters were designed by Zygmunt Pulawski. The Polish fighter force became the first in the world to be armed entirely by all-metal monoplanes, which were exported to several countries. Polish leadership had expected a war with Germany to come by 1936, and had armed accordingly.

By 1939, however, the P.Z.L. fighters were completely outmoded by their German counterparts. When war broke out, Poland had only 397 aircraft it considered "first line" to oppose the Nazi onslaught. These were in fact obsolete, and consisted of 159 fighters and 154 bombers, with the remainder being observation planes.[4]

The Polish Air Force had been plagued by well-intentioned but ill-informed leadership for almost its entire existence. The great Polish hero, Marshal Jozef Pilsudski, regarded aviation as a secondary service, and in August 1929 directed that "aviation is to serve only for reconnaissance and only in this direction should it be used." The succeeding Polish governments continued to downplay aviation. In the four years before the war, the Polish cavalry received twice as much of the tiny defense budget as did aviation.[5]

On September 1, 1939, some 1,600 German aircraft struck Poland. Contrary to most accounts, the Polish Air Force was not eliminated at once, for just before the outbreak of war, all Polish combat units were transferred to forty-three operational airfields that had been prepared in secret, and were stocked with food, ammunition, and fuel. The main operational bases became, in effect, decoy targets.

Because of the disparity in numbers and in the quality of the aircraft of the two air forces, and especially because of a lack of a communications network, Poland offered only a token air defense after the first week of the war. After that time Germany obtained complete air supremacy, even though Polish fighters still took a toll of Luftwaffe liaison planes.

The Soviet Union took advantage of the situation on September 17 to advance to the lines of demarcation previously agreed to by Hitler and Stalin in their infamous nonaggression pact of August 1939, depriving the Polish forces of an opportunity to survive longer by a retreat to the east.

On September 25, General Wolfram von Richthofen conducted the first of the terror-bombing attacks of the European war. German bombers dropped six hundred tons of bombs on Warsaw, cruising like tour buses over the prostrate city. Even obsolete Junkers Ju 52/3ms were brought into play, their crews shoveling incendiary bombs through the cargo doors. Some 1,150 sorties were made, reducing the city to rubble,[6] while German artillery poured in an avalanche of shells. An infantry attack followed, and two days later the city fell.

The P.A.F. had been wiped out, losing 333 aircraft, 83 percent of its total fleet. Thirty percent of its flying personnel and 22 percent of its ground personnel were lost in the first two weeks of the struggle. The Luftwaffe had lost 285 of the 1,600 aircraft it had deployed against Poland, but perhaps more revealing, it had used up 60 percent of its total bomb supply, as well as most of its fuel reserves.[7]

The German success was impressive, but it is important to note what the German military leadership failed to learn from it. Instead of observing that its success stemmed from having a great numerical and qualitative advantage, and that a similar success against a future opponent would depend upon maintaining those advantages, the German High Command just accepted the victory as its due and remained satisfied with the Luftwaffe's status quo.

Germany had denuded its Western defenses for the campaign in Poland, leaving only 30 divisions, of which only 12 were first rate, to face the 110 French divisions and still assembling troops of the British Expeditionary Force. During the month that Poland struggled and

died, France and Britain were stunned by the apparently flawless performance of the German Wehrmacht and did nothing. While they
waited, the Germans redeployed, making up their losses on the
ground and in the air as they prepared for a new battle in the West.

The inactivity of the French and British High Commands forfeited the only chance in the first five years of the war that the Western
Allies could have intervened against Germany on the Continent
with a high probability of success. The only possible reason for this
otherwise inexplicable inactivity is the influence air power exerted
upon national psychology during the interwar period. The French
and British leaders were mesmerized by the possibility of a devastating German air attack on their principal cities and, like rabbits
facing a python, they simply remained quiet and awaited the
inevitable.

The Phony War

In the fine book *The Forgotten Air Force: French Air Doctrine in the
1930s,* author Anthony Christopher Cain makes the point that the
French had, with the best intentions in the world, created a doctrine of reactive air power, in which they attempted to counter every
imaginable security challenge.[8] French doctrine called for its air
arm to conduct every strategic, operational, and tactical task, from
strategic bombing to colonial operations. Given the constrained
budgets of the time, which limited production and training, the
French Air Force could in consequence do none of them well.

The only thing not lacking in the French Air Force was plans for
production and for organization. Of these there was a superfluity,
and no less than five production plans and five reorganizations were
put forward between 1934 and 1939. A sixth and superseding reorganization came just before the outbreak of the war, with the air
force divided into three air armies adapted to the organization of the
ground command.[9] The excessively centralized organization in
effect placed the air force almost entirely at the disposition of individual army commanders, much in the manner of the French
armored forces. Incredibly, the French Air Force administration had
been reorganized so frequently that in its last iteration it was based
upon the *1870* Bouchard report on how to organize an army.[10]

When France and Britain declared war on Germany on September 3, the French First Army, facing Germany, had only 138 Morane-Saulnier M.S. 406 and 94 American Curtiss Hawk H-75 single-seat fighters at its disposal. These were augmented by thirty-seven of the handsome but vulnerable multi-seat Potez 630 and 631 aircraft.

To the immense relief of the French High Command, the Germans did not, as expected, make a violent opening attack on French airfields. The Germans were preoccupied with their conquest of Poland, and more than willing to keep things "quiet on the Western Front." It was the beginning of what the French called the *drôle de guerre*, the British the "phony war," and the Germans the *Sitzkrieg*.

Just as in 1914, Britain deployed a British Expeditionary Force (BEF) to France, this time with a sizeable Air Component composed primarily of obsolescent aircraft. By January 1940, organizational reform had changed the title of these RAF assets to the British Air Force in France (BAFF).

Neither France nor Britain, despite their treaty guarantees, made any serious attempt to assist Poland even by air, preferring instead to remain on the defensive and await the German onslaught—an example of an erroneous lesson learned from World War I. Hitler could not have dared to dream of a strategy more in Germany's interests, for a determined ground assault by France's 110 divisions against the 30-odd German divisions in the West might easily have altered the war's outcome even as Poland surrendered. It was the Rhineland experience once more. The French had overwhelming means at their disposal; the Germans could have put up only token resistance. Unfortunately the French High Command lacked the courage and, perhaps the most important factor in the exercise of air power, the will to act.

Instead, desperately aware of their own weakness, both Britain and France took no major offensive action on the Western Front and kept air activity to a minimum. During the eight months between September 1939 and April 1940, the French lost only sixty-three aircraft, while claiming eighty victories over the Luftwaffe. In terms of fighter losses, the Germans lost thirty-nine, the French thirty-five, and the British eleven.

The French resolutely abstained from bombing German cities, waiting until the desperate days of early June to send a single four-engine Farman N.C. 223 to bomb Berlin. Britain confined RAF Bomber Command to attacks on German naval targets, and in doing so learned a bloody lesson on December 18, 1939, when twenty-four

Vickers Wellingtons were sent on a daylight raid against naval targets in the Wilhelmshaven area.

Up to this point, the Royal Air Force believed that even a small formation of three bombers could, if flown in tight formation, fight their way through enemy fighter opposition to the target. Larger formations seemed to promise even greater defensive capability.

Twenty-two Wellingtons entered the target area, and twelve of these were promptly shot down by defending Messerschmitt Bf 109 and Bf 110 fighters. Five Wellingtons made crash landings on their return flights, and only five landed safely. The disaster convinced RAF Bomber Command that daylight raids were too costly, and that night bombing was the proper method of attack.

As the phony war dragged on, France and Britain frantically attempted to bolster their aviation strength with new equipment. Unfortunately for France, while its Plan V called for the production of 8,059 aircraft by May 1940, it was able to produce only 2,629.[11] Further, a great percentage of these were not combat ready because they lacked essential components such as radios, instruments, and armament. Perhaps most significant of all, the French Air Force had only 67 percent of the pilots it required, and morale was not high among those who were available.

The RAF contribution was better in only one respect, its fighters, but it was on the whole still no match for the Luftwaffe. When the Battle of France opened in May, the BAFF had four squadrons of the vulnerable Bristol Blenheims for reconnaissance, four squadrons of Hawker Hurricanes (one still in the process of converting from the biplane Gloster Gladiator), eight squadrons of the Fairey Battle light bombers for what proved to be suicidal ground attack work, and five squadrons of Westland Lysanders for tactical reconnaissance.[12] Just how unsuitable all but the Hurricanes were would be revealed in the opening days of the campaign. But before this happened, air power would give a dramatic demonstration of its life-or-death importance in the campaigns in Denmark and Norway.

The Scandinavian Campaigns

Air power was decisive in the two northern campaigns, which broke the pleasant if unreal quiet of the phony war. Oddly enough, it took an entirely new war to focus attention on Denmark and

Norway. The Soviet Union invaded Finland on November 30, 1939, expecting to achieve an easy victory. The Finns fought back with skill and tenacity, winning the admiration of the world and confirming Hitler's impression that the Soviet Army would be no match for German forces. (Later, in the depths of the 1942 Russian winter, the record of Hitler's table talk would reveal his gloomy speculation that the poor performance of the Russian troops had been "camouflage" to deceive him as to their real capability.)

The sheer inequity of the contest—the mighty Soviet Union against tiny Finland—aroused public indignation in France and Britain. The two governments were pressured to intervene, and Winston Churchill, in one of his less-forward-thinking moments, suggested that diplomatic relations be broken off with the Soviet Union and that the oil fields in Baku be bombed. In France, where aircraft were instructed not to provoke German reaction by raids on German cities, plans were made to join in bombing the oil fields. Had the oil fields been bombed, air power might have had its greatest influence to date, with the result that Britain and France would have been at war simultaneously with Germany and the Soviet Union.

Norway and Sweden, hoping to preserve their neutrality and their profitable commerce with Germany at all costs, refused a March 2, 1940, British request to allow troops to be sent through to aid Finland. Fortunately for all concerned but the Finns, a revitalized Soviet Army resumed the offensive in February and overwhelmed Finland, which had to sue for peace on March 12, 1940.

Churchill had wanted to mine Norwegian waters from the start of the war because of the vast amount of German shipping traffic carrying iron ore and other materials. The Supreme Allied War Council ordered the mining to take place. It began on April 8, four days after Churchill had been given overall defense responsibilities for Great Britain. He now advocated the seizure of Norway, and hasty preparations were made to put together a combined British, French, and Polish invasion force.

All during this period Grand Admiral Erich Raeder urged Hitler to occupy Norway to safeguard German merchant marine traffic and to establish U-boat bases. Hitler was predisposed to do so, for he had been enraged by Great Britain's violation of Norwegian neutrality on February 16, 1940, when it seized the German supply ship *Altmark* and freed naval prisoners of war taken by the *Graf Spee* on its ill-fated cruise.

It thus developed that both Allied and German forces were en route to invade Norway at the same time. In the event, Hitler moved faster than the Allies, and the German military machine operated with greater efficiency, launching on April 9 a series of attacks that quickly occupied Denmark and key points in Norway. The German armed forces distinguished themselves on land and in the air, even while the German Navy was bravely taking a terrible drubbing at sea. It was a measure of Hitler as gambler that he was willing to challenge the Royal Navy and Norwegian land batteries with his ships, confident in his technique of using airborne forces to capture strategic targets at Oslo and Stavanger and hold them until ground forces could arrive. This was a new and portentous use of air power that would soon see even greater success in the south.

The Germans had the advantage of surprise and of shorter lines of communication and transportation. For their part, the Allies put on a bumbling show of Colonel Blimp incompetence in which ski troops were not provided with skis, and guns were not provided with ammunition. They conducted a colonial-style operation, placing single battalions of troops at individual points, without any thought of gaining air superiority. Each of these penny-packets of troops was lost in turn, as the Germans progressed from south to north under the cover of their air force.

The Luftwaffe streamed into airfields as soon as they were captured all over Norway, and exercised air superiority from the start, crushing the small and ill-equipped Norwegian Air Force, and then besting the limited efforts of the RAF in almost every encounter. It allocated 1,098 aircraft to the campaign, of which 557 were transports, 342 long-range bombers, 39 dive-bombers, and 102 fighters. As each Norwegian airfield was seized, German aircraft deployed to it to begin the next operation.[13] The Japanese used a similar technique in their 1942 conquest of the Malay Peninsula.

Britain ran a tremendous risk, sending three aircraft carriers to the battle, the *Furious,* the *Glorious,* and the *Ark Royal.* The *Glorious* dispatched eighteen Gloster Sea Gladiators of 263 Squadron to Lake Lesjeskog, eighty miles southeast of Trondheim. There the valiant little biplanes were intended to confront the lethal Messerschmitts, flying from a 1,800-foot runway scraped from the snow-covered lake surface. Unfortunately, the battery carts used to start the Sea Gladiator's engines were inoperable, and after a night on the frozen lake, there were only two aircraft available for takeoff before the Germans attacked. After an eight-hour air assault, only five Gladiators remained. The *Glorious* carried away the surviving planes and pilots of the Norwegian campaign, only to be sunk a month later by the battle cruiser *Scharnhorst*, with a loss of 1,400 of the carrier's crew.

The value of air power was proved in one instance by its absence, for the only major British success occurred at Narvik, which was beyond the range of the Luftwaffe. In a brilliant naval engagement, the Royal Navy sank nine German merchant ships and nine destroyers. The Allies landed twelve thousand troops, and the Germans were driven from the city, holding on by their fingertips to the outskirts. After all the defeats, it was a bright moment for the Allies, proving that with the Luftwaffe taken out of the equation, the German Army could be beaten. Unfortunately, on May 10, the Allies were forced to abandon Narvik and all of Norway because of the German onslaught against the Low Countries and France.

The Air Battle of France

On May 10, 1940, Hitler stunned the world by initiating the invasion of Luxembourg, Belgium, the Netherlands, and France. Air power proved to be the sharp edge of the German sword that ripped through Allied defenses with a stunning ferocity.

The Führer had wanted to attack France in the fall of 1939, as soon as possible after the defeat of Poland. The reluctance of his army leaders and the worst winter in decades caused the attack to be postponed, but allowed a brilliant shift in planning. Instead of the variation of the tired Schlieffen plan the Army intended to use, Hitler sanctioned a suggestion by General Erich von Manstein to thrust through the Ardennes forest. This would prove to be a masterstroke.

The delay in the attack was fortunate for the Luftwaffe, enabling it to make up for the losses in aircraft and personnel incurred in the Polish campaign. With an immense industrial effort, the Luftwaffe also acquired the stocks of bombs, fuel, and equipment needed for a major campaign in the West.

It was not obvious at the time, but during the interval between the fall of Poland and the opening battle in France, the German High Command made two errors that would have critical consequences later. The first of these decisions was that the Luftwaffe was appropriately sized for Germany's war aims at about 4,500 front-line aircraft, and that the current production rate of about 9,000 aircraft per year was adequate. Of the 9,000, only about half were combat types. Either unknown to the Luftwaffe High Command, or ignored for political reasons, British aircraft production had already reached German levels and plans were to increase it significantly in the years to come. A subtler, but perhaps more far-reaching, error came in February 1940, when Field Marshal Goering, confident of victory, stopped all work on aircraft projects that could not be finished in time for use in the war. Among those projects were the new jet engines from Heinkel and Junkers, and new jet fighters from Heinkel and Messerschmitt. Had an adequate number of jet fighters been available in 1943 (as they could have been, given appropriate resources for research and production), the air battles over Europe in 1943 and 1944 would almost certainly have resulted in a decisive German victory. If so, the Allies would not have been able to launch the June 6, 1944, invasion, and the war in Europe might have gone on for several more years. Other "what-if" possibilities from this scenario include a separate peace between the Soviet Union and Germany, and the first use of an atomic bomb on Germany rather than on Japan.

When the German May 10 offensive was launched, the Luftwaffe had 4,050 first-line aircraft, including 1,300 long-range bombers (with some of the new Junkers Ju 88As), 380 dive-bombers, 860 Messerschmitt Bf 109s, 250 Messerschmitt Bf 110s, 640 reconnaissance planes, 475 transports, and 45 gliders. Of these, about 2,750 participated in the attack.[14]

The methods of their use would show the stunning effect of the innovative use of air power. The German parachute troops had a tremendous shock effect that unsettled both the Dutch and Belgian armies, and the brilliant glider assault on Fort Eban Emael amazed the world. The Dutch surrendered in five days, the Belgians in eight. Taken together, the two techniques seemed to confirm the myth of Luftwaffe invincibility, as well as the French predisposition to believe that their air force would not survive a German assault.

In comparison, the French Air Force possessed 5,026 planes, of which 2,176 were positioned to meet the German thrust. Of these 1,368 were considered front-line equipment. Only 637 fighters were available.[15] In addition, there were now ten squadrons of RAF Hawker Hurricanes, with about 160 aircraft. Ultimately twelve of the RAF's total of forty operational fighter squadrons would be sent to France, and when more were asked for, the head of RAF Fighter Command, Air Chief Marshal Hugh ("Stuffy") Dowding, would memorably refuse.

A three-to-one ratio is usually preferred for offensive operations, so these numbers show that quantitatively it was not too unequal a contest. As the Bf 110s would not prove to be adequate in fighter-versus-fighter combat, there were 860 German single-seat fighters arrayed against 797 Allied. Unfortunately, there was a pronounced difference in quality. The French Morane-Saulnier M.S. 406 and Curtiss Hawk 75 were substantially inferior to the Bf 109E that now equipped the majority of German single-seat fighter units. The Hurricanes were only marginally inferior to the Bf 109E, and in their combats the decision usually went to the better (or least surprised) pilot. The general introduction of the Bf 109E was extremely important, for it was greatly improved over the D model and contributed much to the Luftwaffe's overwhelming success.

The greatest difference came in morale, where the French were deficient. It was generally known that defeatism was extensive in the French Air Force, not least because of the continual problems with fitting production aircraft with armament and equipment, but most of all because no French equipment was yet a match for the German. General Sir Edward Spears, who was acting as a liaison officer between the RAF Chief of Staff and the French, had written in late May that "this lethargy of the French Air Force is extremely disquieting."

On a visit to General Vuillemin in early June, Air Vice Marshal Sir William Sholto Douglas arrived at Villacoublay airfield, outside of Paris. His task was to discuss what action the RAF and the Royal Navy should take when Italy entered the war.

Somewhat to his chagrin, given what he considered the importance of the mission, no one met him except a flight of German bombers strafing the field where about sixty French fighters were parked. After the German bombers left, Douglas and his party went to the French officers' mess, where to their surprise they found all the French pilots at lunch, ignoring the air raid and apparently unconcerned that several of their fighters were burning on the ramp.[16] The scene stunned Douglas, for he knew that in a similar circumstance, RAF pilots would be fighting for aircraft in which to take off after the attacking Germans.

Thus while the Luftwaffe did have superior aircraft in marginally superior numbers, its greatest advantage lay in its morale and in its organization. On the French side, Vuillemin, commander of the Armée de l'Air, was responsible for the general strategy, but operational decisions were left to his deputy, General Marcel Têtu, who, unfortunately, had no contact with the three primary regional commands. These were at the disposal of individual army and army group commanders, who wanted all efforts directed at the enemy in which they were in direct conflict.[17]

In marked contrast, the Germans had an excellent signal and command system that permitted the rapid shift of fighter and bomber resources to new targets as required. Its efficient ground staff enabled German fighters to fly up to four sorties per day, compared to an average of 0.9 sorties per day for French fighters during the Battle of France.[18]

The Luftwaffe was intent on obtaining air superiority and took an immense step toward doing so with a dawn attack on seventy-two enemy airfields. While claims for victories were inflated, more than two hundred aircraft were destroyed on the ground, and a further blow was struck to French morale.

The British responded bravely, but the totally inadequate Bristol Blenheim and Fairey Battle light bombers suffered appalling losses. As the situation on the ground deteriorated, more and more demands were made upon the RAF component to stop the German advance by blowing up bridges and assaulting armored columns. The Luftwaffe air cover and the excellent flak batteries took a heavy toll. On May 10, thirty-two Battles were dispatched in four waves of eight, attacking a German column that responded with vicious anti-aircraft fire. Twelve Battles were shot down, and the rest were badly damaged. Things got worse. On May 14, every surviving Battle and Blenheim—seventy-one aircraft—was directed to attack the single German pontoon bridge being prepared at Sedan. Some 250 Allied fighters were sent to protect the bombers, but were overwhelmed by a much larger force of German fighters.

Forty of the bombers were shot down and most of the rest badly damaged. Thirty-one other aircraft were shot down that day, including sixteen Hurricanes. This slaughter effectively removed all RAF aircraft but the fighters from the war, and proved once again how costly it can be to economize on defense measures when war at last comes.

The Luftwaffe now played a virtuoso role in air support, with its level bombers, Heinkel He 111s, Dornier Do-17s, and Junkers Ju 88As, attacking road and rail communications far behind the front, while the Junkers Ju 87 Stuka dive-bombers lived up to their awesome reputation in their close air support of the swift-moving panzers. The Stukas effectively replaced cannons for the Germans, because the panzers had moved forward much faster than the horse-drawn artillery could follow. The psychological effect of the screaming dive of the Stukas, followed by the inevitable bomb burst, was tremendous. French troops frequently proved unequal to the strain, breaking and running at the appearance of the Stukas over the battlefield.

The Germans, in just sixteen days, had effectively won the Battle of France. Goering now tasked the Luftwaffe to destroy the Allied forces before they could be evacuated. Exhausted from the campaign in France and the Low Countries, and with ill-prepared fields from which to operate, the tired Luftwaffe nonetheless managed to mount almost two thousand bomber sorties over the seven-day period of the evacuation.

It was not enough, and the German Air Force suffered its first defeat over Dunkirk. Spitfires, flying out of Britain, bested the Luftwaffe and provided the air cover that permitted the operation to succeed. The British put up a slightly smaller number of fighter sorties, but inflicted ninety-two losses, while losing ninety-seven of their own aircraft. The victory came not in the relative exchange, but in the fact that the British were able to evacuate 338,000 British, French, and Belgian troops.

The fighter-versus-fighter conflicts had been conducted at high altitudes, and the very troops that the RAF saved were unaware of the great aerial victory. Instead, once safely back in England, they castigated RAF flyers for their "absence" over Dunkirk.

With the bad experience of Dunkirk behind them, the Germans turned to finish off the French, who still had more guns and tanks than the attacking Nazis, but were completely overwhelmed by the Luftwaffe. The French sued for peace on June 17. The casualties of the ground forces were staggering. The Allies had lost 90,000 dead, 200,000 wounded, and 1.9 million captured or missing. The Germans had about 195,000 casualties, with 30,000 dead.[19]

While the losses on the ground were one-sided, the air battle of France had been extremely costly to both sides. The Germans lost an estimated 1,279 aircraft between May 10 and June 20, including 500 bombers and 300 fighters. The French lost 757 aircraft in combat, while the RAF lost more than 900, including 453 fighters. This number is especially significant when one notes that the eighteen squadrons of Hurricanes that served in France had a nominal strength of 288 aircraft—this meant more than 157 percent losses for the six-week period.

The effect of these losses would not be fully recognized until the Battle of Britain, where a still weary and weakened Luftwaffe was given the task of overcoming a Royal Air Force that was in the process of rebuilding.

In analyzing the influence of air power on the outcome of the Battle of France, it can only be said that its most important functions were to eliminate air opposition and enable the armored units of the German Army to be decisive. Germany might well have won the war against France even if neither side had an air force, but it would not have done so in such a swift, spectacular manner.

The Battle of Britain

When Air Chief Marshal Dowding heard of the French surrender, he said simply, "Thank God, we are now alone."[20] It meant that there would be no more calls to send precious fighters to France to be consumed in a battle already lost. Dowding could now turn his attention to building up the RAF fighter force to face what Winston Churchill had already termed the Battle of Britain.

There were a small number of professional German military men who called for an immediate assault on the United Kingdom. Their argument was that as tired as the German armed forces were, the British were in a far worse state, for the equipment of their army was left behind at Dunkirk, and there was only a single division capable of putting up resistance in Britain. It was felt that landing airborne troops in the South of England could establish more than a bridgehead, but instead would be sufficient to break English resistance. Hitler, however, was too caught up in the euphoria of his victory to contemplate such action. He still dreamed of somehow having Britain as an ally, despite the fact that the British determination to continue in the war was demonstrated by its brutal July 3, 1940, attack on the French Navy at Mers-el-Kebir. Hitler delayed any action, determined to make a generous offer when he made his celebratory speech to the Reichstag on July 19. Incredibly, in the meantime he took a holiday, visiting the World War I battlefield sites where he had served as a lance corporal, a runner, and where he had earned the Iron Cross First Class.

Hitler's Reichstag speech proved to be one of his best, done with a becoming mixture of pride and modesty, as befitted a man who had conquered seven European nations in nine months, six within the last three. But his offer of peace to Great Britain was far from generous, and instead was merely vague. The British provided a negative response within the hour.

Yet the almost one-month interval from the fall of France to Hitler's speech was a priceless gift to Dowding, who used it to rest and reorganize the RAF. The RAF Fighter Command was desperately short of pilots. With 1,456 authorized, it had only 1,094 on strength. Aircraft production was increasing, and the RAF was becoming more adept at returning damaged aircraft to service.[21]

The delay was an equal blessing to the Luftwaffe, which had lost 36 percent of its force (counting severely damaged aircraft) since April 9, when the fighting began in Norway. It had expended 30 percent of each category of bombers, dive-bombers, and Messerschmitt Bf 110s. The Bf 109 fighters had lost 19 percent of their number. Within these losses was concealed a terrible German characteristic of excessive zeal which was to haunt the Luftwaffe throughout the war, and contribute significantly to its ultimate demise. Some 213 Junkers Ju 52/3m transports had been destroyed out of a total of 531 employed. Many of these had been pulled from training bases, and were flown by instructor pilots, whose loss was impossible to make up in the short run. Over the course of the war, Nazi zealots made the same mistake, time and again, sacrificing instructors to "imperative" operational missions and refusing to realize the vital necessity of keeping a viable training system going. This cannibalization of the instructor pool combined with a growing fuel shortage resulted in the decay and eventual death of German flight training.

Among the many titanic battles of World War II, there were only two upon which the direction of the war hinged and that were decided by air power. The Battle of Britain was the first of these, and the Battle of Midway was the second. There were vast differences in these two battles, for Midway took place over a four-day period in which the most important activity was concentrated in just a few hours.

In contrast, the Battle of Britain began in July 1940 with pecking attacks against English Channel shipping. It built slowly but with increasing ferocity until it reached a decisive crescendo on September 15—now celebrated as Battle of Britain Day in the United Kingdom—before settling down into a grueling, deadly, but essentially ineffective night-bombing campaign that lasted until May 1941.

As bloody as the Battle of Britain would be, the importance and influence of air power in 1940 was made obvious by Adolf Hitler in his Directive No. 17 of August 1. In it he stated that the destruction of the Royal Air Force had first priority in defeating Britain, and that he reserved for himself the decision to conduct "terror bombing." The tenor of the directive was dictated in part by the German Navy's insistence that any invasion of Britain was dependent upon securing air superiority to the extent that the Royal Navy could not intervene in the cross-Channel landing. The most competent of Hitler's close military advisors, General Alfred Jodl, agreed with this view.

Directive No. 17 thus provided, not by accident, an impossible criterion. Given the strength of the Royal Navy, and the fact that it would be hurled into the battle at whatever cost, there was no way to prevent its intervention. The German Navy was so badly weakened in the Norwegian campaign that it would scarcely have made an impression on the Royal Navy, and it was too much to ask of the Luftwaffe, even if it had by some means been able to defeat the Royal Air Force.

Although he could not admit it, the directive revealed Hitler's true feelings. He dreaded the thought of a cross-Channel invasion, with all the things that could go wrong, from the thundering guns of the Royal Navy to unseasonable weather that would cut the German invasion forces off from reinforcements. As Hitler himself later remarked, he was a lion on land and a lamb on water.

Up to this point in the war, the Germans had pulled off one surprise after another, keeping their enemies off balance and winning fairly inexpensive victories. It now happened that the German plan of air attack took the exact form for which Great Britain had been preparing. Despite the years of tiny budgets and the delusion of the "Ten Year Rule," the British had been fortunate to have a small number of people in every significant area—aircraft design, armament, radar, ground observer corps, training, and operations—who created just enough of the essential tools to defeat the German attack. Thus it happened that there were eight-gun armed Spitfires and

Hurricanes flowing off the shadow-factory production lines; that the Ground Observer Corps system of reporting aircraft intrusions that had worked in World War I was updated to serve again; and that, most of all, there was an effective radar system in operation which would permit the RAF to use its forces in the most effective and economical manner.

To this fortunate combination of events must be added the factor of Trenchard's legacy, a sense not only of superior capability, but one of superior moral worth, that pervaded the RAF, and gave it such high morale and dashing *élan*.

The Luftwaffe, ever victorious so far, went to war against Britain with enthusiasm, discipline, and skill, and came within days of winning the Battle of Britain. It did so despite the wear and tear from the recent campaigns and the lack of appropriate long-range fighters and four-engine heavy bombers. Where Germany had employed 2,750 of its 4,050 total combat aircraft in the Battle of France, it now had only 2,550 to employ against Great Britain. These consisted of 998 bombers, 261 dive-bombers, 224 Messerschmitt Bf 110s, and 805 Bf 109s, along with other miscellaneous types. Of this mixture, it would soon be discovered that the Ju 87 dive-bombers were far too vulnerable to be used over England, and that the Bf 110 "escort fighters" had themselves to be escorted, as they were helpless against the RAF's total of 704 fighters, of which 620 were Hurricanes and Spitfires.

The Luftwaffe crews fought with courage, and had they been allowed to fight the battle using their hard-won experience, the outcome might have been different. Two things worked against them. Instead of concentrating their efforts solely on Fighter Command, the Luftwaffe attempted to defeat all of the RAF, including Bomber and Coastal Commands. This diluted its efforts severely. And, unfortunately for the Luftwaffe, both Hitler and Goering were used to quick victories, and the concept of deferred gratification was foreign to them. They demanded results and impugned the courage of the crews when the desired results were not forthcoming.

Goering issued the first order of the day in his exalted new rank of Reichsmarschall on August 8. It stated:

> From Reichsmarshall Goering to all units of Luftlotte 2, 3 and 5.
> Operation Adler. Within a short period you will wipe the British Air Force from the sky. Heil Hitler.

The bombastic message did not inspire or motivate air crews who had seen one-third of their friends lost in the last four months, nor ground crews who were working eighteen hours a day under primitive conditions.

Both Goering and Hitler sought to obtain a crushing victory, not in the only way they might have achieved it, a war of attrition in which the larger Luftwaffe eventually wore down the smaller RAF, but instead by shifting objectives. In doing so, they gave the war to the RAF to win. The original strategy of Directive 17 to wipe out the RAF first had been correct, and the Luftwaffe had begun in the appropriate manner with assaults on the radar system and the fighter airfields. Yet Hitler, Goering, and Chief of Staff Jeschonnek all made the same basic error. They did not perceive that the air war was going to be won by *fighters,* not by bombers. If German fighters did not clear the way for the bombers by destroying the RAF, the bombers would *not* "always get through." Instead the RAF fighters would destroy so many bombers that the offensive would have to be called off, and with it, any thought of an invasion.

The aircraft that had been so effective in the continental campaigns, the Bf 109, had too limited a range to undertake sustained cross-Channel operations. It could reach only to London, and there had fuel for only twenty minutes combat. When the RAF withdrew beyond the Bf 109's range, it was invulnerable. Dowding could and did husband its strength so that a maximum number of German aircraft were brought down at the minimum expense to the RAF.

Ironically, Allied leaders would learn nothing from these German mistakes, and instead, would repeat them for many long months in their own air campaigns. They too believed that bombers and not fighters were the route to command of the air, and would not change their beliefs until late in 1943, when losses became unbearable.

Goering had been effective as a bullying executive in his Four Year Plan, hounding intimidated German executives to exert more effort to accelerate rearmament. In that process his mistakes did not matter much, for no one dared to call attention to the problems he caused— they simply worked around them. It was different in the Battle of Britain, in which he personally called off attacks on the radar stations as ineffective, and in which he personally dictated that German fighters fly close escort with the bombers, thus giving away all their advantage in speed and maneuverability. There was no way to deny the results of the daily losses, or the damaged aircraft bringing back badly wounded crew members. Most important, there was no way to deny that every day the RAF still rose to fight. (Inexplicably, the USAAF would make the same mistake with its fighters as did Goering until the arrival of Lieutenant General James Doolittle to command the Eighth Air Force.)

The Reichmarshall's problems were compounded because he was given extremely bad information by Colonel Joseph ("Beppo") Schmid, the superbly optimistic head of the Luftwaffe intelligence section. Unfailing in overestimating RAF losses, Schmid continually failed to identify profitable targets for Luftwaffe sorties. He predicted the demise of the RAF so regularly and so often that it became a joking matter. Despite his failure as an intelligence chief, Schmid went on to other posts in which he served surprisingly well, including that of commanding the air defense of Germany.

On the British side, Hugh Dowding clung slavishly to his plan to survive by defeating the Luftwaffe in the air, allowing radar to direct his carefully hoarded fighter squadrons to attack German formations at precisely the point of greatest advantage. He watched his declining strength with despair, but knew that he had some advantages. His fighter production was accelerating and although his pilot pool was declining, those who safely parachuted from their aircraft could be returned to combat. He reluctantly turned to the use of more pilots from Bomber and Coastal Commands, and to the use of Polish and Czech pilots. Dowding was pleasantly surprised by how successful they were.

In the end, the piece of drama that saved the RAF and Great Britain came about as a legacy of the two-decade-long fear of the bombing of capital cities. On August 24, German bombers en route to strike Rochester became lost and dropped bombs on London by mistake—the first since the last Gotha raid on May 19, 1918. Churchill had been waiting for just such a *faux pas* and had placed Bomber Command on standby to bomb Berlin within twelve hours of a strike on London. The RAF sent eighty-one aircraft, twin-engine Hampden, Wellington, and Whitley bombers, to Berlin. As Churchill had hoped, the raid angered Hitler, and he ordered reprisal raids on London, beginning on September 7.

The effect of these raids on London was severe, with many casualties and much property damage. But the effect on Fighter Command was miraculous, for they had been removed as the Luftwaffe's primary objective, and were now able to concentrate on attacking the German bombers. The initiative of battle had been handed gratuitously by Hitler to the RAF, which did its job so well that the Germans were ultimately forced to shift to night attacks, with the consequent loss of accuracy. It was the beginning of what the British would call "the Blitz." RAF Fighter Command had been saved, and within weeks it would be obvious that the Battle of Britain had been won.

Beppo Schmid's continuous recalculations of the day that the RAF would finally be broken was shifted at last to September 15. But it was the Luftwaffe that had been broken, for on that date it could manage an attack only by 277 bombers, in three separate waves— hardly a saturation effort, and one the British were more than prepared to meet. Thirty-five bombers were shot down, along with twenty fighters.

The effect of this rebuff was startling, and underlines clearly just how influential air power had become. Hitler postponed the invasion of Great Britain indefinitely (it was to prove to be a permanent postponement), and the Luftwaffe switched more and more to night attacks, sending only the faster Junkers Ju 88s and Messerschmitt Bf 109s in fewer and fewer day raids.

The Battle Won and the Lessons Learned

The Luftwaffe lost the Battle of Britain, and with it Germany lost its best chance of winning the war. While it is true that Britain would probably not have surrendered even if it had lost the British Isles, the conquest would have left Germany in a much better position in which to deal with the Soviet Union.

The Battle of Britain was costly to both combatants. The German Air Force lost 1,733 aircraft and almost 3,000 air crew members. The RAF Fighter Command lost 1,017 aircraft and 537 pilots. Bomber Command and Coastal Command lost another 248 aircraft, which with their larger crews, cost almost 1,000 lives.[22]

Yet in truth, the battle turned upon personalities, and it was fortunate for the Allies that where Hitler had Goering as his air commander, Churchill had Dowding. The two men could not have been more different. Goering was a sycophantic toady to Hitler. He suffered from morphine addiction and had been a patient committed to the Langbro lunatic asylum in Sweden. Goering was vain, impatient, indifferent to the casualties of his forces, and vindictive in his messages to them. The Reichsmarshall still possessed the outlook of a World War I fighter pilot captain, and was unable to understand either the scope of the battle or its many variables. Even after the Germans had been engaged in battle for weeks, and despite the fact that Germany possessed its own radar system, they did not fully appreciate just how Fighter Command was using radar against them.

In sharp contrast, Dowding was plainspoken to the extreme and had heroically opposed the requests of the Air Ministry and of Churchill himself to sacrifice more squadrons in the Battle of France. Dowding was modest, patient, immensely concerned about the casualties, and unswervingly encouraging to all under his command. He did, it was true, have some eccentric characteristics (believing that he could communicate with God and with pilots killed in action being one of them), but he knew how to use the weapons he had at hand, and he knew how to manage his fractious commanders who had vastly different views on how to fight the war. The vicious and sometimes unscrupulous methods of Air Vice-Marshal Trafford Leigh-Mallory, Commander of 12 Group against Dowding and the commander of the 11 Group, Air Vice-Marshal Keith Park, would have unhinged a lesser man. In the end Dowding's methods were successful, and so close was the margin of victory that it might be doubted if any other person, using any other methods, might have done so well.

In the curious and often cynical way history has of not treating people properly, Goering was allowed by Hitler to continue after his defeat, living in sybaritic luxury. He had already failed, in everyone's eyes, over Dunkirk, and the second failure over Great Britain should have caused his dismissal. But he had a political image that Hitler did not wish to tarnish.

Again in sharp contrast, Dowding was unceremoniously sacked on November 24, 1940, and replaced by Sholto Douglas. He was given no recognition upon leaving Fighter Command or upon his subsequent retirement. In May 1943, he was made Lord Dowding of Bentley Priory, a small reward for a man who led so brilliantly those few to whom so many owed so much. The last honor, which he deserved more than any other, to be made a Marshal of the Royal Air Force, was denied him.

If the results of the Battle of Britain were adverse for Germany, the failure to draw the correct conclusions from it proved to be catastrophic. Germany still failed to perceive the requirement for a vast increase in the size of its air force, with the concomitant increases in aircraft production and pilot training. In what would be called denial in a human being, the German High Command turned from its defeat over England to a minor campaign in the Balkans and then to the calamitous error of attacking the Soviet Union on June 22, 1941.

Britain also drew faulty conclusions from the German effort. Although the British were aware of just how imprecise the German bombing had been, how relatively little critical damage had been done, and how their British morale had been maintained during the Blitz, they did not profit from their knowledge. Instead Britain embarked upon a night-bombing campaign over Germany, believing somehow that RAF bombers would bomb accurately, and that the German people would not be as morally tough as the British.

Neither side seemed capable of learning from their vast and costly exertions.

Chapter Seven

The Growth of Air Power, 1941-43

In retrospect, it is impossible to understand how Germany could have decided to go to war against the huge, unknown adversary that was the Soviet Union while still at war with Great Britain—unless one attributes it to Hitler's boundless ego and unquenchable desire for *lebensraum*. To undertake such a vast operation with the same inadequately sized Luftwaffe with which Germany had begun the invasion of France bordered on madness, as both Goering and Milch recognized. Most Luftwaffe commanders were appalled by the decision, including the Chief of Air Staff, Generaloberst Hans Jeschonnek, a Nazi so devoted that he would not communicate his misgivings to Goering or to Hitler. (Undeniably brilliant, Jeschonnek rose from his promotion to colonel on November 1, 1938, to become in July 1940, the youngest colonel general in the German armed services.)

In the summer of 1941, the Luftwaffe had about 4,300 combat aircraft. These had to be spread thinly about the new German empire, which now stretched from the Arctic Circle to the Spanish border, and from the coast of France to the new frontiers in the East. Only about 2,770 aircraft were available for Operation Barbarossa, the assault on the Soviet Union.[1] This was almost exactly the same number that had been allocated to the campaign in France, where the main attack was primarily concentrated on a narrow front that ranged from as little as thirty to a maximum of a hundred miles. The front in the Soviet Union was almost a thousand miles long when war began, and as the German Army advanced, would expand to almost eighteen hundred miles. As events would prove, the front would soon become deeper than German aircraft could fly. Further, Germany would soon have to provide for additional requirements for the Mediterranean theater and for the defense of the Reich.

219

The Luftwaffe had moderately improved its fighter force with the introduction of the Bf 109F, perhaps the best of the long Messerschmitt series. It was also operating the latest models of the same types of bombers that had proved inadequate over England. They would initially prove adequate, but fail in the long run against improved Soviet air power.

Hitler had promised that he had only to "kick down the door" of the Soviet Union and the entire structure would collapse. Initially it seemed that he was correct, and even so hardened a pessimist as General Franz Halder, Chief of the General Staff, would say on July 3, 1941, that, "It is thus probably no overstatement to say that the Russian Campaign has been won in the space of two weeks."[2]

The German successes on the ground outdid anything previously seen in the war, and the Luftwaffe kept pace, destroying more than five thousand Russian aircraft by October 5. Much of the German success stemmed from the lack of Soviet Air Force leadership. So many senior leaders had been killed in Stalin's bloody purges that those remaining were ill-trained and so frightened of Stalin that death in battle was preferable to taking the chance on making a wrong decision.

The German attack caught the Soviets at a strangely opportune moment in their rearming process, for most of the aircraft that were destroyed in the air or on the ground were obsolescent. The Germans were opposed for the most part by the same Polikarpov I-15 and I-16 fighters that had fought in Spain. There were many new Soviet designs coming along, however, including the Yakovlev Yak-1, Mikoyan and Guryevich MiG-3, Lavochkin LaGG-3, Petlyakov Pe-2, and the formidable Ilyushin Il-2 Shturmovik. These were available in relatively small quantities when the war started and suffered some losses. Thus the German aerial victory, while remarkable, was over the aircraft that the Soviet Union could most easily afford losing.

The new types, along with even more advanced aircraft, would be built in vast numbers in factories created by the most amazing industrial migration in history. The Soviet State Defense Committee ordered the movement of no less than fifteen hundred industrial enterprises from the path of the German attack to the east beyond the Ural Mountains. Entire factories were moved, and a labor force of ten million, suffering incredible hardships, was transported with them. With minimum food, no heat, and long hours, the workers erected the factories on new sites in the east and began building new aircraft before the roofs were on the buildings. Aircraft manufacture naturally fell during the period of the move, but it was back to normal within ninety days. In 1942, the first full year of their move, the transplanted factories produced more than twenty-five thousand aircraft, far more than the settled factories in Germany were doing.[3]

The Luftwaffe carried the German Army to the gates of Moscow. After that point it became overextended, and while the Luftwaffe could for many months obtain air superiority on limited sections of the front by means of its admirable mobility, it ultimately was worn down.

Now essentially a fire brigade, the Luftwaffe rushed to whatever section of the front was most threatened. It did so well in some instances, such as the aerial supply of troops trapped at Demyansk, that it was then tasked to the impossible—the aerial supply of the Sixth Army at Stalingrad.

Local German air superiority was maintained through 1943 by means of slightly better aircraft combined with more combat experience, better training, and higher morale. After that point, the Voyenno-vozdushnye sily (VVS), the Soviet Air Force, increasingly held air superiority as it grew in numbers, quality, experience, training, and, most important, morale.

The turning point may be said to have occurred during the Battle of the Kuban, the April 17 through June 7, 1943, struggle in the North Caucasus. It was there that the Luftwaffe mode of operation was changed from doing what it *wished* to do offensively to doing what it *had* to do to provide support to the German Army.

The Luftwaffe had experienced a remarkable resurgence after the debacle at Stalingrad, where, at the end, it could put up only 350 sorties a day against thousands by the Soviets. By April 1943 it was capable of a thousand sorties a day and more. Total Luftwaffe numbers had reached a peak for the war, with six thousand aircraft, but only twenty-five hundred of them could be allocated to the Eastern Front, and of these, only about six hundred were fighters.

The VVS had also grown in strength, with large numbers of Lend-Lease aircraft available, including Douglas A-20s, Bell P-39s, and Supermarine Spitfires. It had as well its own new Yakovlev fighters, and most important, it was also supplied with the greatest close air support aircraft of the war, the Ilyushin Il-2 Shturmovik. Artillery has always been a favorite instrument of Russian policy, and the Red Air Force used the Il-2 as a formidable piece of flying artillery. Stalin had sent a message to the factories producing it saying that the "Il-2 is as needed by the Red Army as air or bread . . . I demand production of more Il-2s; this is my last warning!"[4] Stalin's threats were never ignored, and more than 36,000 Il-2s were built. They were extremely effective in destroying German armor and personnel.

The Soviet and German air forces were, for almost the last time, fairly evenly matched in numbers over the Kuban, but for the first time the VVS adopted new tactics that demonstrated newfound skills that startled the Luftwaffe.

The huge Kuban ground battle involved hundreds of thousands of troops but eventually ground down to a stalemate. When the ground battle was over, the air war was evaluated, and it was found that the Russians had lost 2,800 aircraft to "only" 800 of the Luftwaffe. Yet the 3.5-to-1 exchange ratio was a Pyrrhic victory for the Luftwaffe, for the VVS could sustain its losses much more readily than could the Germans. In 1942, the Germans had produced 15,409 aircraft for use on three fronts (the Soviet Union, North Africa, and the defense of the Reich). In that same year the Soviets had produced 25,240 for one front, and had in addition 3,000 Lend-Lease aircraft provided to them.

It was now apparent that the Soviets had long understood the scale of operations that air power required to be effective, and that, because of their previous successes, the Germans only now became aware of the need. Germany had already begun a massive production program under the leadership of Albert Speer, Minister of Armaments and War Production, but it would not only be too little and too late, it would be conducted under the disruptive effects of the very aerial bombardment it was supposed to prevent.

The Germans would make one further attempt to regain the initiative on the Eastern Front, at the Battle of Kursk in July 1943. Kursk, a small city some three hundred miles southwest of Moscow, was the site of a huge salient in the German lines. Hitler wished to pinch off this bulge, measuring some 100 miles deep and 150 across, in the hope of spoiling the imminent Soviet summer offensive. The Red Army intelligence immediately became aware of his intention, and an elaborate fortress was prepared at Kursk, with eight concentric rings of defense. The Soviets concentrated nine field armies, twenty thousand artillery pieces, thousands of tanks, and millions of mines within those rings. The VVS provided 2,900 aircraft for the theater, 940 of them the inimitable Shturmovik anti-tank aircraft.

Hitler's staff, including the author of the 1940 offensive into France, General von Manstein, pleaded with him to call off the assault, but he was adamant. The Luftwaffe stripped other fronts to amass two thousand aircraft, yet only six hundred of them were fighters, and fighters decided the outcome of the struggle.

The Battle of Kursk became the biggest tank battle in history until that time, with more than six thousand engaged, but after initial successes, the German Army ground to a halt, largely due to the hordes of Il-2s that circled the German tanks like the Native Americans used to circle the immigrant wagon trains. There were now so many Soviet fighters, including the formidable Yakovlev Yak-9 and Lavochkin LaGG-5, that German fighters could not break through and interrupt the Shturmovik's terrible fire.[5]

It was the last offensive gasp by the Luftwaffe; never again would it combine with panzer units to thrust an armored arm deep into enemy territory. From Kursk on, it was fighting a death battle. By April 1945, there were some 7,500 Red Air Force aircraft positioned for the attack on Berlin, with fewer than 400 Luftwaffe fighters remaining to oppose them.

The Germans had attempted too much with too little, depending upon high-quality aircraft and proficient, well-experienced combat crew members to prevail. This was enough to secure air superiority in a surprise attack against a demoralized opponent. Germany eventually realized that it had erred in planning the size of its air force and consequently in the size of its industry, training, logistics base, and so on. It attempted to recover in 1943 and 1944, and made substantial gains despite the bombing. It was far too little and far too late, for the tide of war had shifted, and it was no longer possible to catch up by any means, including advanced new technologies. In short, the Luftwaffe was initially successful, but was doomed to fail spectacularly in the end because of its leaders' poor planning.

The Japanese Air Force would make the same mistake and meet the same fate.

A Tough Fight for Six Months

One of the least remarked upon aspects of air power is that an ill-founded confidence in its possession sometimes causes military leaders to make errors on a colossal scale. For example, Hitler might not have invaded the Soviet Union if he had not been certain that his Luftwaffe would win and maintain air superiority for him. Evidence for this misconception may be found in his refusal to invade Great Britain for that very reason. This phenomenon, making fatal errors based on an erring confidence on one's own air power, characterized the career of the most famous of all Japanese military men of World War II, Admiral Isoroku Yamamoto (1884-1943). He would make a number of errors of the greatest magnitude, including the conduct of the Battle of Midway, which reversed the course of the war. But because of his stature and his death in battle, he would never lose the admiration of the Japanese. Oddly enough, he is usually portrayed in admiring tones even in the histories of his wartime enemy, the United States.

As a young officer, Yamamoto had been wounded in the May 26-27, 1905, Battle of Tsushima, a heroic start to a famous career. Despite this baptism of battleship glory, he learned to fly in the early 1920s, soloing in a trainer. His talents put him on a fast track. As the Naval Attaché in the Japanese Embassy in the United States in the mid-1920s, he observed the industrial power of America and there realized that carriers were beginning to eclipse battleships in strategic importance. Against much opposition from traditionalist "big gun" officers in the Japanese Navy, he fostered the idea of the carrier strike force. As he moved up the career ladder, he became captain of two famous ships, the cruiser *Isuzu* and the aircraft carrier *Akagi*. He next commanded the First Carrier Division before becoming Chief of the Japanese Navy's Aeronautics Department. During this swift progress he became a leading proponent of naval air power, not a popular position in Japan at the time, when national policy was always to build battleships that were larger and more powerful than those of rival navies.

Following the same path that it had followed in establishing all of its modern industries, Japan had first imported aircraft, then imported foreign engineers to build aircraft under license. By the early 1930s, the Land of the Rising Sun was well on its way to creating an indigenous aircraft industry, and Yamamoto used his growing authority to elicit new and modern designs. He became Minister of the Navy and then, in 1939, Chief of Naval Aviation Headquarters.

In a September 1940 conference with Premier Fumimaro Konoe at the latter's private residence, Yamamoto, now the Commander in Chief of the Combined Fleet and the First Fleet, was asked what the

Navy's prospects were in the event of a war with America. Yamamoto replied, "If we are ordered to do it, then I can guarantee to put up a tough fight for the first six months, but I have absolutely no confidence as to what would happen if it went on for two or three years. It is too late to do anything about the Tripartite Pact [the alliance of Japan, Germany, and Italy] now but I hope at least that you'll make every effort to avoid war with America."[6] (He made similar remarks on other occasions, including one statement in which he promised to "run wild" for six months.)

It was at this point in his career that Yamamoto made the first and most crucial of the several mistakes he would make before his death in 1943. He bitterly opposed a war against the United States because he knew from his deep understanding of the American manufacturing potential that Japan could not possibly win. Unfortunately, the degree of his opposition did not extend to resigning his position in protest. Yamamoto was held in very high esteem, and the resignation of the Commander in Chief of the Japanese Navy would have created a political firestorm that might have forced the Japanese government to reconsider its options.

Instead of resigning, he acquiesced, insisting on the execution of the strike on Pearl Harbor that he had called upon his staff to plan. It was an act that would stir and unite the people of the United States in a way that almost nothing else could have done, as Yamamoto must have known.

It was Japan's intent to build a defensive ring that encompassed the natural resources it needed to survive, and which would theoretically be impossible to assail. At the height of the Japanese expansion in mid-1942, this ring ran on a line from Manchuria through coastal China to Burma's frontier, then south along a perimeter that included the former Dutch East Indies, New Guinea, and the Solomon Islands. The line then went north to the Gilberts and up to Attu in the Aleutians.

The Japanese government bet its empire on the hope that this defensive perimeter, combined with the stunning defeats administered at Bataan, Hong Kong, Singapore, the Dutch East Indies, and elsewhere, would convince the United States and Britain that a negotiated peace was in their best interests.

Yamamoto did indeed put up a tough fight for the first six months, seasoning the triumphal march with such remarkable feats as the sinking of the *Repulse* and the *Prince of Wales* with land-based air power on December 10, 1941. Called Force Z and commanded by Admiral Tom Phillips, the two Royal Navy ships, with an escort of four destroyers, sailed without air cover. Phillips believed that a well-fought capital ship was able to defend itself against air attacks. He learned differently when attacked by twenty-six Mitsubishi G4M1s and sixty Mitsubishi G3M2s of the Japanese Navy's First Air Group. Of these, thirty-four G4Ms carried armor-piercing bombs; the remainder carried the deadly, long-range, Type 91, twenty-one-inch torpedoes. The two huge capital ships were sunk within two hours, causing general despair in the Allied camp. The Japanese lost four aircraft.[7]

A flexible thinker, Yamamoto had pioneered the operation of Japanese naval air force aircraft from land bases, not confining them exclusively to carrier operations. This method of operation was to prove invaluable as the Japanese fought their way swiftly down through Southeast Asia. The Japanese invasion forces would operate under the cover of carriers, but as soon as they had captured or made an airfield, naval aircraft would begin to operate out of shore bases. The technique enabled the Japanese, with relatively few aircraft and few troops, to defeat the Allied forces in a leap-frog sequence of battles that carried Japan almost to Australia.

In creating the carrier task force, Yamamoto had authored a new form of naval warfare, one that would serve Japan well for six brilliant months of conflict. Yet in one of the least remarked upon but most important anomalies of the war, Yamamoto had inadvertently forced his enemy, the United States, to do the same. In this case it was not the force of his personality that effected the change. Instead it was the fact that while his carrier strike force sank the American battleship fleet at Pearl Harbor, it did not sink the United States carriers, which were, by chance, not in port. The carriers were thus the only weapon (besides submarines) available to the Americans, who quickly applied them in a series of ripostes that led in June 1942, to the Battle of Midway. These successes would lead to a mammoth American building program for aircraft carriers and aircraft on a scale that provided true air power in its most lethal form, and which would defeat Japan in almost every subsequent encounter.

The United States was in shock at the long series of defeats from an enemy that had previously been given little respect. Now, however, the Japanese military seemed invincible, and its aircraft, such as the Mitsubishi A6M Zero, were perceived to be the best in the world. President Franklin D. Roosevelt wanted to do something for American morale, and called for a strike on Japan.

The result was the April 18, 1942, attack of sixteen North American B-25s. Led by then-Lieutenant Colonel Jimmy Doolittle, the twin-engine Army aircraft took off from the carrier *Hornet* and struck targets in Kobe, Osaka, Nagoya, Tokyo, and Yokohama. The physical damage was minimal, for the planes carried only three 500-pound high-explosive bombs and one 500-pound incendiary cluster. All of the aircraft were subsequently lost. Three crewmen died in crashes, and the Japanese captured eight in China. Of these, three were summarily executed as "examples," and a fourth died in prison.

The raid had the desired effect upon American morale—it was the first good news in the entire war, and Doolittle and his surviving crew members were celebrated.

The damage was so light and the news media so well controlled that the raid had little effect upon the morale of the Japanese people. It did have great effect upon the Japanese Imperial High Command, which felt it had lost face. Admiral Yamamoto recognized that while it was probably a one-of-a-kind raid, it did mean that the American carrier force was an entity to be recognized, and he therefore felt impelled to lure the American fleet into a decisive battle at Midway. He felt so strongly about this need that when faced with opposition by both his Navy staff and the Japanese Army, he threatened to resign. His opposition gave in, allowing him to make the second of his great mistakes. The third and fourth would follow shortly in the massive plan he created for the battle.

The May 4-8, 1942, Battle of the Coral Sea was the first ever fought entirely by air power and in which the opposing fleets never came in sight of each other.

The battle would be fought with surprisingly few aircraft on each side, and without the ability on either side to secure air superiority. Intending to invade Port Moresby on the south coast of New Guinea, the Japanese introduced about 150 land-based aircraft, and their striking force included the big carriers *Shokaku* and *Zuikaku,* along with two heavy cruisers and six destroyers. Unknown to them, the Americans interposed Task Force 17 with the *Yorktown,* three cruisers, and four destroyers, and Task Force 11, with the *Lexington,* three cruisers, and two destroyers. Each side had additional auxiliary craft in support.

The Japanese possessed the superior fighter plane, for its Mitsubishi Zero was the best carrier-based fighter plane in the world at the time. The U.S. Navy's Grumman F4F Wildcats were rugged, and when fought in pairs, could hold their own with the Zeros. The dive-bombers were evenly matched, with the Japanese Aichi D3A Val being slightly less modern than the Douglas SBD Dauntless, but possessing an essentially equal capability. The Japanese torpedo plane, the Nakajima N5N Jill, was demonstrably superior to the elderly American Douglas TBD Devastator.

When the battle was over, the Japanese had scored an apparent tactical victory, for they sank the grand old carrier *Lexington,* and severely damaged the *Yorktown,* while only losing the much smaller carrier *Shoho.* Two large, thirty-knot aircraft carriers, the *Shokaku* and the *Zuikaku,* were so badly damaged that they would not be ready for the next big battle. Thanks to Herculean effort on the part of repair crews, the *Yorktown would* be ready, much to Yamamoto's surprise and dismay.

In strategic terms, the Japanese had lost the Battle of the Coral Sea, for they were forced to pull back from their intended invasion of New Guinea. Strangely enough, given his intelligence and his experience, Yamamoto made his third mistake, one that would also ultimately cost him his life. He did not—as he almost certainly should have—infer from the sudden and surprising appearance of the United States fleet that the Japanese naval codes might be compromised. Instead, he began planning the Battle of Midway, and in doing so, repeated the errors of the Battle of the Coral Sea. In both instances he did not suspect that Japanese radio traffic was being read and understood, and in both instances divided his forces, a violation of the fundamental principle of concentration of mass.

The division of forces was a reflection of his ill-founded confidence in Japanese air power, as can be seen in the way he earmarked his aircraft carriers for the operation. He had an immense 165-ship naval force at his disposal for the Battle of Midway. His headquarters were on the world's most powerful warship, the 68,000-ton *Yamato.* There were also six other battleships, five aircraft carriers, ten heavy cruisers, four light cruisers, forty-four destroyers, and a host of smaller warships and auxiliary craft. He diluted his strength by splitting his force into five separate groups, which were then split again into sixteen individual units. The most important of the groups, the Striking Force, consisted of four of the carriers that had attacked

Pearl Harbor—*Soryu, Kaga, Akagi,* and *Hiryu.* They carried a total of about 330 aircraft of the same type that attacked Pearl Harbor, and once again all under the overall command of Admiral Chuichi Nagumo. A second force that included the older carrier *Hosho* was detached for an essentially meaningless attack on the Aleutians, in the vain, almost feckless, hope that the American fleet would be lured away from Midway. The Main Body, with the seven battleships, positioned itself to go to the aid of either the Striking Force, or the Aleutian task force. The two other forces included a screening force of sixteen submarines that did not arrive in time to affect the battle, and the Military Occupation Force, twelve troop transports carrying the five thousand officers and men intended to take and hold Midway.

While Yamamoto divided his large fleet, Admiral Chester Nimitz concentrated his much smaller force. Knowing the Japanese intent from intercepted radio messages, Nimitz placed his carrier strike force, consisting of Task Force 17 with the *Yorktown* (only partially recovered from the battering it had taken in the Battle of the Coral Sea but ready to launch aircraft) and Task Force 16 with the *Enterprise* and *Hornet,* in a position to strike Yamamoto's carriers. He gave the task force commanders, Rear Admirals Frank Jack Fletcher and Raymond A. Spruance, the following extremely rigorous instructions:

"You will be governed by the principle of calculated risk, which you will interpret to mean the avoidance of exposure of your force to attack by superior enemy forces without good prospect of inflicting, as a result of such exposure, greater damage on the enemy."[8]

It was a close-run thing. The Japanese made a ferocious attack on Midway, confident that there were no enemy carriers within striking distance. Land-based American aircraft, including lumbering Consolidated PBYs used as torpedo planes, attacked the Japanese fleet, slowing it for critical moments. Then the final curtain dropped when the *Enterprise* and *Hornet* launched sixty-eight Douglas SBD Dauntless dive-bombers, twenty-nine Douglas TBD torpedo planes, and twenty Grumman F4F fighters, followed by the *Yorktown* launching seventeen SBDs, twelve TBDs, and six F4Fs just thirty minutes later.

The outcome of the battle had turned on intelligence most of all, for thanks to dedicated American code-breakers like then-Commander Joseph J. Rochefort, the Japanese intentions had been known. It turned also upon luck, for the spotting of the Japanese fleet by Lieutenant Commander Wade C. McClusky Jr. was purely a matter of his happening to have chanced to turn in the right direction at the right time. But most of all it depended upon gallantry, for the Devastator torpedo bombers had continued to press home their attack even when it was evident that their losses would be high. Doing so brought the Japanese Zero fighter combat air patrol down low, which enabled the Douglas Dauntless dive-bombers to make their runs with great success.

All four Japanese carriers were destroyed by the gallant actions of American torpedo planes and dive-bombers. The United States lost the *Yorktown,* but Midway was saved. It was a decisive defeat that changed the course of the war, for the Japanese never won another major campaign against the United States. The Battle of Midway serves, with the Battle of Britain, as a prime example of the influence of air power on history.

Yamamoto would go on to make further errors, particularly during the bitter Battle of Guadalcanal. There the Japanese Navy fought some brilliant winning naval engagements, but Yamamoto insisted on providing reinforcements in a piecemeal manner and never in the strength necessary. Despite repeated attempts, the Japanese were never able to drive the American forces from their grip on the vital Henderson Field, the air base from which United States air power could dictate the eventual course of the battle.

Perhaps realizing just how true his prediction of fighting well for just six months had been, Yamamoto became ever more remote. He continued to believe in the integrity of Japanese cryptography, and made his final mistake of broadcasting the itinerary of a proposed inspection and morale-raising trip to Bougainville. The message was intercepted and interpreted, and the task of killing Yamamoto was given to the U.S. Army Air Forces 339th Fighter Squadron, commanded by Major John Mitchell. Mitchell led eighteen Lockheed P-38s on a demanding and dangerous low-level, over-water mission of 435 miles that ended in a perfect interception. Flying as he usually did in a Mitsubishi G4M Betty, Yamamoto was shot down and killed, his plane crashing into the jungle. The accompanying bomber of the same type was also shot down. The victory over Yamamoto was credited for years to Captain Thomas Lanphier, but recent intensive analysis indicates that then-Lieutenant Rex Barber was the probable victor.

Yamamoto died in the same manner that he had lost the war for Japan, unable to see that his codes had been compromised, and with faith in the power of the Japanese Naval Air Force. His death may have saved him much embarrassment, for there would eventually have had to be recognition of the fatal mistakes he had made in the battles of Midway and Guadalcanal.

The admiral's ashes were returned to Japan in two boxes, and he received a state funeral. One box was interred in the Tama Cemetery, next to the grave of Admiral Heihachiro Togo, under whom he had served at Tsushima thirty-eight years earlier. The second box was buried in the Chokoji Zen temple in Nagaoka. So it was that even in death, Yamamoto split his forces.

Under Yamamoto's leadership, Japan had created a small, proficient air force ideally suited for dealing with ill-equipped opponents such as the Chinese. It also operated well against the poorly organized and equipped American, British, and Dutch forces in 1941. Yamamoto lacked the vision and Japan the resources to match the air-power potential of the United States. This fact became increasingly evident in 1943, overwhelmingly so in 1944, and catastrophically so in 1945.

Air Power in the Mediterranean Campaigns

Ironically, as the homeland of the most famous of air-power philosophers, Italy had within its power the ability to use air power to influence history immediately upon its entrance into the war. Had the Italians applied all of their efforts to the capture of Malta in June 1940, rather than engaging in the humiliating struggles with a moribund France, it might have altered the conduct of all of the subsequent Mediterranean campaigns. With strong units of the Regia Aeronautica and the Luftwaffe based in Malta, the Mediterranean would in truth have become what Mussolini referred to as "Mare Nostrum"—our sea. This would have destabilized the British position in Africa and probably have convinced Spain to enter the war. It would have precluded the intervention of the British in Greece, and that being so, Germany would not have been compelled to undertake the Balkan campaign that delayed the invasion of the Soviet Union by several critical weeks. But Italy did not have the foresight—or the appetite—to take Malta in 1940, or later in 1941 and 1942 when it might still have been possible.

Instead of becoming a pivotal point in the war, the Mediterranean campaigns, despite their cost in blood and equipment, were mere footnotes to the overall conduct of the war. To put the matter in the perspective with which Hitler regarded it, the Germans were engaging approximately eight enemy divisions in North Africa at a time when they were engaging some 360 enemy divisions in the Soviet Union. There was no comparison in the critical importance of the two theaters.

The campaigns in North Africa came about as a series of whims and preferences on the part of national leaders. It was a whim of Mussolini to extend his African empire. He tried to do so by attacking with vastly superior numbers a small but tough British force. To his dismay, the British promptly defeated his Italian legions. It was a whim of Hitler not to see his Axis partner embarrassed, so that he dispatched the Afrika Korps with just enough resources to redress the situation temporarily, but not enough to gain a decisive victory. It was Winston Churchill's preference to fight the Germans anywhere but on the continent of Europe, for he dreaded the repetition of the horrors of World War I. He gladly reinforced the theater, for it was the only place that the British could engage the Nazi and Italian forces on anything like equal terms. It was Franklin D. Roosevelt's preference that American troops get into battle against the Germans as soon as possible, and North Africa was the most logical place to begin.

The four-year-long North African campaigns did not change the outcome of the war, and in fact may have prolonged it. The United States did learn invasion techniques from it, and American troops were blooded, but given the resources poured into it and into the subsequent invasions of Sicily and Italy, it was probably a net loss to the Allies overall. The European war was decided mainly on the Eastern Front, with great help from the Allied bombing campaign and the opening of the Western Front with the invasion of France in 1944.

For the purposes of this book, it can therefore be concluded that while air power was a decisive factor in the outcome of the campaigns in the Mediterranean, air power did not have a notable influence on history as a result of battles in this theater. It happened in North Africa that whoever had air superiority at a specific time tended to win the campaign conducted at that time. It was not until 1942 that air superiority was established once and for all by the Allied powers, and from that point on the defeat of the Axis forces in the Mediterranean was only a matter of time. Perhaps the greatest Allied advantage from the campaign was the improvement in close air assault tactics.

The German Army was probably the best in the world for most of the war, and certainly no army was superior to it in defensive operations. In 1943, after the German disasters at Stalingrad, Kursk, and in Tunisia, a new situation developed. The German Army found that while it could not win battles without air power, it could still fight tough defensive battles without any air power at all. During the long agonizing retreat from Sicily and up the Italian boot, the German Luftwaffe was a token force, useful only occasionally for reconnaissance or for strikes against particularly sensitive targets such as the Allied beachheads at Salerno and Anzio. For the most part, the German ground forces just gritted their teeth, dug in, and died as Allied fighters and bombers roamed the battlefield.

The absence of the Luftwaffe was due in large part to the increased demand for fighters for the air defense of the Reich and for the Eastern Front. Germany was at war on too many fronts, and its air force had been kept so small for so long that there was no possibility of recovery, despite an almost miraculous surge in production.

Air Power over Europe: Round the Clock Bombing

The air war in Europe grew slowly from 1939 on, with each side learning from the other as the war progressed. The bombing of Germany had begun in 1939 with low-key attacks around the very perimeter of occupied Europe. After the German conquest of Europe, the British turned to costly daylight fighter sweeps that were eventually abandoned as nonproductive and a night bombing campaign that grew in intensity year by year.

When the United States Army Air Force entered the war, it did so with all the enthusiasm of the true zealot, for its leaders believed utterly in the efficacy of precision daylight bombing and were determined to prove their point in combat.

Although a young service, compared to the ground forces or the Navy, the USAAF had strongly held convictions about bombing, stemming in large part from the considered efforts of a relatively small group of officers who, as mentioned earlier, had been students and/or faculty members of the United States Army Air Corps Tactical School (ACTS). There is no little irony in the fact that this same group was responsible for two eventualities, one negative and one positive. The first of these was an error of colossal importance that is rarely remarked upon, one that cost thousands of lives before it was corrected in the field. The second of these was a tremendous success, and responsible in great part for the ultimate United States air superiority.

The Air Corps Tactical School had been founded in 1926, succeeding the Air Service Tactical School of 1922, and the Air Service Field Officers School of 1920. The ACTS was the highest educational establishment within the service at that time, and in the relatively small air service of the day, attendance was vital for promotion. This was especially true, for promotions were extremely slow, and a competent, well-thought-of officer might expect to be a first lieutenant for ten or twelve years in the ordinary course of events.

As a result, the best and brightest sought to attend the ACTS, and if possible, stay on for a tour as an instructor. A veritable galaxy of stars was created as future general officers such as Orville A. Anderson, Frank M. Andrews, Lewis H. Brereton, Claire L. Chennault, Ira C. Eaker, Harold L. George, George C. Kenney, William E. Kepner, Hugh J. Knerr, Laurence S. Kuter, Joseph T. McNarney, Robert Olds, Carl Spatz (later changed to Spaatz), Kenneth N. Walker, and Oscar Westover attended and often taught at the school.

General Billy Mitchell's ideas on air superiority were of course well regarded, but within a remarkably short period of time, the school developed its own concepts on carrying the war to the enemy's capital, commerce, and industrial centers.[9] These concepts did not derive from Giulio Douhet, whose influence was minimal, but from the realization that an independent service required a war-winning arm, and that could only be the bombing arm.

By 1926, the faculty at ACTS considered bombardment aviation to be the most important element of air power, replacing pursuit aviation. This was the beginning of a two-part fundamental error in thinking that would dictate United States air-power policy for decades to come. The first part was the conviction that bombers were supremely capable of a performance that could not be equaled by pursuit (fighter) aircraft. The second part was the consignment of pursuits to short-range interceptor duty, for the protection of American cities and coastal defenses. This latter reflected the total lack of consideration given to pursuit aviation, for there was at that time no country, much less any enemy, that possessed bombers with the range to strike the United States, and thus required defense against.

The intellectual process moved swiftly, and by 1930 the ACTS position was that the goal of the Air Corps should be entirely strategic with a minimum of effort expended on the battlefield or in defensive pursuit operations. It should be noted that this view was the exact opposite of the Army as a whole, which saw to it that a large portion of the Air Corps' budget was still spent on observation and pursuit aircraft.

In 1933, Major Donald Wilson originated what would today be called asymmetric warfare, postulating that an air campaign could strike at certain vital centers in an enemy's economy, and thus disrupt whole industries. An intensive study was made of United States industry, with the result that transportation, steel, iron ore, and electric power were identified as the industries most susceptible to such attacks not only here but, by inference, in other industrial nations as well.

Certain technological developments confirmed the ACTS thinkers in their beliefs. The arrival of the all-metal, monoplane bomber in the form first of the Boeing B-9 and then the much more capable Martin B-10 seemed to prove that the pursuit aircraft was no longer important. The B-10 had better performance than the Boeing P-26A, at the time the "hottest" Air Corps fighter, thus confirming the rather ingenuous view that no pursuit plane could ever be built that would have performance comparable to a bomber. In 1933, an air umpire of the war game exercises being conducted at Wright Field, Ohio, wrote that "due to increased speeds and limitless space it is impossible for fighters to intercept bombers, and therefore it is inconsistent with the employment of air force to develop fighters."[10] This judgment was immensely reinforced with the appearance in 1935 of the Boeing Model 299, the prototype of the B-17 series of bombers.

Pursuit aviation still had its advocates, most notably then-Captain Claire L. Chennault, but his attempts to prove that military maneuver rules and decisions were biased in favor of bombers were rebuffed.

In addition to the remarkable new bombers, much better bombsights had been developed, including the Sperry and the Norden. With the latter, it was possible, under ideal conditions, to hit small targets precisely from high altitudes. The operative words here are "under ideal conditions" which would rarely be found in combat.

By now, most of the senior officers in the Air Corps believed (just as their counterparts in the Royal Air Force did) that bomber formations were "invincible" and that their massed firepower could beat off any fighter resistance, permitting them to penetrate to the vital centers of the enemy. They were also convinced that they could find the key targets, and from high altitude drop bombs that would destroy them. Left out of the equation were improved enemy fighters, adverse weather, antiaircraft artillery, masking devices (such as smoke screens), the effect of winds on the fall of bombs through different altitudes, and many other variables, some of which were impossible to forecast. One of these was that radar would be adapted to air defense requirements. Another was the surprising ability of an energetic enemy to repair damaged factories quickly, and to continue production of war materials under appalling work conditions. (Machine tools, for example, were virtually impossible to destroy, and could function in factories bereft of roofs and walls.)

Curiously enough, during this entire period, none of the bomber aircraft, including the B-17, had anything approaching intercontinental range, and all would have required nonexistent foreign bases from which to operate. The only countries against which they could have been employed otherwise were Canada and Mexico—neither of which figured in any war plans.

Thus a phantom doctrine, impossible to fulfill, took control of procurement, training, research, and attitude. The Army Air Corps became a bomber force, despite the fact that the official doctrine of the Army, as presented in Army Air Corps Field Manual FM 1-5, clearly stated that air operations were to be planned and executed in accordance with the overall strategic plan for the surface campaign.

The unofficial doctrine developed by the alumni of ACTS would prevail for the first years of the war, under the genuinely excellent leadership of those same alumni. The USAAF would suffer severely because it was essentially an amateur approach, developed in peacetime conditions and by men who lacked the experience to anticipate the hard realities of actual warfare. And, somewhat unusually, the greatest harm came from a passive failure: they did not do the research necessary to develop a fighter with adequate range to accompany the bomber.

Some officers, such as Chennault and Major Gerald E. Brower, saw the need for a long-range fighter, and pressed for the funds to develop one. It was admittedly a difficult task and an early attempt, the Bell YFM-1 Airacuda, was a resounding failure. Unfortunately, the focus on bombers prevented the development of even such long-proven range-extension devices as drop tanks. In May 1939, the Air Corps, concerned about the fire hazard implicit in a droppable fuel tank, issued an order forbidding tactical aircraft to carry such tanks.

Pursuit aircraft, like all others, were designed to specific requirements established by the Air Corps. When drop tanks were forbidden, some manufacturers did not include in their new offerings the fundamental plumbing and connections that made carrying drop tanks possible.

As World War II unfolded in Europe, the United States Army Air Corps found itself with four fighters under development. They were promising in speed, maneuverability, and firepower, but were significantly lacking in range and in many of the requirements for modern combat, including such things as armor, self-sealing tanks, and adequate radios.

The four aircraft included the Curtiss P-40, Lockheed P-38, Bell P-39, and Republic P-47. The famous North American P-51 had not yet debuted. Neither the P-40 nor the P-39 were suitable for European operations, but performed good work in other theaters, including the Mediterranean and Pacific. There was a high demand for both the P-47 and the P-38 to be based in the United Kingdom. The P-47 had been designed without any provision for drop tanks, and on internal fuel had the ability to escort bombers for less than two hundred miles. The P-38, without tanks, could reach out to about three hundred miles—that is, as far as Paris.

On February 20, 1942, General Arnold ordered the full development of drop tanks for the P-38, P-47, and the P-51, which was only beginning to come into service. There were many delays, as successively larger tanks were tested and deployed, but the effects were remarkable. The P-47, suitably modified so that it could carry two 150-gallon drop tanks, could reach out to 450 miles—that is, as far as Hannover. With the same two tanks, the P-38 could accompany the bombers for more than 500 miles—all the way to Berlin. And perhaps even more remarkable, the P-51, with an additional internal tank and two 75-gallon drop tanks, could also range out for 500 miles.

These range figures are for aircraft flying relatively close escort to the bombers—the same erroneous tactic used by the Germans in the Battle of Britain. In the effort to extend fighter coverage, other tactics were evolved, including phasing the arrival of the aircraft in

waves at designated points along the bombers' routes. This technique extended the effective range of the P-38 and the P-51 to 600
miles—a remarkable increase in just two years.[11]

Once the tanks were dropped, the P-47 and P-38 could handle
the average German fighter plane; when the P-51 "was clean," it was
clearly superior to most German fighters. But the arrival of this true
example of a long-range escort fighter would be delayed until well
into 1943, at grievous cost to the USAAF.

Offsetting the major errors in assuming an "invincible" bomber
formation and relegating fighters to interceptor work was the
remarkable work done by a small team of ACTS alumni. It consisted of Colonel Harold L. George, Major Laurence S. Kuter, Major
Haywood S. Hansell Jr., and Lieutenant Colonel Kenneth Walker.
All would become general officers. Walker taught the credo, "A
well-organized, well-planned, and well-flown air force attack will
constitute an offensive that cannot be stopped." He was killed in just
such an attack on Rabaul on January 5, 1943, and was awarded the
Medal of Honor posthumously.

The four men strongly believed that precision daylight bombing was
feasible to pinpoint attacks on specific high-value targets. During July
1941, at the orders of the Commanding General of the Army Air Forces,
they became the Air War Plans Division, and were tasked to come up
with a proposal detailing the resources necessary to win the war.

Colonel George and his team created a plan that came to be
known as AWPD/1. It called for air operations in defense of the
Western Hemisphere, relentless air attacks against Germany, and
strategic defense in the Pacific theater.

For the attack on Germany, the planning team listed 154 strategic bombing targets, including eighteen aircraft assembly factories,
twenty-seven synthetic petroleum plants, fifty electrical generating
stations, forty-seven key points in the transportation system, and
twelve aluminum and magnesium factories.

Despite the relatively small American aircraft industry, AWPD/1
stated that the USAAF could launch a campaign in less than a year,
which was far less than half the time necessary to prepare a conventional ground army for war in Europe. The plan postulated that
six months of strategic bombing of enemy targets, together with
neutralization of the Luftwaffe, submarine and other naval facilities,
would render a land campaign unnecessary.

This optimistic assessment reflected ACTS thinking, and it assumed the neutralization of the Luftwaffe would be easier than proved to be the case. But to achieve these objectives, AWPD/1 made extraordinarily accurate calculations for the forces required. It stated that 13,000 medium, heavy, and very heavy bombers would be required worldwide—at a time when there were still only a handful of B-17s in operation.

Further, after decades during which the USAAF had fewer than 2,000 operational aircraft, the plan called for a total of 63,500 operational aircraft including trainers, reconnaissance, light bombers, dive-bombers, cargo planes, and so forth, and not counting replacements. After years when the personnel strength of the Air Corps numbered only in the tens of thousands, Kuter calculated the manpower requirements at 2,160,000 men, more than Pershing's entire AEF in World War I.

There were other, even more mind-boggling projections, including the loss each month of 20 percent of the aircraft and 15 percent of the personnel. Fortunately, while the aircraft and personnel requirements were very accurate, the loss projections were not.

These projections, which would have been considered sheer lunacy only twelve months earlier, were accepted in September 1941 and became the basis for awarding contracts to industry. This action was a tribute both to senior American military commanders and to Roosevelt's leadership of a country not yet unified by the Japanese attack on Pearl Harbor.

Not exactly coincidentally, acceptance of the AWPD/1 projections meant that an intensive strategic bombing offensive was now the policy not only of ACTS, but also of the United States. And, as far-fetched as the calculations seemed at the time, when the war was over, it was found that the AWPD/1 had estimated the number of combat aircraft within 2 percent and the total number of officers and men within $5\frac{1}{2}$ per cent.[12]

On September 9, 1942, responding again to a request from President Roosevelt, a similar group prepared AWPD/42, Requirement for Air Ascendancy. This action reflected a change in doctrinal thinking in which the air campaign was no longer to win the war but rather to prepare the way for the ground campaign. It was predicated upon obtaining air superiority by destroying the Luftwaffe in combat. As such, it predicted that "our current type bombers can penetrate German defenses to the limit of their radius of operations without excessive losses."[13] Yet the doctrinal wheel had not turned finally in favor of fighter operation—it had simply begun to recognize the fact that there were now the resources available to create the correct (that is, long-range) fighter force while continuing to undertake bomber operations.

Getting Started

The United States, anxious to make its mark in the air war, established the Eighth Air Force in 1942. The first American raid, coming in token form, took place on July 4 of that year when six American and six British crews raided four enemy airfields in Holland, using Douglas Bostons (RAF versions of the A-20 Havoc). The first United States heavy bomber raid came on August 17, with the commanding general of the Eighth Air Force, Brigadier General Ira Eaker, taking part. The Americans did not bomb Germany until January 27, when, as in the ill-fated British raid of December 1939, the target was Wilhelmshaven. Ninety-one bombers were dispatched, fifty-five made attacks, and three were destroyed. Damage to the Germans was minimal.

As minor as this effort was, compared to later raids, it was the start of a process that over the next thirty months would bring Germany to its knees. What no one knew on either side at the time was that the vital key to the success of the offensive would not be bombers, but fighters. From Douhet's time on, leaders in every air force, and their political bosses, had believed that the bomber would dictate the course of battle. In the bloody skies over Europe, there was proven, late in the game, a rule that still stands today: There must be fighters in order to win air superiority. Once that goal is achieved, the bombers can bomb without restraint. This lesson, so hard learned in World War II, has been forgotten again and again, not so much by the military as by the legislatures that control military funding.

The year 1943 was a disappointing one for the Eighth Air Force, even as it grew in strength and capability. Losses began to average as much as 8 percent per mission, which meant that the average crew member statistically had no chance to complete the specified twenty-five missions required before being sent home. Despite feverish efforts to build up the Eighth in size, its strength was constantly siphoned off for other missions, including the campaigns in North Africa.

A relentless barrage of criticism came from Washington on the performance of the Eighth Air Force. President Franklin D. Roosevelt, the Chief of Staff, General George C. Marshall, and the Commanding General of the United States Army Air Forces, General Henry ("Hap") Arnold, all complained that not enough missions were being flown and that insufficient damage was being done to the Germans. At one point they complained not only about the high casualties, but also about the number of crews landing damaged aircraft in Sweden or Switzerland.

One telling reason for the complaints was that the aerial campaign was a political sop to Joseph Stalin, the only substitute available for the second front that he demanded. The Soviet Union had borne the brunt of the fighting since June 22, 1941. Stalin pointed out this fact on every occasion, and sometimes hinted that unless a second front were forthcoming he might be forced to reach an accommodation with the Germans, the thing the Western Allies feared above all others. So, in a curious fashion, Allied air power was more influential on the historical process than ever before at a time when it was still relatively weak. The combined bombing campaign, first announced at the January 1943 Casablanca Conference, was not only a statement of policy, it was a palliative to Stalin's justified anger over the absence of a second front on the European continent.

The relatively low level of effort came about because the Eighth was in a learning process. It was true that hundreds of aircraft and hundreds of newly trained crews had been sent to Britain. What was not understood was that these crews had not been trained to the level necessary for combat in instrument flying, bombing, formation flying, and gunnery. Nor was it realized how severe the shortages would be of spare parts, tools, and air crews. Then, towering above all these problems was the weather, which during all but the short summer allowed an average of only five bombing days per month. In brief, it was not sufficient to provide a crew with perhaps three hundred hours flight training, then give them a B-17 or a B-24 to fly across the Atlantic to Europe. The German enemy was professional and efficient, and the bomber crews had to be taught combat flying, a lesson soon learned and never forgotten by a young wing commander, then-Colonel Curtis E. LeMay.

LeMay insisted on intense training. Working with Brigadier General Laurence S. Kuter, he developed the combat box and combat wing formations that were intended both to increase defensive firepower and improve bombing accuracy. In the combat box, eighteen to twenty-one bombers flew as a group, with three groups to a combat wing. With fifty-four bombers in tight formation, an attacking German fighter would be covered by up to 540 fifty-caliber machine guns.

With training and the hard experience of combat missions, the Eighth began to dispatch more and more aircraft on major missions, rising from 91 in the January attack on Wilhelmshaven to 380 in an August attack on Bochum/Bonn. Losses were high, with 128 shot down in July alone, meaning that 1,280 well-trained crewmen were killed or taken as prisoners of war.

As the Eighth built up toward the powerful machine it would become in 1944, Germany committed more and more of the Luftwaffe fighters to the defense of the Reich, pulling them away from where they were vitally needed on the Eastern Front. All German defenses grew, including radar installations, and particularly antiaircraft guns. So it was that by mid-1944, the bombing campaign did, in the words of the German Minister of War Production, Albert Speer, constitute a second front. In a postwar interview he stated that the bombing required the Reich's antiaircraft defenses to receive two million men, 30 percent of artillery output, 20 percent of heavy ammunition, 50 percent of electronic equipment, and 33 percent of optical equipment. The most important single weapon dedicated to air defense was the magnificent dual-purpose eighty-eight-millimeter guns. Seventy-five percent of these were assigned to anti-aircraft duties rather than to anti-tank duties on the Eastern Front, where they were so desperately needed. Unfortunately for the Eighth Air Force, the full import of its effect was not yet known. Stalin was far from satisfied, and the Eighth continued to be heavily criticized by Roosevelt, Marshal, and Arnold for not doing enough.

The Eighth's air war over Germany was a slugging contest, much less of a technological war than the Royal Air Force's night-bombing campaign. The errors of the ACTS doctrine and the failure to discover the need for a long-range fighter now came into play, revealing the downside of an advocacy system within the services. Proponents had seen to it that the emphasis in training and procurement had gone to the bomber, at the expense of the fighter. As a direct result, there were no fighters available that could escort the bombers to and from targets in the German heartland.

Unfortunately, doctrine, pride, and wartime necessity demanded that the bombers attempt to live up to their billing, and on the sheer strength of their numbers and their combined firepower, undertake missions deep within Germany.

On July 24, 1943, the Eighth Air Force made a series of attacks on airfields and aircraft factories, attempting to carry out Douhet's concept of destroying the enemy in his lair. The raids included the longest one to date, a 1,900-mile, round-trip sortie against targets in Norway. Also included were strikes on Kiel, Hannover, Hamburg, Kassel, and Warnemünde. Eighth Air Force Commander Eaker had 330 aircraft on strength, and in that week they flew 1,720 sorties. Of these, 1,080 struck the target, and 97 aircraft were lost, a terrible 8.99 percent of the attacking force. No less than 330 German fighters were claimed shot down. Unfortunately, the number 97 was genuine, while the number 330 was not.[14] It was inevitable in attacks on bomber formations that there would be multiple claims for every aircraft shot down, more for probables, and even more for wishful thinking. Actual German losses were relatively light, although the Luftwaffe did react by bringing in more fighters from the Eastern Front.

Daytime Air Superiority Won—by the Luftwaffe

The pressure on the Eighth Air Force became overwhelming despite its grudging participation in out-of-theater missions such as the August 1, 1943, raid on the Ploesti oil fields, when 54 out of 177 attacking planes were lost.

A decision was made to send the bombers on long missions to Regensburg and Schweinfurt in the full knowledge that fighter escort would be available only for the initial legs into German-occupied Europe, and the final legs out. This was the championship title bout, the chance to prove the theory that the bomber advocates had advanced. Unfortunately, the Luftwaffe was attempting to prove some theories of its own, including the importance of concentrating fighters en masse, flying line-abreast head-on attacks, and making as many sorties as possible by landing at the nearest flying field for refueling and rearming rather than returning to home base.

LeMay, newly promoted to brigadier general, led the 4th Bombardment Wing to attack Regensburg with 146 aircraft. The plan called for 230 planes of the 1st Bombardment Wing, under

Brigadier General Robert B. Williams, to take off ten minutes after the last of LeMay's planes had departed, and attack the vital ball bearing plants in Schweinfurt. The idea was that the 4th Bomb Wing would draw in most of the Nazi fighters, which would have to land to refuel and rearm and thus miss the opportunity to strike the 1st Bomb Wing.

Weather intervened, and the 1st Bomb Wing took off three and a half hours late, which meant that the Luftwaffe had plenty of time to attend to both incursions. German fighters attacked continuously from the point the American escort fighters left, all the way to the targets and all the way back to the point where the second wave of American escort fighters were waiting.

LeMay was in the lead plane, a Boeing B-17F of the 97th Bomb Group, and he saw to it that three hundred tons of bombs were dropped accurately on the Messerschmitt factory at Regensburg. Production was disrupted for five months, and the fuselage jigs for the top-secret Messerschmitt Me 262 jet fighter were destroyed. LeMay led his group on over the Alps to land in North Africa, after losing twenty-four aircraft—16.4 percent of the force.

The 1st Bomb Wing fared even worse, losing 36 out of the 183 aircraft it put over Schweinfurt, a startling 19.7-percent loss rate. The 1st did inflict significant damage on the plant, but the Germans were resilient, making up the losses with purchases from Sweden, and substituting other types of bearings where possible.

The two battles were an outstanding Luftwaffe victory, but were not interpreted as such by the German High Command. The combination of the recent devastating bombing of Hamburg and the coincidence of a British raid on Peenemünde on the night of August 17-18 infuriated Hitler. He savaged Goering, who responded as usual by berating Jeschonnek. The latter committed suicide rather than continue to be blamed for things over which he no longer had control.

The heavy losses forced the Eighth Air Force temporarily to concentrate on targets where escorts could be provided. Then on October 14, the Eighth went back to Schweinfurt, again with fighter escorts for only the route to and from Aachen. From that point on the Eighth's bombers were escorted only by the Luftwaffe, which shot down 60 out of the 229 aircraft in the attacking force, a horrendous 26.5-percent loss rate. Another seventeen B-17s were scrapped after return to the United Kingdom, and 121 more were damaged. Neither the Eighth nor any other air force could sustain such losses, and the Luftwaffe had achieved daylight air superiority. Fighters had unquestionably prevailed against bombers, which were not invincible. They did, in fact, always get through, but at an unbearable cost.

Bomber Command's Grueling Night Battle against the Luftwaffe

Early daytime raids had convinced the Royal Air Force Bomber Command that it was impossible to conduct daytime strategic raids against Germany. It shifted immediately to night raids, and for a period of time sincerely believed that those raids were severely damaging the German capacity to wage war.

The German Ruhr became a particularly attractive target, not least because the steel mills and armament factories were relatively easy to find, and were well within the bomb range of British aircraft. Unfortunately, equipment and training of the Bomber Command crews was not adequate to strike accurately, with as few as one-third of attacking forces ever getting within five miles of the intended target. Despite this situation, Britain had no other means of attacking Germany, and first priority was given to the production of heavy bombers, including the Short Stirling, Handley Page Halifax, and Avro Lancaster. The Chief of Staff of the Royal Air Force, the admirable Air Chief Marshal Sir Charles Portal, had once headed Bomber Command himself, and he now endorsed a report which stated that with a force of four thousand heavy bombers, Germany could be driven out of the war in six months. This report did not promise an early end to the war, however, for there were currently only 506 heavy bombers at Bomber Command's disposal—getting to the magic 4,000 number would take years.[15]

Air Chief Marshal Sir Arthur Harris was given command of Bomber Command in February 1942, and quickly determined that the only solution to the attack on Germany was night area bombing, with the intent of destroying the German will to fight not by precisely destroying strategic factories, but by destroying as many houses and killing as many people as possible, civilians as well as military. (There was a persistent refusal on all sides to recognize that bombing often had the reverse effect of raising the enemy population's will to resist.)

Harris built up Bomber Command, hastening its re-equipment with four-engine heavy bombers and adopting each new element of technology as it appeared. The night-bombing campaign was a bitter technical contest with the Luftwaffe. For the most part, British technical expertise was well ahead of the German, as successive types of improved bombing equipment were fielded, including navigational aids such as GEE and OBOE and the introduction of H2S (for the code name "Home Sweet Home") airborne radar. The most impressive improvements came in the form of radar spoofing devices, such as Window (simple foil strips called chaff today) and the use of electronic countermeasures.

Yet the Germans were resilient, and the experience of their night-fighter crews did much to offset British technical superiority. The German crews were also fighting over their homeland, and they could see the devastation that the British bombers were causing on every mission, and this made them fly with a grim determination to halt the stream of enemy aircraft.

The strain on both British and German airmen was tremendous. It has been pointed out that while a Navy ship may be in a fleet action once or twice a year and an Army division might fight for six to eight weeks before being relieved, the Bomber Command squadrons went into battle every night that weather and moonlight permitted, engaging the enemy as often as ten to twenty times a month, for month after month. American bomber crews were relieved after a certain number of missions, initially twenty-five, then thirty-five, and finally fifty, as opposition eased. RAF bomber crews were assigned instructional or other duties after thirty missions, and then returned for another twenty combat sorties. The German crews had no such "tours of duty"; they flew until they were killed or the war ended. The air war over Germany was a savage, bloody battle that exacted a high casualty rate from its participants. The total wartime losses for the three combatants were strikingly similar, with the Germans suffering 80,588, the British 78,287, and the Americans 79,625 casualties.[16]

Despite an inability to achieve decisive results and despite heavy casualties, Harris inspired a fierce if inexplicable loyalty in his crews. The term inexplicable is apropos because Harris was not personally a warm man, he did not extensively cultivate his crews as a more charismatic leader might have done, and he sent them to their deaths night after night.

Under Harris, Bomber Command made one notable raid after another, including the thousand-plane raid on Cologne on May 30, 1942, the terrifying assault against Hamburg, in which some forty-five thousand were killed and almost that many injured, and culminating in the notorious attack on Dresden in 1945. He would begin a campaign against Berlin in August 1943 that would increase over time, reaching a crescendo in 1944. That campaign would bankrupt his philosophy of area bombing and give the Luftwaffe its last major victory—aerial superiority in the night skies of Germany.

One Final Chance

One surprising aspect of air power was the manner in which a little air power in the right spot at the right time could have an effect all out of proportion to the assets involved. This was true in the Battle of Britain, and even more so in the Battle of Midway, in which a relative handful of aircraft decided the battle.

The opposite was also true. There were instances in the war where a campaign was lost because it lacked just a few aircraft that would have contributed decisive results. Perhaps the most important instance of this phenomenon was the Battle of the Atlantic, where a comparative handful of German submarines came within just months of forcing Great Britain to its knees.

Germany began the war with a tiny fleet of fifty-nine submarines of which only thirty-six were oceangoing types. This meant that the German Navy could keep only a few at sea at a time. Initially the number could be as few as six, but as the war proceeded, and submarine production accelerated, there came to be as many as a hundred U-boats at sea in 1943.

The U-boat fleet was centrally controlled by radio from the headquarters of Admiral Karl Doenitz, a veteran submariner from World War I. Doenitz introduced the wolf-pack tactics by which German submarines stalked a convoy and then attacked simultaneously in as great a number as possible. The success of this tactic was so great that by March 1943 Doenitz believed that he had almost defeated England, as he had promised he would do. In that one month alone, German U-boats sank 105 ships of 590,234 tons, a rate of loss that was unsustainable by Britain. Much of the U-boats' success stemmed from aerial reconnaissance reports.

In 1937, Germany had pointed the way to the future of passenger aircraft with the four-engine Focke Wulf Fw 200. Called the Condor, and designed by the famous Kurt Tank, the aircraft made several record flights including an eye-opening Berlin-to-New York flight in 1938. The Condors were quickly modified for military duties and became active in sinking ships, accounting for some eighty-five vessels totaling 363,000 tons between August 1940 and April 1941. Winston Churchill called the Condor the "scourge of the Atlantic."[17]

Yet the Condors performed their greatest service when they detected convoys and reported their presence back to Doenitz's headquarters. Unfortunately for the Germans, Reichsmarshall Goering resented the use of Luftwaffe assets to help the Navy. As a result, the Condor received a low priority, with only twenty-six aircraft being completed in 1940, and another fifty-eight in 1941.

Production was increased to eighty-four in the following year, but operational losses were so great that there were rarely more than twenty-five Condors available for action at any one time. The last year of production was 1943, when seventy-six were manufactured.

Had the Germans been foresighted enough to accelerate Condor production early in the war, there might have been enough in service in 1942 and 1943 to have allowed Doenitz to carry out his plan of starving Britain into submission. If, for example, 50 percent of the effort given to the Battle of Britain and the subsequent Blitz had been applied to the Battle of the Atlantic, Germany might well have won the war against Britain before beginning its war against the Soviet Union.

The Allies were equally shortsighted in their allocation of aircraft to the Battle of the Atlantic. The United States and Great Britain had waged the war against submarines with relatively short-range aircraft such as the Consolidated PBY Catalina, Short Sunderland, and Lockheed Hudson. "Bomber" Harris had fought against allocating any of his long-range four-engine bombers to the task. As a result, there remained a vast area of ocean south of Greenland where Allied aerial coverage did not reach. The Consolidated B-24 Liberator was ideally suited as an antisubmarine aircraft, for it had a long range and could carry as many as twenty-four depth charges. The allocation of B-24s to antisubmarine work was delayed until the early spring of 1943. They arrived just in time to combine with a number of other antisubmarine warfare devices that included airborne radar, far more proficient escort groups, and the increased efficiency of radio detection methods. This combination would in March 1943 dash the cup of prospective victory from Doenitz's lips, and completely reverse the course of the Battle of the Atlantic.

It will be seen that air power while essential in all theaters had not yet been applied at the scale and with the ferocity that would elicit a full measure of its effectiveness. That full measure would come, with terrible implications for the future, in the next two years.

Chapter Eight

True Air Superiority, Then Absolute Air Supremacy, 1944-45

By 1944, the war had lasted long enough for tremendous sums to have been spent upon military aeronautics. Air power had evolved so far beyond the most extreme force that Douhet, Trenchard, Mitchell, and others had prophesied that their most dire predictions now seemed almost innocent in comparison.

It was abundantly evident that the exercise of air power required far more than a fleet of bombers flown by adventuresome young amateurs, as envisioned by Douhet and others. Instead, air power demanded the dedication of entire industries—aeronautical, electronic, munitions—and the talents of thousands of scientists. It further required extraordinary numbers of aircraft, at least an order of magnitude more than any air-power prophet had envisaged. These massive numbers in their turn required millions of spare parts, modification kits, untold tons of fuel, and similar massive quantities of every ordinary support item down to rations and clothing for the millions of personnel involved. Air power required an entirely new infrastructure of bases, plus navigation, meteorological, and communication systems far more capable than anything previously imagined. Most of all, air power required courageous, well-trained, and proficient air and ground crews who were intelligently led by professionals. These leaders had to understand how to apply their air power, knowing full well that thousands under their command would die to achieve their mission.

Each combatant nation reached some level of this new measure of air power, and each by different means. The Soviet Union attained it by its usual methods: a ruthless massive exploitation of its people and material resources at whatever cost to repel the Nazi invaders.

251

It saw air power as it saw artillery and mass infantry advances, an instrument to be used in such quantities that any opponent was simply swamped by the sheer magnitude of the effort. Losses were unimportant—there were always more planes and more men—and there was a finite number of Nazis.

Britain had reached a measure of air power by devoting an estimated one-third of its national war effort to Bomber Command's campaigns. Not only was there never any great assurance of success, there were, early on, indications that the bomber campaign was not achieving the desired results. But the slaughter of the 1914-18 war, the tragedies of the Somme, of Ypres, of Passchendaele, made an invasion of continental Europe the last thing Britain wished to undertake. Bereft of any real alternative for striking Germany, and thus aiding the struggling Soviet Union, Britain placed its bets on the efficacy of a bombing campaign. In the process, it created one of the great military commands of the war, RAF Bomber Command, a dedicated force, incredibly brave in the face of terrible losses, but not equipped for most of the war to do the job for which it was tasked.[1]

Japan had great difficulty in adapting to the demands of modern warfare. It wanted World War II to be fought on terms acceptable to Japan, meaning it wanted to fight weak opponents with its small, highly trained forces. When, by mid-1942, it perceived that the war was going to be fought on the terms the United States imposed, Japan tried to achieve the maximum amount of air power within its considerable capacity. It had talented designers and engineers, a loyal work force, and a country utterly dedicated to the pursuit of the war. It did succeed partially in moving toward a more powerful degree of air power by demanding even more of its work force and adopting a wholesale system of decentralization that permitted virtually every household to become a "shadow factory." Women were inducted into the work force on a vast scale and were paid at a rate approximately 50 percent that of the comparable male wage. Japan was forced, however, to accept a decreased level of quality in return for higher production, which had adverse effects in the field, where Japanese in-commission rates were typically much lower than those of the United States, adding to the quantitative imbalance.

Germany reached its upper levels of both quality and quantity in air power while enduring the most extensive bombing campaigns in history. It was able to do so by the intense employment of slave labor from captured nations to extract the most from its previously underutilized industrial capacity. Germany had overbuilt its aircraft industry before the war, not with the conscious knowledge of having the overcapacity in an emergency, but rather to achieve its production goals with a normal one-shift work week. It maintained this one-shift approach long after Britain and the United States had gone to a twenty-four-hour-day, seven-day-week schedule, and departed from it only long after it was realized that a much bigger Luftwaffe was required. In April 1942 more than 90 percent of German industry was on a single-shift, five-and-one-half-day week. Not until March 1944 were German aircraft plants placed on double shifts with a seven-day work week.[2]

An intricate system of subcontracting was devised to allow dispersed factories dedicated to the production of specific components to raise production levels. It was costly in terms of increased labor expenses, difficulties in keeping track of changes, additional expenses in tooling, and its great dependence on road, rail, and canal transportation. But the system worked well enough until it fell victim to the attacks of long-range fighters in late 1944 and early 1945. These long-range fighters would do more to disrupt German production efforts than the massive aerial bombing had done—a turn of events totally unforeseen either by Germany or the Allies.

Germany increased production by taking advantage of the talents of gifted—if utterly immoral—managers such as Albert Speer, Karl-Otto Saur, and Erhard Milch. These men succeeded in "rationalizing" its industry, putting key lower-level management decisions in the hands of the factory owners and workers, reducing the number of types of aircraft, restraining the German penchant for changes in production aircraft, and, in 1944, deciding at last to concentrate on the production of fighters. The result was a massive surge in production in 1944, reaching a rate of forty thousand per year. Unfortunately for Germany, this increased production came at a time when fuel supplies were critically short both for operations and for training.

The Allied situation was far better. Britain not only had control of its own airspace, it had pilots streaming in from training in all parts of the Empire and in the United States. The Soviet Union had vast reaches of territory where flight training could be conducted undisturbed except by weather. The United States was immune to air attack and had hundreds of flight schools. In aching contrast, Germany's flight schools were by 1944 almost out of business, turning out students with a hundred hours flying time or less, because of short-ages of fuel and instructors. German flying schools were also subject to air attack, and more than one German cadet, out on a solo mission, was caught and shot down by marauding American or British fighters.

The failure to increase German fighter production early on was generally recognized as a significant factor in its final defeat. In a postwar interview, Field Marshal Milch said that his greatest regret was the "140,000 un-built fighters" that Germany could have had if it had done in 1938 what it finally did in 1943 and 1944. His esti-mate is probably high, but it is indicative of the failure of German planners to recognize the gigantic scale of operations that true air power required—and was in fact achievable.[3]

The Germans, in desperation, did introduce "miracle weapons" such as the V-1 pilotless flying bomb (a cruise missile in today's terms) and the V-2 ballistic missile. If Germany had been able to maintain air superiority, and manufacture the V-1 on the schedule (operational by January 1, 1944) and the quantity (8,000 per month) Hitler had demanded, it might in fact have influenced invasion operations, if not the course of the war. The V-2 in contrast, was an enormous waste of resources that could better have been applied building jet fighters. The V-2 was actually the hobby-shop project of German scientists who were more interested in going to space than going to war. When appropriated for war purposes, the V-2 became the world's first ballis-tic missile, and had a deadly effect upon morale in Great Britain. Had the Germans had a complementary nuclear program, it might have been decisive, but in the last analysis, the baleful V-2, produced large-ly by concentration camp labor, was a mistake for Germany but a post-war research boon to the United States and the Soviet Union.

The United States had arrived at its overwhelming air superiority by means of its unparalleled industrial capacity, its unrestricted fund-ing, and the limitless reservoir of energy that the decade-long Depression had dammed up. The United States was fortunate that its aviation engineers, managers, and entrepreneurs had been enthusiasts who somehow kept their small companies going despite the economic doldrums. Even the "big" names in American aviation, such as Boeing, Curtiss, Douglas, Grumman, Lockheed, and Martin, were relatively small, with a few million dollars in capitalization and only a few hundred or a few thousand workers at the start of the war. They expanded quickly, with Lockheed, for example, going from about 3,000 in 1939 to 91,000 by 1943.[4] What was surprising was the manner in which small older firms and brand new firms just entering the market place grew and prospered. Smaller older firms such as Aeronca, Piper, Waco, and others made invaluable contributions, while new firms such as McDonnell and Northrop would prove to be major assets to the industry.

None of it could have happened without the human factor. People flocked to work in the aircraft industry, reveling in the sheer pleasure of having a worthwhile job at a good wage in a good cause. The social ramifications were enormous, with minorities and women entering the work force in unparalleled numbers. Nor were they confined to unskilled jobs; instead, training programs enfranchised them with skills never before open to them. Production levels in all arms soared to new heights as a result, but nowhere more than in the aviation industry, which reached a peak in 1944 with a rate of 100,000 aircraft per year, and, (slightly reduced because of cancellations) an actual output of 96,000. In the course of the war, the United States would build 325,000 aircraft of all types. The Ford Motor Company had been slow to come to war work, but by 1945, the Willow Run bomber plant was turning out one Consolidated B-24 every hour.

These new levels of air power would be exercised in the first six months of 1944 in two notable air campaigns. In one, the resilient Luftwaffe won its final major victory, achieving air superiority at night over the Reich after more than four years of struggle. This triumph would not have significant effect on the war or on history, for by the time the Battle of Berlin was concluded, Germany's defeat was inevitable.

In the other notable campaign, the United States Army Air Forces led the way in blowing the Luftwaffe out of the sky, rendering it a spent force, able to put up only limited resistance at great intervals. This victory had an immense effect upon history, for it permitted the invasion of Europe, secured Germany's defeat on the Western Front, expedited the Soviet victory on the Eastern Front, and established a pattern for the future in which the air forces of the United States would be the primary protector of the free world.

The Night Campaign against Berlin: Last Victory for the Luftwaffe

When Bomber Command began its preliminary offensive against

Berlin in late August 1943, it had on strength about seven hundred four-engine bombers, approximately twice the number available to the Eighth Air Force. Where in the past its bombers had formed a 350-mile-long bomber stream that took hours to fly over a target, they now streamed across a city in about twenty-minutes, flying in a dense wedge no more than seventy miles long. Elaborate bomb-dropping techniques evolved, which included special Pathfinder crews to mark target areas accurately with a variety of sophisticated markers, and a "Master of Ceremonies" who orbited the target at great risk and directed incoming bombers as to where best to place their bombs. Successively more sophisticated electronic countermeasure (ECM) devices were available in abundance to jam enemy radar and communications. And while the bombers headed in, specialized de Havilland Mosquito night-fighters sought to eliminate their Nazi counterparts. Most raids were assisted by elaborate spoof sorties that diverted German resources and hid the ultimate target for as long as possible.

Yet despite setbacks, the Luftwaffe night-fighter force had grown both in numbers and in skill, supplementing its radar-equipped night-fighters with single-engine fighters using Major Hajo Herrmann's *Wilde Sau* (Wild Boar) techniques. When the British "Window" chaff system knocked out German radars, Herrmann realized that ordinary day-fighters could operate at night, using the flames of German cities as the background against which RAF bombers could be spotted. It was risky, for the single-engine aircraft were tricky to land at night on the darkened airfields, but it filled a huge gap in German defenses when there was no other evident solution. The Germans adapted their radar to handle the British ECM countermeasures, and were sometimes innovative enough to find a way to use the enemy ECM to guide their night-fighters to the bombers.

And the Germans did in the air what they did on the ground—make up any disadvantage in numbers or technology with the lives of their servicemen. The air crews, often inadequately trained, flew against tremendous odds, in hazardous weather, in inferior equipment, and they died in great numbers. As with the German day-fighter force, the process of attrition quickly eliminated less-well-trained and adept pilots. Those who remained became more and more proficient, until they too, in the ordinary course of events, were killed in combat or by an accident.

Air Chief Marshal Sir Arthur Harris was nicknamed "Bomber" by the press, to which he was utterly indifferent. His crews nicknamed him "Butcher," a seemingly awful term, but one they applied in a strange, almost affectionate way, indicating their understanding that he was doing a job that had to be done rather than expressing resentment against him. Harris longed to prove his theory that the Germans could be "de-housed," that the obliteration of one city after another would do more than just damage German productivity, but would instead bring an end to the war. To him, Berlin was the ultimate target, for it was not only the capital of Germany, it was the symbol of Hitler's evil government.

Harris launched three attacks against Berlin in August 1943, with a total of 1,719 sorties, using primarily four-engine bombers, and most of these the superb Avro Lancaster. Bomber Command lost 123 aircraft, a 7-percent loss rate. On November 3, he wrote to Winston Churchill, saying: "We can wreck Berlin from end to end if the USAAF will come in on it. It will cost between 400-500 aircraft. It will cost Germany the war."[5] The USAAF did not come in on the Battle of Berlin, however, not making its first major raid on the city until March 6, 1944. A decision had been made at Eighth Air Force to minimize deep incursions into Germany, with their inevitable losses, until adequate fighter escort could be provided.

Harris began what he considered to be the formal Battle of Berlin on the night of November 18-19, 1943, and waged it without relaxation until March 1944. In those four months, Bomber Command flew 20,224 sorties, during which about 2,700 Bomber Command aircraft were lost or heavily damaged. Of these 1,047 were shot down over Germany. There were 9,111 sorties against Berlin, with 492 aircraft missing, 954 damaged, and 95 written off upon return.[6] The final major battle over Berlin came on March 24, 1944, when just over 800 bombers were dispatched and 73 were lost. While this dire 9-percent loss rate was being digested, the climactic battle came, not over Berlin but Nuremburg. On the night of March 30-31, Bomber Command put a force of 976 four-engine bombers and 15 Mosquitoes over Nuremburg in perfect weather. Ninety-six aircraft were shot down, with 960 crewmen killed or captured. The raid, with its almost 10-percent loss rate, had resulted in only 138 German civilian deaths. It was clear to many, including Winston Churchill, once bombing's biggest backer, that the RAF bombing campaign was no longer worth the price that was being paid for it.

Harris and his supporters always maintained that the Battle of Berlin was not a defeat and that the RAF could have carried on, had it not been for the shift in mission to bombing the French transportation system. Yet the fact remains that at the crucial moment over Berlin, it was Bomber Command and not the Luftwaffe that stood down.

At that late date in the war, the Luftwaffe appeared to have won air superiority in the night skies over Germany. Harris had been defeated, but was spared the ignominy of admission by the swift pace of the war. In the spring of 1944, the requirements for the planned invasion of Europe, Operation Overlord, resulted in Harris's having to place Bomber Command at the disposal of General Dwight D. Eisenhower, the overall Allied commander.

On March 25, 1944, Eisenhower directed both Bomber Command and the Eighth Air Force to concentrate their efforts on softening up enemy resistance by bombing the transportation system that connected Germany to the coming battlefield on France's coastline. When that campaign was over and area bombing of Germany could be resumed, Harris and Bomber Command would be the beneficiaries of the great American daytime victory over the Luftwaffe. By that time, area bombing of Germany had become of questionable military value. Yet Germany had rebounded from apparent abject defeat before, as with the Christmas offensive that became known as the Battle of the Bulge. The retreating German armies were still huge and still possessed a great military potential against an unwary opponent. They were being led by men who had nothing to lose, so the habit of bombing cities was continued, in the hope of interfering with their movement. There was also, unquestionably, an element of vengeance, a desire to mete out to the Germans what they had so freely done to the British. The bombing was carried on until April 1945, and included among its terrible assaults Dresden, the subject of intense controversy ever since.

The controversy over Dresden began with a March 28, 1945, memo from Winston Churchill to the Chief of Air Staff, Air Marshall Sir Charles Portal, stating that Dresden was a "serious query against the conduct of Allied bombing"—an indication that Churchill had anticipated the drift of public opinion. In 1963, the controversial author David Irving wrote in *The Destruction of Dresden* that 135,000 had been killed—erring by about 100,000 according to more accurate accounts. His book, combined with Kurt Vonnegutt's *Slaughter House Five*, argued that it was an unnecessary and excessive reaction.

The inference was that it was a personal, vindictive, and bloody-minded act by Bomber Harris, who was in turn a metaphor for all the vindictive and bloody-minded air force leaders who bombed not to win wars but for the sheer pleasure of killing.

The controversy stems in part from the fact that the critics make their decisions in peacetime, without any responsibility for prosecuting a war. In contrast, the Allied commanders had been fighting for more than five years, and even in its death throes, Germany was proving resilient. It had in the past year introduced the V-1, the V-2, the Messerschmitt Me 262, and the snorkel submarine. It was still killing as many Allied soldiers and civilians as it could, and was still conducting an as yet undefined but horrifying holocaust on the Jewish population. No one knew what last resource it might have—there were even fears that it might have somehow availed itself of an atomic bomb.

So great was the remaining danger that requests for the raid on Dresden had come from Prime Minister Winston Churchill, and reportedly, from Joseph Stalin as well. The Allied Supreme Commander, General Eisenhower, was informed, and a USAAF raid was laid on for the following day. The chain of command ran from Churchill down through the Chief of the Air Staff, Air Chief Marshal Charles Portal, and through Air Vice Marshal Sir Sidney Bufton, the Chairman of the Combined Strategic Targets Committee, to Harris. These men did not see Dresden as a quaint provincial city; they saw it for what it was, a key transportation hub for the Eastern Front, and a collection of munitions. Notwithstanding this viewpoint, Harris took the trouble to have his deputy, Air Vice Marshall Sir Richard Saundby, check to make sure that Dresden should be on the target list.[7]

The top-level decision to bomb Dresden also had the unstated requirement to demonstrate to the Soviet Union both the Allied desire to help—and the Allied ability to inflict punishment by bombing. The bombing of Dresden, then, was like any bombing raid from the first feeble leaflet drops to the atomic bomb on Nagasaki: a terrible waste. It would have been better if none of them had ever taken place—but there happened to be a war on.

The Quest for Air Superiority: Operation Argument

Air power and its influence have always turned on the capability of individuals. Yet the daytime air war over Germany saw an extremely capable individual, Ira Eaker, unable to establish air superiority solely because he was attempting to do it with the wrong tools. Eaker was fulfilling the Air Corps Tactical School doctrine of bomber invincibility, using his limited resources to the maximum. Unfortunately, air superiority and the free exercise of air power were not to be achieved until bitter bloody experience at last called forth the long-range fighters that would do the job. The pervasive and insidious influence of the ACTS doctrine of bomber supremacy can be inferred from the fact that no urgent requests were made for two groups of the aircraft most suitable for the task, Lockheed P-38s that were available in the United States. (Other P-38 groups had been sent to fight in North Africa.)

When the Eighth Air Force began operation, it was originally commanded by Major General Carl A. ("Tooey") Spaatz and consisted of the VIII Bomber Command under Brigadier General Eaker (who had flown with Spaatz on the famed 1929 endurance flight of the *Question Mark*), and VIII Fighter Command, under World War I ace Brigadier General Frank O'Driscoll ("Monk") Hunter, who with his dramatic mustache and military flair was the very image of the glamorous fighter leader.

The Eighth Air Force grew from six men and no airplanes in February 1942 to 8,000 aircraft and 400,000 personnel by June 1944. Eaker became Commander of the Eighth Air Force in December 1942. His articulate voice at the Casablanca Conference convinced Churchill to stop pressing for the USAAF to join Bomber Command in the night-bombing role, and instead to complement it in "round-the-clock" bombing, a phrase Eaker used that appealed to the wordsmith in Churchill.

Eaker worked well with the RAF and with the British people, to whom he had endeared himself with his now famous arrival speech in which he said only, "We won't do much talking until we've done more fighting. After we've gone, we hope you'll be glad we came." But despite his truly magnificent efforts, he never received the assets capable of doing what General Arnold constantly demanded of him. It may have been that Eaker was not quite ruthless enough with his subordinates. Neither his replacement at VIII Bomber Command, Brigadier General Newton Longfellow, nor the VIII Fighter Command's Hunter, were obtaining the maximum results with their equipment. Hunter used his aircraft for short-range fighter sweeps, which the Luftwaffe simply ignored. Eaker reluctantly replaced them, with Brigadier General Frank Armstrong Jr., and Brigadier General William ("Bill") Kepner, respectively, but Eaker's own command was already forfeited.

His longtime friend and co-author, Arnold, bit the bullet and replaced Eaker on January 6, 1944, with Major General James H. ("Jimmy") Doolittle, a man who had previously been regarded as an outsider. Doolittle had offended the regular corps of officers by resigning his commission in 1930, after spending ten years as a first lieutenant, to provide for his family with a more lucrative career in the business world. (In fairness, it must be noted that in those ten years, Doolittle became one of the most famous flyers in the world. He performed the first outside loop in an aircraft that he had instrumented himself to record the pressures and the stress. He earned three degrees, including a Doctor of Science in aeronautics from the Massachusetts Institute of Technology. During the same period, he made many record flights, won the Schneider Trophy, and most important of all, initiated the science of instrument flying. The sheer brilliance of his performance was not rewarded with promotion solely because there were too many people senior to him on the Army promotion list.)

Doolittle, called "the master of the calculated risk" by his biographer, Carroll V. Glines, visited VIII Fighter Command headquarters soon after his arrival and saw in Kepner's office a sign reading, THE FIRST DUTY OF THE EIGHTH AIR FORCE FIGHTERS IS TO BRING BOMBERS BACK ALIVE. He told Kepner that the sign was no longer in effect, that he should take it down and put one up reading, THE FIRST DUTY OF THE EIGHTH AIR FORCE FIGHTERS IS TO DESTROY GERMAN FIGHTERS.[8]

And there lay the secret of air superiority in a nutshell. Instead of bomber formations being invincible, they were now bait to lure German fighters into the air where they could be destroyed by Eighth Air Force fighters. This was to be the secret of air superiority, a pragmatic recognition of first things first. It was not a product of years of study and the formulation of doctrine. It was an unvarnished look at the real world of air warfare as it existed in early 1944. (Doolittle, ever the modest warrior, always insisted that Eaker would have done equally well if he had been fortunate enough to have had sufficient equipment of the right type. When, in 1985 Doolittle and Eaker were both honored with promotion to full four-star general rank, Doolittle insisted that Eaker's be awarded first to maintain Eaker's seniority.)

Kepner and his men welcomed Doolittle's sweeping directive. They were being re-equipped with a new fighter, the North American P-51B Mustang, itself a product of two sets of improbable circumstances in which individuals played key roles.

In the first of these, the Anglo-French Purchasing Commission had invited North American Aviation to produce Curtiss P-40 fighters under license. North American was a relatively new company, and a lucrative contract to produce fighters without any risk capital whatsoever must have been tempting to the company president, James H. ("Dutch") Kindelberger. However, he consulted with his lead designers who convinced him that a more modern fighter could be designed and put into production before the P-40 could.

The British were not enamored of the P-40's performance, and Sir Henry Self, the Director of the Purchasing Commission, agreed to a contract for four hundred new North American fighters, to be delivered at $37,509.45 each, and armed with eight machine guns. The prototype had to be ready in 120 days. (When the first contract arrived, it was for 320 aircraft.)

The North American team responded brilliantly with a beautiful new fighter that featured a laminar-flow wing and an innovative low-drag radiator system. (The laminar flow wing was the product of NACA research, and points up the value of a government-supported research agency.) The first aircraft rolled out in 102 days, but had to wait eighteen days for the delivery of the engine.[9] The first flight was made on October 26, 1940, with veteran test pilot Vance Breese at the controls.

It was soon evident that the NA-73, as it was designated, was the best American fighter yet produced, but the USAAF ordered only two, as XP-51s, for test purposes. The Mustang, as it was called, entered RAF service in April 1942, equipped with the American Allison engine, which lacked the two-speed, two-stage supercharging necessary for high-altitude work. Instead, it excelled in high-speed, low-altitude missions. Its future was forecast in October, when it became the first American fighter to penetrate Germany, flying a reconnaissance mission to Dortmund.

The second improbable circumstance, which raised the Mustang from a good, well-liked, low-level fighter to perhaps the best piston-engine fighter of the war, occurred when Major Thomas Hitchcock, a famous polo player serving as an assistant air attaché at the American embassy in London, suggested that the best available engine, the Rolls-Royce Merlin, be installed in the Mustang.

It was a superb idea, and after considerable testing and modification, the North American P-51B emerged. It outperformed the Messerschmitt Bf 109F and G and the Focke Wulf FW 190 in almost all important flight characteristics. Best of all, with an additional eighty-five-gallon internal tank and two seventy-five-gallon drop tanks, it could escort bombers all the way to Berlin and back. Fuel had to be used out of the new internal tank first, to keep the center of gravity within limits, but by the time that fuel was used, and the two external tanks emptied and dropped, the P-51 could whip any German piston-engine fighter it encountered. The first sortie of the P-51B was with the 354th Fighter Group on November 11, 1943. On December 13, the group escorted 710 bombers in a raid on Kiel, a round-trip distance of 980 miles.

The Eighth Air Force now had the weapon with which to defeat the Luftwaffe. There were other good fighters in the Eighth, including ever-increasing numbers of the Republic P-47 and two Lockheed P-38 groups, but neither had the Mustang's range. One of the unforeseen benefits of the Mustang's taking on the aerial superiority role was that it would free the P-47 to become one of the all-time great attack aircraft. Further, once the P-51 had won air superiority, both the P-47 and the P-51 had a free run against the German transportation system.

The Fight for Air Superiority

In some respects the Eighth Air Force and the Luftwaffe were like two champion boxers who fought each other repeatedly, each learning from the other, each growing in strength and proficiency, and, for a long time, neither able to muster a true knockout blow.

The Germans had been forced to denude the most dangerous and critical battle area, the Eastern Front, to protect against the growing British and American onslaught. They also had to force Hitler to agree at last to cease production of bombers. The German leader was an eye-for-an-eye man who believed the British would stop bombing only when he bombed them back. His insistence on continued bomber production badly hurt German fighter production, and it was not until the failure of Operation Steinbock, the final, pathetic Luftwaffe bombing campaign against England, that he finally agreed to cease building bombers in favor of fighters.

The Luftwaffe had managed to gather 550 bombers together for Steinbock, including thirty-five of the trouble-prone Heinkel He 177 heavy bombers. Led by Major General Dietrich Peltz, the campaign began with a total of 270 sorties on January 21, 1944, and continued in fitful fashion until April 18. Most raids consisted of 100 to 170 aircraft, and while losses were high, bombing accuracy was low. When the campaign was concluded, Germany had fewer than 130 bombers with which to contend the coming invasion.[10] In its bumbling way, Operation Steinbock was an instruction manual on how not to use air power, for it was conducted with inadequate resources, ill-trained crews, and no means with which to attempt to gain air superiority.

Establishing True Air Power

By February 1944, the Eighth Air Force had finally grown to the point where its dismal in-commission rate did not prevent it from putting a lot of bombers over Germany. It now had 1,852 heavy bombers of which 1,046 were serviceable—a lackluster 56 percent in-commission rate. (When Eaker had only 350 bombers, a similar low in-commission rate meant that he had a striking force of 196, too few to do much damage—except to his reputation.)

The Eighth was also supplemented by the Fifteenth Air Force, which operated out of Italy with 835 heavy bombers. Of these, 570 were serviceable, a more reasonable 68 percent in-commission rate. With a combined effort, 1,600 heavy bombers could be placed over Germany.[11]

The Luftwaffe had responded to the growing strength of the Eighth's incursions in 1943 in the only way it could, by increasing its flak installations and building up its fighter force at the expense of other fronts. In January 1943, the Luftwaffe had 635 single-engine and 410 twin-engine fighters, a total of 1,045, for the defense of the Reich, which left it with 395 single-engine and 50 twin-engine fighters on the Eastern Front—a pathetically small number given the enormous size of the front and the rising strength of the Soviet Air Force. By January 1944, the Luftwaffe had 870 single-engine and 780 twin-engine fighters (a total of 1,650) in the defense of the Reich, while strength on the Eastern Front had declined to 425 fighters, of which only 345 were single engine.[12]

Germany's fighter aircraft production was rising at a rate even faster than Allied estimates. The USAAF decided that in addition to attacking the aircraft industry, the Luftwaffe also had to be worn down by attrition to reduce the so-called "production-wastage differential."[13] In plainer words, the objective was to shoot down more German planes than could be built to replace them.

The weather began to clear over Germany on February 19, and Operation Argument was put into play, with Bomber Command, Eighth Air Force, and Fifteenth Air Force joining in. One of the primary objects of the attacks was to get the German Air Force into the air and destroy it, with the bombers serving as bait.

The American long-range fighters adopted new tactics, reaching out beyond the bomber stream to attack German units as they were forming up, then dropping down to some of the most hazardous duty in the war, strafing enemy air bases that were hotly defended by many antiaircraft guns.

Aptly called "Big Week," the battle went on for seven days, with the Luftwaffe bravely rising each day to meet new defeats. By February 25, the Eighth and Fifteenth Air Forces had flown more than 3,800 sorties and dropped almost 10,000 tons of bombs. The loss rate was high—just under 6 percent—with 226 heavy bombers shot down. The USAAF fighter loss rate was minimal, with only 28 aircraft lost out of 3,673 missions.

It was a different story for the Luftwaffe, which lost 2,121 aircraft in February, and would lose a further 2,115 in March.[14] Even more devastating to the Luftwaffe, however, was its loss in experienced pilots, especially its *Experten,* the high-scoring aces with a hundred victories or more. The effect of these losses was devastating, and put an impossible demand on the Luftwaffe replacement program. As more pilots were killed, their replacements were brought in with less and less training; these less-well-trained pilots were killed even more rapidly, accelerating the downward spiral to impotence. The obvious decline in the quality of Luftwaffe pilots was noted in many intelligence debriefings of Allied pilots, with comments made about enemy pilots flying straight ahead when under attack and others bailing out before an attack even began.

From the end of Big Week on, the Luftwaffe took up the challenge less and less frequently, as it tried to husband its dwindling supplies of pilots and fuel. Ironically, fighter production continued to soar, but losses to airfield and factory attacks were also soaring. The effectiveness of the suppression techniques was evident in the case of the Messerschmitt Me 262, the superb jet fighter that the Germans began introducing in 1944. Of some 1,340 built, only about 315 ever got into combat, the rest being destroyed by bombing before they could be used.[15]

Yet the Luftwaffe even in decline had recuperative powers, and would occasionally strike out—it was like a wounded shark that has been brought on deck in a boat, dying, but still capable of lashing with both teeth and tail. On March 6, 1944, when the Americans made their first major raid on Berlin, the Luftwaffe destroyed 69 of the 660 aircraft attacking.

The Big Week victory over the Luftwaffe opened up new avenues for the Eighth Air Force and Bomber Command in bombing and for RAF and USAAF fighters in strafing. The bombing statistics are revealing, indicating that true air power was reached in 1944, for the first time in history. Never before had there been at one time a similar degree of aerial dominance and also the capability to deliver so much destructive power. The combined effort of the RAF and the Eighth Air Force, through the end of 1943, had resulted in 293,566 tons of bombs being dropped on the Nazi empire. This jumped in 1944 to a total of 1,154,897 tons; in the five months of war in 1945, the total reached 461,212 tons. In grand total terms, the Allies put down 1,909,405 tons of bombs in 793,700 sorties on occupied Europe.[16] (In contrast, the Germans had dropped 58,702 tons of bombs on the United Kingdom in what seemed at the time like a massive bombing campaign in 1940 and 1941, and a total of only 74,172 in the course of the war, less than 4 percent of the Allied total.[17])

Of the almost two million tons of bombs, a staggering 76 percent of the total tonnage (1,451,147 tons) had been dropped on Germany in the last seventeen months of the war. Ironically, the ability to deliver this devastating tonnage in the final months came about as a result of air superiority won not by bombing the enemy factories into oblivion, but instead, by utilizing the long-range fighter, which hammered the Luftwaffe into virtual impotence. Many of the later bomber missions were flown without seeing a single enemy fighter.

The full extent of that air superiority was revealed on D-Day— the invasion of Europe—when General Eisenhower promised his troops that any aircraft they saw would be friendly. He was almost completely correct, although the Germans made a few hundred sorties. In contrast, between June 6 and September 1, 1944, the Allied air forces flew almost 500,000 sorties, in which 4,100 aircraft were lost, mostly to ground fire and to accidents. The Luftwaffe was unable to respond, and most of the aircraft that had been flown in to bases in France specifically to repel the invasion were destroyed en route or after landing.

The German forces awaiting the invasion had been positioned according to the concepts of Field Marshal Gerd von Rundstedt—a relatively thin line of troops in the West Wall, with reserves, particularly armor, held back to be committed only when the "main invasion" took place. Field Marshal Erwin Rommel held the opposite view; having experienced the effects of Allied air power firsthand in North Africa, he wanted the entire German force to be as close to the front as possible, for he warned that moving them forward would prove impossible. Hitler agreed with von Runstedt, and, as usual, reserved to himself the right to release the forces. Although Hitler had intuitively predicted that Normandy would be the invasion spot, an elaborate Allied spoof convinced him that the main attack was intended for the Pas de Calais area.

Rommel proved to be correct. The landing at Normandy was the only Allied invasion point, and when Hitler at last committed his armored forces, the Allied fighter-bombers tore them to bits. Reinforcements could travel only at night, and with these delays, Germany's sole opportunity to repel the invasion was lost. Under the cover of tactical air power, the bridgehead grew day by day, contained only by the fanatic Nazi resistance.

Allied bombers assisted in the breakout from Normandy with controversial carpet-bombing tactics that, while not always precise and sometimes inflicting friendly fire casualties, were nonetheless devastating to entrenched German defenders. As Field Marshal Gunther von Kluge reported to Hitler, "The psychological effect on the fighting forces, especially the infantry, of such a mass of bombs raining down on them with all the force of elemental nature, is a factor which must be given serious consideration. It is not in the least important whether such a carpet of bombs is dropped on good or bad troops."[18]

With the breakout, the fighter-bombers assumed a new role, sometimes acting as flanking guards for advancing American armor, often with pilots riding in tanks as land-borne forward air controllers.

In France as in Italy, Germany demonstrated its new and ugly anti-air-power doctrine. Simply stated, the new doctrine postulated that soldiers could fight a strong defensive battle even without air power, even though in the end, many would die, and the battle would be lost. Similar circumstances would force Japan to adopt the same bloody doctrine on its road to defeat.

As the Allies advanced, the German radar system was pushed back so that there was even less time to alert the dwindling fighter force. The only advantage to the Luftwaffe was that, as it retreated, more and better-equipped bases were found in Germany, and there were more antiaircraft weapons available for defense.

The diminishment of the Luftwaffe's threat permitted tactical aviation to come into its own in the advance across France, as the fighter-bomber became the preferred weapon for the close air support role, for which the Republic P-47 was particularly suited. The P-47 was extremely rugged and had a 2,000-horsepower Pratt & Whitney R-2800 engine that could take enormous damage and still run well enough to get the airplane back to its home field. As the war had progressed, cooperation between the armies and the air forces had improved enormously, so tactical aircraft became an on-call service for advancing armored units, standing in aerial cab ranks, awaiting targets.

The value of the tactic was proved in such slaughters as the mid-August 1944 Falaise Gap massacre, when fleeing enemy columns, the remnants of some twenty German divisions, were first halted then decimated by wave after wave of fighter-bombers, particularly the very effective British Hawker Typhoon. Forced to abandon their vehicles and guns, only about half the enemy force made it back to its own territory.

Meanwhile, over Germany, the Luftwaffe conserved its strength as best it could, staying on the ground except for raids on the most critical targets, trying to put together enough numbers to make its attacks meaningful. To the Mustangs and Thunderbolts that now roamed German skies with near impunity from aerial opposition, everything was now a target, from the dangerous airfields down to a courier on a bicycle.

The attacks on the airfields were by far the most hazardous, and experienced pilots carefully planned such attacks to maximize surprise and minimize the response of the antiaircraft guns. The concept was to make one sudden whirlwind attack and leave—if they came back for a second pass, they were almost certain to be shot down. Even on the "one pass and haul ass" attacks, many pilots were lost or captured, including some leading aces, such as then-Major Francis ("Gabby") Gabreski.

But the greatest and most surprising triumph, the one that at last shut down the indefatigable German industry, was that of tactical fighter-bombers over the German transportation system. The fighter-bombers came in at low levels, making surprising raid on trains, canal barges, trucks, and automobiles. They shot them up with abandon and with a minimum of hazard, although the trains and even the barges sometimes had flak accompanying them, and often blew up just as the fighters passed overhead. Even in so powerful a nation as Germany, which had assiduously ransacked the territories it had conquered for equipment, there was a finite number of locomotives, railcars, trucks, and barges, and the marauding fighters eventually destroyed most of them. This left German industry with a host of dispersed factories making components for which it could not receive raw materials and from which it could not deliver finished parts.

Hitler had anticipated the problem, and had begun the construction of huge underground facilities in which raw materials would be brought in one end, and jet fighters flown out the other. A great deal of money and effort was spent in constructing these last-ditch efforts, but to no avail—the war was long over before they could be brought to practical use. Hitler had also correctly estimated the hardiness of the German populace, reassuring Speer on one occasion that as long as the German worker had a hole to live in and a board for a roof, he would go on working, sustained by vaporous propaganda on "miracle weapons."

It was in Hitler's Berlin bunker where for the first time a totally unexpected aspect of the influence of air power on history manifested itself. All of the air-power philosophers had assumed that when air power had reached its peak and wreaked havoc upon an enemy nation, the populace would rise up, and the enemy government would admit its defeat. Quite the contrary happened. The people did not rise up because a totalitarian government still had severe reprisal methods that included the slaughter of entire families for any ill-considered action by one member. And the Nazi leaders would not contemplate surrender, no matter how utterly hopeless the situation, because they preferred to remain in power, skulking in an underground shelter, for as many more days or weeks as possible. Thus even when air power had been demonstrated absolutely, when the war was totally and obviously lost, maniacal leaders permitted thousands of ordinary soldiers and civilians to die just to delay their own fate a little longer.

The bombers had run out of worthwhile targets in April, and were stood down or assigned to more positive duties such as dropping food supplies to starving citizens of Holland. The fighters were still in demand, however, for die-hard German contingents were still attempting to slow the Allied progress, and it made sense to use the freely available air power to eliminate them rather than lose lives in a frontal assault. The last fighter-versus-fighter engagements took place on May 8, 1945, the day of Germany's surrender.

Air power had been demonstrated at last over Germany. Not even the most avid advocate could claim the victory for air power alone, but not even the most stubborn anti-air-power critic could deny that its role had been essential. The German Army was generally admitted to be the best in the world, and it probably fought better without air power than any other army could have done. Letters and reports from German soldiers are filled with complaints about the "unfair" American infantry that would halt at the first sign of opposition and summon air power to blow any resistance out of the way. It was not at all unfair, it was the only intelligent way to fight the war, and ironically, it was the way Germany initiated the fighting. The difference was that where the Germans once had a few hundred Stukas, the Allies now possessed thousands of fighter-bombers.

The quality of the American effort stemmed in large part from the brilliant leadership of Brigadier General Pete Quesada. A veteran of the 1927 *Question Mark* endurance flight, Quesada had established the IX Fighter Command in October 1943. He instilled in it his ideas of tactics, and with the creation of IX Tactical Air Command in June 1944, blazed a trail across Europe, providing flank coverage to armored columns, decimating German resistance, and ranging over the German transport system. His IX TAC became the pattern for other USAAF tactical air commands. Despite a bitter feud with Lieutenant General Hoyt Vandenberg, Quesada emerged from the war as the biggest contributor to the cooperative success of American air and armored units.[19]

In the Pacific War, on the other side of the world, the United

States would use air power initially in much the same way as in Germany, with both naval air forces and the USAAF supplementing the advance of Marine and Army units. Ultimately, however, the greatest expression of air power to date would be found in the employment of the Boeing B-29. Within months, the ultimate in air power would be found in the combination of that airplane and nuclear weapons.

Air Power in the Pacific

Control of American forces in the Pacific theater of war was divided between two towering personalities, the colorful, flamboyant General Douglas MacArthur and the quiet, reserved Admiral Chester Nimitz. To preserve their respective egos and to insure the least amount of friction, the Pacific theater was divided into the Southwest Pacific Area under MacArthur and the Pacific Ocean Area under Nimitz. MacArthur was to move in an arc from Guadalcanal up through New Guinea to the Philippines. Nimitz was to take a central route, through the Gilbert, Marshall, and Mariana island groups. Fortunately both men were convinced of the value of air power, and both were content to let their experts wield it.

The first hint of the scale in which American air power would be applied in the Pacific was seen in the first six months of 1943, when nine new aircraft carriers joined the Pacific Fleet. They were mere harbingers of what was to come in United States naval air power, for by 1945, there were no less than fourteen large fleet carriers and sixty-five light aircraft carriers in operation against the Japanese homeland. By then, Japan lacked pilots who could take off and land from the four carriers (two large and two small) that remained afloat.

As the American carrier forces became a true strategic force in 1944-45, they grew bolder in tactics, doing routinely what experts had previously deemed impossible, taking on and defeating land-based air power. The Japanese had so heavily fortified Truk, the so-called Gibraltar of the Pacific, that an invasion would have been very difficult. On February 17, 1944, Vice Admiral Marc A. Mitscher's powerful Task Force 58 (TF 58) attacked with its fifteen carriers and 956 aircraft. In a series of smashing blows, it eliminated Japanese air power and sank 200,000 tons of merchant shipping. On February 22, Mitscher shifted his attack to the Marianas, destroying more than 150 aircraft and sinking many ships. In less than a week, Mitscher had demonstrated that his sea-borne air power could dominate Japanese land-based air power. His success confirmed a previously made decision to bypass Truk, and not invade. Abandoned without air power, Truk was changed from a fortress to a prison, with a garrison Japan could not evacuate, reinforce, or supply.

Japan was now in a position where its last hope of defending its remaining island outposts such as Saipan was the almost suicidal choice of seeking out an engagement to destroy the United States fleet. The Imperial Navy was still powerful in prewar terms, for it possessed five fleet carriers, four smaller carriers, five battleships, thirteen cruisers, and forty-two other ships. The battleships included the most powerful in the world, the 68,000-ton *Musashi* and *Yamato,* each armed with nine powerful (if not technically superior) 18.1-inch guns. In Japanese war games, this massive fleet always performed admirably—real warfare would prove to be quite different. The Japanese also possessed 222 fighters (late models of the Zero), 113 dive-bombers, and 95 torpedo bombers. These planes, however, were not flown by veteran experts as they had been in the first days of the war—instead there was a mere sprinkling of experienced leaders among a mass of poorly trained pilots.

The Japanese also planned to use 100 land-based planes in their attack on the United States fleet, operating them out of the Marianas. Mitscher took care of these by launching a preemptive strike on June 11 that destroyed the land-based aircraft in a single attack. Four days later, another American force, Task Group 58.1, under Rear Admiral Joseph James ("Jocko") Clark, began a series of strikes that ranged all the way up to Iwo Jima, destroying 175 additional aircraft. All of this was but a preliminary to the June 19-20 Battle of the Philippine Sea. There American naval air power triumphed completely in what became known as the "Great Marianas Turkey Shoot." Some four hundred Japanese aircraft were either shot down or lost on the three aircraft carriers that were sunk. Saipan fell on July 9, Tinian on August 1, and Guam on August 10, completing the conquest of the Marianas. Work immediately began on the airfields from which Boeing B-29s would batter Japan into submission.

There was one major naval battle to come, in Leyte Gulf. There, in a last "death charge," sixty-four ships of the Japanese Imperial fleet set out to engage 219 ships of the United States Navy, using a typically too-complex Japanese battle plan. The battle raged across thousands of square miles of ocean and ended in two results: the utter and final defeat of the Japanese Navy and the introduction of suicide tactics with the Kamikaze attacks. The latter would become Japan's futile last hope, inflicting terrible casualties on American forces at Iwo Jima and Okinawa, captured on March 26 and July 2, 1945, respectively. In both places, the Japanese resisted fiercely, forcing U.S. Marine and Army units to fight for every foot of land at a terrible cost in lives.

The United States Navy's success exposed for the second time the curious contradiction in the study of the influence of air power on history. Air power, no matter how brutally applied, once again appeared unable to convince defeated leaders to surrender. In Japan, as in Nazi Germany, as long as the leaders could be safely ensconced in bombproof bunkers, they went into apparent denial about losing the war, clinging to chimerical belief in Kamikaze sacrifice. Rather than admit defeat, they much preferred to expose their military and civilian populace to endless casualties just to prolong their existence and their power a few months longer.

Army Air Forces Operations

Under the command of one of the great fighting airmen of World War II, Lieutenant General George Churchill Kenney, the Fifth Air Force had grown from a ragtag collection of cast-off aircraft into a formidable force that hammered out a path for General Douglas MacArthur's armies in the Southwest Pacific. Kenney proved once again the pivotal importance of personality in the exercise of air power. He had the gift for getting along not only with MacArthur, but also with MacArthur's even more difficult Chief of Staff, Major General Richard K. Sutherland. With MacArthur, Kenney did it with charm, logic, and performance; with Sutherland, he did it with a quick exposure of a titanium hand in a silken glove. But Kenney's talents for getting the best out of people did not extend upward only; he extracted the utmost from the people who worked for him, for he had the capacity to listen. He had some superb co-workers, including Kenneth Walker, who had helped prepare AWPD/1, and the tough, often irascible, Brigadier General Ennis C. Whitehead. He also had a protégé, Major Paul I. ("Pappy") Gunn, who was a master of unorthodox field modifications, a talent sorely needed in the early days of the war.

Under Kenney, the Fifth Air Force rocked Japanese shipping with low-level skip-bombing attacks, and destroyed Japanese aircraft on the ground with parafrag (parachute-retarded fragmentation) bombs. The innovative Pappy Gunn supervised the installation of seventy-five-millimeter cannon in the nose of North American B-25s for anti-shipping work. In March 1943, the Fifth, working with the Royal Australian Air Force, had been decisive in the Battle of the Bismarck Sea. The Japanese had been desperate to reinforce their army in New Guinea, and sent eight transports and five escort ships to do so. All were sunk, and Tokyo wrote off the Japanese Army in New Guinea.

The reason for the triumph was more than just having air power available. Kenney had seen to it that there had been many practice missions for just such an eventuality, and the Battle of the Bismarck Sea proved conclusively that naval operations in the face of enemy air superiority were tantamount to suicide.

With successes like these behind him, Kenney became a close strategic advisor to MacArthur in the invasion of the Philippines where MacArthur's drive from the south and Nimitz's drive across the central Pacific coincided in the fall of 1944. There American naval air power and the USAAF decided the outcome of the land campaign.

The earliest efforts of American air power in the Pacific theater had come with the work of Claire Chennault and his American Volunteer Group (AVG), the famous Flying Tigers, in China, defending the Burma Road. There, beginning in December 1941, Chennault had the satisfaction of seeing the pursuit tactics he had advocated without success at the Air Corps Tactical School proved in combat. The AVG was absorbed into the USAAF on July 4, 1942, with Chennault ultimately becoming a major general commanding the Fourteenth Air Force. The Fourteenth conducted an unremitting aerial campaign against Japan until the close of the war.

China also became the operating location of the Twentieth Air Force, which was to conduct Boeing B-29 operations against Japan. President Roosevelt had promised Generalissimo Chiang Kai-shek personally that bombing operations against Japan would begin before November 1944. The Twentieth Air Force had been organized by Hap Arnold himself, and remained under his direct command with Major General Haywood S. ("Possum") Hansell Jr. as his Chief of Staff. Hansell was a graduate of ACTS, and had flown with Chennault on the "Three Men on the Flying Trapeze" flying team. A founding member of the "bomber mafia," Hansell had done yeoman work on AWPD/1 and AWPD/42. In Europe he had successfully commanded both Boeing B-17 and Martin B-26 bomber wings. By the time it was operational, XX Bomber Command had 20,000 officers and men to operate the first increment of approximately 150 B-29s. It was in effect, a testing ground for the B-29 bombing campaign.

XX Bomber Command conducted initial operations from China, led by the man responsible for the successful B-29 program, Major General Kenneth B. ("K. B.") Wolfe. Operations from China were extremely difficult because of the unreliability of the B-29's Wright R-3350 engines and of the intrinsically unsolvable problem of flying the mammoth quantities of fuel and bombs across the Himalayas to the operating fields in Chengtu, China. B-29s had to be pressed into service as tankers and transports, consuming fuel as they carried fuel, defeating the object of fielding a strong force of the aircraft. The first combat mission, to Bangkok, was flown on June 5, 1944, and the first strike on Japan was made against the Yawata steel works on June 15. The results of this and subsequent raids were unsatisfactory, as there was not enough fuel and bombs available to send an adequate number of B-29s, and there were long stand-downs between raids as supplies were accumulated. Wolfe was relieved of command, and Major General Curtis E. LeMay was given the task of leading the B-29s against Japan.

LeMay undertook a substantial reorganization of training and tactics, but it was simply too difficult to conduct successful operations out of China against Japan. He felt that the entire project had been unsound from the start and was frustrated by the failure to obtain better results. The Japanese made the situation worse with their last successful land-based offensive, which forced XX Bomber Command to pull out of China in January and return to bases in India. On January 18, 1945, LeMay went to the Marianas to assume command of the XXI Bomber Command, into which XX Bomber Command would ultimately be absorbed.

The XXI Bomber Command had previously been commanded by Hansell, who began operations from the Marianas on November 23, 1944. The high winds and weather of Japan conspired against the success of Hansell's high-altitude precision bombing tactics, however, which achieved limited results. In the USAAF, if an officer worked for Hap Arnold, he had to deliver results no matter how far back his friendship reached, and so Arnold dismissed Hansell. (It is worth mentioning that the military leaders of the United States, a democracy, were notably more severe in their demands for performance than were their counterparts in totalitarian Germany and especially in Imperial Japan. In both of those nations, old-school ties, family connections, and a feudal sense of *noblesse oblige* often kept commanders in positions where they had failed so that they would not "lose face.") LeMay continued Hansell's conventional tactics, but in the back of his mind was a plan to switch to nighttime, low-level area bombing attacks intended to burn the combustible Japanese cities to the ground.

The continued efforts at precision bombing not only yielded poor results, they were met with increasing opposition. In a series of raids through February, twenty-nine B-29s were lost to fighters and ten more to either flak or fighters. In addition, the B-29s were still having development difficulties, and no fewer than twenty-one crashed because of operational problems—engine fires for the most part. A further fifteen were simply missing, down somewhere over the trackless ocean. When LeMay looked at the balance sheet, it read seventy-five aircraft lost, with their 825 precious crew members. In return, so little damage had been done to the Japanese that their military leaders began to think the B-29 raids were an actual advantage to them, siphoning off huge amounts of American resources that might have been better applied.

In Kenneth P. Werrell's *Blankets of Fire,* a quote by Colonel Cecil Combs, a key officer at Twentieth Air Force Headquarters reveals that LeMay knew his trade, having done it personally and learning it the hard way. He knew what he wanted of his people, he knew what he could expect of his planes, and he knew how to train to get what he wanted. And, in Combs's words, "He was a hardheaded bastard."[20]

LeMay, after long consideration, decided to adopt the tactics that he and his staff had not only planned but tested. There were many advantages to night area bombing, for the Japanese had few nightfighters, and their antiaircraft guns were designed to work against high-altitude intruders. Flying at low levels meant burning less fuel and putting strain on the still unreliable Wright engines. LeMay dismayed many when he ordered some guns and ammunition to be deleted. The off-loading of 8,000 pounds of ammunition allowed the bomb loads to be increased by 3,200 pounds up to much as 13,000 pounds per plane.[21]

The major test of LeMay's theory came on March 9-10 in an attack on Tokyo, with 334 B-29s (about 100 more than on any previous raid) carrying about 1,700 tons of primarily incendiary bombs. The attack was made at altitudes ranging from 4,900 to 9,200 feet, and was focused on a twelve-square-mile area where the population density was an incredible 103,000 persons per square mile. The lead squadron acted as pathfinders, each one dropping 180 of the new seventy-pound M47 napalm bombs. These were intended to start major fires that would mobilize the Japanese fire-fighting equipment and get them committed to different locations in the city. Following aircraft carried 500-pound cluster bombs, each with thirty-eight of the smaller six-pound M69 bombs. The fires would suddenly be much more widespread, and the fire equipment would be unable to concentrate on the most serious blazes.

These small incendiary bombs were themselves a metaphor for the gigantic differential in strength between the United States and Japan and underlined how utterly foolish the Japanese leaders had been to provoke a war. The United States had not only developed a massive fleet of Boeing B-29 aircraft, surpassing anything the Japanese could build, they had deployed it halfway around the world, equipping it with precision radar, magnificent bombsights, and these devilishly capable incendiary bombs for use against targets which were intrinsically flammable. In contrast, the Japanese lacked antiaircraft guns, radar, night-fighters, an adequate fire-fighting force, hospitals, and bomb shelters. Perhaps the most pathetic inequity could be found in the scale and size of the reprisal Japanese air offensive against the United States—small bombs dropped from a tiny submarine-launched aircraft, and a handful of explosive-laden paper balloons, set loose to drift on air currents across the Pacific to land in the forests of the American West.

XXI Bomber Command's first night raid on Tokyo induced a gigantic firestorm that swept the city, destroying 261,171 buildings and killing more than 83,000 people. Another 160,000 received injuries. The Japanese defense had been weak; some forty aircraft succeeded in making interceptions, but had little effect. Fourteen B-29s were destroyed, but only two by enemy action, the figures reflecting both the weak Japanese defenses and the intrinsic hazard of the still not fully developed B-29s.

At this point all of the theories of the air-power philosophers broke down. The Tokyo firestorm—and the implicit threat to all Japanese cities—was a horror greater than anything that even H. G. Wells might have penned, but the populace, though stricken with the enormity of the tragedy, did not rise up, nor did the Japanese government even remotely consider surrender. Instead, blinded by the unthinking and completely artificial martial spirit that had held it captive on every battlefield since Guadalcanal, the government vowed to fight on, promising to repel any invasion by the self-sacrifice of its men, women, and children.

LeMay had gambled his career, and it paid off. He began a relentless bombing campaign that reduced Japan's cities to ashes, beginning with an attack on Nagoya, Japan's third-largest city on March 11, followed by another on Osaka, the second-largest city, on March 13. Three days later, the target was the relatively untouched Kobe, with its population of 1,000,000. The cigar-smoking general, called by many "the best air combat leader in history," drove his men hard, flying them an average of sixty hours a month to generate the sorties necessary to burn one city after another. LeMay was determined to prove that air power could win wars. When USAAF Headquarters sent him a prioritized list of thirty-three Japanese cities to attack in order to smooth the way for the invasion of the main islands of Japan, LeMay replied, "I consider that for the first time strategic air bombardment faces a situation where its strength is proportionate to the magnitude of its task. I feel that the destruction of Japan's ability to wage war lies within the capacity of this command, provided its maximum effort is exerted unstintingly during the next six months."[22]

This was the first instance of an air commander making such a statement; in the past, all of the prophets of air power, and all of those who exercised it, talked only about the potential to achieve such results in the future. It was the mark of LeMay's leadership that he recognized the scope of the effort necessary to achieve a victory through air power, and that he knew that he could with great exertion attain that level of effort. His position was far different from Goering's, Harris's, Eaker's, or Doolittle's. Each of them had been faced with a superfluity of targets that were far more difficult to destroy, and they faced much more capable enemy opposition. The Germans did not begin to have even a small proportion of the number of aircraft required, and even the Allies had, until late in 1944, an insufficient quantity of aircraft equipment. These differences in no way demean LeMay's assessment or his performance. A lesser man might have cried out about his casualties and demanded many bombers before he could promise victory. LeMay did not hedge; instead, he did as he would do through much of his career, understand exactly what the equipment and crew members under his command were capable of, then task them to achieve their maximum capabilities.

Nor was his campaign without its problems. XXI Bomber Command ran out of incendiaries, and LeMay was required to divert effort to suppress the Kamikaze attacks on Okinawa by attacking their bases in Kanoya. In the same time period, the XXI also achieved remarkable (and too often unremarked upon) success with a superb mining campaign.

And as his strength grew, Japanese resistance became ever more feeble. A successful precision bombing campaign had destroyed some 70 percent of Japanese aircraft engine manufacturing capacity, and turned XXI Bomber Command once more toward urban areas. On May 11, LeMay resumed attacks against Japanese cities, with the intention of destroying so much of Japan that an invasion would not be necessary. The major cities were ravaged with fire bombs as 6,690 B-29 sorties dropped 41,592 tons of bombs on Tokyo, Nagoya, Kobe, Osaka, and Yokohama. Smaller cities were also attacked, bringing the burned-out area of Japanese cities to an estimated ninety-four square miles—fifty-six of these in Tokyo alone. The cost in B-29s was an acceptable 136 aircraft, a loss rate of only 2 percent. As the major cities turned gray in their ashes, XXI Bomber Command attacked secondary cities that housed any war-making potential whatsoever. It also dropped millions of leaflets urging the Japanese public to surrender before they were killed by bombs or starved to death. Death by starvation was the greatest threat, for American submarines, mines (including many laid by B-29s), and aircraft had almost eliminated the entire Japanese merchant marine, down to small fishing boats, and imported food was impossible to obtain. To make matters worse, the Japanese rice harvest was disastrous, yielding almost 50 percent less than in previous years.

General LeMay believed that he could force Japan to surrender with conventional firebombing attacks, but he was not going to have the chance to have his theory validated. A decision had been made before July 1941 to create an atomic bomb before the Germans were able to do so. The mammoth $2-billion program paid off at

Alamagordo, New Mexico, on July 16, 1945, with the detonation of the world's first atomic bomb. The news was vitally important to President Harry S Truman, still a novice after just three months in office, for it permitted him to plan on defeating Japan without requiring Soviet assistance to do so. He shared the news with Winston Churchill, but not with Joseph Stalin—who already had full information on the project from his spies in the United States.

Using the bomb against Japan was fraught with moral consequences. There was never any question in Truman's mind that the bomb should be used if it would save American lives, but he wanted Japan to have an opportunity to surrender if possible before the bomb was dropped. An ultimatum was issued on July 26, 1945, at the Potsdam Conference calling for the Japanese to surrender and promising prompt and utter destruction if they did not. The new Japanese Prime Minister, Suzuki Kantaro, responded using the term *mokusatsu,* by which he meant to convey the Japanese equivalent of "no comment." Interpreters, however, understood the word to be contemptuous rejection of the Potsdam Declaration—and the die was cast for dropping the atomic bomb.

Ultimate Air Power

The $2-billion American investment in the atomic bomb depended entirely upon the $3-billion investment in the B-29, for there was then no other aircraft capable of delivering it. Specially picked Boeing B-29s built at the Martin factory in Omaha, Nebraska, were modified to carry the bomb, and a special unit, the 509th Composite Group, was selected to fly those B-29s. Commanded by Colonel Paul Tibbetts, a veteran of the Eighth Air Force, the men of the 509th were given extraordinary training without being told what their mission was until two days before the bomb was to be dropped—and even then they were not told that it was to be an atomic bomb.

A list of targets was drawn up, made up of the largest cities which had the least damage already done to them. These included Kyoto, Hiroshima, Niigata, and Kokura, but Kyoto was dropped from the list because of its cultural significance to the Japanese. Nagasaki was substituted for Kyoto, with fateful results.

Hiroshima's population had been greatly reduced by mass

evacuations, but there were still many military installations, and like all Japanese cities, it was geared entirely to the war effort. It also had the positive feature that there were no Allied prisoner of war camps in the area.

The American air superiority was now so great that Tibbetts felt secure even though only seven B-29 aircraft were assigned to his mission. These included the bomb-drop aircraft (soon to be named *Enola Gay* after Tibbett's mother) and two escort planes carrying observers. Three other aircraft were assigned duty as weather planes, with one aircraft retained as spare.

The *Enola Gay* took off at 0245 in the morning on August 6, 1945. Released at 0915, from 31,600 feet and at an airspeed of 328 miles per hour, the first nuclear weapon ever dropped in combat fell toward Hiroshima. It exploded fifty seconds later, at an altitude of 1,900 feet, with a force of 20,000 tons of TNT. Almost five square miles of the Hiroshima city center were wiped out, and almost 80,000 people were killed and another 80,000 were injured.

The reaction of the Japanese government was confused; officially they denigrated the power of the attack, saying only that it was a new bomb "which should not be made light of."

There was only one atomic weapon remaining, and a decision was made to use it on August 9, in part to give the impression that there was a full stock of nuclear bombs to follow. This time the aircraft was *Bock's Car,* flown by Major Charles W. Sweeney and his crew. Weather impeded an attack on Kokura, the primary target, and Sweeney flew the B-29 to Nagasaki where the bad weather cleared just enough to allow a visual sighting to be made and the bomb to be dropped. This time there were 35,000 people killed and another 60,000 wounded.

As the stunned Japanese were digesting this second blow, the Soviet Union lived up to its wartime treaties—and to its desire for revenge—declaring war on Japan on August 8. All of the major powers were now arrayed against Japan, which had no allies, and no prospect for anything but defeat. Incredibly, the majority of Japanese leaders still argued against surrender. Japan still had almost 5,000,000 regular troops under arms as well as huge paramilitary forces. There were still 3,250 combat planes and 8,000 Kamikaze suicide planes available to attack the invasion force.[23] As the Japanese cabinet members debated, B-29s flew the length and breadth of Japan, not dropping bombs but leaflets telling the Japanese people of the Potsdam Declaration, of the Soviet Union's declaration of war, and of the true nature of the atomic bomb.

On August 10, the Japanese announced that they would be willing to accept the terms of the Potsdam Declaration provided that it did not prejudice the prerogatives of the emperor as their sovereign. The routine bombing attacks that had continued were now stopped in the hope that negotiations would proceed. When nothing further was heard from the Japanese leaders, bombing was resumed, with LeMay putting 828 bombers and 128 fighters over Tokyo on August 14-15.

While the bombers were in the air, Emperor Hirohito himself stopped the arguments of his cabinet by insisting that the Potsdam Declaration be accepted. Before the last B-29 had returned from the last mission on August 15, the Japanese surrendered. (Some militant Japanese still rose in revolt, slaughtering dozens before they were subdued.) On September 2, the surrender was signed on the deck of the U.S.S. *Missouri*, in Tokyo Bay. In the two-week interval, the B-29s had another mission, dropping 5,000 tons of supplies to the more than 63,000 prisoners of war in camps in Japan, China, and Korea.

The great triumph of air power was that it averted the necessity for an invasion. Estimates vary widely over the cost of an invasion. Some scenarios say that there would have been hundreds of thousands of American casualties, while others say that there would have been "merely" tens of thousands. Most agree that millions of Japanese would have died resisting the invasion as they had resisted invasions of all the island bases, and that, inevitably, the newly completed third atomic bomb would have been dropped before the end of August. There are two significant points that are often overlooked, and which themselves make an airtight case for dropping the atomic bomb. The first of these is that the rice crop failure and the inability to import food spelled death by starvation for as many as 6,000,000 Japanese if an invasion had been necessary. The second is that the Japanese still held millions of nationals from other countries under their tight military control, and they still exploited them with war-crime behavior. Had the war lasted another six months— as it surely would have if an invasion had been required—hundreds of thousands and perhaps millions more Chinese, Vietnamese, Burmese, Indonesians, and others would have died under Japan's cruel rule. (In account after account, Japanese behavior became quite correct when the surrender was announced, the captors at long last realizing that there might be reprisals.)

The Influence of Air Power in World War II

It belabors the obvious to say that air power was influential on history during World War II, but it is instructive to recapitulate some of the most important aspects of the phenomenon, with particular regard to their effect upon the future.

First and foremost, incorrect ideas about air power led to political miscalculations of the first water by many nations. These miscalculations usually included imputing too much to air power (always at a time when there really was no true air power anywhere) and also imputing too little to it. The Germans imputed too much to air power in the Battle of Britain; they imputed too little to it in the attack on the Soviet Union. The British imputed too little to it in their early battles in France and North Africa, and far too much to it in their own great bomber offensive. The Japanese imputed far too much to it in starting the war, and far too little in their ultimate defeat. Only the United States and the Soviet Union measured it with some skill. The Soviet Union tailored air power to its powerful land armies, using it as an essential ingredient in its combined arms assault. The United States was wealthy enough to use air power on the scale in which it was needed, which was vastly greater than any country had ever imagined, and far beyond the means of almost all of them.

Air power enabled the ground forces of the United States and its allies to win in Europe. In the Pacific, air power joined with naval and ground forces to beat Japan back to a point to which air power could become the decisive weapon. The combined arms of the American Army and Navy, and to a lesser degree, America's allies, were necessary to establish the bases from which B-29 operations could demolish Japan with conventional bombs. Once those bases were available, air power was decisively influential.

In the hands of well-equipped and able practitioners, air power had at last achieved what its philosophers and prophets had so hopefully claimed for it. The Cold War, which broke out so soon after the end of World War II, would reveal that air power had become captive to its new potential in a way that no one could have imagined.

Chapter Nine

The Cold War, 1945-62

Adolph Hitler began World War II with the intention of obtaining colonies in the east. Joseph Stalin ended World War II with the complete defeat of Germany, and the acquisition of a series of buffer states that became, if not Soviet colonies, at least compliant client states that were exploited ruthlessly.

In this turnabout of historical events, air power had been of enormous consequence. None of the air-power theorists nor even any of the air-power practitioners could ever have imagined that air power would reach the ultimate heights that it did in the summer of 1945—"ultimate" meaning the combination of air superiority, the atomic bomb, and a long-range delivery system, the B-29. Yet oddly enough, instead of becoming a major new factor in world politics, ultimate air power had, for the moment at least, become a non sequitur, unnecessary in a world in which the aggressive national states of Germany and Japan had been defeated, and where there seemed to be at least the prospect of peace for the immediate future.

It is worthwhile to stop for a moment and consider what might have been the case with ultimate air power in 1945 if it had not been the sole possession of the United States, but instead that of Germany or Japan or the Soviet Union. And—not to put too fine a point on it—what it might have been even if it were in the possession of the United Kingdom, or France, or Italy. It is entirely possible that some other country, possessed of such limitless power, might have used it to settle old scores, retain its colonial empire, expand its territories, and in general become an international bully. The United States did none of these things. In fact, it did something very different: it virtually discarded ultimate air power in a headlong return to a peace that also promised prosperity. It should not have done so, for there were early signs that

285

all might not be well in the future relations of the Western Allies and the Soviet Union.

These signs were the first steps toward the Cold War that would dominate the political scene for most of the remainder of the twentieth century, and in which air power would play a dual role as the ultimate strategic and indispensable tactical weapon.

The maturing of air power into its ultimate form in August 1945 meant that all of the theories of air power in the past had to be reviewed for their contemporary relevance and that new theories of air power had to be established. Many new ideas were put forward over the next fifty years, but few would be put into practice because the political and military rivalry of the Soviet Union and the United States dominated the real world of air power. Not until 1991 would an emerging new theory of air power be both defined and demonstrated.

Hidden in the results of a series of conferences held by the "Big Three," consisting then of President Roosevelt, Prime Minister Churchill, and Premier Stalin, were the first steps to the Cold War. The three wartime leaders met at Tehran in November 1943 and at Yalta in February 1945. The Big Three met again at Potsdam in August 1945, but two of the members had changed. Truman had succeeded Roosevelt, who had died on April 12 of that year, and—in the midst of the conference—Labor Party leader Clement Attlee replaced the old warhorse Churchill as a result of a fit of post-war British ingratitude.

In all of the negotiations that took place at the three conferences, Stalin possessed immense advantages that he exploited later to the maximum extent possible. At Tehran, Roosevelt and Churchill were fully aware that Stalin's forces were bearing the brunt of Hitler's wrath, and that the greatest danger they faced was a separate peace between Germany and the Soviet Union. They had to make concessions to ensure that the Soviet Union remained in the war. By Yalta, things had changed radically. The Western Allies had at last made good their promises to invade Europe, but by February 1945, massive Soviet armies, three hundred divisions strong, were successful everywhere and had swarmed to within forty miles of Berlin. At Potsdam in August 1945, the inner strength of the Western Allies was buoyed by the knowledge that the United States had successfully tested the atomic bomb, but Stalin's three hundred powerful divisions were still an unanswerable argument.

Another advantage of Stalin's was his intention to abandon any agreements made at the conferences as soon as it suited him to do so. Notwithstanding this intention, and the massive Red Army, there were some good results from the series of meetings, including the establishment of the United Nations and agreement on how Germany was to be divided for its occupation.

It is worth recounting exactly how far and how quickly Stalin had moved to expand the influence of the Soviet Union. He had absorbed pieces of Finland and much of Poland in 1939, then swallowed up Estonia, Lithuania, and Latvia in 1940, along with parts of Rumania. In 1944, Finland again had to grant territorial and trade concessions that made it dependent on the Soviet Union. In March 1945, King Michael of Rumania was forced to appoint a Communist-controlled government under Petru Groza, the first step toward King Michael's overthrow and the establishment of a completely Communist government. The following events then occurred:

June 28, 1945: A pro-Soviet government was established in Poland.

September 2, 1945: Trained and backed by the Soviet Union, Ho Chi Minh declared the independence of Vietnam from France.

November 10, 1945: Communist Enver Hoxha became the premier of Albania.

November 18, 1945: A Communist-controlled government was installed in Bulgaria.

January 31, 1946: Yugoslavia adopted a Soviet-style constitution.

February 9, 1946: Stalin announced that Communism and capitalism could not coexist.

March 5, 1946: Churchill made his "Iron Curtain" speech in Fulton, Missouri.

January 19, 1947: A manipulated election in Poland established a Communist majority.

May 31, 1947: Communists won a general election in Hungary.

February 25, 1948: A Communist coup in Czechoslovakia ended a democracy there.

April 1, 1948: The first elements of the Berlin Blockade were in place.

September 9, 1948: Communist Kim Il Sung was placed in power in North Korea.

All this was but the start of a worldwide extension of Communism, in a seemingly unstoppable tide, at a time when the United States seemingly still possessed a decisive military advantage.

For the general public, the Cold War has come to be regarded as beginning formally with Churchill's inimitable March 5, 1946, speech in which he said, "From Stettin in the Baltic to Trieste in the Adriatic, an iron curtain has descended across the Continent. Behind that line lie all the capitals of the ancient states of central and eastern Europe, Warsaw, Berlin, Prague, Vienna, Budapest, Belgrade, Bucharest and Sofia, all those famous cities and the populations around them lie in what I might call the Soviet sphere and all are subject, in one form or another, not only to Soviet influence, but to a very high and increasing measure of control from Moscow. "[1]

The term "Iron Curtain" caught on immediately. In later years the phrase's origin was pursued relentlessly, being first attributed to an article in the February 23, 1945, issue of *Das Reich* by German Propaganda Minister Joseph Goebbels, in which he warned that an "iron curtain would descend immediately" upon the territory the Soviet Union then occupied if the German people failed in their attempts to repel the invaders. There were earlier examples of the phrase as well, but Churchill's meaning was clear: the Soviet Union had complete control of the eastern frontiers of its buffer zone, and no one could know or alter events that occurred behind those frontiers. There was also the implicit threat that the Soviet Union would inevitably seek to expand its Iron Curtain westward, to the English Channel and beyond.

The Western Allies made attempts to strengthen their own position, including the February 12, 1947, articulation of the Truman Doctrine, which offered aid to countries threatened by Communism. This action was followed on June 5 by the announcement of the European Recovery Program. Although Truman could in all modesty have lent his own name to the plan, he was politically savvy enough to let it be known as the Marshall Plan, after his universally popular Secretary of State, George C. Marshall. The Soviet Union was offered participation in the Marshall Plan, but declined and forbade its client states to join in. Defensively, preliminary steps were taken to form what eventually became the North Atlantic Treaty Organization (NATO).

Curiously, considering the massive importance that can be imputed to the influence of air power on the events leading up to and during World War II, air power had virtually no influence in the later gigantic Soviet expansion, other than being an integral part of Stalin's massive forces. The reason was simple. The Western Allies, weary of war, had demobilized at an incredible rate, and no longer possessed a significant amount of air power. There remained only the threat of atomic retaliation, based on the sole possession of nuclear weapons and their delivery system by the United States. Fortunately, the threat was sufficient to deter the Soviet Union in the early years of the Cold War from even more predatory aggression, for in reality, the actual nuclear capability of the United States was limited.

The Demand for Demobilization

The United States had not been at war as long as its Allies had, nor had it suffered nearly as much in terms of casualties and physical damage. The war had in fact pulled the United States at last from the grip of the Great Depression, and the country was bursting with both a pent-up demand for consumer goods, and the banked wherewithal to buy them. Two terrible enemies had been defeated, and the Soviet Union had been presented since December 7, 1941, as a good, loyal ally, with governmental and social institutions not unlike those of the United States. Stalin's image as an implacable tyrant had been smoothed over into one of an amiable "Uncle Joe," still a dictator, but one who had been properly contained by the agreements made at Yalta and Potsdam.

There was therefore tremendous public demand for all troops to be brought home and demobilized as soon as possible. This public outcry was translated into congressional action, and there began the greatest unilateral disarmament in history. The Army and Navy were immediately affected, but demobilization had the most adverse effect upon the United States Army Air Force, because of the higher degree of technical skills needed by its members.

The USAAF had 2,253,000 military and 318,514 civilian personnel on-strength on the day Japan surrendered. Within five months, the totals had fallen to 888,769 military personnel. This figure fell to 303,600 by May 1947, when there were still about 110,000 civilians employed.

The stark reduction in numbers does not tell the whole story. Where there had been 350,000 mechanics, there were now less than 35,000. This meant that in-commission rates (the number of aircraft serviceable) fell to an embarrassing 18 percent—and that high only because most of the aircraft were brand new and scarcely flown. The USAAF had fallen from a worldwide strength of more than 70,000 aircraft to 25,000, and of these, only 4,750 were ready for combat. Even this small number—about the size of the Luftwaffe in 1943—was dispersed on a global basis.

But, again, numbers did not tell the true story. Where on August 15, 1945, the USAAF had 218 groups of all types, most of them combat ready, by December 1946, it had fifty-two groups—of which only *two* were combat ready. The USAAF had become the most powerful air force in the history of the world in the forty-four months after Pearl Harbor. It took only sixteen months to render it virtually powerless.

Britain's demobilization was slightly less hasty than America's, because it still required armed forces to maintain order in its fast-diminishing empire. In terms of stopping Soviet aggression, however, the RAF was as impotent as USAAF conventional forces.

Perhaps the only offset to the demobilization factor was the reorganization of the armed forces of the United States by the National Security Act of 1947, which established the United States Air Force as a separate service. The new service became independent on September 18, 1947, with the swearing in of the first Secretary of the Air Force, Stuart W. Symington. He would soon have his hands full. One of his principal problems would be the long and bitter struggle with the United States Navy over roles and missions. The Navy protested the USAF's possession of long-range bombers such as the B-36 in what became known as the "Revolt of the Admirals."[2] Ultimately, as will be noted below, the Navy sought to have its own strategic and tactical nuclear capability.

The Soviet Union now determined that it would move the Western Allies from the zones they occupied in West Berlin by placing a stranglehold on their supply lines. It began on April 1, 1948, with restrictions on road and rail traffic. Then on June 22, the seventh anniversary of Hitler's invasion of the Soviet Union, all barge, rail, and road traffic into West Berlin was halted. The Soviets backed up this land and water blockade with thirty full-strength army divisions—as many as 400,000 troops— supported by a capable tactical air force. The United States had only 60,000 troops in Europe, of which only a fraction were in combat units.

In terms of air power, the new USAF was bankrupt. As a show of force, parts of four B-29 bombardment groups were sent to Britain. It was a bluff, as they brought no atomic bombs with them, but the Soviet Union could not be sure about that. A token force of sixteen Lockheed F-80 jet fighters was flown to Germany.

The Western Allies seemed to have two alternatives, fight or flight. Under the guidance of General Lucius D. Clay, a third alternative was recommended to President Truman: the aerial supply of basic commodities to the citizens of West Berlin until the matter could be resolved diplomatically. Clay then asked the commander of United States Air Forces in Europe, Major General Curtis E. LeMay, if in fact West Berlin could be supplied with the estimated 4,500 tons of supplies it needed daily—almost eight times that which had been required but never delivered to the German Sixth Army in Stalingrad.

LeMay responded that the USAF could do anything, and initiated an immediate airlift that marshaled 102 Douglas C-47s and two Douglas C-54s. On June 26 the first eighty tons of supplies, primarily medicine, were flown in. This would build to a vast flow of aircraft, men, and supplies to provide air power with its first victory of the Cold War, and do so without dropping a single bomb.

Major General William H. Tunner, who had distinguished himself in the massive supply of China over the Himalayan "Hump," was brought in to oversee the airlift. Backed by the entire air force, Tunner standardized equipment, selecting the four-engine Douglas C-54 as the primary transport and then establishing an efficient system in which an aircraft was landing at West Berlin airports every ninety seconds.

The C-54s were not designed to carry coal, grain, and other bulk supplies, but they did it so effectively that airlift totals reached 2,000 tons per day by July 31, and then 5,583 tons per day by September 18. As the totals built, the rations issued to West Berlin citizens increased, and Soviet embarrassment mounted.

Ineffective attempts were made to disrupt the steady, conveyor belt-like flow of C-54s streaming in orbits through the clearly defined airways into Berlin. Soviet fighter planes buzzed the transports, and false radio signals were transmitted to confuse them, to no avail.

On April 15, 1949, 1,398 aircraft brought in a staggering 12,940 tons of goods, more than West Berlin would have received by rail, road, and canal before the Berlin Blockade began. The Soviet Union ended the blockade on May 12, recognizing that it had suffered a humiliating diplomatic defeat. The airlift continued until September 30, 1949, by which time it had delivered 2,325,000 tons of supplies in 275,000 sorties. The airlift, to which the Royal Air Force made a major contribution, was expensive, costing more than $200 million. More serious were the twelve crashes that claimed thirty-one American lives.[3]

The influence of air power on subsequent history in the Berlin Airlift is difficult to overestimate. First and foremost it established the respective roles of the United States and the Soviet Union in the world. The Soviet Union was seen as repressive, hostile to the citizens of West Berlin, and willing to use starvation tactics to enforce its bullying methods of blockade. The United States was seen as brave, for standing up to an overwhelming force, and technologically clever, for it created the miracle of the airlift virtually overnight. Most important of all, the United States was seen as humane—it was spending its money and the lives of its airman on the behalf of a defeated enemy populace.

This was the beginning of the largely unheralded history of compassionate relief missions that have seen the USAF on the spot with relief supplies and remedial measures all over the world, whether the trouble is earthquake, fire, flood, civil war, famine, plague, or anything else. It is worth noting that the number of lives saved by these compassionate missions, especially those that involve fighting insect-borne disease or fighting famine by enhancing agriculture, far exceeds the total number of lives lost to all hostile air action in history.

The peaceful resolution of the Berlin Blockade had a curious by-product. The battle-less Berlin airlift seemed to reduce Soviet interest in an open clash of arms with the United States. While it would continuously build up its forces and those of its satellite states, and thus present the continuous threat that Red armies might suddenly spill past the frontiers and race to the Channel coast, it directed more of its energies into a changed strategy. The Soviet Union now tried to expand Communism by supporting "freedom" movements around the world, particularly in countries that were shaking off their previous masters. The greatest success came in China, but there were active Communist cells fomenting revolution elsewhere in Asia, Africa, Central America, and South America. And wherever possible, the Soviet Union would seek to embroil the United States in wars with Soviet client states serving as proxies. This strategy would be only too successful.

The crisis in Europe seemed to be temporarily quelled. In the Far East, however, there were disquieting events. On October 1, 1949, Mao Zedong proclaimed the People's Republic of China, with

America's longtime ally, Chiang Kai-Shek, scuttling with his dwindling forces to Formosa (Taiwan). On January 14, 1950, Ho Chi Minh declared the Democratic Republic of Vietnam and was promptly recognized by the Soviet Union and Communist China. Then, on June 25, 1950, with the implicit backing of both Stalin and Mao Zedong, Kim Il Sung ordered North Korean troops to invade South Korea.

Korea and the Conundrum of Ultimate Air Power

Six columns of North Korean People's Army (NKPA) troops had swept across the border, overwhelming the token South Korean defenses with well-trained, well-equipped divisions that were armed and fought in the fashion of Soviet troops. Kim Il Sung's intent was to capture Seoul, then drive all the way through South Korea to the sea. He would then announce that all of Korea had been reunited under his rule.

Stalin, Mao Zedong, and Kim Il Sung all believed that the United States would not intervene. They based their belief primarily on an assurance given by Secretary of State Dean Acheson at the National Press Club on January 12, 1950, that the United States would defend only the area specified in an earlier National Security Council memorandum, NSC 48/2. The memorandum specified that Japan, the Ryukus, and the Philippines would be defended, but South Korea was not mentioned. The Communists took him at his word, and were surprised when President Truman announced that the United States would defend South Korea. Truman, displaying the savvy political acumen that had brought him to be first a senator, then vice-president, finessed the United States Congress by calling the intervention a "police action" and not a war. He then maneuvered a resolution past a potential Soviet veto through the United Nations Security Council that established a joint United Nations Command to be allied to South Korea. The United States would provide the vast majority of forces—but it was not officially at war.

Yet even Truman's speedy actions were almost too late, for the North Korean Army had pushed the South Koreans and a token UN force into the tiny Pusan Perimeter, where it looked like they would soon either be captured or backed into the sea. The president turned to the only thing he had to stem the tide: air power.

It may be said of United States air power in the Korean War that while it did not achieve victory, it averted defeat three times. The first time occurred in the days after the war began, when obsolescent aircraft, most veterans of World War II, flew out of Japan to slow down the advancing North Korean forces. The second time came after the massive intervention by Communist China in November 1950, when the UN forces were again pushed almost into the sea, and air power would again slow down, then halt the advance. The third time would come after the UN forces had once again established a front running roughly just above the Thirty-Eighth Parallel, and the only thing that restrained the enormous Communist forces from breaking through was close air support at the front and the interdiction of their supply lines by American air power.

Avoiding defeat was an exceedingly close-run thing, for the United States was depending upon a World War II-style air force to prevent World War III. If, in the first months of the war, the North Korean troops had not outrun their supply lines by such a large margin, it is doubtful that the available handful of North American F-51s, North American F-82s, Douglas B-26s, Lockheed F-80s, and Boeing B-29s could have stopped them. But stop them they did, and in doing so they prepared the way for General of the Army Douglas MacArthur's masterful counterstroke at Inchon, launched on September 15, 1950. As Commander in Chief of the UN forces, MacArthur insisted on a risky flank attack that was perilous in the extreme, but which went off very well.

Carried away by his success, MacArthur ordered that the victorious UN forces drive the North Koreans all the way back to the Yalu River on their northern border with Red China. It was a disastrous mistake, compounded by MacArthur's failure to heed China's clear warnings that it would intervene unless the northward advance was halted.

The intervention came in November, with overwhelming effect, and, as noted above, once again almost pushed the UN into the sea. The Chinese assault was highlighted by the introduction of the top jet fighter of the Soviet Union, the swept-wing MiG-15. Flown by Soviet pilots, it immediately altered the air war, and forced the United States to respond with its own premier fighter, the North American F-86 Sabre. Flights of the two aircraft engaged in swirling dogfights over the triangle of land surrounding the Yalu River and called MiG Alley by American pilots.

In considering Korea, the aviation world's attention became (and has largely remained) fixed on the contest between Sabre and MiG, for it recaptured in part the glamour and the color of the dogfights of earlier times. Air superiority was still the *sine qua non* of air power, and the Sabres were able to maintain it although greatly outnumbered and fighting at an immense geographical disadvantage. (The Communist pilots could take off and land from air bases in the Chinese sanctuary for which the Yalu River marked the border. Most combat was conducted within gliding distances of those bases, while the F-86s had to fly all the way up the peninsula from bases in South Korea.) As a direct result of this air superiority, the remainder of the UN air forces could interdict Chinese Communist supplies and furnish close air support, thus equalizing the great difference in the number of troops.

Yet the contest of the future, the struggle that would redefine air power over the next four decades, was not over the Yalu—it was in the home territories of the United States and the Soviet Union. As important as the outcome of the air battles over Korea were—and they would largely determine the outcome of the battle for Korea itself—it paled into insignificance compared to a potential nuclear battle between the homelands of the United States and the Soviet Union.

The possession of ultimate air power was now a conundrum. While the United States did possess ultimate air power as defined over Hiroshima and Nagasaki, it did not choose to use it. The United States had long-range aircraft capable of penetrating the defenses of both the Soviet Union and Red China with nuclear weapons, but was inhibited from doing so for many reasons. One was a sense of national morality—atomic weapons could not be used lightly. Another more pragmatic reason was that the number of nuclear weapons at its disposal was still limited, as were the carriers, and both of the potential enemies were vast in area and population. If war was thrust upon it, and if nuclear weapons were used successfully, the United States still did not have an army that could follow up the bombings with an invasion and occupation.

As a result, the Korean War was fought with conventional means. The results were effective, particularly when, in 1953, attacks were extended to the dams that were essential both to the hydroelectric system and to agriculture. A different set of circumstances began to prevail when President Dwight D. Eisenhower replaced Truman in 1953. Eisenhower did not believe that the Soviet Union was in any condition to take part in another war, and he instructed his Secretary of State, John Foster Dulles, to communicate to the Indian Premier, Jawaharlal Nehru, that he was prepared to use atomic weapons if an agreement on a peace treaty could not soon be reached at Panmunjom. The message was of course promptly relayed to North Korea, which then began serious negotiations resulting in the cease-fire agreement that became effective on July 27, 1953. Knowledge of Eisenhower's wartime successes conditioned this decision; the Communists presumed that with his military experience, he was not averse to using nuclear weapons.

There was yet another critically important factor in all of the American military and political considerations, and that was the gradual but relentless increase in the Soviet Union's capability to attack the United States with its own nuclear weapons. The announcement of the discovery that the Soviet Union had exploded an atomic bomb came as a stunning surprise on September 23, 1949. Unaware of the extent of Soviet espionage and the number of traitors in the United States' nuclear program, loyal American scientists had estimated that it would be 1953 or later before the Soviet Union could explode a test atomic weapon. (By August 1953, the Soviets had successfully tested a hydrogen bomb.)

And, just as the Soviet atomic capability was revealed, the United States became increasingly aware that the Soviet Air Force had acquired the means to deliver the bomb, thanks to a directive from Stalin.

Joseph Stalin had meant many things to the development of Soviet air power. He had been a source of funds during the prewar years and had saved the entire industry by ordering its forced removal to beyond the Urals. He had intervened to accelerate production of the Shturmovik, and had graciously allowed talented designers such as Andrei Tupolev to continue working in jail, rather than killing them for suspected treason as was his usual custom. The Soviet dictator had asked the United States on three occasions for the delivery of B-29s under the provisions of Lend-Lease, but had been refused. When the Soviet Union acquired four examples of Boeing B-29s that landed there after being damaged in raids on Japan, he ordered Soviet engineering teams to reverse-engineer them, copying them as exactly as possible given the difference in Soviet and American materials and tools. Tupolev was assigned the task of copying the aircraft, while A. D. Shvetsov was told to copy the Wright R-3350 engines.

The massive endeavor was insulting to the capability of Soviet engineers and designers, who felt they could have created an aircraft of equivalent performance in less time. But Stalin was intuitively correct; the B-29, with its pressurized cabin, turbocharged engines, and central fire-control system, was far more sophisticated than any previous Soviet airplane. The task of reverse-engineering the B-29 and its components revitalized the Soviet aviation industry. When this revitalization was combined with the information gained from German sources after World War II, and, perhaps more important, with the political coup by which Britain's Sir Stafford Cripps sanctioned the sale of fifty-five Rolls-Royce Nene jet engines, Soviet aviation was given a ten-year boost in progress that would have profound effects upon both political and scientific events.

The Tupolev Tu-4, as the copy was called, first flew on June 3, 1947. It was followed by some four hundred additional aircraft, of which three hundred were in service by 1950.[4] These aircraft had the capacity for a one-way nuclear attack on the United States, a horrifying possibility that had never before existed.

As a result of this situation, the second USAF Chief of Staff, General Hoyt S. Vandenberg, had to prepare not for what he thought the Soviets might do, but what he knew they could do, however improbable it might seem. (The performance of the Tu-4 for a one-way mission was marginal—but a Soviet nuclear attack could have been made.) Thus, even as a critical air war was being fought in Korea, the focus of the United States Air Force had to be on defense of the national air space and upon a retaliatory force. The situation introduced revolutionary changes in thinking, for the Congress was at last persuaded that the military budget had to be increased significantly in peacetime. And from this point on, the USAF had to become a permanent force in being, rather than, as in the past, a small regular force that would be augmented by reserve forces during a protracted buildup in the event of war.

This small beginning set into motion the largest, most expensive, and potentially the most catastrophic arms race in history, that of the United States and the Soviet Union. It would continue for another four decades, until the abrupt collapse of the USSR on December 25, 1991. In the intervening forty years, both nations would raise the capability of air power by an order of magnitude—and both nations would be inhibited by the specter of what came to be known as MAD or mutually assured destruction.

In the United States, there began an immediate buildup of the Strategic Air Command (SAC) and the Air Defense Command (ADC), both of which had been established, along with the Tactical Air Command (TAC), in 1946. Because of the severely limited defense budgets, none of the three commands had flourished initially. On October 19, 1948, Curtis E. LeMay, now a lieutenant general, became Commander in Chief of the Strategic Air Command, a position he would hold until June 30, 1957, the longest tenure of any United States military commander since General Winfield Scott who served as the Army's senior general from 1852 to 1861. LeMay would build SAC into the strongest and most important military force in history, with one purpose in mind: to deter the Soviet Union from exercising its avowed first-strike policy.

LeMay's goal was to make the Strategic Air Command so obviously powerful that the Soviet Union would know that there was no possibility of making a first strike on the United States without receiving, in swift return, an overwhelming retaliatory strike that would wipe it out of existence. It is of key importance to note that unlike Hitler or Hirohito, relatively safe from conventional bombs in their underground bunkers, the Soviet leaders knew that in a full-fledged atomic attack, they would be killed as well as their enemies—a sobering incentive to find ways to avoid war.

LeMay succeeded on the basis of his wartime experience, using classic "sweat instead of blood" techniques that demanded the utmost professional effort from the crews under his command. SAC's buildup under LeMay's guidance was extraordinary, particularly because he insisted on such very high standards at every level and in every unit. When he arrived at SAC, he found a mixed force of 837 aircraft, only 70 of which had an intercontinental capability. The bulk of his bomber force was B-29s. When he left SAC to become Vice Chief of Staff in 1957, he left behind the most superbly trained and equipped air force in history, with 3,040 aircraft, including 1,543 Boeing B-47 Stratojets (the six-jet, swept-wing bomber that revolutionized aviation), 380 of the magnificent eight-engine B-52 Stratofortresses, and, perhaps most important of all, a fleet of 971 tankers, including 182 of the brand-new and highly efficient Boeing KC-135s.

The cigar-smoking general had led huge formations of B-17s into Germany during World War II, flying together for protection. Now his jet bombers were designed to strike enemy targets alone or perhaps in cells of three aircraft, with each one carrying within its bomb bay nuclear bombs with the destructive firepower equivalent to a thousand-plane raid from World War II.

SAC worked hard, and LeMay was proud of it. He flaunted its capability, flying B-52s around the world nonstop and fostering publicity that dramatized how quickly his force could be scrambled into action. None of this show of force was for self-aggrandizement—it was all intended to convince the Soviet Union that any first strike would be suicidal. It worked.

Air power now had to have a two-part definition: strategic and tactical. The world was divided into two main opposing camps: one headed by the United States, and one headed by the Soviet Union. There was a third camp of nonaligned powers that were wooed by the two superpowers, as they came to be called.

Each of the superpowers was supported by alliances and by client states: the United States by NATO, and the Soviet Union by the Warsaw Pact nations. In this situation, strategic air power became the protector of peace, not by the preemptive attacks that the early prophets had deemed essential, but by promising such total retaliation that any would be attacker was deterred. But this mutual deterrence did not apply to the smaller wars that occurred with bewildering frequency all around the world. In these smaller conflicts tactical air power still had to win air superiority over the battlefield so that actions in support of ground forces could be flown with impunity. Thus it was that both the USAF and the Soviet Air Force had to build up strategic and tactical forces to handle both eventualities.

In the same year that LeMay left SAC to become Vice Chief of Staff, there occurred the most significant aerospace event of the second part of the twentieth century—the orbiting of a satellite by the Soviet Union. On October 4, 1957, the little silver Sputnik sent an innocuous but ominous beeping message to the world that everything had changed. The Soviet Union had clearly surpassed the United States in the technical field of rocketry, and it was obvious that the technology that could place a satellite in orbit could also create an intercontinental ballistic missile that could place nuclear warheads halfway around the globe. And, on the off chance that anyone had missed the obvious, Soviet Premier Nikita Khrushchev gloatingly repeated that fact on several occasions.

In today's world where hosts of satellites have every country under constant surveillance, it is difficult to recall just how totally uninformed the United States was about the Soviet Union in the pre-satellite years. Soviet security was airtight, the borders were guarded, few foreign visitors were admitted, and those who were admitted were kept under constant scrutiny. The Soviet Union practiced disinformation with great skill, even to the point that there were no reliable tourist maps of Moscow or Leningrad. The only available maps were those made from photos taken by German reconnaissance planes before and during World War II. As a result, the United States had no accurate knowledge of the number of bombers possessed by the Soviet Union, and even more important, it had little knowledge about the state of the Soviet ICBM development.

The Race to Aerospace Power

The space race began with a series of Soviet triumphs and American failures. This gave rise to jokes by comedian Bob Hope and others that in the Soviet rocket program "their German rocket scientists were better than our German rocket scientists."

While the joke was not literally true (it is generally agreed that the United States obtained the cream of the German scientific crop), both the American and Soviet programs were founded on the German missile programs of World War II, and fostered by the German scientists who were eagerly snapped up by both countries at the end of the war.

The Soviet Union had some initial advantages, in that it did not face the bitter interservice rivalry that characterized the disputes over which service would control the missile programs within the United States. After much wrangling, a decision was made on November 26, 1956, assigning the responsibility for various types of missiles among the services. The USAF received responsibility for the operational employment of intercontinental ballistic missiles and a joint assignment, with the Army, for intermediate-range ballistic missiles.

The USAF was pleased with the responsibility, for it saw missiles merely as "unmanned bombers" and had already done a significant amount of research work. Unknown at the time, however, was the fact that the responsibility would cause significant problems within the USAF when missiles became a larger element of the force structure. These problems are covered at length in Carl H. Builder's *The Icarus Syndrome,* in which the author postulates that senior Air Force leaders, almost every one a veteran pilot, resented the "intrusion" of the missile upon the mission of the piloted aircraft. Builder goes so far as to state that the leaders only grudgingly accepted missiles and satellites as a means to air-power ends, but also that their true affection was not for air power—but for airplanes.[5]

Fortunately, there was within the ranks of the USAF a brilliant aviator, then-Brigadier General Bernard A. Schriever, who loved airplanes but saw the ICBM as a means not only to aerospace power superiority, but as the key to the exploration of space.

Made aware of the immense Soviet effort in ICBM development, but unable to obtain exact information on its status, President Dwight D. Eisenhower gave top priority to the development of the ICBM by the USAF. Schriever was appointed Commander of the Western Development Division (WDD) and allowed to handpick his staff.

He immediately enlisted the assistance of the academic, scientific, and industrial communities, and established an organization that ultimately dwarfed the atomic bomb project in funding and number of employees. Further, the ICBM, although an even more difficult scientific challenge than the atomic bomb had been, was far more urgently needed. The United States, at however great a cost, would ultimately have defeated Japan even if the atomic bomb project had failed. There was every reason to believe that the Soviet Union was far advanced in rocketry and pulling equal in both atomic and hydrogen bombs. If the Soviet Union was the first to field a fleet of ICBMs, it would have the United States at its mercy—and mercy was not a commodity for which the USSR was noted.

Schriever had picked the Convair Atlas as the first missile to be developed. Not everything went smoothly; the first launch of the Atlas on June 11, 1957, followed what had become a classic American pattern: a first launch failure. But Schriever persisted, and the third launch on December 17, 1957, was successful. In the interval between the first and third launches the first series of Soviet space successes had occurred, and Congress at last provided unlimited funding.

Schriever, only forty-seven, had courageously taken the risk of concurrent development, production, and operations in the most sophisticated project in history. Within the first two years, he was coordinating the talents of 18,000 scientists, 17 prime contractors, 200 subcontractors, and 3,500 suppliers, all employing an estimated 70,000 people, and all initially focused on building the Atlas ICBM. Later Schriever's team would extend their talents to improving the Atlas and to creating a series of missiles.

The speed and efficiency of Schriever and his team was dazzling, especially in comparison to other military and even commercial development programs. During the same general period, the prime contractor for the Atlas, Convair, took ten years to develop the admittedly advanced F-102 fighter, at a time when it was customary for General Motors to take five years just to introduce a new model Chevrolet. In contrast, Schriever guided the USAF and the newly born missile industry to four complete new missile systems within a period of eight years. These included the Atlas, Titan, and Minuteman ICBMs and the Thor intermediate-range ballistic missile. The Thor was essentially a shorter-range spin-off of the Atlas. The Titan series was larger and more sophisticated, but still powered by liquid-fueled rockets. The Minuteman was an immense leap ahead, being a solid-fuel rocket that made it easier to manufacture, deploy, store, maintain, and launch.

The Strategic Air Command folded the new missile strength into its retaliatory capability as swiftly as it became available. By early 1959 three Atlas squadrons were operational, with a total of eighteen missiles among them. Two years later there were seven Atlas and three Titan squadrons. By 1962 there were thirteen Atlas, twelve Titan, and eight Minuteman squadrons, with a total of 637 missiles. By 1984, there were no less than 1,000 Minuteman and 54 Titan missiles in service—a bewildering, overwhelming strength—and but one part of an American strategic triad, for there were also 262 B-52s and 60 General Dynamics FB-111 strategic bombers and the burgeoning strength of the United States Navy's submarine-launched ballistic missile force.[6]

In February 1957, well before the first success of the Atlas, Schriever had announced that at least 90 percent of the developments of the ballistic missile program could be applied to space vehicles. The Atlas, Titan, and Thor missiles all became stalwart launch vehicles for satellites, with the Atlas and the Thor (Delta) developing into commercial systems of immense importance.

Developing the ICBMs had not been inexpensive; in 1970 dollars, more than $17 billion was spent on the ICBMs compared to $2 billion on manned aircraft procurement during the same decade of procurement.[7]

The Department of Defense was justifiably proud of the buildup in strength of its missile forces, but it was completely in the dark as to how well the Soviet Union was progressing. Soviet security was virtually impenetrable, and no one had any verifiable information on Soviet strategic forces.

Soviet Air Power

The Soviet Air Force had been substantially reorganized after World War II under the leadership of a new Commander in Chief, Marshal of Aviation Konstantin A. Vershinin. Stalin had imprisoned the previous commander, Marshal of Aviation Alexander A. Nivikov, on the usual charges of treachery.

The Soviet Union had different requirements from those of the United States, and its air force was structured in a different manner. About 857 of the Tu-4 Bull bombers became the basis for Long-Range Aviation, a rough counterpart to the Strategic Air Command, but one that never achieved the same degree of proficiency. The Soviet Union was always defense-minded, with the result that the Fighter Aviation of the Defense Forces was established to intercept incoming aircraft. But close air support remained dear to the Soviet Union's heart, and the Frontal Aviation division was dedicated to it. The Soviet Navy had expanded considerably, and although it still had no carriers, it required a force, Naval Aviation, to operate with it. The final element of the Soviet Air Force was the Aviation of the Airborne Troops.[8]

Marshal Vershinin's first task was to bring the Red Air Force to the technological level of its potential adversaries, the United States and Britain. At the end of World War II, the Red Air Force had been even more thorough in its exploitation of German engineering than had the United States. The Soviet Union did not demobilize to the extent that the United States did, and it maintained the production of military aircraft at the rate of ten thousand per year at a time when the United States was building fewer than a thousand combat aircraft annually. Much of the production was allocated to satellite air forces, which were pleasantly surprised to be equipped with modern, first-line equipment rather than obsolete castoffs as was usually the case. These aircraft were also used to influence the politics of neutral nations, particularly in the Middle East, where Egypt and Syria in particular received large quantities of MiG-15s and other first-line aircraft. Such largess became a competitive bribery process between the United States and the Soviet Union, each one bringing client states under its wing by equipping their armed forces. Thus it was that some third-world countries, unable to feed themselves, would still have modern missile-armed jet fighters on their flight lines.

The Red Air Force treated the Korean War as it had treated the Spanish Civil War, as a perfect place to train its pilots for combat. It began rotating pilots through on so regular a basis that the Americans were able to tell when a new "class" had arrived. Recent research by Western scholars into the Soviet archives indicate that the Red Air Force did much better in Korea than American reports would indicate, so much so that the long-held belief that the F-86s shot down MiG-15s at the rate of ten to one is now suspect.

Veterans of the Soviet Air Force in fact claim to have won the air war in Korea, basing their claim that they achieved their primary objective of shooting down bombers and preventing them from attacking strategic targets by forcing the B-29s out of daylight attacks. They are particularly proud that no Soviet jet fell to B-29 gunners, despite many claims to the contrary. Their success in halting the daylight bombing campaign cast serious doubts on the thirty-year-old claim that the bomber would always get through.

Seeing this situation, the Soviet Union turned away from building bombers on a scale equivalent to the United States, and began to emphasize the intercontinental ballistic missile. They also began arming their limited force of bombers with cruise missiles—the Kelt, Kipper, and Kangaroo missiles (NATO code names) were all being carried by the 1960s.[9]

Shortly after the end of the Korean War, the best estimates of the Soviet Air Force indicated that it possessed about 10,000 jet fighters, 5,000 tactical jet bombers, and 1,500 medium and heavy bombers, including 750 of the Tupolev Tu-16 Badger, a twin-jet equivalent to the Boeing B-47, and less than 100 of the impressive-looking but ultimately disappointing Myasishchev M-4, a four-engine jet intended to correspond to the B-52. The most successful Soviet heavy bomber effort came with the huge, four-turboprop Tupolev Tu-20 developed into the Tu-95. Given the NATO code name "Bear," the Tupolev bomber first flew in 1954, and will likely remain in service well into the twenty-first century, with about 545 being built.

Like the United States, the Soviet Union had seized upon the German V-2 weapon as the basis to begin the development of an ICBM. These initial developments lent themselves to short-range tactical missiles initially, and were built originally at a great rate, approaching two thousand missiles per year. Later under the guidance of the great Sergei Korolyov, the Soviet Union developed indigenous missile systems that ultimately matched or exceeded the performance of their American counterparts. Born in Kiev in 1907, Korolyov was caught up in Stalin's purges, and spent six years of his life in Siberia. Reinstated as a colonel in the Red Army in 1945, he became as important to the Red Air Force as General Schriever had become to the USAF. The vehicles that Korolyov designed as ICBMs could also be modified into use as launchers for space craft, which were the designers' real passion. Korolyov died at the age of fifty-nine, and many say that his death was a primary reason for the failure of the Soviet effort to place a man on the moon.

The major military problem facing the United States was learning exactly how far the Soviet Union had progressed with its missile force. In 1960, John F. Kennedy made much of an alleged "missile gap" in his run for the presidency. President Eisenhower was in the invidious position of knowing that Kennedy was wrong, but was unable to say so because it would compromise American intelligence sources.

Eisenhower, along with other American military leaders, had been appalled by the growth in Soviet air power, and frustrated by their inability to determine just how great a threat it was. Secretly, and with great personal courage, for the political risk was enormous, Eisenhower had authorized the development of two invaluable information-gathering systems. One of these, the Lockheed U-2 spy plane, provided an immense amount of information initially, but later caused him immense embarrassment and a dressing down by Soviet Premier Khrushchev. The other, the CORONA (aka DISCOVERER) satellite, would become the greatest intelligence bonanza in the history of warfare.

These two developments, the U-2 and the DISCOVERER, heralded an entirely new era in the history of air power, influencing history beyond the dreams of any previous aviation prophet or practitioner.

The new technologies would also present enormous challenges for those who wished to articulate the air-power doctrines and philosophies of the future, for changes and improvements in equipment now began to occur so rapidly that it was difficult to keep a theory of air power current.

Satellites for gathering intelligence were the first step in this invasion of space. Great galaxies of satellite systems, for communication, meteorology, and navigation, followed. The new systems were complementary and revolutionized air power (among many other things). They would also change the ways wars could be fought. And because the computer revolution was occurring simultaneously, it became possible to integrate the information supplied by all of these systems in ground and airborne platforms from which both air and ground battles could be controlled.

Intelligence Gathering and the Space Age

The United States had been far more successful in gathering information on Japan during World War II than it had been in gathering information on the Soviet Union. It had virtually no clandestine intelligence (although the Soviet Union maintained an aggressive and successful clandestine campaign against the United States), and the information from the occasional defector was usually either stale or incorrect.

For the first time since 1812, a foreign power seemed to have the wherewithal to launch a direct attack on the United States. It therefore became absolutely necessary to create a photoreconnaissance aircraft that could fly over the Soviet Union and determine if an attack was being prepared, an extremely dangerous mission that could be viewed by the Soviets as an act of war. They were very conscious that the Germans had conducted such reconnaissance flights before their June 22, 1941, invasion.

Acutely aware of the danger, USAF Major John Seaberg, working at Wright-Patterson Air Force Base, believed that the jet engine had reached a stage where a high-altitude, long-range aircraft could be built. Fortunately, the necessary equipment had also materialized in the form of a high-resolution camera developed by Dr. Edwin Land (of Polaroid fame). The camera could use new Hycon Corporation lenses, and Mylar-based film developed by Eastman Kodak.

In March 1953, the Air Force established a requirement for a single-seat spy plane capable of operating at altitudes of greater than seventy thousand feet. The Bell X-16 won the competition for the aircraft, but no one had reckoned with Lockheed's famous engineer, Kelly Johnson, who presided over a secret engineering shop colloquially called the Skunk Works after a mythical workshop in cartoonist Al Capp's comic strip *Lil Abner.*

Johnson, perhaps the greatest aeronautical engineer of his time, bulled his way through the monumental red tape by promising the delivery of the first aircraft in eight months, and the delivery of twenty aircraft for $22 million despite the fact that Bell already had a contract for its X-16. Johnson's offer was accepted, the X-16 program was killed, and on August 1, 1955, the famous Lockheed test pilot, Tony LeVier, made the official first flight.

The U-2 was a fragile aircraft, with a long, slender wing, narrow fuselage, and a bicycle-style landing gear. Weight considerations prevented installation of a pressurized cockpit, so the pilot was forced to wear an uncomfortable pressure suit through the long missions. The U-2 proved to be a dangerous aircraft to fly. It demanded extremely high piloting skills and was unforgiving of any error. There were many losses, and many pilots died in the U-2. All the while, NACA provided a cover story that the U-2 was making high-altitude research flights.

The first U-2 spy flight took place on June 20, 1956, from Weisbaden, Germany, on a route that took it over Warsaw and Prague. Then on July 4, Leningrad and Moscow were overflown. The results were sensational—the photographs peered into the heart of Soviet defenses and industry.

There had been some hopes that Soviet radar could not detect the high-flying U-2, but this was not the case, and the Soviet foreign ministry bitterly protested the invasion of its territory. The United States "stonewalled," denying that such flights were taking place, and ignoring the Soviet threats of military reprisals. The heart of the matter was that the Soviets were unwilling to admit that they could not stop the flights after the hundreds of billions of rubles they had spent on their air defense system.

In the next four years, the U-2s made forty overflights as well as many flights around the periphery of the country. On one of these flights, a pilot noted a previously undisclosed railroad spur; he elected to follow it, and found the supersecret Baikonur Cosmodrome—a bit of sleuthing that the later satellites could not do. Sensors were soon added to the U-2 to bring back invaluable electronic information.

The information bonanza the U-2s brought back revealed not only that the Soviet bomber fleet was far less numerous than believed, but that the Soviet ICBM development, while serious and advanced in some areas, was in general not as far along as feared.

The U-2 overflights ended on May 1, 1960, when Francis Gary Powers was shot down near Sverdlovsk by the blast effect of a volley of fourteen SA-2 surface-to-air missiles. Khrushchev used the incident to mortify President Eisenhower at a Paris summit meeting.

Powers was given a Soviet show trial and sentenced to ten years in a labor camp for espionage. He was later exchanged for the notorious Soviet spy, Rudolph Abel.

Although flights over the Soviet Union were discontinued, the U-2 continued to be improved over time and will likely see service well into the twenty-first century. It performed its most important duties in 1962, when as an expression of a new concept of air power, it brought the greatest possible influence to bear upon world history.

CORONA: The First Successful Spy Satellites

The successful ICBM program had prompted the United States Air Force to issue a contract in October 1956 to the Lockheed Corporation to develop the Advanced (satellite) Reconnaissance System, that would transmit digitized images directly to ground stations. Progress was slow, and in 1958, President Eisenhower approved an interim system to return the photographs on film via a recoverable capsule. The program was launched under the public code name DISCOVERER, and masked as an effort to use space vehicles to learn more about the earth's environment. The actual program was run by the USAF and the Central Intelligence Agency (CIA) and had the code name CORONA.

The technical challenge was great, and there were no less than twelve well-publicized mission failures. Because today's media seems to find a hysterical delight in pointing to government program failures, no similar contemporary effort could survive such a series of catastrophes without demands for cancellation. On August 18, 1960, DISCOVERER XIV succeeded in exposing twenty pounds of film over the Soviet Union. The capsule was ejected from the satellite and picked up in midair by a USAF Fairchild C-119, flying at 8,500 feet over the Pacific Ocean.

In its first successful mission, the CORONA satellite in seventeen orbits photographed more of the Soviet Union than had been obtained by all of the U-2 overflights. The film, while lacking the resolution of U-2 photos, revealed sixty-four new airfields and twenty-six new surface-to-air missile sites, along with invaluable targeting information for the Strategic Air Command.

Four of the next five CORONA launches failed, but in 1961, seven out of eleven missions were successful to a degree beyond the wildest hopes of anyone in the CIA or the Air Force. It was as if the Cold War were a poker game, and a big mirror had just been installed behind the Soviet Union, revealing all its cards. The full results of the CORONA program were not revealed until the 1990s.

The equipment on board CORONA satellites was continually improved, and specialized satellites were introduced to provide data sought for particular purposes. The 145th and final CORONA launch took place on May 25, 1972, and six days later, two reentry vehicles carrying 160 pounds of film were recovered. The resolution was such that a print seven feet wide and one hundred feet long was sharp from end to end. CORONA had furnished photographic coverage of 750 million nautical square miles of the earth's surface.

In the early years of the Cold War, the United States had been continually surprised by Soviet developments, from the appearance of new and formidable jets over the annual Moscow air show to the successive detonations of atomic and thermonuclear bombs to the stunning success of Sputnik. An overwhelming fear had grown of Soviet capability in bombers and ICBMs, fears that had to be responded to in the United States' defense budget.

These fears were partly dispelled by the U-2 flights, but by June 1964, CORONA had photographed all twenty-five Soviet ICBM complexes and offered convincing evidence that there was neither a missile nor a bomber gap and that United States strategic nuclear forces were already adequate for any task that might be levied upon them. This knowledge permitted a reduction in defense spending and a reallocation of the defense budget, both of which more than compensated for all of the costs involved in the DISCOVERER/ CORONA projects. In the words of the Director of Central Intelligence, Robert Gates, in November 1999, for the United States "during the last two-thirds of the Cold War . . . there were no more strategic surprises."[10]

It is impossible to overestimate the importance of the CORONA satellites, nor to comprehend their incredible effects upon history. By far the most important of these effects was the prevention of the United States from making a fatal miscalculation about Soviet capabilities and intentions. Ironically, CORONA thus proved to be almost as great an advantage to the Soviet Union as the United States, for it ruled out an inadvertent escalation that might have led to an all-out nuclear exchange.

The success of CORONA signaled the maturation of air power into aerospace power, a process that had begun with Sputnik and would accelerate over time for it was inextricably linked with Moore's Law and the swift progress of computers. In 1964, semiconductor engineer Gordon Moore observed that the amount of information storable on a given amount of silicon had roughly doubled every year since the technology was invented. This relationship held until 1970, when the doubling period slowed to about eighteen months, a rate it has since sustained. Experience indicates that Moore's Law is apparently self-fulfilling, for each increase in capacity gives the ability to improve performance. The improvements in satellite systems and in weaponry since CORONA support this concept, and would make it possible for aerospace power to reach beyond the heights it has demonstrated in the Persian Gulf War, Kosovo, and Afghanistan.

Yet before CORONA had fully developed, it happened that an older, tried-and-true piece of reconnaissance equipment, the Lockheed U-2, would provide critical information on the most dangerous flashpoint of the entire Cold War: the Cuban Missile Crisis.

Approach to Armageddon

It might be said that in some respects the Cold War was conducted somewhat along the lines of a family quarrel, in which some misconduct was permissible, and some impermissible. It was permissible, for example, to build up huge quantities of nuclear weapons, and it was also permissible to provide large quantities of conventional arms to allies. Providing nuclear arms to allies, however, was impermissible. It was permissible to build up huge forces of Soviet intermediate-range ballistic missiles (IRBMs) that threatened all of Europe, for the European states were presumably protected by the retaliatory capability of the United States. This capability included the installation of American IRBMs in Turkey—which the Soviets somehow regarded as impermissible.

All this information is background to the stark fact that United States intelligence sources had begun reporting that the Soviet Union was installing offensive weapons in Cuba, reports that Soviet officials persistently denied, saying that they were installing only defensive weapons in their Caribbean client's homeland.

Cuba was attractive to the Soviet Union, for it offered a conduit for operations into Central and South America. After Fidel Castro had seized power in January 1959, he began to move openly toward the Soviet sphere of influence. The situation became worse when President John F. Kennedy supported the abortive Bay of Pigs invasion of Cuba by Cuban exile counterrevolutionaries in April 1961.

By 1962, the Soviet Union was well on the way to turning Cuba, only ninety miles from the United States mainland, into an advance base in the Western Hemisphere, supplying Mobile Medium-Range Ballistic Missiles (MMRBM), IRBMs, and Ilyushin Il-28 bombers. Defensive weapons were also supplied, including SA-2 surface-to-air (SAM) missiles and more than fifty MiG fighters.

On October 14, 1962, two expert U-2 pilots of the 4080th Strategic Reconnaissance Wing, Majors Richard S. Heyser and Rudolf Anderson Jr., brought back conclusive evidence that the Soviet Union was building offensive missile sites in the San Cristóbal area. Follow-up flights revealed that sites for both 1,000-mile-range MRBM and 2,000-mile-range IRBM were being prepared. The assembly of the Il-28 bombers was clearly in progress. It was estimated that within two weeks, the Soviet Union would have a minimum of two dozen missiles capable of reaching every heavily populated area in the Western Hemisphere.

President Kennedy was faced with a series of problems, beginning with finding some way to force the removal of the Soviet offensive capability without unleashing World War III and without repeating the Bay of Pigs fiasco. The full array of military options was considered, from a large-scale air attack taking out missiles, bombers, and other weapons in a single massive strike to a "surgical strike" aimed at eliminating only key installations. ("Surgical strike" was the favorite choice of non-flyers, who were unaware of how difficult such a strike was with the weapons of the day. In another thirty years and the arrival of precision-guided munitions, surgical strikes would become the *sine qua non* of United States warfare.) Other options included an invasion by conventional forces or a blockade.

After consulting with his most trusted advisors, President Kennedy decided on the blockade option, choosing for diplomatic purposes to call it a "naval quarantine." All American military forces, particularly the Strategic Air Command, were put on full military alert.

In the most important and most dramatic address of his career, President Kennedy addressed the nation and the world by television on the evening of October 22. He stated clearly that the United States recognized that it was not dealing with Cuba, but with the Soviet Union, and that the country was prepared to use the full weight of its war-making capability to insure that all offensive weapons were removed from Cuba. He added that the naval quarantine would not be lifted until the Soviet missiles had been removed and the sites destroyed. He then stated, "It shall be the policy of the United States to regard any nuclear missile launched from Cuba against any nation in the Western Hemisphere as an attack by the Soviet Union on the United States, requiring a full retaliatory response upon the Soviet Union."[11]

It was a tough statement reflecting the president's confidence in the capability of United States aerospace power. In the next few days the Soviet Union signaled its intentions by not attempting to cross the five-hundred-mile boundary line of the naval quarantine. There followed an exchange of messages, varying in tone, but revealing Soviet awareness that a miscalculation could result in a nuclear exchange. Sadly, on October 27, Major Anderson, who had discovered the satellite emplacements, was shot down and killed by an SA-2 missile.

While messages were being exchanged, private diplomatic conversations were proceeding, and Khrushchev was assured that the United States would not invade Cuba and that the previously determined plans to remove IRBMs from Turkey would be carried out. On October 28 Khrushchev accepted the United States' demands that the missiles be removed and the sites be destroyed, and the immediate crisis was over, although additional pressure had to be applied to obtain the removal of the forty-two Il-28 bombers. Extensive reconnaissance saw that the Soviets were bulldozing the missile sites, and when United States Navy vessels boarded departing

Soviet ships, they were shown that there were indeed missiles on board being returned to the USSR.

Secretary of State Dean Rusk made a public statement that the United States and the Soviet Union had stood eyeball to eyeball, and the USSR had blinked. It was perhaps too glib a characterization, but the entire episode was politically disastrous for Khrushchev, who lost face within his own Communist Party. Red China took careful note of the incident, decided that Khrushchev was soft, and began backing away from the close relations that the two nations had previously enjoyed.

In later analyses of the crisis, two unlikely characters, General Curtis E. LeMay, then USAF Chief of Staff, and Premier Nikita Khrushchev found themselves in agreement about the importance of the American nuclear capability. Khrushchev stated, "About twenty percent of all Strategic Air Command planes, carrying atomic and hydrogen bombs, were kept aloft around the clock." The thought of these aircraft, orbiting on his borders, had contributed to his backing away from war. LeMay stated that the success of the American effort was due to SAC's superior nuclear power and President Kennedy's obvious willingness to use it, if required.[12] The effectiveness of United States nuclear power was further augmented by the fact that arrangements had been made to conduct a war from an airborne command post if required.

Aftermath and Prelude

The Cuban Missile Crisis was the first instance in which aerospace power played such an important role in first precipitating and then resolving a military confrontation. The most important effect of aerospace power on history was of course the avoidance of a nuclear exchange. The very success of the United States efforts carried within it the seeds of a future disaster, one that would see aerospace power greatly expanded, but at the same time, thwarted by the ill-founded conclusions drawn by the same men who had participated in the decisions affecting the Cuban Missile Crisis.

President Kennedy's advisors included Defense Secretary Robert S. McNamara, National Security Advisor McGeorge Bundy, and Chairman of the Joint Chiefs of Staff, Maxwell D. Taylor. Pleased with the success of their counsel on Cuba, they came away with a very inflated sense of their own value in managing the crisis, and more important, with confidence in the techniques used to respond to the behavior of the enemy. This led them to confuse strategy with crisis management, two very different disciplines. They would give advice using these techniques in reaching their conclusions on how to deal with the North Vietnamese, and as a direct result, plunge the United States into a long, bitter, and losing war in Southeast Asia that would forfeit the capability of air power in favor of a series of mistaken efforts to "send signals" to an enemy whom they did not even begin to understand.

Thanks in large part to the bad advice given by these Cuban Missile Crisis veterans, American participation in the Vietnam War became a textbook on how *not* to use air or aerospace power.

Chapter Ten

The Cold War, 1963-73

Doctrine as Its Own Enemy

The remarkable surge in the strategic power of the Soviet Union, as evidenced by its bomber and missile strength, was not at the expense of its tactical forces. The Soviet Union maintained a huge army, equipped with massive numbers of tanks and artillery pieces, and supported by large and effective air forces. Its allies in the Warsaw Pact were similarly well equipped.

As a measure of the scale of Soviet effort, in 1970 it operated about 1,300 ICBMS, 700 IRBMs, 160 SLBMs, and 190 long-range bombers. The Red Air Force had more than 10,000 aircraft including 725 medium bombers and 4,000 tactical aircraft, for light bombing and close air support. For air defense, there were 3,300 operational interceptors and an immense antiaircraft and surface-to-air missile system. The latter included 8,000 SA-2 Guidelines, plus additional numbers of shorter range missiles. At least sixty-seven Galosh antiballistic missile launchers were in place around Moscow. The Soviet population of 244 million generated a Gross National Product of about $466 billion, of which $39.8 billion (8.5 percent), was allocated to defense. (These were official figures; unofficial estimates put the percentage much higher.)

The Soviet Army was estimated to be 2,000,000 men, with almost 17,000 tanks and an immense amount of artillery. The Army was organized into 157 divisions, and could mobilize another 70 divisions, completely equipped, in less than thirty days. The Soviet Navy was not yet a "blue water" surface navy, but it consisted of 475,000 personnel and had 290 conventional and 80 nuclear-powered submarines.

In comparison, in the same time period the United States possessed 1,044 ICBMs, 656 SLBMs, and 540 strategic bombers. The

USAF had about 6,000 additional aircraft, including 700 interceptors and 1,000 tactical aircraft in the United States. An additional 3,000 aircraft of all types were dedicated to operations in Southeast Asia. The United States Army had a strength of 1,363,000, but was hopelessly outnumbered in tanks and artillery. It did excel in helicopter strength, however, with almost 9,000 in its inventory. The key numbers, however, would not ultimately be men, planes, or tanks but these: a smaller population of 205 million generated a Gross National Product of $932 billion. The annual defense outlay in the midst of war was $72 billion, or only about 7.7 percent of GNP.[1]

It was first perceived in the early years of the Ronald Reagan presidency that the relative percent of Gross Domestic Product (GDP) spent on defense would be the ultimate key to victory in the Cold War. The Soviet desire to be militarily strong everywhere would speed its ultimate collapse, as its economy was not strong enough to bear the costs of such strategic commitment or extensive weaponry. The overemphasis on military spending destroyed any chance of creating a strong domestic economy. The Soviet populace suffered extremes of hardship endurable only so long as they were unaware of what was happening in the free world. With the advent of mass means of communication, including television, they swiftly became aware of what they were missing. Those who directed the Soviet system lived well, which perhaps prevented them from understanding that without a strong domestic economy, the tax base was insufficient to fund profligate military spending.

In contrast, while the United States did not spend a markedly smaller percentage of its GDP on defense, its economy was so robust that it generated a civilian economy unmatched in history. In doing so, the United States took some deliberate risks. There was, for example, nothing in the United States to compare with the massive Soviet civil defense efforts, and this deficiency would have been of overwhelming importance if a nuclear exchange had occurred. Instead, it was fortunate for all that instead of nuclear explosions there was an economic implosion in the Soviet Union that brought it down with a whimper and not a bang on Christmas Day, 1991.

The Korean War, where the outcome quite literally depended upon the efficacy of American tactical air power, should have led the United States to the development of a similar balance of forces as that of the Soviet Union even if not one of such extravagant scale.

The senior Red delegate at Panmunjom, Lieutenant General Nam II, stated that it was the interdiction of Red Army supplies that forced the half of the combined North Korean and Chinese forces, rather than the close air support.[2] The general made similar remarks several times in his comments, and while his choice of terms was sometimes confusing, it was clear that he meant that the interdiction of supplies by American air power had sapped the Red forces of the strength necessary to defeat the outnumbered UN forces.

Unfortunately for the furtherance of tactical air power or a balance of forces, the predominance of the Strategic Air Command began to have a counterproductive effect on the Air Force as a whole. As SAC matured, its success caused its procedures to be emulated by other Air Force elements, not always with good effect. In 1954, when the former Commander of Far East Air Forces, General Otto P. ("Opie") Weyland took over, he announced his decision to make the Tactical Air Command the equivalent of SAC. It followed that TAC would procure aircraft such as the Republic F-105, designed for the nuclear mission. TAC's training would henceforth focus on the nuclear mission to the detriment of training in conventional methods of bomb delivery and in air-to-air combat. This trend was emphasized when a former SAC commander, General Walter C. Sweeney Jr., assumed command of TAC on August 1, 1961. Sweeney brought a much needed discipline and rigor to TAC, but he also insisted on the importance of delivering tactical nuclear weapons. There were many veterans, including mavericks such as then-Colonel Robin Olds, who campaigned internally for training in "tried and true" tactics (that is, dropping conventional bombs and obtaining air superiority in dogfights), but they were in the minority, and their ideas were overlooked. Sweeney's appointment was also a symptom of how influential SAC was becoming throughout the Air Force, as generals brought up under LeMay were sent to command other organizations.

The United States Navy, determined not to be phased out of existence by Air Force technology, also pursued a nuclear course, bringing in large aircraft such as the Douglas AD-3 Skywarrior for that role.[3] Fortunately, the Navy also believed in power projection through conventional means, and continued to field aircraft such as the Douglas A-4 Skyhawk and the Grumman A-6B Intruder for the tactical role. The requirement of carriers to provide a fleet defense capability also led to the employment of sophisticated fighters such as the McDonnell F-4 Phantom and the Vought F-8 Crusader, both, particularly the Crusader, useful in the air superiority role.

The United States' nuclear mind-set persisted even through low-level crises such as those in Lebanon and Taiwan in 1958. In Lebanon, the Combined Air Strike Force (CASF), which had been first established in 1955, was dispatched as a deterrent to a Muslim uprising and/or an invasion of Lebanon by Syria or Iraq.[4] The CASF consisted of about a hundred aircraft, including fighters, bombers, reconnaissance aircraft, and tankers. It was in concept not unlike today's Air Expeditionary Forces, but smaller in scale. The show of strength eventually caused the situation to cool down.

In a similar way, President Eisenhower signaled his intention to defend Taiwan from Red Chinese attack by dispatching the Seventh Fleet and a squadron of the brand-new and red-hot Lockheed F-104s. Combat ensued, with United States and Nationalist Chinese pilots giving the Red Chinese Air Force a severe drubbing, shooting down thirty-three planes.[5]

The success of these actions should have fostered a greater realization within the USAF of the need for tactical forces to fight conventional (i.e., non-nuclear) wars. The unfortunate assumption was made that the tactical forces were successful in their mission only because they operated under the umbrella of the massive nuclear air power of the United States. Because of this mental set, when the USAF was forced—against its wishes—to begin to intervene in Southeast Asia, it did not have the proper equipment or training to do so. Instead of being able to put capable, well-trained counterinsurgency forces in the field, it was forced to improvise. United States naval aviation had equipment more suited to the contest, but it too was limited in the number of aircraft carriers that it could maintain on station for any given period of time.

A Cautionary Note

The premise of this book is to reflect on the influence of air power on history, a particularly difficult task to do in relation to the Vietnam War for a variety of reasons. First and foremost of these is the passion that the war still elicits from both those who fought it with such desperate effort and those who protested it so vehemently.

Another factor is the large number of books that have appeared in recent years that have examined air power and found it wanting, most often concentrating upon lack of effectiveness of bombing campaigns. Written by scholars and less often by military officers, many of the books have a subtext in which the immorality of bombing is highlighted. Those that do so often receive the greatest critical acclaim, for it is easy to appreciate the view that bombing, and indeed, all warfare, is immoral.

Yet in the world in which we live, war is a fact of life. It always has been, and it seems as if it always will be. When nations need to defend their interests, they do so with what they believe to be the most effective means at their command, and for most nations since 1918, those means include bombing.

The bombing campaigns of the Vietnam War have been much examined, and the general consensus of many of the books is that bombing was not effective because the war was ultimately lost. Nothing could be further from the truth. Air power was the only means by which the United States could sustain its own ground forces and those of its ally, the Republic of Vietnam, in the field. Just as in the Korean War, where military victory was also forfeited to political considerations, air power succeeded in Vietnam by preventing military defeat. It did so by gaining numerous small land victories in the field, including four of vital, history-shaping, importance.

The more numerous small victories include the thousands of situations in which the arrival of air power won the battle for United States or South Vietnamese troops in contact with Communist forces. Perhaps the most dramatic of these were the nighttime relief of outposts under attack by the timely arrival of airborne gunships, first Douglas AC-47s and then Fairchild AC-119s and Lockheed AC-130s. It was the proud boast of gunship crews that no outpost was ever taken when a gunship was on hand to prevent it. There were many other examples, from the firepower of army helicopters supporting troops being evacuated from landing zones to the heavy weapons of the McDonnell F-4s demolishing enemy troops ringing a besieged hamlet to the extended engagements of Douglas A-1Es during rescue operations. It is impossible to estimate the number of lives these actions saved, nor the spin they put on the history of the war.

Yet these all pale when compared to the four major instances in which an air-power victory prevented defeat in the field. The first of these was the aerial relief of Khe Sahn. The brilliant North Vietnamese defense minister, General Vo Nguyen Giap, planned to surround the base. His purpose was to effect a second Dien Bien Phu, the 1954 battle that saw the defeat of the French in Vietnam. Air power helped turn his plans into a costly defeat. The second was helping suppress the bloody military blunder that was the abortive Tet Offensive of 1968, a battle that quite literally wiped out Viet Cong capability for the rest of the war. The third was the magnificent effort in which air power was rapidly recalled back into the theater, helping to stop the controversial March 1972 "Easter Offensive" of the North Vietnamese regular army. The fourth was the most important, the final, definite defeat administered by air power to the North Vietnamese during the eleven-day bombing campaign of December 1972.

In short, air power had a profound influence on history in the Vietnam War, by preventing the outright military defeat that would have occurred in its absence. There is a genuine possibility that if air power had been applied with a stronger political will from the start of the war, it could have done more than prevent military defeat—it might have actually won the war. What it could not do, however, was prevent the shameful political defeat that was administered to the United States by North Vietnam in the course of negotiations. The United States abandoned the Republic of Vietnam to defend itself against the Democratic Republic of Vietnam in January 1973. The Republic of Vietnam, lacking United States air power, was no longer able to do so and succumbed to a final attack in the spring of 1975.

The Slow Slide to Involvement

It has happened more than once that air power has influenced history not so much by what it could do, but by what politicians thought it could do. It may be said that the United States aerial involvement in the Vietnam War came about because American governmental officials felt secure in the immense nuclear power they possessed, which had grown from the less than 2,000 nuclear weapons that President Eisenhower had at his disposal in 1953, to 26,500 by 1962.[6] With this enormous strength at their ultimate disposal, those officials were more than willing to exert diplomatic and military pressure with token gestures of conventional air power. In theory it was much like the gunboat diplomacy of the Royal Navy in the previous century. Then a minor British force could be sent to deal with colonial problems because it was implicit that the entire weight of the Royal Navy would be employed if the minor force met with difficulty.

Military officers, particularly in the USAF, were well aware of the limitations of air power and never had the same level of confidence that these token forces could accomplish the jobs they were asked to do. They were also all too aware of how conflicts sometimes escalated rapidly beyond the control of anyone involved. There was strong opposition to the idea of intervening in Southeast Asia throughout the military establishment, an opinion top civilian leaders in the Departments of Defense or State did not share.

The first step in the escalation process seemed harmless enough. After the French were forced from their former colony in 1954, the newly established nation of South Vietnam sought assistance from the United States. A 925-man Military Assistance Group (MAG) was in place by 1955 to train the Army of the Republic of Vietnam (ARVN.)

For the next six years, the United States Air Force had no formal involvement in Vietnam. Then-President Kennedy authorized the establishment of a mobile control and reporting post at Tan Son Nhut Air Base near Saigon. It began operation on October 5, 1961, and was soon followed by a detachment with the code name Farm Gate. Consisting of 155 officers and airmen equipped with four Douglas RB-26s, four Douglas SC-47s, and eight North American T-28s, the Farm Gate contingent began arriving at Bien Hoa Air Base on November 15. The official mission was to train the South Vietnamese Air Force, but the Farm Gate crews were soon flying combat missions. It was the thin edge of what would become a bloody eleven-year wedge.

Operation Mule Train followed Farm Gate in January 1962, to provide troop carrier and cargo capability in the form of sixteen Fairchild C-123 twin-engine transports. In the same month, the first detachment of Operation Ranch Hand would arrive. Ranch Hand used the C-123 to conduct the highly controversial Agent Orange defoliant operations that Secretary McNamara authorized on November 3, 1961.

This cautious escalation was not without its costs, for several aircraft were lost. The first of these was a Fairchild C-123 on a training mission that crashed on February 2, 1961, killing its crew of three. Thousands more aircraft would be lost in the course of the Vietnam War.

The tempo of air-power operations did not increase substantially until after the August 2, 1964, Gulf of Tonkin incident when North Vietnamese torpedo boats were reported to have attacked the destroyer USS *Maddox*. President Lyndon B. Johnson ordered retaliatory raids on North Vietnamese bases by carrier aircraft, and the air war in Vietnam began to pick up speed. In Operation Pierce Arrow, sixty-four sorties were flown from the USS *Ticonderoga* and the USS *Constellation* on August 5, striking North Vietnamese petroleum storage facilities and naval vessels.[7]

Side Effects of the Success in Cuba

Many of President Kennedy's advisers (too many, according to some) had been held over when he was succeeded by President Johnson. Many of these same advisers had worked to the successful conclusion of the Cuban Missile Crisis, and they had the false impression that they could use the same negotiating tactics with the North Vietnamese that had been successful with the Soviet Union. It was their intention to "teach" the North Vietnamese leaders that their political aspirations to absorb South Vietnam would have to be changed because they were opposed by the United States. This concept would have disastrous effect, for it resulted in air power being applied in too small doses over too long a period of time. The United States became, in effect, North Vietnam's personal trainer, instructing it in penny-packet lessons on how best to defend against attack.

While the decisions of the president were always final, and while many others contributed to the decision-making process, there is no question that Secretary of Defense Robert S. McNamara guided the United States into the war in Southeast Asia. Unfortunately, McNamara chose to base United States strategy on the obvious—and fatally flawed—fiction that the war was merely a civilian insurrection in South Vietnam that pitted a rebel National Liberation Front (Viet Cong) movement against the South Vietnamese government. Yet McNamara knew very well that the war was in fact a deliberate attempt by North Vietnam's inspirational leader Chairman Ho Chi Minh to overthrow the South Vietnamese government and establish a unified Communist state under his leadership.

One aspect of McNamara's insurgency viewpoint was that the Viet Cong were to be considered a rebellious opposition party to the

South Vietnamese government, when in fact they were directed from Hanoi, and included a large number of North Vietnamese troops who were inserted into South Vietnam to terrorize rather than persuade. Because there were rebellions going on all over the world, McNamara saw the war in Vietnam as a laboratory, a learning experience. He believed that by using the methods of quantitative analysis that had given him a meteoric career at the Ford Motor Company he would be able to analyze the results of operations in Vietnam. This learning experience would presumably teach the United States how to handle future insurgencies elsewhere in the world. He ignored the human factor entirely, a grave mistake given the redoubtable fighting qualities of the North Vietnamese and their dedication to their mission.

The situation in Vietnam was in many ways parallel to that of Korea in 1950. Both Korea and Vietnam were bordered on the north by Communist China. Both had formerly been occupied by a foreign power. Both were divided in half with most of the limited industrial capacity in the North. In both instances, the northern portion of the country was militant, with an army well trained and well equipped by the Soviet Union, while the southern portion had an army that was poorly trained and poorly equipped by the United States. The militant North was ruled by a strong, determined Communist government, while the South was ruled by a weak and only theoretically democratic government. Both the Soviet Union and Red China subsidized North Vietnam, while the South looked to the United States for assistance.

There were also significant differences that affected the outcome of the conflict. This time, the United States was not operating under the umbrella of the United Nations. It was supported by some of its allies, but there was not the consensus of United Nations action.

Korea was a peninsula bounded on one side by the Yellow Sea and on the other by the Sea of Japan—and both bodies of water were controlled by Allied naval forces. Vietnam was bordered on the west by Laos and Cambodia, through which was established the most famous supply route in history, the Ho Chi Minh Trail, to support the insurgents in South Vietnam. Yet perhaps the most important difference up to the time of the Tet Offensive in 1968 was the Viet Cong guerrilla movement for which there was no counterpart in Korea. The guerrillas were largely imported from North Korea as a terrorist movement that used threats and force to intimidate the native population and recruit from it. It was considerably less important after the massive defeat of the Tet Offensive.

Secretary McNamara intended to use carrot-and-stick tactics to teach the North Vietnamese to cease the policies they had steadfastly and successfully followed since 1945. He planned to offer concessions for "good" North Vietnamese behavior, and varying degrees of punishment for varying degrees of "bad" behavior. The concept of "flexible response" was introduced, in which military responses were to be graduated, so that a Viet Cong (or North Vietnamese) transgression would be met by a response just slightly sharper than the transgression. If the next transgression were more serious, then the next response would be more serious. In effect, McNamara put aside the tremendous economic and military power of the United States to fight tit-for-tat slogan warfare. He was seeking to elicit a Pavlovian response from a tough North Vietnamese government that was composed in large part of intellectual revolutionaries who had been successful in their thirty-year struggle against both the Japanese and the French. In the end, it would be the Vietnamese ringing the bell, with the United States salivating at the prospect of peace.

McNamara had erroneously assumed that North Vietnam was a mere pawn of Red China, and he sought to avoid the possibility of war with China by pretending to deal only with his fictional insurrection in South Vietnam. War with China was a genuine concern for President Lyndon B. Johnson, as well. Unfortunately, neither man ever assessed the Red Chinese means or intentions; had they done so, they would have learned that war on behalf of Red China's hated enemy, the Vietnamese, was unlikely in the extreme. Further, they completely missed the point that in his determination to unite Vietnam under his own regime, Ho Chi Minh would fight China as readily as he fought the French and the United States.

McNamara's entire concept was based on an appalling ignorance of the quality of the North Vietnamese people and their battle-hardened leaders. Neither he nor any member of his staff was personally familiar with the Vietnamese culture, and none had learned anything of the psychology of the enemy. Worst of all, safe in the confines of their air-conditioned Washington offices, none of them had any idea of the ruthless determination and the skill with which the North Vietnamese had fought and would fight. The concept of "teaching" the North Vietnamese was a snobbish, condescending power play that might have worked in the automobile industry from which McNamara came, but was totally inappropriate for conducting a war against a formidable enemy. Ironically, the North Vietnamese leaders had incisive insight into American culture and psychology, and indeed, correctly believed that they would win their war, not by military force of arms (they were in fact continually defeated in the field) but by the waning of support by the American public.

Nonetheless, such was McNamara's influence that he was able to persuade both Presidents Kennedy and Johnson to fight the war as an insurrection and thus abandon traditional military strategy. He agreed with General Maxwell Taylor that while the air war against North Vietnam was to be limited, an ever-increasing number of United States Army troops would be brought in to fight a land campaign. This, despite later innovations in the use of air-mobile troops, was a "traditional war."

When after seven years and thousands of casualties it became apparent to all that the war could not be won in the manner in which it was being fought, McNamara advocated abandoning South Vietnam to its own fate. He had his own personal "bug out" when he left the government on February 29, 1968, to head the World Bank. Years later his best-selling autobiography would reveal that he had believed all along that the war could not be won. (Struck by the cynicism of a man who would make money writing about losing a war for which he bore substantial responsibility, some suggested that profits from the book be given to organizations supporting Vietnam veterans. McNamara declined.)

The most bizarre aspect of the war being run by politicians was the way the bombing was conducted. At Tuesday afternoon meetings in the White House, the president and McNamara would decide on targets and perhaps on the weight of bomb loads and the munitions to be used. The fact that they were twelve thousand miles from the scene of the action, and that their orders had to pass through numerous headquarters before being realized, did not discomfort them. To the troops in the field, who knew the enemy positions intimately and who saw how often the missions were useless, the process appeared insane.

One set of statistics will reveal exactly how skewed the thinking in Washington was. During the war in Southeast Asia, the United States dropped eight million tons of bombs, twice the tonnage dropped by all the warring powers during World War II. Because of

McNamara's insistence that it was a war against insurgents, more than 90 percent of this figure was dropped on the country of America's ally, South Vietnam, while only 10 percent was dropped on the country of America's enemy, North Vietnam.

This abysmal computation, 7.2 million tons of bombs on friendly South Vietnam and 1.8 million tons on enemy North Vietnam, is an absolute indication of the political madness with which the war was conducted.

In addition to the misdirected bomb tonnage, all traditional concepts of the employment of mass, surprise, and the selection of appropriate objectives were tossed aside in an orgy of too-clever "signal sending." For years there prevailed within Washington the hope that sending signals such as the bombing halts would result in the North Vietnamese becoming more tractable. The North Vietnamese did not interpret the signals as an avenue to compromise; instead they saw them as what they were, signs of weakness, showing that will and purpose were lacking in United States top leadership. Every such signal, instead of leading to some understanding, led to stiffened resistance by the North Vietnamese.

McNamara and his associates in government thus succeeded in forfeiting all the enormous advantages that American air power possessed, in part by imposing rules of engagement that gave every advantage to the enemy. These varied from time to time, and many were altered after McNamara left office, but they were very restrictive, as some brief examples will indicate.

The United States military leadership was not without blame. Generals who knew that McNamara and his colleagues were wrong in their methods should have resigned their positions and gone public with their beliefs. Instead, most went supinely along with the misdirection.

The greatest danger to American aircraft came from surface-to-air missiles, primarily the SA-2 Guideline. The SAM sites were off-limits while under construction for fear that the Soviet advisers installing the sites might be injured. They remained off-limits to attack even after being completed, and could not be attacked until such time as the enemy radar had acquired the United States aircraft as a target and had switched from the radar-surveillance mode to the track mode, seconds before it was going to fire its missiles. Even then, however, missile sites could not be attacked if they were located in a populated area or on a dike of the widespread irrigation system. Naturally enough, these became the favored place to install weapons. SAM sites within ten miles of Hanoi or Haiphong were off-limits entirely. The air bases from which the enemy MiG fighters flew were off limits to attack on all but a few occasions when such attacks were sanctioned. This meant that enemy fighters could sit in perfect safety in full view of American aircraft, taking off, attacking, and landing at times of their own choosing. It was forbidden to attack shipping in Haiphong's harbor, even though it made much more sense to sink a ship carrying three-hundred trucks with one mission rather than take a thousand missions to destroy the trucks one by one as they came down the infamous Ho Chi Minh Trail. There were many other rules, all conducive to enemy safety, all dangerous to American flyers; if these rules were broken, the United States military men were punished, sometimes by court-martial.

With the full use of air power forfeited, McNamara next saw to it that the United States was engaged instead in the type of conflict that almost all American military leaders condemned, a long land war in Southeast Asia in which more than 500,000 troops were eventually employed and in which more than 58,000 casualties would be incurred. In doing so, McNamara followed the advice of General Maxwell Taylor, who was Chairman of the Joint Chiefs of Staff for President Kennedy. It must be noted that McNamara's policies were exactly contrary to the advice of a man with combat experience in World War II, Korea, and the Cold War, the USAF Chief of Staff, General Curtis LeMay. LeMay, like most military leaders, had bitterly opposed entering the conflict in Vietnam. Once entered, however, LeMay advocated winning the war in 1965 with a massive conventional bombing campaign directed against ninety-four North Vietnamese targets. The attack was to begin with airfields, with petroleum manufacturing and storage facilities, the industrial system, and then the road and transportation network to follow.[8] Unfortunately, both McNamara and Kennedy regarded LeMay as a saber-rattling Neanderthal, whose hard-won experience in warfare was to be ignored. LeMay retired on January 31, 1965, being replaced by General John P. McConnell as Chief of Staff. The likeable McConnell lacked LeMay's combat experience and did not have the personal wherewithal to challenge McNamara, in part because of a drinking problem.

McNamara decided that the war was to be conducted like corporate accounting, with minute attention directed to the number of sorties flown, bombs dropped, and bodies counted, along with other totally irrelevant but highly quantifiable details. In the muddled process, it escaped notice that McNamara was not concentrating on the ends of achieving strategic objectives, but was instead focused on those means that could be statistically quantified.

It thus happened that the American Secretary of Defense neutered United States air power, allowing it to be employed at an enormous cost of blood and treasure, but insuring by incredibly stupid policy decisions that it could not secure a victory. The possibility of whether or not a victory could be secured by air power was debated all through the long agony of the Vietnamese war. But, as will be shown below, it was finally proved beyond any shadow of a doubt that air power could achieve victory in Vietnam in the eleven-day Linebacker II campaign of December 1972.

Air Power in Vietnam

Air-power naysayers are quick to point out that air power was not successful in bringing about victory in the Vietnam War. Air-power loyalists insist that air power was not applied correctly for almost the entire war, and that when it was, in December 1972, it worked. Other Air Force loyalists will protest that the Air Force did not have the right combination of doctrine, equipment, and training for combat in Vietnam, and there is much truth to the charge.

United States naval aviation, in contrast, was well suited for the war, given the limitations of the rotation of task force assets and the requirements for self-defense. It had virtual immunity from North Vietnamese or Viet Cong attack, and possessed aircraft well suited for the mission with which it was charged. Unfortunately, even after the experience presumably gained in World War II and Korea, it proved impossible to conduct joint operations of USAF and naval aviation forces under a single air combat controller. Ostensibly there were too many conflicting demands, including the Navy requirement to allocate resources to fleet defense and communication incompatibility, but the real reason resided in the old bugaboo, service rivalry. As a result, it was necessary to resort to the primitive device of allocating targets to the Air Force and to the Navy by separate geographic areas (called Route Packages), rather than allocating targets on the basis of importance and the concerted use of all resources.

In the long conflict in Southeast Asia, there were many bombing campaigns, most with intriguing operational names, such as Flaming Dart, Commando Hunt, or Steel Tiger. The latter two campaigns were serious attempts to halt the flow of men and supplies from North Vietnam through Laos and Cambodia into South Vietnam. A good assessment can be made of the importance of air power in the Vietnam War by comparing the two major bombing campaigns against North Vietnam. The first of these was Operation Rolling Thunder, conducted from 1965 through 1968. It was followed by a four-year halt to bombing North (but not South) Vietnam. The second phase to be reviewed consists of President Richard M. Nixon's two 1972 bombing campaigns, Linebacker and Linebacker II.

Operation Rolling Thunder

The administration's confidence in the air power of the USAF and the United States Navy was great, so that very high goals were set. President Johnson expected Rolling Thunder to do three things. It was first of all to help create a viable state in South Vietnam, no easy task considering the corruption and political infighting that was endemic there. It was, by means of the restrictions placed upon it, to avoid provoking a war with either or both the USSR and Red China. And finally, always a politician, Johnson decreed that it was to be of such a constrained nature as not to excite the concerns of the American public.

Johnson's military *eminence grise,* Secretary McNamara, thought that the president's objectives could be met by Rolling Thunder because it would raise morale in South Vietnam and make sustaining the flow of supplies from North Vietnam too expensive. It is worth pointing out here that neither Johnson nor McNamara thought of air power in terms of *defeating* the North Vietnamese. It was the most critical error they could have made.

The plan for Rolling Thunder was subtle. The flow of supplies to South Vietnam would be struck at the southernmost part of North Vietnam. If the flow did not stop, heavier strikes, farther north would be made. This gradual increase in intensity was to signal the enemy that he should stop sending supplies south, or things would get worse. It became a characteristic of United States policy that in any attack planned on North Vietnam, civilian policymakers selected the weakest option available.[9]

There were many major faults with the plan. First of all, it forfeited the classic military advantages of both surprise and intensity in the attacks. Second, it assumed that the enemy could be bluffed, an assumption for which there was no basis to be found in the previous years of successful fighting. Third, Secretary McNamara and his civilian staff who arrogantly agreed with World War I French Premier Georges Clemenceau's observation that war was too important to be left to generals, maintained command and control. They determined targets, ordnance loads, and tactics, and then passed these decisions to the president for his approval or disapproval. The Joint Chiefs of Staff could suggest alterations, but their military input was often ignored. Fourth, it was based on no knowledge of the minimum amount of supplies that were necessary to sustain operations in the South. In actual practice, the hardy Viet Cong could get by on only a fraction of what they were receiving, a fraction that could be delivered, if necessary, not by trucks or bicycles, but on foot. Fifth, it did not take into consideration the fact that the destruction of supplies in any quantities was meaningless to the North Vietnamese, who had the boundless resources of both China and the Soviet Union to draw upon. Both of those countries were delighted to see the United States involved in the war, frittering time, attention, and assets on a corner of the world that was far from such critical hot centers of gravity as Taiwan or Berlin. Finally, the most disastrous aspect of the plan was that it gave the enemy time to gather more defensive resources and to train its people in the operation of radar systems, antiaircraft weapons, surface-to-air missiles, and even jet fighters. North Vietnam took advantage of Rolling Thunder to learn American methods, to grow stronger, and to become a much more difficult opponent.

The campaign began in February 1965, and by June there had been a complete inversion of tactical and strategic air power by the United States. In that month, Strategic Air Command B-52s began flying tactical bombing missions in Operation Arc Light, operating first from Andersen Air Base, Guam, and later also from U Tapao Royal Thai Air Force Base in Thailand. Arc Light B-52s dropped their thunderous loads of bombs on enemy bases and supply lines in South Vietnam and ultimately became useful in close air support.

They were described as the most feared weapon of the war by captured Viet Cong, for the first notice of their presence was the explosion of bombs, the B-52s flying too high to be seen or heard. Unfortunately, this was true only when there happened to be Viet Cong in the target area. All too often, warned by the incredible information network that the Viet Cong possessed, the bombs just cratered jungle areas empty of all enemy troops.

While the strategic bombers were flying tactical missions in the South, tactical bombers, Republic F-105s and later McDonnell F-4s, along with Navy attack aircraft, were flying Rolling Thunder's strategic missions against North Vietnam. An essential new role developed for the suppression of enemy air defenses, and a new breed of combat crew emerged to fly the "Iron Hand" and "Wild Weasel" missions to seek out and defeat the enemy SAM sites.

Whatever momentum Rolling Thunder had begun to gather was brought to a screeching stop when President Johnson declared a bombing halt from December 24, 1965, to January 31, 1966, to include both Christmas and Tet holiday periods. He had previously declared the first bombing halt in May, in the hopes that it signaled United States willingness to negotiate with the North Vietnamese. The invariable North Vietnamese reaction to a bombing halt was to accelerate repairs to bomb damage and to increase the flow of men and goods to the South as much as possible.

The next phase of Rolling Thunder began in January 1966 and lasted until August. This time, acting on the advice of the Joint Chiefs of Staff (JCS), the attack was focused on the petroleum resources of the North. Although many North Vietnamese installations were destroyed, the campaign itself was a failure because of the wealth of oil available to the North from its allies.

As Rolling Thunder rolled on, reputations began to fade, and faith was lost at the highest levels that the war could be won. The JCS was now given more weight in target selection, and it recommended attacks on what Bomber Harris had termed "panacea targets"— ports, locks and dams, industry, and the power system. McNamara, growing indifferent and aware that Johnson was losing confidence in him and in the conduct of the war, acquiesced. The president approved attacks only on industry and the power system, neither of which was as vital to North Vietnam as they had been to Germany. Attacks on ports would have been far more successful, but there were Red Chinese and Soviet vessels in the ports, and Johnson did not dare take the risk. It has been pointed out that the effort against Haiphong might have been successful if only the dredge that cleared the channels for shipping had been sunk, but not even this relatively safe option was selected.

All through Rolling Thunder, Secretary McNamara believed that North Vietnam would be made aware that supporting insurgency in the South was too expensive to continue. He reported that for the period of February 1965 through October 1966, Rolling Thunder had cost the North Vietnamese an estimated $150 million. This would have been a great expense for an impoverished country, if the losses in trucks, rice, oil, SAMs, and everything else not been replenished by China and the Soviet Union, who competed with each other like jealous suitors in lavishing aid on North Vietnam. The other side of the war's profit and loss statement revealed that the effort was costing the United States $250 million per *month*. And in spite of this level of expenditure, Secretary McNamara noted that he perceived "no significant impact on the war in South Vietnam."[10]

The decision based on this analysis was to spend more money. From 1965 to 1966, Rolling Thunder sorties rose from 55,000 to 110,000, while costs rose from $460 million to $1.2 billion, for both ammunition and aircraft were becoming more sophisticated and more expensive. The futile effort continued until November 1, 1968, when President Johnson halted the bombing of North Vietnam north of the Nineteenth Parallel, and called a halt to his own administration by announcing that he would not run for reelection.

The point must be made that Rolling Thunder was a failure despite the incredible bravery of the air crews who fought to carry it out and the hard work of the ground crews who made it possible. But it was not a failure of air power—it was instead a classic example of how *not* to use air power. Had the resources expended during Rolling Thunder, plus the resources that had been expended in South Vietnam, been applied in a carefully thought out unrestricted bombing campaign against North Vietnam, the war would have ended on American terms long before December 1968. This is not a hypothetical "what-if" situation; it is based on the hard fact that four years later, when North Vietnam was far stronger, it was beaten into the ground by just such an air campaign.

It is intoxicating to think what air power's influence on history might have been if Johnson had elected to defeat North Vietnam in the manner described above. He almost certainly would have been reelected, perhaps even fulfilling his dream of the "Great Society," and there might never have been a Nixon presidency. The terrible division within America prompted by the Vietnam War might never have grown so wide and so bitter. The people of South Vietnam would not have experienced the harsh punishments handed out by the conquerors from the North—and the people of North Vietnam would have had a chance to get rid of the shabby, impoverished relic of their Communist government.

Rolling Thunder revealed that there were serious shortcomings in contemporary USAF and Navy aircraft that needed to be rectified. But more than anything else, Rolling Thunder was a crash course for the North Vietnamese in strengthening their defenses. When the bombing of the North was resumed after an almost four-year interval, the North Vietnamese would possess the most sophisticated and powerful integrated air-defense system in history.

The Limits of Air Power, or the Limits of Political Will?

Some observers have used the Vietnam War as a measure of the limits of air power. To do so, they have thoughtfully considered the achievements of air power in the light of the objectives of the American commander in chief. Thus, for example, the use of United States air power in Vietnam during John F. Kennedy's brief tenure might be regarded as successful, as it helped sustain South Vietnamese morale at a time when there were rapid changes in the South Vietnamese government. In contrast, the employment of air power on a vastly greater scale would have to be considered as having limited success during President Johnson's tenure, because it failed to achieve Johnson's objective of stopping North Vietnamese efforts to subvert South Vietnam. During the Nixon presidency, air power was used as a lever to achieve his objective of permitting the United States to disengage formally from the war, and therefore should also be considered a success.

The difficulty with this approach is that it does not really measure the limits of air power, but measures instead the limits of the politicians who controlled its use. When politicians are too unknowledgeable about the use of air power, or are too timorous to employ air power to its full capability, it is unreasonable to say that it was the limitations of air power that precluded success. To repeat the obvious, the unsatisfactory results of the Vietnam War do not reflect the limitations of air power but do reflect the limitations of the politicians employing it for most of the war.

This assessment does not imply that air power is limitless in its power to achieve military results. Air power has to be properly applied by professional practitioners in circumstances in which they judge that it can prevail. The preceding paragraph *does* imply that in the Vietnam War, air power, properly applied, could have won that conflict for the United States and South Vietnam. To validate this point of view, it is necessary to review the effects of air power as applied to Linebacker and Linebacker II operations.

Air Power Unleashed: The Linebacker Operations

The most famous supply route in history, the Ho Chi Minh Trail, consisted of many supply lines that ranged from a foot track to paved roads, and included river passages. These lines led from ports in North Vietnam to a thousand distribution points in South Vietnam. There were three principal routes: The first trail ferried troops by truck to Laos, from which they infiltrated on foot into South Vietnam. The second trail also ran through Laos, and was used primarily by trucks crossing through the Mu Gia and Nape passes. The third route used both trucks and boats, and passed through Cambodia.[11]

The ability of American air power to stem the flow of supplies down the Ho Chi Minh Trail was irrevocably crippled when the decision was made not to attack shipping in Haiphong and other North Vietnamese ports. Instead of destroying supplies at their source and inhibiting their further importation, the civilian leaders in Washington elected to spend billions of dollars and far too much blood to interdict the Ho Chi Minh Trail. There resulted the curious spectacle of the most sophisticated aircraft, armament, and electronic equipment being directed against inexpensive Russian trucks, bicycles, and even porters carrying rice on their backs.

It was a losing battle, insane on the face of it, and recognized as futile by those who were tasked to fight it. Yet suppression of the Ho Chi Minh Trail, became, with the attempts to defeat Viet Cong and North Vietnamese troops in South Vietnam, the principal focus of American air power during the almost four years of the bombing halt. It was not a target that leaders in either the USAF or in naval aviation would have chosen; they knew that it was a misapplication of air power, and they bitterly resented its high costs in men, equipment, and ultimately, public esteem.

Early during this interval, in July 1969, Richard Nixon, making his first foreign trip as president, announced in a speech at Guam that "we will keep our treaty commitments" to Asian nations, but cautioned that "as far as the problems of internal security and military defense, except for a major power employing nuclear weapons, the United States . . . has a right to expect that this problem will be increasingly handled by . . . the Asian nations themselves."[12]

Nixon was moved to make this statement because after seven years of McNamara's guidance, the war was irrevocably lost politically no matter what happened in the field. The greatest evidence of this fact was the Tet Offensive, which was a crushing defeat for the Communist forces, who lost 45,000 killed of the 84,000 troops participating. Despite this terrible loss, media of the United States turned Tet from a crushing tactical defeat into a smashing strategic victory for the North Vietnamese. Just at the moment when the North Vietnamese were at their weakest and most vulnerable, they were gratuitously handed a propaganda victory that ultimately decided the outcome of the war.

The speech at Guam became known as the Nixon Doctrine and was interpreted, against protests to the contrary, that it meant that the United States was withdrawing support from Vietnam—which was indeed the case.

In two earlier statements, one by General Creighton Abrams in 1968, and another by Secretary of Defense Melvin Laird in the spring of 1969, the word "Vietnamization" was introduced. This became generally accepted as a code word for the training and reequipping of the South Vietnamese Army so that it could defend its homeland against North Vietnam without American forces, particularly air power, taking part. It also meant many other things, including improving the South Vietnamese political system and creating a viable economy.[13]

The United States continued engaging in both open and secret discussions with the North Vietnamese leaders. The American negotiating position was weakened by the progressive withdrawal of

United States forces that had fallen by April 1972 to 69,000, most of whom were not combat types. The North Vietnamese had been fighting for three decades, and their leaders, mostly military men, preferred a military victory that would cap their effort with glory, rather than a negotiated settlement, even if the ends they reached were the same.

It became evident in late 1971 that the North Vietnamese were going to invade South Vietnam. They also stepped up action in South Vietnam, shelling Saigon. The North Vietnamese anticipated that the prevalent antiwar feeling in the United States would preclude an American military response, particularly in the face of support for the offensive from China and the Soviet Union. They overlooked a factor that would be crucial. The regular troops of the North Vietnamese Army would require vastly greater quantities of supplies than that required by the Viet Cong guerrillas. It would be essential to keep a steady flow of fuel, munitions, and food to keep them fit for battle.

The offensive opened on March 30, 1972, and while the North Vietnamese advanced in a three-pronged drive and succeeded in defeating the initial ARVN forces, the offensive soon fell into a pattern. The North Vietnamese advance ran out of steam for lack of supplies, ARVN resistance stiffened, and United States air power, newly recalled to the region, forced the North Vietnamese to withdraw, pursued by ARVN forces. When the offensive ended, both sides claimed victory, but two facts had emerged. The first was that North Vietnam retained large areas of South Vietnamese territory, enabling it to prepare for another invasion. The second was that Vietnamization had failed because American air power was still the *sine qua non* of South Vietnamese resistance.[14]

The code name for the employment of American air power was Linebacker, a tip of the hat to Nixon's fondness for football. In March, additional fighters were flown into the theater, followed by a massive buildup of bombers in April and May. These aircraft were augmented by six carriers, *Constellation, Coral Sea, Kitty Hawk, Hancock, Midway,* and *Saratoga* on station in the Gulf of Tonkin.

Unlike Rolling Thunder, Linebacker was not designed to send a message but to deliver ordnance that would slow down, then halt the invasion, and force the North Vietnamese to negotiate a peace settlement. Linebacker featured strikes on the standard North Vietnamese targets including transportation, petroleum storage, and power generation, but was expanded to mining harbors and rivers.

Air power was once again in the hands of politicians, but politicians of a different mind-set. While it is true that Secretary of Defense Laird and the Director of the Central Intelligence Agency, Richard Helms, were still cautious about provoking China and the Soviet Union and believed that the battle had to be won in South Vietnam, Nixon and his Secretary of State, Henry Kissinger, were determined not to take half measures.[15] Nonetheless, half measures were taken, as the bulk of the bombing was assigned once again to fighter-bombers. The B-52s were assigned targets north of the Demilitarized Zone, but were not to attack Hanoi and Haiphong.

The order for Linebacker was signed on May 8, issued with some assurance because of the bold and quite successful diplomatic initiatives Nixon had undertaken with both the Soviet Union and Red China. The president was confident that neither country would make more than pro-forma objections to a new bombing campaign.

Except for the failure to apply the full strength of the B-52 weapon, Linebacker represented in large part what the Joint Chiefs of Staff had wanted to do since 1964. The attacks began on May 10, and featured a glimpse into warfare's future with the employment of both electro-optically and laser-guided bombs. Among their achievements was the destruction of the previously invulnerable Paul Doumer bridge.

The results of Linebacker became evident early in June, as enemy columns suffered supply shortages, and the ARVN were able to score more successes. For many observers, this made Linebacker an even more significant demonstration of air power than Linebacker II. The North Vietnamese indicated their willingness to resume peace talks, and when these seemed to be making satisfactory progress, Nixon called a bombing halt in October as a gesture of goodwill.

As in every previous bombing halt, the North Vietnamese interpreted the gesture as a sign of weakness and became less cooperative at the peace table even as they accelerated building a store of supplies for a renewed offensive.

Linebacker II

The North Vietnamese had enjoyed "political air superiority" for most of the war. The term is an odious one, as it reveals that political shortsightedness handed air superiority to the enemy even as thousands of lives and billions of dollars were being spent in the air war. Linebacker and Linebacker II reversed the situation, seizing air superiority and making the most of it. President Nixon now used air power as had been advocated by General Curtis LeMay in 1963, and subsequently by Generals John P. McConnell, Earle Wheeler, and John Ryan, along with Admiral U. S. Grant Sharp. Air power was to be directed at its highest intensity and in all its forms against the enemy's most important political and military targets. The object was perhaps ignoble: to force the enemy to agree to allow the United States to withdraw under the umbrella of a formal peace treaty, rather than simply to be thrown out of the country militarily.

The Paris peace negotiations broke down on December 13, 1972, and President Nixon issued an ultimatum to the Democratic Republic of Vietnam (DRV) that it must return to the negotiating tables within seventy-two hours—or severe measures would be taken. Hanoi rejected the ultimatum, and Nixon ordered that the full array of United States air power be assembled for Linebacker II. (As the South Vietnamese, fearing betrayal, had also withdrawn from the talks, Linebacker II was designed to reassure them, so that they would agree to a settlement.)

The force included Boeing B-52s, General Dynamics F-111s, McDonnell Douglas F-4s, Vought A-7s, McDonnell Douglas EB-66s, Republic F-105 Wild Weasels, Douglas A-4s, Grumman A-6s, Vought F-8s, and a complete array of tanker, search and rescue, and electronic countermeasure aircraft.

The principal weight of the attack was to come from B-52s attacking targets in Hanoi and Haiphong. The first day called for 129 B-52 sorties; the second for 93, and the third for 99. Then B-52 pressure would be applied at the highest level possible.

Mines were sewn in Haiphong harbor on December 14, and the first B-52 in the bomber force took off from Andersen Air Base on Guam on December 18. The raids would be a learning experience for SAC, which had dictated that the bombers were not to take evasive action from either SAMs or MiGs on the long run in from the Initial Point (IP) to bomb release. This costly measure was enforced to ensure that the main targets were hit with a minimum of collateral damage.

With four years to prepare, and a very limited geographical area to defend, the North Vietnamese were ready with the most powerful integrated air-defense system in history.

On the first night of operations, three B-52s were shot down by SAMs out of the 129 engaged in the mission, for a 2.3-percent loss rate. SAC rigidity was revealed on the second day, when the ninety-one missions were run with exactly the same procedures—aircraft attacking in three-ship cells (radar formations) over a seventy-mile-long axis. This time six B-52s were shot down and a seventh badly damaged—an unacceptable 6.6-percent loss rate, and 7.7-percent loss rate if the badly damaged aircraft is counted.

The losses dictated a change in tactics, and on each of the next two nights, only thirty-three B-52s attacked, and emphasis was shifted to destroying SAM installations and storage facilities. From December 20 to December 24, three more B-52s were shot down, but enemy resistance was perceptibly weakening.[16]

After a thirty-six-hour stand-down for Christmas, bombing was resumed, with the intensity and the focus of the bombing stunning North Vietnamese leaders, who for the first time could see real air power in action.

December 26 saw renewed bombing, with new tactics. This time 120 B-52s struck ten different targets within a fifteen-minute period—the results were devastating, and the North Vietnamese leaders inquired of Washington if January 8 would be a suitable day for resuming negotiations. Two more B-52s were lost to SAMs, a sad but acceptable 1.7-percent loss rate.

Sixty B-52 sorties were flown in each of the next three nights, with the last two B-52s being lost on December 27. North Vietnam was defenseless; its SAM inventory had been depleted, and its remaining MiGs were a negligible force.

Linebacker II was the very essence of air power influencing history: North Vietnam agreed to all of Washington's requirements for beginning negotiations again, and President Nixon ordered the end of Linebacker II by forbidding all bombing above the Twentieth Parallel.

The B-52s had flown 729 sorties, dropped 15,000 tons of bombs, with 15 B-52s shot down for an overall loss rate of 2.0 percent. The North Vietnamese had fired 1,240 SAMs to destroy the fifteen B-52s, a kill rate of 1.2 percent. Twelve other aircraft were lost in the supporting missions.

The bombing brought tremendous joy to one portion of Hanoi's population—the prisoners of war who had been treated so cruelly for so long. Later, upon their release after the armistice, they reported the pure ecstasy in hearing the B-52s' bombs, and in seeing the terror in the eyes of their guards, some of whom sought refuge in the prisoners' cells.

Vice Admiral James B. Stockdale, a prisoner of war and a Medal of Honor recipient, had this to say about the effects of the bombing: "One look at any Vietnamese officer's face told the whole story. It telegraphed hopelessness, accommodation, remorse, fear. The shock was there; our enemy's will was broken."[17]

The USAF had proved that B-52s, supported by tactical air assets, were able to meet and decisively defeat the enemy. The result of Linebacker II was exactly what had been predicted by those who had advocated the full application of air power against North Vietnam: a military victory. If, as could have readily been done, the B-52 campaign had been extended, it could have attacked the previously off-limit dikes and continued to plow the rubble of urban and industrial areas. The result would have been a complete crippling of the North Vietnamese economy, as limited as it had been. The North Vietnamese could then have been subject to invasion by ARVN forces supported by United States air power. The South Vietnamese could at the very least have retaken the areas that the North Vietnamese had occupied during the two 1972 offensives.

The Paris Peace Accords were signed on January 27, 1973, and within sixty days, 591 American prisoners of war had been released and were back in the United States. American forces continued their drawdown, with the principal effort being Military Airlift Command aircraft attempting to recoup some small portion of the vast amounts of supplies still stored in South Vietnam.

In the spring of 1975, after waiting for what Secretary of State Henry Kissinger described as "a decent interval" of about two years, Hanoi knew that it no longer faced a threat of retaliation from United States air power. It invaded South Vietnam and entered Saigon on April 30, 1975, uniting the two Vietnams under Hanoi's totalitarian control.[18]

There are many who argue that Linebacker II could have been launched in 1964 or 1965, when there were far fewer North Vietnamese defenses, and would have achieved a military victory. There might well have been associated political and military costs, but had air power been used as it could have been used in 1964, and was used in 1972, the war would have cost far less in lives, money, and civil unrest. Others maintain that the war in Vietnam could never have been won, no matter how air power had been applied. When one considers the results of Linebacker II, and the possible outcome of its extension over even a few weeks, it is difficult to accept the latter argument.

Conclusion

For the purposes of this book, the Vietnam War has to be regarded as an example of the way in which the misuse of air power influenced history. The most unfortunate humanitarian aspect is that the failure to use air power properly resulted in the consignment of all of the people of Vietnam to the Communist camp, keeping them there long after the Communist system had imploded in the Soviet Union. Now, as Red China moves more toward a capitalistic economic system, Vietnam remains with Cuba as a vestigial remnant of the failed Communist system.

Chapter Eleven

Post World War II Middle-East Conflicts, Terror, and the Modern Air War

The Israeli Defense Force Air Force (IDF/AF) was quite literally born in battle, and while it did not have decisive effect on the 1948-49 war of independence that established Israel as a sovereign state, it did dictate how Israel would subsequently develop and use its air force. The exercise of that air force's power would become a determining factor in the subsequent history of the Middle East, and indeed, the world. It would not only influence the action of Israel's Arab enemies, it would become of considerable and sometimes overriding importance to France, Britain, the United States, and the Soviet Union. In addition, the technological by-products of the Israeli Air Force would be sought by many nations, including China and North Korea.

At the birth of its independence, Israel was less than 270 miles long at its extreme points, and less than fifteen miles wide at its narrowest point. This diminutive size posed almost insuperable problems for its ground forces, which could be attacked anywhere around its perimeter, but offered a tremendous advantage to its Air Force, which could depart the country in an instant in any direction to attack its foes. (The small size of the country was a double-edged sword, however, for the Air Force had little time in which to react to an attack. One Israeli officer said that "Israel is like a stationary aircraft carrier, permanently stationed in hostile waters.")

Israel's first major exercise in the use of air power came in the Suez Canal fiasco. The president of Egypt, Gamal Abdel Nasser, who continually threatened Israel with extinction, had sponsored fedayeen terrorist attacks and formed a military alliance with Syria. The

Soviet Union sought to extend its influence in the Middle East by funneling massive military aid to Egypt, including great quantities of armor and two hundred modern jet aircraft. Emboldened, Nasser nationalized the Suez Canal on July 26, 1956, and announced the abrogation of the Anglo-Egyptian treaty.

France and Britain, both infuriated and mortified, solicited Israel's help in a joint operation. It happened that Israel had already determined to take military action against Egypt, Syria, and Jordan, who had formed a joint military command to attack Israel.

At 3:00 P.M. on October 29, 1955, the Israelis launched an aerial attack, disrupting Egyptian communications and dropping 395 men of the crack Israeli 202nd Parachute Brigade at the entrance to Mitla Pass, deep in the Sinai desert. Future Prime Minister Lieutenant Colonel Ariel ("Arik") Sharon commanded the 202nd. Following up with a series of swift military movements, the Israelis conquered the entire Sinai as well as the Gaza Strip.

The French and British then played their cards, calling for a withdrawal of both Egyptian and Israeli forces, and making a massive air attack that destroyed more than a hundred Egyptian aircraft. On November 5, an invasion followed, intended to take the Suez Canal and reverse Nasser's nationalization.

To the utter amazement of France and Britain, the United States and the Soviet Union joined together in the United Nations Security Council to denounce their actions. Britain immediately agreed to a humiliating cease-fire, and France soon followed suit. What had started off as an incisive Anglo-French military operation to seize the Suez ended in a fiasco that vastly increased the prestige of Nasser in the Arab world.

The Anglo-French debacle was a perfect illustration of ill-founded confidence in the influence of air power. The combined air power of France, Britain, and Israel was dominant over Egypt—but impotent in the halls of the UN. Nonetheless, the stage was set for a demonstration of the influence and the decisiveness of air power in the next Arab/Israeli war.

The Six-Day War, June 1967

Despite—or perhaps because of—Nasser's constant threats to obliterate Israel, his prestige began to dim by 1967, and he found himself at odds with much of the Arab world, including Yemen, Saudi Arabia, and Jordan. In an effort to regain his popularity, he placed seven divisions, with close to 85,000 men, on the Israeli border, and closed the Straits of Tiran to Israel, an act of war that defied the mandate of the United Nations.

King Hussein of Jordan placed Jordan's armed forces under Nasser's command, and Iraq did the same. Other Arab states sent contingents of troops, arms, and funds as a gesture of support of the one aim upon which all agreed: the destruction of Israel.

The crisis was aggravated when French President Charles de Gaulle sought to curry favor with the Arab nations by cutting off all weapon supplies to Israel, for many years the primary customer for French export arms. The Egyptian threat soon built to an intolerable level (more than 100,000 men, 900 tanks, 1,000 artillery pieces, and 385 combat aircraft, mostly late model MiG-17, -19, and -21 fighters). The Soviet Union supplied Tupolev Tu 16 and Ilyushin Il-28 jet bombers that could reach Tel Aviv within minutes after take-off from Egyptian airfields.

The fate of Israel was about to be decided in a conflict of power personalities. The charismatic Israeli Minister of Defense, Moshe Dayan, knew that the situation was far more critical than it had been in 1956, but he was held back by the curiously passive actions of Israeli Prime Minister Levi Eshkol. Yitzhak Rabin, the IDF Chief of Staff, supported Eshkol in his surprising restraint. The situation in fact overstressed Rabin, who suffered a nervous collapse that caused him to be replaced by the much more aggressive Major General Ezer Weizman, who had commanded the IDF/AF from 1956 to 1966.

Weizman agreed with Dayan about the crisis they faced, and they, with the commander of the IDF/AF, Brigadier General Mordechai Hod, developed plans for a preemptive strike, which they believed to be the only solution to their dilemma.

As a result of this planning, the IDF/AF began the war on June 5, 1967, with a devastating series of attacks. Ten waves of forty Dassault fighters and fighter-bombers took off in ten-minute intervals, one flight for each of the most important Egyptian airfields. As soon as the bombs were dropped and the ammunition exhausted in strafing runs, the planes returned to be rearmed and refueled at breakneck speed for another sortie, with Jordanian and Syrian targets now included. By nightfall, more than 1,000 Israeli sorties had destroyed

350 enemy aircraft, demolished their airfields, and left their armor open for attack. On June 10, the totally defeated Arab nations sullenly accepted a UN-imposed cease-fire.[1]

The effect upon history was fantastic, and continues to this day. For the first time in its existence, Israel had borders that prevented its being overrun by armor in a single day. The Suez Canal became (until 1973) the world's most effective anti-tank trap. But perhaps more important than anything else, the war moved the Soviet Union firmly into the Middle East picture, as it once again rallied to the support of Arab states, providing them with unlimited arms for the next round in the battle.

Israel, deprived of arms from France, turned to the United States for equipment, receiving the remarkable Douglas A-4H Skyhawk and McDonnell F-4E Phantom aircraft to replace their Dassault-built fighters. The economic and political implications of this new flow of arms were enormously important for the future, for the Middle East was now as critical a point of potential conflict for the two superpowers as Southeast Asia.

The War of Attrition, July 1967 to August 1970

The Soviet Union always gave assistance with a heavy hand of advice accompanied by attempts to insinuate its culture as well as its military and political philosophy into the client nations. Even as it provided the Arab states with modern aircraft, armor, and artillery, it offered new ideas. One was critically important. It was the Soviet contention that masses of surface-to-air missiles (SAMs) could neutralize the Israeli air superiority. Arab ground forces, with their vastly superior numbers, could then overwhelm their common enemy.

The effectiveness of the idea was tested during the so-called War of Attrition, with its continuous exchange of artillery fire and the heavy losses inflicted on the Israeli Air Force by SAMs. The three-year battle became a training ground for the Yom Kippur War of 1973, for it showed that one form of air power, massive amounts of antiaircraft artillery and SAMs, could neutralize the traditional form of aerial bombardment. The Soviet Union, understanding that there was no conceivable way that Arab air forces could ever match either the training or the *élan* of the Israeli Air Force, counseled Egypt and Syria on the wisdom of accepting huge quantities of antiaircraft and SAMs to create virtually impenetrable defenses. They also sent destabilizing weapons such as Scud missiles, a primitive development of the German V-2 but still a factor to contend with in the Middle East today.

The gifts were laden by thousands of Soviet advisors, and by an increasing Soviet say in Arab policy, including veto rights on the firing of Scud missiles.

As has happened so often in history, personal elements combined to affect the exercise of air power, and its subsequent influence on history. In this case, the President of Egypt, Anwar Sadat, saw the logic of the Soviet advice, and decided to adopt it in a plan that called not for the invasion and defeat of Israel—as everyone demanded—but instead for the seizure of a strip of land on the eastern side of the Suez Canal. Sadat planned a war of limited scope and duration—his aim was to regain Arab dignity by seizing a portion of the Sinai, then force a diplomatic settlement in the United Nations that would require Israel to return the Sinai to Egypt. Sadat, by force of his personality and by limited disclosure, kept his idea secret from almost everyone, an exceedingly rare event in Arab politics. This secrecy extended even to his Syrian ally, President Hafiz al-Assad, who would be furious when he finally discovered that Sadat's objectives were so limited.

Sadat's wily insight that a political solution could be achieved by combining those limited war objectives with a sophisticated integrated defense system was complemented perfectly by Israeli hubris. After the smashing victory of the Six Day War, the Israeli military, and even the nation of Israel, suffered from what the pre-Midway Japanese called "the victory disease"—an utter assurance that they could not be defeated. Israel persisted in this delusion even after the War of Attrition, where it failed to pick up on the potential of mass SAM defenses, and the requirement of electronic equipment to suppress enemy missile radar. This was a massive failure not only of intelligence but also of leadership, for Israeli leaders continued to emphasize the acquisition of armor over virtually every other arm.

Israeli intelligence assumed that the Egyptians would not go to war until the Arab air forces were able to gain air superiority over Israel. They knew that this objective had not been achieved, and therefore ignored the obvious military buildup on its frontiers with Egypt and Syria, attributing them to routine maneuvers.[2]

Egypt and Syria had not only imported vast quantities of Soviet supplies, they had greatly improved the fighting qualities of their armies. They launched their war of revenge at two o'clock in the afternoon of October 6, 1973. In the east, Egyptian forces swarmed across the Suez Canal. In the north, well-trained and well-led Syrian forces swept down toward the Golan Heights. Both Egyptian and Syrian troops fought well, surprising the Israeli Army with defeat in every battle, and most important of all, bringing their incredible antiaircraft and SAM defenses along with them.

Israel expected the usual formula to apply: the Israeli Air Force would first blunt the Arab attack, then destroy the Arab Air Force and prepare the way for the Israeli Army counterattack. None of this happened, for the Soviet Union had advised Sadat correctly: Arab antiaircraft artillery and SAMs shot the Israeli Air Force out of the sky, while their newly inspired armies gave the Israeli ground forces more than they could handle. The Israeli armored forte of the past, the slashing tank counterattack, proved useless, as the Arab soldiers were provided with masses of anti-tank missiles that turned the Israeli tanks into blazing torches. The anti-tank weapon system that proved so deadly to Israeli armor was called the Sagger. The Sagger was a wire-guided missile literally flown by a gunner who operated a joystick, watching the missile's flight and steering it right/left/up/down toward the target. The Sagger had an effective range of about a mile, perfect for desert terrain. Because the "gunner/pilot" could be located up to a hundred yards from the missile launcher, the Sagger was fairly safe to fire. Infantrymen carried the whole system in a suitcase-size package. The Arab forces thus added the densest anti-tank missile defense capability to their highly effective air-defense system.

The Arab forces could probably have completely overrun the state of Israel within a few days, but were held back by Sadat's strategy of just taking a strip of the Sinai and holding it. Even so, the Israeli High Command had vastly underestimated its requirements for ammunition and for aircraft losses and was rapidly approaching the dreaded "red-line," the point where there were no longer sufficient supplies and ammunition to keep on fighting.

Israel turned to the United States, and after much argument, succeeded in obtaining an airlift of supplies that eventually helped it turn the tide. Implicit in Israel's demand for assistance was the threat to use its nuclear weapons if all else failed.

The American decision to provide an airlift signaled to the world its support of Israel, while its Lockheed C-5s and C-141s brought in lifesaving amounts of ammunition and supplies. This assistance enabled Israel to reverse the tide of the war by an inversion of tactics. In the past, Israeli aircraft had always cleared the way for Israeli armor. The reverse was now true. Israeli armor lashed out to destroy the Egyptian SAM missile batteries, thus allowing the Israeli Air Force to conduct the kind of campaign it preferred against Egyptian armor and entrenched positions.

Amid the clamor of war, the threat of ultimate air power manifested itself twice. The first was Israel's threat to use nuclear weapons that had two great effects. It let it be known (allegedly through a known Russian mole in Israeli intelligence) that it intended to use nuclear weapons against Damascus if the Syrian attack was not halted, and for otherwise inexplicable reasons, the Syrian forces retreated. Israel's threat was also made known to Washington, and is considered by many historians to be the vital factor in expediting the airlift that followed.

The second near-instance of using ultimate air power came when the United States responded to a perceived Soviet threat by issuing a Defense Readiness Condition (Def Con) III alert about midnight on October 24. This action placed the nation in a state of increased readiness, and might have triggered a Soviet response that could have heightened the crisis. Fortunately in both instances, the crises passed without resort to nuclear arms.[3]

The war came to an end when Israeli forces at last broke through Arab lines and surrounded Egyptian forces in the east while routing Syrian forces in the north. On October 28, Egyptian and Israeli military officials met for the first time in twenty-five years to discuss disengagement. An agonizingly slow armistice process followed under UN jurisdiction in which the combatant forces were gradually drawn apart with UN peacekeeping forces acting as a buffer.

Despite the ultimate military defeat, Sadat had achieved most of his goals, and on March 26, 1979, signed a peace treaty for Egypt with Israel in the White House, under President Jimmy Carter's beaming smile. It was a partial step toward peace, but one that left the problem of Palestine unresolved.

In the following years, Israel continued to depend upon its Air Force for military superiority in the Middle East, but took care to improve its capability against antiaircraft and SAM defenses.

In 1981, the Israeli Air Force undertook a mission whose implications for history can never be fully measured. It sent six McDonnell

Douglas F-15s and eight General Dynamics F-16s from its Etzion Air Base in the Sinai to bomb an Iraqi nuclear power plant twelve miles south of Baghdad. The purpose was to prevent Iraq from developing a nuclear weapon. The F-16s dropped a total of sixteen one-ton bombs on the reactor dome and its surrounding buildings. The attack removed Iraq's immediate capability to build a bomb, and delayed any such activity for years. Although the strike received international condemnation as a violation of Iraq's sovereignty, its colossal importance was not fully appreciated until the Persian Gulf War in 1991, when Iraqi possession of a nuclear weapon might have permanently altered the political and military dynamics of the Middle East. It is, of course, even more important today.

Nonetheless, the limits of air power have been clearly defined in the Middle East. The Israeli Air Force is able to maintain Israel's sovereignty by preventing its Arab neighbors from (to date) launching another major war against it. The IDF/AF scored the most one-sided victory in modern aviation history with its savage defeat of the Syrian Air Force in August 1982, shooting down eighty-five fighters and great numbers of helicopters without suffering a single loss.[4] The air battle was a part of the ill-starred struggle by Israel to eliminate Palestinian Liberation Organization (PLO) forces in Lebanon. And, while called upon for reprisal efforts, air power is obviously not a tool that can resolve the problems still presented by the Palestinian question.

Before turning to another area of Middle Eastern warfare, it will be seen below that Israel showed the greatest restraint imaginable during the 1991 Persian Gulf War, by refusing to have the IDF/AF intervene even when Scud missiles were falling on Israeli territory.

Air Power in the Iraq-Iran War, 1980-88

The vast distance between the Western and the Middle Eastern military mind-set was demonstrated by the manner in which air power was either ill-used or ignored in the long, eight-year struggle between Iraq and Iran.

By his ruthless suppression of opposition, Saddam Hussein had turned Iraq into a compliant police state; his opposition was purged with a thorough ferocity that made Stalin's similar efforts in the 1930s seem merciful. It was his grandiose intent to conquer Iran as a first step toward dominating the Arab world, and presenting Iraq as a superpower equivalent to the United States or the USSR.

Iraq attacked Iran, which was four times its size and had three times the population, as a means of settling old political and religious scores and taking advantage of the unrest caused by the removal of the Shah and the beginning of the Ayatollah Ruhollah Kohmeini's regime. In 1980, both countries had sizeable air forces. The Iranian Islamic Air Force (IIAF) had 77 Grumman F-14A Tomcats for home defense, 188 McDonnell Douglas Phantom II fighter-bombers, and 166 Northrop F-5E/F fighter-bombers, along with a surprisingly large inventory of support aircraft that included tankers. The Iraqi Air Force (IQAF) was equipped with 300 combat aircraft, including 80 MiG-23 fighter-bombers, 40 Sukhoi Su-7b fighter-bombers, 40 Sukhoi Su-20 fighter-bombers, and 115 MiG-21 fighter-interceptors.[5]

The opening attack by the IQAF drew on lessons hard learned in the Arab/Israeli war of 1967. Iraqi planes attacked ten different Iranian airfields on September 22, 1980, while Iraqi armor drove into disputed border territory.

There followed an eight-year-long struggle in which the respective air forces flew many missions against enemy targets, but always on a small scale, usually with no more than six aircraft involved. Neither side attempted to gain air superiority by eliminating the enemy in air combat, and, in truth, the airmen of neither side showed either desire or aptitude for battle. The training and tactics that the United States had provided the Royal Iranian Air Force had residual effect with the Islamic Iranian Air Force, and gradually the Iranians gained dominance over the Iraqi Air Force, which, as it would in its next war, dispersed its aircraft to neutral countries to escape attack. Neither side practiced the use of air power in support of ground attacks. Despite the inclusion of terror tactics involving Scud missiles and chemical weapons, air power became a virtual non-issue in the war. Some observers believed that both sides regarded air power as a means not to win the war, but instead as a measure to avoid losing it.[6] One of the major ironies of the war was the clandestine maintenance support Israel provided Iran to keep its aircraft and other sophisticated weapons operating.

The difficulty in understanding the misuse of air power by both Iraq and Iran is found in the general difficulty of the Western mind to understand the Muslim culture. What the West defined as misuse was apparently the correct use to both Iraq and Iran. It is a mystery to the West, but no greater mystery than the fact that the two nations, with their long history of hostility, could endure an eight-year war with its many thousands of casualties, and yet still be able to rally to the common causes of obliterating Israel and opposing the United States. Ultimately Iraq (with, ironically enough, the help of United States intelligence and weaponry) wore Iran down and led to a peace that did not significantly alter the pre-war conditions.

The ill use of air power in the Iran and Iraq war would serve as a backdrop to the creation of a new definition of air power in the Persian Gulf War.

The United States Reinvention of Air Power after Vietnam

Earlier passages in this book have called attention to the fact that individuals can often shape the development and exercise of a nation's air power. Nowhere was this fact more spectacularly true than in the air forces of the United States in the post-Vietnam era.

There were many reasons for this situation, not least of which was the bitterness about the way air power had been misapplied in the Vietnam War. Added to this controversy was the general demand that new aircraft be developed to overcome the deficiencies of those used in Southeast Asia. Thus aircraft such as the McDonnell Douglas F-15 Eagle, General Dynamics F-16 Fighting Falcon, Fairchild Republic A-10 Thunderbolt II, and Grumman F-14 Tomcat would emerge as a fourth generation of jet aircraft, superior to the latest generation of aircraft of all nations, including those of the Soviet Union.

The demand for new aircraft was complemented by the realization that much of the new technology developed in the later years of the Vietnam War—including precision-guided munitions and equipment to suppress enemy air defenses—could be further exploited. Another capability, stealth, was also in the works, unknown to all but a few.

In the United States Air Force there was a major revolution in leadership underway. The Air Force had been dominated by "bomber generals" for generations, from the very first Chief of Staff, General Carl A. Spaatz, in September 1947, down through the ninth chief, General David C. Jones, in 1974.

Jones was a visionary leader who also had a sure political instinct. He introduced significant organizational changes not only within the Air Force, but later, as two-term Chairman of the Joint Chiefs of Staff (JCS), in other services, and in NATO. Many of his concepts were incorporated into the important Goldwater-Nichols Act of 1987 that increased the power of the JCS and placed greater war-making capability in the hands of theater commanders.

Jones also had a technical bent, and championed the development of airborne command and control aircraft and precision-guided munitions. He thus started the transition from the typical bomber-oriented air force to an air force of the space age, a critical factor whose fruits would first be realized in the Persian Gulf War.

Jones changed the climate of the Air Staff so much that he was succeeded as Chief by General Lew Allen Jr., a scientist with a doctorate in nuclear physics. Allen advocated the development of cruise missiles, satellite programs, and such new weapons as the McDonnell Douglas F-15, General Dynamics F-16, and Rockwell B-1B.

The cycle of change was completed in 1982, when a veteran fighter pilot, the well-liked General Charles A. Gabriel, became Chief of Staff. From that point on, the Air Force became increasingly a "fighter air force" in contrast to its earlier years. Every Chief of Staff who followed Gabriel came from the fighter-pilot community.

It was perhaps inevitable that the revolution in planning and equipping for modern war should come from that community. The Strategic Air Command had been the dominant factor for years and had done its job perfectly by deterring war. As time passed, however, SAC became rigid and doctrinaire and thus far less likely to produce the next generation of planners who would be receptive to the advent of space-related weaponry and to new ideas in management. Had the reverse been true, had fighter advocates dominated for all those years, it would have been the bomber advocates who came up with the new and the revolutionary ideas. And it may well be that this very process is working now, with new ideas for the employment of bombers beginning to take precedence over the fighter.

General Wilbur ("Bill") Creech was the fighter pilot who orchestrated the revolution in Air Force management, demonstrating his technique as Commander, Tactical Air Command. Creech preached decentralization of management to obtain the maximum flexibility, responsiveness, and feeling of "ownership" by the air and ground crews. He advocated obtaining both leadership and commitment from everyone at every level. Finally, he insisted on planning for the highest quality in every action from painting barracks to attacking a target.

Bill Creech also led in military tactics, insisting on ultrarealistic training and emphasizing that modern antiaircraft artillery and SAM defenses made the previous "go-low" tactics obsolete. He insisted instead on the development of means to take out enemy SAMs in the first attack so that subsequent aircraft could operate at either high or low altitudes according to their assessment of the target. These tactics would pay off in the Persian Gulf War, and Creech would be recognized as their author by no less a person than General Charles A. ("Chuck") Horner, the air commander.[7]

Air-Power Philosophers in the Modern Era

The first two generations of air-power philosophers were relatively few in number, and for the most part practitioners rather than academics. The first generation included Douhet, Trenchard, and Mitchell whose concepts were put into use in one form or another by military men of the second generation, including Arnold, Walker, Hansell, Kuter, Harris, Yamamoto, and others. One of the best known of the second generation philosophers was Alexander P. de Seversky, whose real merit lay not with his ideas, most of which were derivative, but in his genius to put those ideas in front of the American public. The third generation of philosophers did not have much of a philosophy to boast about, for theirs was the era of mutual assured destruction, of which the premier advocate was General Curtis LeMay.

But beginning with the Vietnam War, there emerged a host of philosophers, academics for the most part, but with many of the academics being military officers. Air-power philosophy and doctrine began to be evaluated and written about much as were other academic disciplines, with seminars, papers, journals, and books appearing in droves. Often of the highest caliber, some of the work was devoted to analyzing the philosophers of the past, some to deducing an air-power philosophy from past campaigns, and some to prophesying the future of air power. Many of them have been cited in the present work, and they include in part works by John Boyd, Mark A. Clodfelter, Benjamin S. Lambeth, Phillip S. Meilinger, Karl P. Mueller, and John Warden.

These philosophers were faced with a far different and more receptive world than their predecessors in many respects, for their audience included an intelligent and well-read population of military leaders who accepted the concept of air power for the most part, and were willing to have its nuances examined. In biblical terms, if Douhet, Mitchell, and Trenchard were St. John the Baptist announcing a coming, the current air-power philosophers are more in the mode of St. Augustine, preaching to a (not always receptive) choir.

In at least one instance, a philosopher of air power had the pleasure of seeing the ideas he put forward as theory materialize as fact in actual combat. This philosopher was Colonel John Warden, who flew 226 combat missions in Vietnam as a forward air controller, and later commanded the 36th Tactical Fighter Wing at Bitburg Air Base, Germany.

Colonel Warden asserted in his 1988 book *The Air Campaign: Planning for Combat* that aerospace leaders should focus on translating national political objectives and strategic military goals into theater campaign plans. As logical as this assertion sounds, it was rarely practiced in the past. Warden believed that air power could achieve those objectives and goals swiftly and at minimum costs. Just as Douhet, Mitchell, and Trenchard had emphasized "vital centers," Warden emphasized striking at the enemy's center of gravity (COG), i.e. attacking the enemy where he is most vulnerable, and where an attack will be decisive. (This is the opposite of the great nineteenth-century military philosopher Carl von Clausewitz's concept of the center of gravity, which was always the center of greatest strength.)

Warden developed a model of five concentric rings. Each ring depicted individual COGs, ranging outward from leadership at the center to successive rings of organic essentials, infrastructures, population, and fielded forces.[8]

Given today's capabilities with stealth aircraft and precision-guided munitions, it was Warden's belief that well-planned strikes could take out the leadership ring, not necessarily by killing everyone involved, but by cutting off their ability to control their forces and thus inducing a physical paralysis that would lead to surrender. His thesis also included the idea that successful removal of other COGs (for example, fielded forces) would put the leadership under such severe psychological pressure that the same sort of paralysis would ensue.

Warden put forward his ideas in the Pentagon's famed Directorate of Plans ("Checkmate") Division, and they were adopted for the first phase of Operation Desert Storm against Iraq in the Persian Gulf War, so he was perhaps the only air-power philosopher who saw his ideas promptly executed in action, at least in part. Critics of Warden's plan (called "Instant Thunder" to contrast it to "Rolling Thunder" of the Vietnam War) considered it too optimistic, and faulted it for failing to consider ground operations sufficiently. The most glaring defect, and one that resonates even at the time of this writing, is that the air campaign was not designed to remove Iraqui leader Saddam Hussein from power, and of course, did not do so. It may be that the greatest benefit of Warden's planning and philosophy was that it put the USAF on course for a sudden and massive attack on Iraq and its forces, rather than falling prey to the "Rolling Thunderish" plan of gradually escalating attacks that the Tactical Air Command had hurriedly put forward.[9]

In the end, Warden's plan was retained in part, with one of his Checkmate planners, then-Lieutenant Colonel David A. Deptula, serving as part of a planning staff. This staff assisted Brigadier General Buster C. Glosson in meeting the demand for an executable air campaign.

In looking back over air-power philosophy, however, one finds that although the terms may be different, the basic idea has remained the same: air power permits the avoidance of a long war and high attrition by striking at the heart of the enemy and paralyzing his ability to fight. The greatest differences lie not in the philosophies of various periods, but in the means that philosophers of those periods had at hand. If, for example, Trenchard had somehow been presented with stealth bombers and precision-guided munitions, he would almost certainly have modified his plans from attacking industrial centers to making exactly the same sort of surgical strikes that Warden and others now call for. The same is true for Douhet, Mitchell, Arnold, Harris, LeMay, and the others. They articulated philosophies of air power based on the resources that were available to them, or, more accurately, that they thought they could obtain in the relatively near future. Not one of these leaders would have preferred to slaughter tens of thousands of soldiers and civilians if they could instead have killed the ten or twenty key people who stood in the way of peace. The means were simply not available to them, and hence their philosophies of air power were bound to be less precise.

The most important fact to focus upon in considering the relative merit of the various philosophies of air power is that the means to achieve true air power did not occur until 1945, and the means to achieve true air power without the use of nuclear weapons did not occur until 1991.

Sadly, the means to achieve true air power may not be available to future leaders, not because of a loss of technical expertise, but because of the change in the nature of warfare. With the battle no longer between alliances of great nations, or between two superpowers, or even between a great power and a rogue state such as Iraq, but instead between the civilized world and terrorists, even modern stealth and precision-guided weapons may not be the answer. The concept of killing or paralyzing the leaders of a nation is not fully equivalent to the killing of the leaders of an extraterritorial organization such as al-Qaeda. The difference lies in the nature of the commitment of those led to their leaders' cause. It may even become the case that the leaders will not be able to control their followers, and that death or "paralysis" of a few leaders will mean nothing at all in terms of ending the struggle.

Ironically, with the persistent and increasing threat of rogue nations developing weapons of mass destruction, the industrialized nations may be thrust back into an age when the chosen response will inevitably be nuclear weapons, with the contemporary concerns about collateral damage ruthlessly put aside in the battle for survival.

Air Power in the Persian Gulf War

It is far too early to assess the influence of air power on history in terms of the Gulf War, but it is possible to examine the effect of air power on the outcome of that war, upon the Cold War, and upon subsequent Major Regional Contingencies (MRC). The survey will also give insight into the fact that there is no guarantee that air power will always be applied effectively, despite the demonstration of "how to" in the Gulf War, and the subsequent major improvements in technology.

Iraq had expended more than $40 billion and 100,000 lives during the eight-year war with Iran. In an attempt to recover economically,

Saddam Hussein ordered Iraqi forces to invade and occupy Kuwait on August 2, 1990, precipitating the Gulf War. The Iraqis confiscated all moveable assets and annexed Kuwait as an integral part of Iraq.

In this situation, the initial response of the United States could only be air power, in the form of forty-eight McDonnell Douglas F-15C/D Eagles of the First Tactical Fighter Wing. On August 7, 1990, they flew nonstop from Langley Air Force Base, Virginia, to Dhahran, Saudi Arabia, in the longest operational fighter deployment in history. Six to seven in-flight refuelings were required on the flights, which lasted from fourteen to seventeen hours. Another twenty combat squadrons followed in the next few days.

It was a meaningful show of force, and it signaled to Saddam and to the world that the United States meant business. There was nothing to stop Saddam from invading and seizing Saudi Arabia; his tanks could have covered the two-hundred-mile distance between the Kuwaiti border and Dhahran in less than a day. He still possessed the fourth-largest army and the sixth-largest air force in the world. But he did not move, almost certainly because of the message sent by the F-15s.

President George Bush began a concerted effort to construct an international coalition for what would become known as Operation Desert Shield, which was intended to protect Saudi Arabia and build up the forces necessary to evict Iraq from Kuwait. He also set in motion a modus operandi that would serve well. The president, in consultation with his advisers, would set the objectives, then leave it to the military team headed by the Chairman of the Joint Chiefs of Staff, General Colin Powell, and the Central Command's commander, General H. Norman Schwarzkopf, to carry it out. The essential air power element of this plan was contained in the decision that there would be a single Joint Forces Air Component Commander (JFACC) to control all air operations. General Horner was given the task, and he executed it ably.

There immediately began an explosive buildup of resources, with 398 fighters in place by September 11. This number would build to 652 by the January 17 kickoff date of Desert Storm, the actual air operation against Iraq.

Lockheed C-5s and C-141s were soon landing at the rate of one every seven minutes at Dhahran. These aircraft were joined by elements of the Civil Reserve Air Fleet (never used previously), which provided thirty-nine aircraft from sixteen airlines. This military airlift became a vast aerial aluminum conveyor belt from airports all over the world directly to the Gulf. It would outstrip all previous airlifts, reaching a rate of 17 million ton-miles per day, ten times that of the peak of the Berlin Airlift.

The fighters and the transports were obvious. Less obvious was a revolutionary shift in warfare when the Air Force Space Command positioned satellites of the Defense Satellite Communication System to establish communication links for Desert Shield. With this system and the NavStar Global Positioning System, the battlefield was now cloaked with an enveloping power that transcended Iraqi understanding.

On January 17, 1991, Desert Shield became Desert Storm, with three different forms of attack: Special Operations helicopters, stealth fighters, and cruise missiles. All of the elements of modern warfare were now in play—intelligence, navigation, weather forecast and communications from space, superb airborne command and control aircraft, stealth attack aircraft, and precision-guided munitions.

Two units of six helicopters each crossed the border at 2:20 A.M. and took out specific radar sites to punch an initial hole in the Iraqi air-defense system. Lockheed F-117A Nighthawk stealth fighters followed to attack targets deep within Iraq with precision-guided munitions of uncanny accuracy. No one knew for sure that stealth would work, but it functioned perfectly on the first night, and every night thereafter. The third element of the one-two-three strike was a flood of thirty-five CALCM (Conventional Air Launched Cruise Missiles) fired from Boeing B-52s that had taken off from Barksdale Air Force Base, Louisiana, fifteen hours (and many refuelings) before. The B-52s were airborne for thirty-five hours, performing the longest combat mission in history up to that time. CALCMs were joined by TLAMS (Tomahawk Land Attack Missiles) launched from naval vessels.

This combination of helicopters, F-117s, and cruise missiles opened the way for a blinding attack by 650 coalition aircraft, including 400 strike planes. Within the first twenty-four hours of Desert Storm, the coalition forces had established air superiority, decapitated Saddam's command and control system, shut down Iraq's electrical production, and destroyed many SAM sites and antiaircraft batteries.

The coalition air forces targeted electrical plants, command centers, roads, bridges, and government structures, each chosen with the maximum consideration of avoiding collateral damage to the civilian populace.

There followed forty-three days of sustained attacks, during which the coalition flew 109,876 sorties and dropped more than 85,000 tons of bombs. Air Force tankers flew 15,434 sorties, conducted 45,955 refuelings, most within a very small area, and many within the actual combat zone.[10] About 7,400 tons of precision munitions were expended, of which about 30 percent was dropped by the F-117As. This small percentage of the total (about 9 percent) accounted for 75 percent of the damage.[11] It was warfare on a scale of size and a measure of precision that was totally without precedent.

So successful was the air campaign that when the massive ground campaign was launched on February 24, the way was so well prepared for it that only a hundred hours were required to achieve the degree of victory desired by the Bush administration. During those hundred hours, air power continued to support the advance of ground forces.

In the afterglow of victory, the principal leaders of the coalition, including President Bush, General Powell, and his Secretary of Defense, Dick Cheney, made comments to the effect that the war had been won by air power. Due deference was paid to the bravery and skill of the ground and sea components, but the fact was obvious—particularly to the Soviet Union—that United States air power had transformed warfare, and that no other country, including those of the coalition, had anything to compare to it. It was the advent of "differential air power" in which the power of the United States' air forces meet all criteria for applying air power as an instrument of national policy.[12]

Perhaps the most monumental influence of the Gulf War was upon the perception of the leaders of the Soviet Union, both military and political. The United States' *tour de force* in the Gulf War served notice to the world that a new age of warfare had arrived. The general effect upon an already shaky Soviet Union was immense. Economics and political expediency dictated a change in doctrine that had been fundamental to the Soviet Union for decades that wars would be won by offensive action, with a first strike the preferred option. The Gulf War showed clearly that the Soviet Union was perhaps one or more generations behind the United States in technology, and that in the future, Soviet forces would have to be on the defensive and to center planning around a counterattack.

This led, after the dissolution of Communism in the Soviet Union on (ironically) December 25, 1991, to a position in which the security policy of the new Russian Federation would be based on the prevention of war.[13]

There has unfortunately been an unrealistic reaction to the situation by the Russian military, which still seeks somehow to wrest superpower status from the wreckage of the Russian economy. Formerly, the Soviet military was the instrument of Soviet policy; now there is an increasing trend toward the Russian military dictating policy and doctrine. This new doctrine once again espouses preemptive warfare combined with the threat of early use of nuclear weapons. It also guarantees the 25 million ethnic Russians living in former Soviet states protection from any kind of retaliation, a posture troublingly reminiscent of Adolph Hitler's attitude toward ethnic Germans living in Czechoslovakia and Poland before World War II.

Given the desperate condition of the economy of the Russian Federation, the military doctrine is currently no more than a dream, moving in a direction opposite to national policy.[14] But this situation could change with the emergence of a strong (and perhaps oil-based) economy that would permit military spending to be vastly increased.

Air Power in Small Wars

It would be convenient if this book on the influence of air power could end with its apotheosis, air power in the Gulf War. In the years that followed there were new emergencies in new locations—Bosnia, Serbia, and Afghanistan—that required a response. These responses were hampered by the severe drawdown in United States and NATO military strength and a weak (and during the Bill Clinton years, a vacillating) American presidential administration severely troubled by domestic issues. Nonetheless, air power was able to eventually force solutions, though not without tremendous economic cost.

The collapse of the Soviet Union had effect upon its neighbors. Yugoslavia, which had prospered as an independent Communist state under Marshal Tito, was divided into Bosnia and Herzegovina, Croatia, Slovenia, and Macedonia, with Serbia and Montenegro comprising a rump Yugoslavia. Internal ethnic problems with a Muslim minority were exacerbated by aggression from Serbia led by Slobodan Milosevic, now under indictment as a war criminal.

After many negotiations and many warnings, the United Nations sanctioned operations by North Atlantic Treaty Organization (NATO) forces, to halt the ethnic cleansing which had reached vicious proportions. For two years, beginning in April 1993, NATO air operations (Operation Deny Flight) in Bosnia were tinged with failure because they were inadequately planned and encumbered by United Nations constraints reminiscent of the rules of engagement of the Vietnam War. Air-power effectiveness was proven again in Operation Deliberate Force, conducted from August 30 to September 20, 1995, and designed to force the Bosnian Serb Army to cease shelling UN-designated "safe areas" throughout Bosnia. As NATO's first sustained air operation, Deliberate Force saw 293 aircraft of eight NATO countries fly 3,515 sorties, of which 750 were strike sorties. The result was an uncertain truce that forced the Bosnian Serbs to remove their heavy weapons from specified areas, provided access to Sarajevo, and led ultimately to the Dayton peace accords.[15]

Two years later there followed another air war, this time for Kosovo. The campaign, Operation Allied Force, was intended to protect ethnic Albanians in the Serbian province of Kosovo from Serb aggression, with the objective again of ending ethnic cleansing.

Allied Force was supposed to be a short campaign with limited objectives, and as a result NATO aircraft focused initially on the Yugoslav Integrated Air Defense System, which, while older, was well experienced. To restrict losses to antiaircraft artillery, Lieutenant General Michael Short, the NATO air commander, restricted NATO flights to a minimum altitude of fifteen thousand feet.

Yugoslav President Milosevic intensified his ethnic cleansing atrocities, and the NATO air effort was increased to target his military forces south of the Forty-Fourth Parallel. The campaign now began to assume a bumbling appearance that was reminiscent of the Vietnam War. Relatively high claims of damage to Serbian forces were made, but these could not be substantiated after the fighting stopped. Further, it was impossible to conceal the widespread disagreement between NATO's military Commander in Chief, American General Wesley Clark, and his superiors in the Pentagon, nor with Clark's disagreement with General Short, who wanted a more intensive campaign. This desire conflicted with the wishes of the NATO allies who had opted for a gradualist approach in the bombing.

Clark asked for more air resources, and a ground campaign capability as well. The Clinton administration was strongly opposed to any thought of a ground campaign, but did supply additional air assets.

Strong NATO air attacks did not begin until the fourth week of the campaign, and on May 3 a significant attack by USAF F-117s destroyed much of Yugoslavia's electric power production. Although there were embarrassments, such as the bombing of the Chinese Embassy on May 7, the bombing campaign continued at the rate of about 250 sorties per day, and seemed to be having effect upon the Yugoslav economy.

On June 9, Milosevic agreed to NATO demands, and after seventy-eight days the bombing was halted. Yet many observers believe that Milosevic's capitulation had more to do with an increase in Kosovo Liberation Army action and a word of warning from Russia than the bombing itself.[16]

Terrorism and Technology

The terror attacks of September 11, 2001, upon the World Trade Center and the Pentagon, with the subsequent campaign against the Taliban and al-Qaeda in Afghanistan may prove to be the ultimate test of the influence of air power on history.

The situation is unusual in that it pits a shadowy world of terrorism, using suicide bombers to strike innocent civilians, against the most modern technological giant in the world. Unlike the Cold War, where the opposition leaders were rational and concerned about their own survival as well as the survival of their nation, the terrorist leaders are (to the Western mind) irrational and unpredictable. And again, unlike the Cold War, where weapons of mass destruction were kept in check because of the certainty of massive retaliation, the terrorists are not inhibited by the thought of them or their countrymen being destroyed, but in fact welcome death as martyrdom.

Brilliantly employed air power to date has been able to eject the Taliban from power and to hound the al-Qaeda from cave to cave, causing casualties and destroying supplies. It has not as yet been able to influence the nations that support the terrorists to cease that support. It is possible that if air strikes like those conducted in Afghanistan were extended against countries supporting terrorism (for example Iraq, Iran, Syria, and Lebanon), such support might be diminished.

Unfortunately, this action is unlikely. While surgical air strikes can take out command and control centers, oil production facilities, and so forth, they cannot extinguish an international extremist Muslim conspiracy that seems to support, actively or passively, the terrorist movement. The most obvious analogy is the Vietnam War, where technology was thrown against the myriad porters on the Ho Chi Minh Trail and failed. Against a Muslim terrorism that is now growing from Morocco on the Atlantic across the world to the Philippines and Indonesia, and is imbedded in Western countries as well, a purist, surgical technology intended to harm only practicing terrorists, simply cannot win.

The ideal solution would be a twofold miracle: the resolution of the Palestinian problem with a meaningful settlement among the Arabs and Israel, and a booming new economy that would lift Muslim nations from their fatal poverty toward a less violently confrontational view of life. Either miracle is unlikely, and it may be assumed that two are impossible.

The greatest question is whether containment, which served in the half-century Cold War against Communism, will work against terrorism. One would hope that the West, led by the United States in alignment with the United Nations, will somehow muddle through perhaps decades of threats, of inconvenience, of expense, and even some level of physical harm from the terrorists. During this time there may be changes in the fervor and the direction of the Muslim world, signs of which are already apparent in Iran. If terrorist acts never again reached the horror of the attack on the World Trade Center and the Pentagon, and if even the lower-level attacks such as the suicide bombing in Israel were to diminish steadily over the years, the situation might, in half a century, resolve itself without radical action.

One method that might ultimately lead to such a hopeful solution would be a huge modern Marshall Plan, in which the West and the wealthy Arab nations would provide the capital, resources, and leadership to energize the economies of Arab nations all over the world, bringing them up from their terrible poverty, and offering hope to their young. If in this effort, both sides would put aside conflict, and direct their military budgets into constructive channels of improved industry and agriculture, the problem might be solved, not in fifty years but perhaps in twenty.

Such a possibility is no doubt Pollyannish. The real question, of course, is whether the terrorists and their sponsoring nations will have the restraint necessary to permit the West to be even grudgingly temperate in its actions. The impetus toward the use of a major weapon of mass destruction is great; if the September 11 attacks were a high point in terrorism, a nuclear weapon exploded in a major Western capital—Washington, London, Paris—would be the apotheosis of terrorism. Given this trend, restraining terrorists is doubtful, even though they and the nations that support them are painfully aware that there are at least two devastating methods that the United States, with or without a United Nations coalition, could use. The first would be to conduct full-scale bombing campaigns without regard to collateral damage that would force nations supporting terrorism to desist or be destroyed. The second is even more horrifying, a reversion to the use of nuclear weapons against known terrorist camps and against nations supporting terrorism. This action would be have to taken first as a threat, then as a deliberate measure of war, to end in the cruelest and most forcible manner possible the threat of international terrorism.

Given that United States defense spending has declined on a steady basis since before the Gulf War, and given that the intervening MRCs have placed a continual drain on resources, the first option, full-scale bombing campaigns, may be impossible to execute. There are roughly 21 Northrop-Grumman B-2s, 85 Boeing B-52s, and about 50 Boeing B-1Bs in the American heavy bomber force. With the most efficient employment possible, there are simply not enough bombers to conduct an extended bombing campaign over several countries. Nor are there sufficient Air Force and Navy tactical aircraft to conduct such a campaign.

It may therefore be that an unrestrained terrorism, one that employs weapons of mass destruction, could bring upon itself the ultimate terror, nuclear and thermonuclear weapons put reluctantly to use to destroy not only terrorism but also, and necessarily, the states that support it.

One can only hope that terrorists will opt for restraint.

Chapter 12

Iraq: Air and Space Power

A new epoch in warfare opened with the brilliant operations of the United States armed services in Operation Enduring Freedom. This all-out pursuit of Al-Qaeda terrorists and the eradication of the oppressive Taliban regime in Afghanistan only hinted at the almost unbelievable proficiency—and ferocity—with which those services (and those of their coalition allies) would operate in Operation Iraqi Freedom (OIF). This new war, intended to overthrow the regime of Saddam Hussein, began on the night of March 19/20, 2003 with a surprise air attack intended to "decapitate" the regime.

There followed a brilliant land, sea and air combined operation that swiftly defeated Iraqi forces and allowed President George W. Bush to announce the cessation of combat operations on May 1. A low level but painful resistance by die-hard Ba'athist members and criminal elements continued, and will undoubtedly do so for a long time to come.

Operation Iraqi Freedom was a unique display of technological power, administered with an unprecedented compassionate concern to avoid collateral damage. It is perhaps the first war ever waged in which hostile actions were waged solely against the truly evil regime in power, and where so much care was taken to shield the captive population from harm.

The armed forces of Iraq, formidable on paper, were overwhelmed by a precisely executed war plan that sought to win by effects based operations (EBO) rather than by inflicting massive damage upon the enemy.

A totally new system of warfare emerged, in which land forces moved forward as swiftly as possible, without concern for protecting supply columns or combating enemy forces on their flanks. These land forces occupied key areas, depending upon the quick reaction of continuously on-call air power to protect them. The coalition air forces were maintained on a constant alert, operating over the entire area of responsibility (AOR) night and day, ready to respond to any evidence of enemy movement.

Within a very short period, this new system evolved even further. In some instances, the presence and exercise of air power forced the enemy to move to positions more suitable for an attack by coalition land forces. In other instances, the movements of the ground forces were such as to force the Iraqi forces to move in turn—and thus be exposed to devastating attack from the air.

The coalition forces achieved information dominance through the unparalleled use of its Command, Control, Communications, Computers, Intelligence, Surveillance and Reconnaissance (C⁴ISR) capabilities. The combination of at least fifty satellite systems and a wide variety of manned and unmanned aircraft provided a stream of intelligence that gave coalition leaders a common picture of the battle on all fronts. For the first time in history, the commanders of land, sea and air elements all saw exactly the same record of events. They could communicate with each other on an instantaneous basis, and take actions in full harmony with those of all other components.

Measures toward air superiority were taken well before the war, during the long years of Operation Northern Watch and Operation Southern Watch. This patrolling of the "no-fly" zones was dictated to Iraq as a result of its defeat in the 1991 Gulf War. During that period, United States and coalition forces became very familiar with Iraqi targets, air defense systems, and tactics.

This familiarity permitted a true air supremacy to be established at the very start of the war. It was so absolute that Saddam Hussein elected not to send his air force of some 300 fighters into battle. Instead, he moved them to what he hoped would be protected areas, going so far as to bury some in the desert sand. (About 150 aircraft remained hidden in the sand long after May 1, a situation that shows how easily vials of anthrax or small nuclear elements can be hidden.)

The fruits of air and information dominance were harvested by a combination of two additional technological advances. The information received from all of the C⁴ISR assets was used in conjunction with the Global Positioning System (GPS) to pinpoint the locations of Iraqi targets, down to the movement of individual truck and tanks. Once located, the coalition air forces were able to use precision-guided munitions (PGMs) to destroy the target.

The brilliant achievements of the war were played out against a media that held a very jaundiced view of the operation. Almost immediately after the war began, there was wide spread commentary to the effect that Operation Iraqi Freedom was "bogged down", and that Baghdad would become a Stalingrad-like graveyard for coalition forces. Almost nightly, the clamoring talking heads on television raised all the manifold possibilities of what was going wrong, and how huge an error the United States had made.

As the previous chapters have shown, air-power theorists have searched since the early days of World War I for the means to strategically paralyze the enemy. The answer was found late in World War II with the deployment of the Boeing B-29 and nuclear weapons. Yet so terrible was the destructive capability of nuclear weapons that the United States and the Soviet Union, each armed to the teeth with a super-abundance of nuclear power, were able to confront each other for almost half a century and never go to war. Nuclear weapons carried with them the implicit threat of Mutually Assured Destruction, and were therefore never used in the Cold War.

The incredible technology displayed in Operation Iraqi Freedom meant that present-day air practitioners of air power were able to go well beyond the most sophisticated concepts of Giulio Douhet, Billy Mitchell, Hugh Trenchard and even Curtis E. LeMay. Intimate knowledge of and proficiency with the advanced technology at their disposal permitted modern leaders to undertake entirely new methods. This proved to be a double advantage, as Saddam Hussein was convinced that the strategy and tactics that worked so well for the coalition in 1991 would be used again.

Instead, he was surprised and disconcerted when the armed forces of the coalition employed asymmetric, network centric warfare[1] in an unmatched demonstration of both joint operations (Army, Air Force, Navy, Marine and Coast Guard) and combined operations (U.S., U.K. and other forces).

Two other factors helped the concept succeed. The first was obvious even to on-lookers. Space-based technology was effectively integrated with every aspect of military operations. The second was far more subtle, for Operation Iraqi Freedom saw the fullest expression of the "Total Force" concept in which reservists and National Guard members fight alongside the regular components.[2] (Operation Iraqi Freedom may well have stretched the "Total Force" concept to the limit, as Secretary of Defense Donald Rumsfeld has already called for a complete reorganization of both the National Guard and Reserve Forces.)

Traditional warfare calls for an invading army to outnumber defenders by a ratio of at least three to one. During Operation Iraqi Freedom, that ratio was reversed to about one to two. This seemed to defy the doctrine enunciated by Colin Powell, part of which stated that force was always to be employed in overwhelming strength. Far fewer personnel were in used in OIF than were employed in 1991, yet their amazing use of advanced technology made them an overwhelming force of another kind.

Another vital use of air and information dominance was the ability to employ large numbers of special operations forces (SOF) within Iraq well before the war. They continued to operate through the war and still do to this day, operating alone, or in concert with military units. These SOF actions, combined with brilliant target selection and expert bombing execution by means of laser-guided and other precision devices, provided an entirely new method of battlefield preparation.

There was no need this time for the forty-three days of bombing required by Operation Desert Storm. Instead, aerial attacks were conducted with incredible precision and economy. This permitted the relatively small Army and Marine forces (the famous "boots on the ground" element) to seize critical points before the Iraqis were even aware that they were in danger. As a result, the Iraqis were kept constantly off balance, always several days and several miles behind their opponents.

The air war was conducted on two levels, one of which was the precisely executed bombing of carefully selected targets in Baghdad. This was well recorded and commentated on by the media, particularly that of the Arab world. The other level was the relentlessly savage hammering of Iraqi ground forces wherever they were found, far away from any television camera. This relatively anonymous part of the air war worked to the disadvantage of the coalition air forces in terms of recognition for their accomplishments.

The situation was far different with the ground forces, where embedded reporters rode to the front in armored vehicles, and thus reported the ground advances on an almost hourly basis.

Yet it was the continuous air attacks that sapped the strength of the Iraqi divisions, taking them far below the 50 percent level that is usually regarded as adequate for their elimination as a coherent fighting force. One estimate had Saddam's main battle tank force of some 700 reduced to a few dozen by May 1.

An unusual aspect of the air war, never envisaged by any previous generation of air-power philosophers, was the order-of-magnitude increase in the ability of fighters, bombers and even unmanned aerial vehicles to take out targets. The Northrop Grumman B-2A Spirit was able to strike as many as sixteen different targets with precision-guided munitions in a single raid. Yet it was the Boeing B-1B, long an object of scorn by critics of the defense department, and the veteran Boeing B-52 that did even more spectacular work, placing large quantities of precision-guided munitions on a large number of targets in a single sortie. In one instance, the Northrop Grumman B-2A stealth bomber demonstrated its versatility by dropping a bomb load of unguided bombs on a target.

Background to the War

The United States was certain that Iraq had possessed and used weapons of mass destruction in the past. The future use of such weapons, either locally against Israel or another neighboring state, or by provision of such weapons to al-Qaeda or other terrorists, was potentially fatal to the United States. President George W. Bush was determined to eliminate all doubt by removing Saddam Hussein's cruel and repressive regime.

He was opposed in the United Nations by a number of countries, including Russia, France and Germany. Each of those countries had its own rationale for wishing to keep Saddam Hussein in power, despite the fact that all three nations had voted for UN Resolution 1441. Iraqi violations of that resolution had already provided adequate justification for military intervention. Despite this opposition in the United Nations, President Bush was determined to make Saddam Hussein, live up to the requirements of UN Resolution 1441.

On March 17, President Bush delivered a unique ultimatum to

Saddam Hussein, calling for him to step down, and to leave Iraq, with his sons, within forty-eight hours. Failing to do so would lead to United States intervention.

All United Nations personnel, including the inspectors searching for Iraqi weapons of mass destruction, were asked to leave. There was a general exodus as embassies closed and thousands of foreign workers left.

Iraq rejected Bush's ultimatum, and threatened a world-wide holy war jihad against the United States. As the time limit expired, the buzz words "Shock and Awe" gained prominence. The initial air attacks on Iraq were supposed to be of such a catastrophic nature that those of Desert Storm would be seen as mild in comparison.

Worries abounded in the press. The number of coalition troops was held to be far too small and the cry for "more boots on the ground" increased, with visions of the Vietnam War and of the Soviet Union's Afghanistan disaster continuously invoked. There was also a mindless claim that war on Iraq might provoke retaliation from al-Qaeda—as if an invitation was required.

Pessimism deepened with the March 2 decision of the Turkish Parliament to refuse access to the U.S. 4th Infantry Division (Mechanized), which subsequently had to be diverted south to Kuwait. Some military commentators thought that the Turkish refusal endangered the entire war plan, insisting that at least 60,000 troops had to invade Iraq from the north to assure victory.

On the eve of Operation Iraqi Freedom, Saddam had a total of about 400,000 soldiers, far fewer than the almost 1,000,000 men he mustered at one time. Most of his soldiers were conscripts, used in seventeen regular army divisions for internal security. They were considered not only to be untrustworthy, but a threat to the regime. His real strength was supposed to lie in his six Republican Guard divisions, which were given special treatment as well as the best equipment and the best training.

The Iraqi Army still possessed as many as 2,000 tanks, including perhaps 700 T-72 tanks. There were also nearly 4,000 light tanks and armored personnel carriers, and 2,000 heavy self-propelled artillery pieces. Although he had far fewer surface-to-air missiles than in 1991, Saddam still had about 1,000 of the smaller, man-portable SA-7/14/16s and 400 of the larger SA-2, SA-3, SA-6, SA-8 and Roland varieties. In addition, there were 6,000 antiaircraft guns.

Initially, General Tommy Franks, Central Command commander, had about 230,000 men. Of these, the United States contributed about 190,000 Marine, infantry, airborne, and Special Forces, while the United Kingdom provided 42,000 troops, including Royal Marines and paratroopers. These were joined by 2,000 Australians, including Special Forces troops, and a very small but welcome number of Polish forces. This force would grow to 340,000 in the crucial next three weeks. An important aspect of this force was that there were 8,000 to 10,000 Special Forces troops.

The distinguishing characteristic of this coalition army was the fact that up to 8 percent of its strength was invested in special operation forces, operating clandestinely well before the outbreak of the war, and ranging all over the country. They achieved political, military, economic and psychological successes of great importance, so much so that the composition of United States and perhaps British forces will be altered in the future to include many more Special Forces personnel. This extremely high percentage of Special Forces characterizes the newness, the daring, and the ingeniousness of the war plan and strategy as a whole. (Raising the number of Special Forces from an army is difficult without expanding the size of the army itself. The reason is that so few personnel possess the physical and mental standards required by Special Forces.)

The actions of the special operations forces were and continue to be incredible, and the degree with which things "went right" because of them is remarkable. It is difficult to believe that even a nation as large and wealthy as the United States could field so large a force of capable, fit, intelligent warriors. A force approaching 10,000 personnel from the Army, Navy, Air Force, the United Kingdom, Australia and Poland was more than 50 percent larger than the 6,000 used in Afghanistan and very much larger than the number used in the 1991 Gulf War.[3]

The special operations forces' diplomatic efforts may have transcended their military triumphs. Surprisingly, the brilliant and ever dangerous SOF campaign resulted in light casualties. The actions of the SOF contributed to Iraqi's confusion, and aided Franks' decision to go in early with ground forces. Avoiding "Shock and Awe" was not only sound but brilliant, for it allowed the full employment of effects-based-operations, while at the same time at least attempting to assuage Arab hatred of the United States for its invasion of an Arab country.[4]

General Franks' decision to strike with the relatively small number of forces in the theater prior to a heavy air attack was both brave and correct. Given that everyone was expecting "Shock and Awe", launching the ground war first was the best way to obtain surprise. The surprise was sustained throughout the ground operations, as the Third Army moved swiftly toward Baghdad in a process that approximated John Boyd's theory of the OODA (Observe, Orient, Decide, Act) loop.[5]

As events developed, the attack "went right" because of an imaginative and audacious strategy and plan, air and space dominance, overwhelming C⁴ISR capabilities, tactical surprise, speed, the high quality of coalition troops including their equipment and training, the manner in which U.S. and coalition assets were used and the inferior troops, leadership and planning of the Iraqis.

The surprising success of the weapon systems fielded in Operation Iraqi Freedom came despite a long period of time when defense spending as a percentage of gross domestic product declined steadily, from 5.4 percent in 1992 to 3.0 percent in 2001. (In 2002, it crept back up to 3.4 percent.) During the same period, the military increased its activities in military operations, humanitarian and compassionate relief missions, homeland defense, and other requirements on the order of 300%. As always, the increase was taken "out of the hide" of service personnel by increasing the tempo of operations to an unprecedented degree both in intensity and duration.

When defense spending declines at a time when military operations expand so dramatically, military leaders are forced to continuously trade-off considerations on force structure, personnel, adding new equipment and research and development. The evidence is that these trade-offs have been made judiciously for the past twenty years, although there are some implicit hazards that will be covered later.

The weapon systems employed in Operation Iraqi Freedom were immensely superior to those used in the 1991 Gulf War. The American acquisition process may not be perfect, but compared with other armed forces in the world, and compared with other huge organizations, from the United Nations to the Ford Motor Company to the Catholic Church, the United States military has made many correct decisions that helped raise the nation beyond superpower status. In brief, the American military on the whole buys the right things and what it buys, works.

The increase in the power and capability is so great that no nation in the world, including our staunch ally, the United Kingdom, has the wherewithal to keep up to the same standard. Many nations, despite fielding relatively modern equipment, are so far behind the U.S. standards that their armies, navies and air forces are not interoperable with those of the United States.

The newly demonstrated power of the United States will enable that nation to continue doing good for the world. Never in history has a powerful nation been so altruistic as the United States. To paraphrase Secretary of State Colin Powell, the only land we ever sought from others was enough to bury the men who died in saving their country.

The United States may be able to begin a badly needed economic revolution for the Islamic states. Currently sunk in poverty, the Muslim states have to reorient themselves to the creation of jobs and the advantages of a consumer society, and to turn away from the blind hatred of "infidels."

The War Begins

The war began with an amazing demonstration of flexibility as General Tommy Franks attacked on the ground first ("G" Day) and then in the air ("A" Day). It was a brilliant move that saw the heavy 3rd Infantry Division (Mechanized) race more than 200 miles in a short period of time. The 101st Airborne Division (Airborne Assault) provided additional reach and striking power with many Apache helicopters. The 1st Marine Expeditionary Force launched deep into the desert from the beaches, while United Kingdom forces operated primarily in the south. The union of Army and Marine ground units under one land component commander was unique in history and sets the pattern for the future.

Problems soon arose concerning flank defense and supplies of water, food, ammunition, and fuel. A delay of almost twelve hours occurred. But so swift was the attack that the United States was already inside the Iraqi decision cycle, spreading confusion and anticipating reactions. Air power was used to cover the flanks as the 3rd peeled off individual battalions to stop Iraqi forces from intervening.

Sandstorms Not as Big a Problem as Anticipated

On March 24 100 mile-per-hour sandstorms obscured the battlefield, slowing operations of both land vehicles and helicopters. The combination of aerial sensors and precision-guided munitions made it possible for Boeing B-1B bombers of the 405th Air Expeditionary Wing to continue their operations. The "Bone" as it is called, dropped as many as twenty-four of their Global Positioning System/inertially-guided JDAMs (Joint Direct Attack Munition) on a single mission.

Despite the weather, fourteen hundred strike missions were flown, with the major targets remaining the same: Republican Guard divisions, key command and control facilities and surface-to-surface missile facilities. The venerable Boeing B-52 continued to perform operations from its deployed base.

Despite the sandstorms, any Iraqi vehicle that was detected was immediately identified by the Joint STARS Moving Target Indicator (MTI) systems and its geographic coordinates determined by GPS. Once identified and located, it was destroyed by precision-guided munitions from a coalition aircraft. In a brilliant example of "effects-based operations", the coalition did not resort to blowing up bridges, but instead destroyed troops on the move.

F^2T^2EA: Find, Fix, Track, Target, Engage, Assess

A new and important feature of the war was the development of a target cycle concept that the USAF Chief of Staff, General John P. Jumper has termed "Find, Fix, Track, Target, Engage, Assess (F^2T^2EA)," and is more colorfully known as the "kill chain." Jumper knows that the armed services of the United States have the ability to find targets anywhere in the world, fix them in a database, track them as necessary, designate them as a target, engage them with the appropriate weapon at the appropriate time, then assess the damage done to the target—all in a very compressed period of time. They should also have a similar (if even swifter capacity) to do the same to targets that emerge suddenly from hiding.

Three elements of the equation, F^2 and T (Find, Fix and Track), have been operational for years. They are provided by the following systems: Boeing E-3C Airborne Warning and Control System (AWACS): Northrop Grumman E-8C Joint Surveillance Target Attack Radar System (Joint STARS); Lockheed Martin EP-3; Beech

RC-12 Guardrail; Boeing RC-135 Rivet Joint; General Atomics Aeronautical Systems RQ-1A Predator UAV; Northrop Grumman RQ-4A Global Hawk; and Lockheed Martin U-2.

Once found, the target has to be "fixed," that is, its location must be determined with precision, most often using GPS satellites. Then aircraft with precision-guided munitions attack the target. After the attack, Battle Damage Assessment (BDA) is carried out.

In Operation Iraqi Freedom, the use of PGMs became almost standard, for in the ten years after Operation Desert Storm, a tremendous effort was made by all the services to adapt them to all of their aircraft. Even the Northrop Grumman F-14 Tomcat was given a new mission as the F-14D (the "Bombcat"), using PGMs.

While a wide variety of PGMs were available, including such standards as the Maverick, HARM, and several varieties of laser-guided bomb, increased reliance was placed on the JDAM, which was not only accurate but relatively inexpensive. Other precision munitions used included the AGM-154 Joint Standoff Weapon (JSOW) and the Wind Corrected Munitions Dispenser.

Naval and Marine aviation worked brilliantly in Operation Iraqi Freedom. A case in point was the sterling performance of the Boeing AV8-B Harriers, which were able to take off from the carrier, fly a mission, go to a forward operating base (FOB) to rearm and refuel, fly a mission, and then return to the carrier. This doubled the availability of the aircraft.

The addition of the Litening II ER targeting pod greatly extended the Harrier's capability. The video downlink of the ISR version of the Litening pod was particularly valuable, for it enabled forward air controllers to see what the Harrier pilots saw, and talk them to the targets.

The Boeing F/A-18s did very well with the new Super Hornets functioning in both tanker and fighter roles. They were joined by Northrop Grumman F-14s and a host of support aircraft. The Navy's claim for the effectiveness of carrier task groups was fully supported by their performance.

Under a benevolent umbrella of air power, the ground forces moved forward quickly, Army and Marines working hand in hand. On April 4, the 3rd Infantry Division sent twenty-six M1A1 Abrams tanks and ten Bradley fighting vehicles on a twenty-five-mile run through the streets of south and central Baghdad, amazing not only the Iraqis but the world. Early reports indicated that the "Thunder Run" killed two to three thousand Iraqis who had attempted to interfere with the raid.

The armored spearhead, which paraded within two miles of Saddam's famous bunker and onto his favorite military parade ground, burst the bubble of media and public discontent over the "slow progress" of the war. It demonstrated that with absolute air and information dominance, coalition forces could move when and where they wished, even in the heart of Saddam's citadel, Baghdad.

Instead of slugging it out, the coalition relied on its air power to provide close air support, on a rapid-reaction basis. Ground and airborne forward air controllers (FACs) in a wide variety of aircraft including Boeing A-10s and F-15Es, Lockheed Martin F-16s, Northrop Grumman F-14Bs and Boeing F/A-18s provided round-the-clock cover in and over Baghdad, all armed with precision-guided munitions.[6] In Iraq, close air support was no longer defined by fighter bombers dropping down close to the ground to deliver weapons. Instead, huge bombers, operating at high altitude, delivered weapons with uncanny precision on individual trucks, tanks and bunkers.

On the nineteenth day of the war, April 7, a Boeing B-1B bomber combined with C[4]SIR, GPS and PGMs to attempt to decapitate the regime. Four 2,000-pound JDAMs were dropped, and a 60-foot crater replaced the target, a restaurant in the al Mansur section of western Baghdad where Saddam and his two sons were supposed to be meeting. Although they were not killed in the attack, it was a demonstration of the flexibility and power of modern warfare, one that must have caused every potential enemy of the United States to stop and think.

General Franks used speed almost as a replacement for firepower during the move north to Baghdad. Once inside the city, however, the terrific firepower of both the heavily armed and armored Abrams and Bradleys dominated the battleground.

During and after the war, leaders placed great emphasis on the importance of the Joint Forces Combined Air Operations Center (CAOC) in Prince Sultan, and the $40,000,000 Operations Center at the Al Udeid Air Base near Doha, Qatar. Their success was no accident, for much planning and training had gone into them. During the war they proved their worth, particularly enabling the concept of "jointness" between services to transcend into interactive operations.

Even before the war ended, data was being gathered on the air war. Lieutenant General T. Michael Moseley (who was later selected to become a four-star general and Vice Chief of Staff of the USAF) issued the first data compilation. By April 25, 2003, the coalition was shown to have flown almost 50,000 fixed-wing missions, of which the USAF flew roughly 30,000, the Navy 9,500, the Marines 5,500 and the Royal Air Force and Royal Australian Air Force about 5,000. Of the missions some 36 percent were strike sorties, 20 percent were tanker missions, and 25 percent were airlift missions, with 4 percent miscellaneous.[7]

Of the 28,820 munitions that were dropped, 19,060 were precision-guided, an amazing 66 percent. The aerial refueling figures showed that 417,137,233 gallons of fuel was offloaded by tankers of all the services. Another 195,753,818 gallons of jet fuel were provided by land- and ship-based sources.

Weapons of Mass Destruction

Military operations benefited from the Iraqi failure to use weapons of mass destruction (WMD), for while chemical or biological weapons could have been overcome, they would have impeded progress, perhaps for weeks. It is possible that Iraqi leaders still possessed WMD, but were deterred from their use by repeated coalition warnings that doing so would be a war crime.

The primary military objective for discovering Iraqi weapons of mass destruction was to prevent their use. The failure to find WMD as of the date of this writing has been politically harmful to the United States, particularly to President Bush. It is possible that the Iraqis transported their weapons of mass destruction to Syria or Iran.

Aftermath and Lessons to be Learned

The United States had evolved a new way to fight wars, almost without regard to the skill or size of an opponent. The formula includes complete information dominance through C[4]ISR and complete air dominance that includes loitering platforms equipped with precision-guided munitions. These, when used in combination with swift and powerful land forces, make victory inevitable.

One of the most important lessons learned by the armed services is that joint and combined operations can work well only if the concept is adhered to through all levels from the Commander in Chief down to the newest enlisted person. This was achieved in Operation Iraqi Freedom, but it does not guarantee that it will be achieved in future conflicts.

The success of the coalition forces was made possible in part by the huge, multi-billion dollar long-term investments that had been made in such disparate disciplines as space satellite systems, UAVs and UCAVs, night-fighting equipment, stealth technology, aircraft carriers battle groups, which require the permission of no nation to take up station in international waters, and advanced fighters and bombers.

Problems were encountered in Operation Iraqi Freedom, including fratricide, for which no total solution has emerged, and a significant shortage of tanker aircraft for in-flight refueling. Another difficulty, alluded to earlier, is the age and condition of the helicopter fleets. With many helicopters more than thirty years old, maintenance was a continual problem. Procurement of both tankers and helicopters has been deferred time and again over the years in favor of "combat" equipment, but the United States must now face the fact that both of these invaluable fleets must be updated and replaced.

U.S. bombers are few in number and growing older, but existing plans call for the introduction of a new bomber into the fleet in the 2030 time period. In the meantime the United States will be relying on B-52s that will be approaching 70 years of service, B-1Bs which will be about 45 years old, and youngster B-2As of only thirty-eight years of age. This is dangerous in the extreme, for it is entirely possible that stealth technology may be compromised, and the relatively few bombers we possess will be inadequate for the demands placed on them.

Lessons to be Learned by the Public and by Congress

But the armed services are not the only agencies that can learn lessons from Operation Iraqi Freedom. The American public and the American Congress should learn that previous investments in the defense of the United States have paid off handsomely, and that cuts, particularly in such critical areas as the gathering of "humint"—

human intelligence—were costly, making the United States vulnerable to the terror attacks of September 11, 2001.

The Congress and the public must also recognize that we are engaged in a global war against terrorism. The only way to win this war is to maintain the same degree of advantage that we enjoyed in Iraq over all our future enemies. To do so will require us to invest in our future defenses at a rate higher than has been the case for almost all of the two previous decades. The increase has to be a significantly higher percentage of gross domestic product than is currently being spent (about 3.4 percent). It may need to rise to as much as 7 percent by 2008. After being sustained at that rate for a few years, the costs could easily drop back down to the 3–4 percent range—given that China or a revived Russia does not emerge as a potential foe.

The increase is necessary not only for new equipment. The United States has to increase the total number of regular service personnel, particularly for such elite branches as the Special Forces, SEALS, Rangers, Air Force Special Operations and so on.

Too many Guardsmen and Reservists have been called to duty too often for too long. The entire concept of a Reserve or National Guard force is impractical if the components of those forces are required to be constantly or even repeatedly on duty.

Conclusion

Operation Iraqi Freedom was a brilliant military success, accomplished in spite of a series of what were either diplomatic disasters or simple foreign intransigence, based on resentment of the primacy of the United States in economic and military matters. Although there was a mutual recognition of the importance of land and sea forces in obtaining victory, air power was dominant in a way that was never possible before. The influence of air power upon victory, upon diplomacy and upon world events has never been greater than today.

Air power now promises more than quick and certain victory. It holds out the possibility of a genuine Pax Americana, one unmarred by terrorist threats or aggressive warfare by one state upon another.

Conclusion

It is a shame that technology cannot somehow overcome the threat of terrorism through sheer brilliance, given that in the past it has done so well in overcoming threats that were equally serious at the time. Technology gave air power its (on balance) beneficial influence upon history, and it might be well to review how that influence has, despite the death and destruction of wars, been benign.

Until the question of terrorism is resolved, it may be said that the first and most beneficial influence of air power on history was its contribution to the destruction of Nazi Germany and Imperial Japan. Both of those nations were ruled by malevolent leaders who knowingly and deliberately did great harm to the people of the countries they conquered—and to their own people as well. Had they succeeded in their grandiose aims of conquering the world, the suffering would have been multiplied many times. Yet air power did make the key contributions that led to their defeat, and a badly bruised and shaken world was preserved from what would have been decades of horror and millions of additional deaths.

The second most beneficial influence of air power on history was the containment of the Soviet Union and its ultimate dissolution as Communism foundered in its own economic contradictions. There were major conflicts in that process of containment, but United States air power kept the Cold War cold, and averted a World War III with the hundreds of millions of casualties that would have occurred.

The retaliatory strength of American air power served to keep Soviet and Warsaw Pact tanks within their own borders and prevented a first strike on the United States and its European allies. It gave hope to Soviet satellite nations, who began asserting their independence even as the Soviet Union began to crumble.

Even more remarkably, air power has influenced history the most

383

in totally nonmilitary ways. Air power has fostered international air travel on a grand scale, one that, before the advent of terrorism in its present form, seemed (with electronic media) to be the swiftest way to democratize and internationalize the people of the world. Air power has provided the technology for vast improvements in agriculture, in disease control, and for compassionate relief of disaster victims.

Now air power has translated to aerospace power, as has been amply demonstrated since the Persian Gulf War. The capabilities of meteorological, intelligence-gathering, reconnaissance, and navigational satellite systems have been integrated firmly into modern weapon systems, such as the Boeing E-3 Sentry airborne warning, battle management and command, control and communication aircraft, the Boeing/Northrop Grumman JSTARS land-battle management aircraft, and the Rivet Joint Boeing RC-135 real-time intelligence-gathering aircraft. This integration has gone beyond airborne platforms, however, and can now be found in the individual radar and fire-control systems of fighter, tanker, and transport aircraft. And the philosophy has been taken a step further so that satellite-based commands can now guide individual rounds of precision munitions. There will soon be an airborne laser weapon introduced, capable of stopping a ballistic missile as it ascends from its launch pad.

Yet while space warfare has already influenced the outcome of wars, and is increasingly influential in the development of weapons, it is too early to determine its effect upon history. It remains to be seen if human political genius will be the equal of human technical genius in its use in the future, and thus make air power as space power a continuing positive influence on history.

Appendix

The Earliest Expressions of
Air Power

There are three compelling reasons to study the use of the balloon as an instrument of air power. The first is that, in both Europe and the United States, the use of balloons as a military instrument created conditions of achievement and of failure that were to be repeated all through the history of air power, and consequently it affected air power's influence on history. The second is that perhaps 50 to 60 percent of the problems encountered during the twentieth century in the exercise of air power were encountered in the military use of the balloon more than a hundred years earlier. Most of these problems were solved at the time by the balloon operators. But because there were long interruptions in the use of balloons, there was no corporate memory of either the problems or the solutions, and the same situations were encountered often over time. The third is that vitally important individual personalities were involved in both the creation of problems and their solutions, a situation which would be found again and again, all through the history of air power.

Despite all the difficulties that were encountered, the balloon and its lighter-than-air relatives proved to be long-lived elements of air power with still more uses predicted for the future. What is surprising, perhaps, is how relatively sophisticated were the uses to which balloons were put from the very start.

Balloons at War

Given that humans are so eager to find some new way to inflict harm upon each other, it is surprising that the balloon did not come into general use until the Montgolfier brothers, Joseph Michel and

Jacques Etienne, began their early experiments with hot-air balloons. The Montgolfiers were wealthy French paper manufacturers, long interested in science. The initial efforts with the "lifting power of smoke" led them to their wildly acclaimed public ascension of an unmanned balloon on June 4, 1783. The flight, at Annonay, France, was a tremendous technical achievement as well as a great success. In Etienne's words, "The aerostatic machine was constructed of cloth lined with paper, fastened together on a network of strings fixed to the cloth. It was spherical; its circumference was 110 feet and a wooden frame sixteen feet square held it fixed at the bottom. Its contents were about 22,000 cubic feet of gas, and it accordingly displaced a volume of air weighing 1,980 pounds. The weight of the gas was nearly half the weight of the air, for it weighed 900 pounds, and the machine itself, with the frame, weighed 500 pounds. It was therefore impelled upward with a force of 490 pounds. Two men sufficed to raise it and fill it with gas, but it took eight to hold it down until the signal was given. The different pieces of covering were held together with buttons and buttonholes."[1] (The great pioneer used the term "gas" here because he considered it to be a physical substance similar in effect, if not in substance, to hydrogen. It had not yet occurred to the Montgolfiers that their balloons rose because heated air is less dense, and therefore lighter.)

The first publicly demonstrated balloon rose steadily from the ground to more than a mile in height, floated there with unbelievable grace, and then sank gently to the ground. In a little over ten minutes and perhaps a mile and one-half in distance, the Montgolfiers and their balloon had unleashed a revolution that is still in progress.

And yet all of the elements that constituted this success had been available for hundreds of years. There are reports that indicate that primitive balloons might have been made in China. The Egyptians and even the Incas had the material with which to make a balloon, and the combustible material with which to furnish the necessary heat. Civilizations such as these, which built great structures and had an understanding of astronomy, certainly would have been able to create a balloon—but apparently did not pursue that goal. Other experimenters, including Bartolemeu de Gusmao, created small toy-sized hot-air balloons in the early eighteenth century. What the Montgolfier brothers provided was the insight, persistence, and wherewithal (for balloons have never been inexpensive) to create a method of harnessing the simple physical forces that would lift the balloon and a cargo into the air.

Interest in ballooning spread rapidly, and unlike the invention of the aircraft some 120 years later, there was an air of joyous and cooperative *bonhomie* among the celebrants of the new discipline. Henry Cavendish had discovered both the lifting and the combustible properties of "phlogiston" or "inflammable air" in England in 1766. The gas would be named "hydrogen" by Antoine Lavoisier, and its lifting properties would be soon put to use by Professor Jacques Alexandre César Charles, a Parisian physicist.

As would become customary in the development of air power, one element of technology, in this case the lifting properties of hydrogen, had to be melded with another element to obtain the desired result. It happened that two brothers, Anne-Jean and Marie-Noël Robert, had developed a method of dissolving rubber in linseed oil. When this material was applied over certain cloths (silk or taffeta, for example) as a varnish, the oil evaporated, and the rubber remained to render the cloth impermeable (or almost so) to hydrogen. By early August, the Charles-Robert team had constructed a spherical balloon of red and light-yellow silk. (The original materials were red and white, but the varnish turned the white to light yellow.) Because hydrogen had greater lifting power than hot air, the balloon could be made much smaller, and the initial "aerostat," as it was called, had a diameter of twelve feet and a volume of 943 cubic feet.

Even such a relatively small balloon required a great deal of hydrogen, and the manufacture of the gas was both difficult and dangerous. Hydrogen gas was generated in a hazardous process in which five hundred pounds of dilute sulphuric acid was poured over one thousand pounds of iron filings. Collecting the hydrogen and transferring the gas into the balloon proved troublesome, and it was only after a great deal of effort that the small balloon, appropriately named *Globe*, was filled and transported to the Champs de Mars, later the site of the Eiffel Tower. A tremendous crowd of more than 50,000 gathered, and among the many notable dignitaries was a future president, sixteen-year-old John Quincy Adams, and the American most beloved by the French (if not always by his fellow Americans), Benjamin Franklin. At five o'clock in the afternoon on August 27, 1783, the balloon was released, and the masses cheered as it ascended to be caught by the wind. Franklin's later description can be recaptured today with an ordinary helium-filled toy balloon, for he noted that it appeared to diminish in size as it rose, until it entered the clouds.[2]

To Franklin, at the time America's premier scientist as well as foremost diplomat, the flight of the balloon was filled with both portent and potential. To a scoffer who asked, "Of what use is it?" he made the famous reply, "What is the use of a newborn babe?" But he also immediately realized, as had Joseph Montgolfier, that the balloon could have a military application.

The first Charles balloon had a more adventurous flight than that of the first Montgolfier, for the *Globe* sailed fifteen miles, ascending until the expanding hydrogen burst the envelope, then landing northeast of Paris at Gonesse, the same small town where an ill-fated Air France supersonic Concorde airliner would crash 213 years later. There the terrified peasants attacked the balloon with pitchforks and staves, succeeding in subduing it. Fortunately, all of the action took place where there were no open flames, or the peasants might have been truly convinced that they were dealing with the devil.

Ballooning became immensely popular. There was a flood of experimenters, as well as a flood of merchandisers as the balloon craze swept first France, and then the rest of the continent and Great Britain. Those brave and rich enough to afford it sought ascensions. Those who were not had to be satisfied with the toy balloons sold on the street. The balloon motif was incorporated in jewelry, furniture, clothing, even hairstyles.

Summoned to perform for King Louis XVI, Etienne Montgolfier constructed a huge hot-air balloon, more than fifty-seven feet in height and forty-one feet in diameter, and decorated in a manner fit for a king. On September 18, 1783, at Versailles, with the entire court assembled, the balloon was launched carrying a sheep, a cock, and a duck, the first animals to fly in a man-made conveyance. The intrepid animal aviators survived their two-mile flight, but the danger was implicit.

Louis was immensely pleased, so much so that he awarded the brothers the Legion of Honor, the Order of St. Michael, and an annual pension. He also intimated that he looked forward to the first balloon flight by humans, and a twenty-nine-year-old scientist, Pilâtre de Rozier, volunteered.

Rozier was a thoughtful man who understood the dangers involved. He made a number of tethered test flights to gather experience, including one on October 17, 1783, on which he carried a friend, Andre Giraud de Vilette. Like most passengers on balloon flights, Vilete was exhilarated, but not just with the view of Paris. Instead, he immediately saw the military utility of a balloon being used for observation purposes, and became the first military aviation author by writing an article proclaiming this subject in the *Journal de Paris.* Vilette noted that the fairly inexpensive machine would be useful to an army in observing the enemy's position, maneuvers, movements, and supplies, and could report them by signals.[3] As with most seminal military articles, there was no immediate effect, but the seed had been planted.

The first human flight was planned with pomp and ceremony, and with a launching mechanism that in its own way foreshadowed the immensely complex launch facilities at Cape Canaveral. There was risk implicit in launching a balloon, just as there is in a rocket, for the balloon itself was terribly flammable, and had to be suspended over a roaring fire to be inflated.

As the launch date approached, the king decided that it would be safer if two condemned criminals were sent up on the first flight. If they lived, their sentences would be commuted. If they did not—*c'est la vie,* so to speak. The king's safety-consciousness did not appeal to the swashbuckling Gallic spirit, and Rozier protested bitterly. He asked two friends, the Duchess de Polignac and the Marquis François-Laurent d'Arlandes to intercede. Both were considered favorites of Queen Marie Antoinette, and the duchess was also a friend of the king. They succeeded, the king agreeing with some reluctance, but recognizing the essential French *élan* in the request. Then to the surprise and discomfort of the marquis, who had not contemplated the adventure and was perhaps a little light on *élan,* the king "suggested" that d'Arlandes accompany Rozier on the historic flight.

To obtain the proper balance, Rozier and the Marquis had to place themselves in opposite sides of the balcony-like basket in which they were to ride. The balloon was initially suspended from tall wooden gantries on either side of the fire pit; when it became suitably inflated with hot air, enthusiastic spectators restrained it by holding four guide ropes.

Unlike the utilitarian colors that characterize the Space Shuttle, the balloon was decorated beautifully in blue and gold, displaying signs of the Zodiac, the fleurs-de-lis, and the king's royal monogram, thus being altogether worthy of the king's interest and patronage.

Rozier and the Marquis d'Arlandes took off on November 21 from the Bois de Boulogne to the cheers of a huge crowd. The initial heat for the ascent of their Montgolfier came from the fire pit, which had been fueled with such noxious elements as old shoes and wet straw to generate the maximum amount of smoke—still thought to be the lifting agent. In flight, they sustained the lift with judicious applications of fuel to the fire that was carried on board in the center of the bottom of the balloon. In the next twenty-five minutes, they flew five miles across Paris and overcame the world's first in-flight emergency, putting out the small fires that were burning holes in the envelope of their balloon. The first small aviation steps for humankind had been made in Paris, just 186 years before similar steps would be made on the moon.

Etienne Montgolfier and the Marquis d'Arlandes visited Benjamin Franklin in his home shortly after the flight. Franklin, the venerated representative of the United States to France, waxed enthusiastic, and made the first predictions of what would become known as "vertical envelopment." He suggested that the balloon might in fact give a turn to human affairs, one that would convince rulers of the folly of war. Using the quick mental arithmetic for which he was famous, Franklin estimated that five thousand balloons, each capable of carrying two men, could not cost more than five ships of the line. He concluded that no sovereign could defend his country against such a force, which might appear at any place and any time. (And, given the vagaries of wind and weather, that is probably what would have happened—the dispatched troops would have landed not where they were destined to go, but anywhere and at any time.)

The interest of the king and Franklin in ballooning was repeated all across Europe, and progress in ballooning was rapid. Only eleven days later, the first humans to be carried in a hydrogen balloon took off from the Tuileries Gardens in Paris. Marie-Noël Robert and Professor Charles flew more than twenty-seven miles in just over two hours, landing safely at Nesle-la-Vallée.

There were elements in even these early flights that in later years characterized air power in general, and the European interpretation of air power in particular, tempering its influence on history. Ballooning was perceived as a daring gentleman's sport, something in which only the rich and the privileged could indulge. Most of all, it was obviously dangerous, so that a balloonist was by definition a brave man. For most of the early years of flight, this same combination of danger and elitism combined to attract the best of young nobility in many countries, but especially in France and Germany. When the various national military services first became interested in aviation, many of its early practitioners were drawn from this noble elite. It should be noted that these same members of the noble elite had influence in the governments of their country, with the result that funds were spent far more freely on military aviation in the modern European states and in Russia than in the United States.

Military aviation would soon demand far more pilots than the rich and noble could provide. When more pilots were required, an enormous number of ordinary people were attracted to ballooning, not only because of the danger, but because it was a rich man's sport, the only one in which they would ever have the chance to participate.

As a new sport, ballooning brought with it the opportunity to set records on almost any flight. Rozier flew a Montgolfier to an altitude of 11,700 feet, and distance records were routinely broken, with the Robert brothers and another passenger flying more than one hundred miles from Paris to Beuvry, in the astounding time of six hours and forty minutes.

As always with aviation, record-setting led to equipment improvement, and none did this more effectively than Professor Charles and the brothers Robert, for they soon devised a hydrogen-filled balloon equipped with all the features found on such balloons today. These improvements included a valve on the top of the balloon, to release gas as necessary; ballast to drop, to make the balloon ascend; a rope netting that covered the balloon and to which the passenger basket was attached; and an orifice through which the hydrogen could pass if it became necessary to equalize pressure.

Many more of the Montgolfier (hot-air) and Charles or "Charliere" (hydrogen-filled) balloons were built, and within a few years a series of dazzling flights ensued in Italy, Austria, and even the United States, where the first tethered flight was made in June 1784. So widespread was the enthusiasm that the first regulations governing flight were issued in France in April 1784, prohibiting flights of balloons unless the appropriate safety procedures were followed.

The most compelling flight by far was a cross-Channel flight in 1785 made by one of the first "professional balloonists," Jean-Pierre

Blanchard, and his financial backer, Dr. John Jeffries. As often happened in early aviation, a conflict between greed and ego almost prevented the flight. After allowing Jeffries to finance the balloon in exchange for going on the flight, Blanchard planned to double-cross him by taking off without him. He was concerned (correctly as it developed) that with Jeffries' weight he would be unable to carry sufficient ballast for the trip. The outraged Jeffries forced his way into the Dover Castle launch site. After much argument, he was allowed to join Blanchard on the flight, but only after he promised to leap from the balloon if its safety required him to do so.

The two men flew from west to east to take advantage of the prevailing winds, crossing the English Channel in their hydrogen-filled balloon on January 7, 1785. The trip was not an easy one, for the ballast, as Blanchard had feared, was insufficient. They eluded a dunking only by divesting themselves of their clothing and even their cork lifejackets—a desperate measure indeed, given their wave-skimming circumstances. A sudden freshening of the wind enabled the pair to complete the flight from England to France in two and one-half hours. They brought with them letters, the first air mail.

Honor demanded that this record-setting trip be answered by a flight from France to England, and the king assigned the task to the veteran de Rozier. He had misgivings about the task because of the west-to-east prevailing winds, but nonetheless, he reluctantly obeyed the king's order. He created a new hybrid balloon, one that placed a forty-foot-tall hydrogen-filled balloon above a ten-foot-tall hot-air balloon. It was an obviously unwise combination and given Rozier's competence, the decision is difficult to understand. Some primitive safety precautions had been taken; for example, expanded hydrogen from the Charles was to be vented well below the fire-basket of the Montgolfier, but it was simply too risky.

Rozier, and his passenger, Pierre Ange Romain, launched at 7:00 A.M. on the morning of June 15, 1785. Twenty-three minutes into the flight, at an altitude of five thousand feet, the inevitable happened. The balloons caught fire, and both men perished in the ensuing crash. (In modern times, the term Rozier has been applied to the balloon type most preferred for long-distance flights. The Breitling *Orbiter* 3, which flew around the world in twenty days in 1999, was a Rozier-type balloon. It used inert helium rather than hydrogen, and kerosene burners rather than burning straw.)

Despite Rozier's failure, the flight of Blanchard and Jeffries had made it obvious that England was no longer an island—and that the balloon could well be a practical military tool. Military observers began to write with notable prescience about the possibilities of using balloons in warfare. Some of the proposals might be considered obvious, given that generals had always wished to "see the other side of the hill." But it was soon noted that the balloon would be useful for reconnaissance, gathering intelligence on enemy forces and positions through observation. It became an aid to navigation when used as an airborne marker to guide the advance of reinforcements. Seasoned observers could use the balloon as a platform from which to make maps. Balloons also had defensive purposes, acting as airborne early-warning sentinels to guard against surprise. It was also suggested that a system of signals, including semaphores and flares, be created so that balloons could be used for long-range communications. Given that any balloon observer of the time would also certainly have commented on any observed weather phenomena, one can immediately see that the duties prescribed for balloons have parallels in modern military navigational, intelligence, communication, and meteorological satellites.

But as desirable as innovation is in military journals, it is rarely given equal appreciation in military budgets, and after the first flight of the Montgolfier balloon in Paris, it took ten years and the French Revolution before serious consideration was given to the use of a military balloon.

The great patron of balloonists, King Louis XVI, lost his head to the guillotine on January 21, 1793. The revolutionary government, faced with internal disorder and at war with Austria, Britain, and Prussia, was in such military disarray that drastic remedies were sought. Among these remedies were suggestions for the use of balloons. These suggestions included one by Joseph Montgolfier that huge balloons be used to drop bombs on Toulon, another that balloons would be useful as reconnaissance platforms, and yet another that powered, steerable dirigibles be built for offensive purposes.

Amid all the suggestions, the idea that balloons could be used for observing enemy action was most feasible. On October 25, 1793, an act was passed authorizing sufficient funds to build a balloon and procure the necessary equipment for use by the Republican Army of the North.

This operation, like so many in the history of air power, would succeed or fail based on the talents and energy of the men to whom the
task was assigned. In this instance the choices were excellent for an
engineer, Nicolas Lhomond; a scientist, Nicolas Conte; and a chemist,
Jean Marie-Joseph Coutelle; were given the difficult task of preparing
the hydrogen-generating apparatus. The job, difficult enough by conventional means, was rendered almost impossible by the stipulation
that sulphuric acid not be used, for the limited quantities available of
that commodity were already allotted to other military needs.

The team responded well, using the alternate method of water
decomposition to create the hydrogen. In this process, the hydrogen was isolated from the water by passing steam continuously over
heated iron. This was safer and less expensive, but more time consuming, and it served its purpose well. As a result of the team's success, the Committee for Public Safety passed an act on April 2, 1794,
authorizing what became the 1ère Compagnie d'Aérostiers, the very
first organized air unit in history, and the one from which every air
force, all over the world, descended. Somehow, amid the mixture of
a confused and bloody revolution and bitter wars, the French managed to form this first air unit correctly and with style.

The engineers were a highly regarded element of the French
Army, and the Aérostiers were manned and equipped accordingly.
The chemist, Coutelle, was made the company captain, and he was
assisted by the scientist Lhomond as his lieutenant and by a sergeant
major—always the key person in a military unit. There were two cor-
porals and twenty privates, one of whom was Lhomond's son. These
were not just ordinary recruits, for the personnel were selected for
their knowledge of the arts and sciences. Coutelle made the selec-
tions, and he sought to gain a group with the talent to sketch (for
purposes of observation), and to be able to build equipment,
including hydrogen generators.

Despite the technical nature of their task, the Aérostiers were soldiers first and foremost, and were given the same training as regular troops. Aware of the specialized nature of their calling, however,
Coutelle saw to it that they received special uniforms. The coat,
waistcoat, and breeches were blue, piped with red. The collar and
cuffs were black, with red facings, and the buttons, interestingly,
used infantry instead of engineer patterns. Given that much of the
balloon work was dirty, Coutelle also devised a fatigue uniform of

blue cotton slacks and jacket. He did not want his men to be confused with the ordinary French infantry.[4]

This sensible, straightforward, and effective approach would be sadly missing in many later efforts to use the balloon at war. Coutelle's work became the standard by which the French operated their balloon corps.

He had managed well during a time of rapid change. Authorized on April 2, the unit inflated its balloon, the *Entreprenant (Enterprise)*, and went into action near Maubeuge, in the north of France, near the Belgian border, during the end of May. Austrian and Dutch troops confronted the French, who were commanded by General Jean-Baptiste Jourdan, a short, fat little man of unheroic aspect. The son of a surgeon and a consummate survivor, Jourdan had served King Louis XVI in the American War of Independence. When Louis was beheaded, Jourdan earned laurels as a hero of the French Revolution. After Napoleon came to power, Jourdan rose to the rank of Marshal of the Empire, and still surviving, went on to have his rank confirmed by the restored King of France, Louis XVIII, in 1817.

In his role as hero of the French Revolution, Jourdan, the commander of the Army of the Moselle, welcomed the arrival of Coutelle and his Aérostiers. (There was no little irony in this incident, as Jourdan had the year before summarily dismissed Coutelle's offer of help, advising his superiors in Paris that "a battalion is needed more than a balloon.") Coutelle's persistence and the professional appearance of his troops apparently convinced Jourdan on this occasion, and the *Entreprenant* began the history of aerial reconnaissance on June 2, making the first recorded military combat flight in history. Later in the month, the company moved the balloon to Charleroi in Belgium, covering the intervening twenty miles in just fifteen hours. On June 23, the *Entreprenant* made history again when it took the first general officer aloft, General Antoine Morlot, who used a telescope to discern that the Dutch forces were ready to capitulate in the Battle of Maubeuge.

According to captured enemy deserters, the French were assured that "General Coubourg [the Austrian commander] had cursed the balloon copiously, that he kept saying that 'there's nothing those scoundrels don't invent; there is a spy in that thing and I can't get at him to have him hanged.'"

This engagement is largely forgotten now, but the experience gained there would be invaluable in the pivotal Battle at Fleurus. Fought on June 26, 1794, at the site of an ancient Roman town, it proved to be one of the most significant battles fought during the French Revolution. Two men who shared the same Christian name and would become famous with Napoleon, Jean-Baptiste Jourdan and Jean-Baptiste Kleber, commanded 72,000 troops. They awaited an assault by Dutch and Austrian troops, who, unaware of the strength of the French, made a headlong assault in five columns.

During the battle, the *Entreprenant* was enterprising indeed, remaining aloft for more than nine hours, and once again lifting the intrepid Morlot to view the battle, this time ascending as high as 1,300 feet, far higher above the ground than any other general had ever been. Observations were dropped in message packets from the balloon and immediately conveyed to Jourdan at his field head-quarters. In the inevitable post-mortem on the efficacy of these dis-patches, there were only positive comments. The balloon observa-tions were invaluable, despite the difficulties inherent in transport-ing inflated balloons from point to point. One of the most authori-tative members of the National Constituent Assembly, Deputy Joseph Lakanal, was an expert in the well-developed system of sem-aphore-telegraphs used for communication. He commented that sending an army into battle without a balloon to observe was like fighting a duel blindfolded. Jourdan, however, perhaps conscious of his earlier resistance to the idea of balloons, did not comment at all on its effect in his report. And, in a manner remarkable for any flyer, Coutelle was modest to the point of self-abnegation in his report. In his own words, "I will not claim as do those who praise or blame with exaggeration everything that is new, that the balloon won the battle of Fleurus. On this memorable day, every corps did its full duty. What I can say is, that well served by my glass [telescope, not brandy], despite the oscillation and movement caused by the wind, I was able to distinguish clearly the corps of infantry and cav-alry, the parks of artillery, their movements, and in general the massed troops."[5]

In his place, it would have been the work of a moment for Guilio Douhet or Billy Mitchell to have said: "Without the *Entreprenant*, the battle of Fleurus would have been irredeemably lost. With it, the enemy had no chance for victory." A neutral observer, British Army

Major General John Money, a sometime balloonist himself, and hence perhaps prejudiced, published *A Short Treatise on the Use of Balloons and Field Observateurs in Military Operations* in London in 1803. In this work he stated unequivocally that the Battle of Fleurus had been won because of the balloon observations. Then, in a bit of "what-if" war-gaming, he went on to assert that the British could have kept the colonists in check if England had been able to use balloons during the American Revolution. With an eagle eye for the pertinent, Money went on to say that he would not ask "old generals" about the value of balloons, for he knew their answer would be negative, just as they had in previous years declined the use of light artillery, field telegraphs, and other advances.

Before looking into the subsequent demand for the services of the Aérostiers, let us first stipulate, for the sake of argument, that the balloon did have some effect upon the Battle of Fleurus. In that case, the first application of air power did have influence of importance upon history, for winning the Battle of Fleurus enabled the French to occupy much of Belgium. This victory made the Taliban-like economic and social repressions of the infamous Robespierre seem both cruel and unnecessary. The immediate result was his overthrow and execution on July 27, 1794. While it is indeed a stretch to say that this early exercise of air power by balloon observations at Fleurus was the direct and immediate cause, it is fair to say that it *influenced* the situation and thus has historic import far beyond being a combat mission.

Jourdan may have been silent in his reports, but he nonetheless called for the balloon to accompany his campaign, serving at the Battles of Liège and Brussels. The result of Jourdan's campaign was the occupation of the Rhineland and Holland, with the hotly desired peace negotiations following in 1795.

Subsequent events strengthen the case for the early influence of air power on history. The new French Republic, financially exhausted by the extravagance of the Bourbons and by war and revolution, was so strapped for funds that it often could not provide shoes or arms to its battalions. Nonetheless, not only did it authorize the construction of a new balloon, the *Martial,* it also provided for a balloon depot near Aix-la-Chapelle, complete with supplies and an apparatus for making hydrogen. A second company of balloonists was enrolled, and, most significant, a permanent training school for military aeronautics to be known as École Nationale Aérostatique was established at Meudon. It would go on to become a historic part of French aviation as a research center for many years, and then as the repository of the collection of the French Air Museum.

These were acute, far-thinking steps that could not have been undertaken if the results of aerial observations had not been generally accepted as extremely valuable. They were also, it is sad to say, far-thinking steps that would not be repeated for decades.

The new "balloon school" was a serious endeavor, tripling Coutelle's original company, and operated according to the standards of the French Army, which maintained strict discipline and organization despite the changes brought about by the revolution. The scientist, Nicolas Conte, who had been Coutelle's colleague during the first experiments with balloons and in establishing the first company of Aérostiers, was named to head the school. Coutelle was rewarded with the command of the second company of Aérostiers.

The new unit received two new balloons, the *Hercule* and the *Intrepid,* and went into action with General Charles Pichegru's Army of the Rhine. If Jourdan had been the consummate survivor, Pichegru was the consummate conspirator, whose continual attempts to betray whatever side he was supposed to be serving resulted ultimately in his being strangled in 1804, purportedly on Napoleon's orders. Nonetheless, balloons were used effectively during the siege of Mayence (Mainz) and at the Battle of Mannheim.

The year 1796 saw the second company of Aérostiers fully employed by General Jean-Victor Moreau in battles at Rastadt, Stuttgart, and Donauwerth. Moreau, a brilliant commander, was also a conspirator with royalist sympathies who schemed with Pichegru. It is perhaps no accident that the balloon companies did not fare so well under these commanders, who had things other than victory on their minds.

Part of the problem was one that would become familiar to all future aviation units, and in later years the term "tooth to tail ratio" would be created to describe it. In the balloon company, the "tooth" was the observer, able on days when wind and weather permitted, to make ascensions and obtain data about the enemy. The "tail" was the impedimenta of the balloon company—its wagons, equipment, and personnel that were perforce idle when the balloon could not be used. To a commander hard pressed for infantry, the sight of an inactive balloon company of men, regardless of the color and cut of their uniform, was galling.

The original company, now commanded by Lhomond, continued to be used by Jourdan until the Battle of Wurzburg, where Jourdan suffered one of his rare defeats and the first balloon company was captured by the Austrians.

There now occurred one of the typical events in the development of air power—the inability of a commander to make appropriate use of it. When Coutelle became ill in 1796, responsibility was transferred to a Captain DeLaunay, an officer known for his lackadaisical approach to duty. As a result of DeLaunay's failure, the Commander of the Army, General Louis-Lazare Hoche, thought the balloon to be useless. Hoche was a gruff soldier who had risen like a rocket from the enlisted ranks. Commissioned a captain in 1792, he became a general in 1793. In his usual abrupt manner Hoche requested that the balloon company be removed from his command.

This unfortunate and ill-informed judgment after so much good work sounded the death knell of the French balloon corps. The First Company was returned to French service after the capture of Leoben, and was reorganized under the command of Coutelle. Fate dictated that the new unit be included in Napoleon's army that was being sent to Egypt—a move designed largely to remove the increasingly popular (and thus dangerous) Bonaparte from the continent. The balloon contingent was never used in Egypt, and its equipment was lost when the British sank the French fleet in the Battle of the Nile. On January 18, 1799, the two balloon companies were officially disbanded, and the École Nationale Aérostatique at Meudon was closed. The great French experiment in air power, conducted so well, and with such good effect, had ended.

There were numerous attempts over the next sixty years to use the balloon in warfare, but only one of them was conducted with the full rigor, military discipline, and common sense of the French Aérostier units. That exception was the Austrian use of balloons in the siege of Vienna in 1849. The American efforts during the Civil War, while relatively large scale, lacked the organization and discipline of the first French units.

Had the proper inferences been drawn from the successes the balloon units actually achieved, the conduct and the outcome of the Napoleonic wars might have been far different. But Napoleon, the master technician, who knew well how to use a hill and a telescope, and had called forth such military innovations as food preserved in bottles, standard-size cargo wagons, and mobile command posts, was blind to the advantages of balloon observation, and failed to use it as he might have. Had he done so, he might have had a better fix on the position of "Old Forward," Prussian Field Marshal Gebhard von Blücher, at Waterloo, and the fate of Europe might have been forever altered.

Other Trial Balloons

Advanced thinkers in many armies perceived the intrinsic merits of the balloon, but, too often, those seeking to use the balloon would much underestimate the expense, manpower, and time required to make it effective. This failure would accurately foreshadow the legislative abuse of air power until the present day, for democratic governments traditionally slash spending on aviation in peacetime, only to become embarrassed by a shortage of air power in time of war. Totalitarian governments also underestimate their requirements, but usually to a lesser degree. And even in the age of superpowers, budget cuts inevitably mean reductions in personnel, force strength, training, and the procurement of spare parts that subsequently handicap air power in time of crisis.

France flirted again with balloons on several occasions, sometimes frivolously, as with Lhomond's 1808 proposal to send a fleet of a hundred balloons to England. Each of them was to be a hundred meters in diameter and carry a thousand men, horses, cannon, fuel, and fodder. Word of his plan quickly became known, and there were numerous cartoons depicting the event. Fortunately, given the prevailing winds, Napoleon declined to undertake the operation without a full-scale test, which was never made. If the test had gone ahead, France might inadvertently have invaded Switzerland.

The military balloon was briefly revived during the reign of Napoleon III, and used during the Italian campaign against Austria. Difficulties with supplying hydrogen in the field meant that many of the balloons were the less satisfactory hot-air type. The French reports of the campaign failed to mention the balloon, effectively condemning it.

During the Franco-Prussian War of 1870, the French used the balloon again, not as a weapon of war but as a communications vehicle. Sixty-six balloons were launched during the siege, carrying passengers, messages of state, personal letters, and four hundred homing pigeons out of Paris. The homing pigeons returned with microfilmed letters and documents. The effort was so great that a training school for balloonists had to be started to fill the need for pilots.

Before that surprisingly successful exercise, the balloon was used in tentative fashion by Denmark in 1809, to drop propaganda leaflets over Sweden. The Austrians made a more serious use of it in the siege of Venice in 1849. Daniele Manin had led a revolt by his fellow Venetians against the Austrians in 1848 to create the Venetian republic. A protracted war followed, featuring extraordinary infighting and continual defeats of Italian forces by the Austrians, with the result that Venice came under siege in May 1849. During the course of that siege no less than 60,000 shells fell upon the city from Austrian guns, but none had as much long-term political effect as a handful of ineffectual bombs dropped from the air.

Lieutenant Franz Uchatius, an Austrian artillery officer, envisaged the use of balloons to drop bombs upon the city. He immediately organized two "aerial torpedo" units, each one consisting of one hundred hot-air balloons, each eighteen feet in diameter, and made, like the earliest Montgolfiers, of paper and cloth. Each balloon carried one bomb of his own design, a pear-shaped vessel filled with gunpowder. Uchatius also saw to it that the necessary wind screens (to protect the balloon when tethered close to the ground), wagons, and other equipment were provided. Smaller balloons were used to test the air currents over the city. Tests showed that because the prevailing winds ruled out release from the land, it was necessary to equip a ship so that the balloons could be released from the sea. As a result, the aptly named paddle steamer *Vulkan* became the first aircraft carrier in history. The *Vulkan* was positioned so that the wind would drift the released balloons over the city. The bombs were dropped by a conventional burning fuse mechanism, timed to release the bombs over Venice. (An account in the March 1849 edition of *Scientific American* quotes the Vienna *Presse* as follows, "[T]hey will be fired by electro magnetism by means of a long isolated copper wire with a large galvanic battery placed on the shore. The bomb falls perpendicularly and explodes on reaching the ground." This early version of a modern wire-guided missile seems highly improbable, but Uchatius was unusually creative. (He later became the commander of the Vienna Arsenal and invented, among other things, a new method of casting artillery pieces and, as a military training aid, a forerunner of the motion picture projector he termed the "Lantern Wheel of Light.")

The results of the aerial bombardment were minimal, as might be expected, with the Venetian defenders claiming that only one bomb had dropped within the city. Paradoxically, this air-power nonevent was to have tremendous influence on history, for it set in motion a train of thought that civilian populations would succumb in terror if bombarded by air. The fact that before succumbing the Venetians had endured 60,000 cannon shells (also arriving through the air) was ignored, as was the virtual zero result of the balloon bombs. Instead, the myth grew that bombing by air would place such an emotional strain on the civilian populace that they would panic and surrender. The idea was picked up by Jules Verne and H. G. Wells, and began to be debated by governments. Russia, in particular, sought that bombs from balloons be prohibited. The net result was that the 1907 Hague Convention on Land Warfare included a provision stating: "It is forbidden to attack or bombard by any means whatsoever, towns, villages, dwellings or buildings that are not defended."[6]

The intent of the Hague convention to prevent aerial bombardment was ignored as military leaders in every nation began to plan to use the air weapon as soon as they had the means to do so. Yet the sentiment behind the anti-bombing provision grew stronger and stronger until it became a potent political force, a decider of national existence, in the years before World War II.

How Not to Do It

For most of the nineteenth century, balloonists became entertainers who made money from their profession much as circus aerial artists made money from theirs. Ballooning was also adapted to advertising and even to aerial photography. In Paris, Gaspard Félix Tournachon, who used the dramatic name Nadar professionally, took the first aerial photographs, and was far-sighted enough to patent the concept of aerial mapping by the use of overlapping photographs. In 1863, Nadar created the largest balloon built to that time, *Le Géant* (The Giant). It was 196 feet high and carried a two-story observation car with a built-in photographic studio. Unsuccessful, it gained notoriety rather than fame, but it nonetheless inspired a generation of large balloons.

In the United States there were dozens of balloonists who made names for themselves by public ascensions and long-distance flights. Among this group, there emerged four well-intentioned if often argumentative aeronauts —James Allen, John Wise, John La Mountain, and Thaddeus S. C. Lowe—who were determined to place themselves and their balloons at the service of their country when the Civil War erupted. Fate treated them as unkindly as they treated each other.

If the four balloonists and their followers had cooperated, they might have penetrated the inner workings of the Union high command. Instead, they each operated alone, some with greater success than others, and they failed to make Union commanders realize exactly what it was that they had done, and more important, what they could do. Whatever their success in individual ballooning efforts, their larger failure had an adverse affect upon the appreciation of the potential of air power.

The long-feared Civil War erupted on April 12, 1861, when Confederate forces fired on Fort Sumter. Three days later, President Abraham Lincoln made his optimistic call for the states to provide 75,000 militiamen for what everyone believed would be a short war. James Allen, a thirty-seven-year-old native Rhode Islander, immediately volunteered his services. Allen had been flying balloons since 1857, and was widely recognized as "the New England Aeronaut." Despite his greatest efforts, Allen's career as the first United States military balloonist would be a failure. He was caught in the classic dilemma faced by air-power advocates of all ages. On the one hand, the novelty of his equipment was expected to work wonders upon the battlefield. On the other, the lack of experience and the pressures of time resulted in Allen's going to war with balloons designed for fair-weather air-show work, supported by detailed units composed of men who were completely ignorant of balloon operations. Failure under these circumstances was inevitable, and the same circumstances would be found in the future.

Allen himself was apparently an able man, well liked, and adaptable to circumstance. Later in the war, when Thaddeus S. C. Lowe brought a balloon corps into existence, Allen served well, twice becoming corps commander, at Malvern Hill and again at Chancellorsville.

Veteran John Wise, a self-taught balloonist who made his first balloon at the age of twenty-seven, followed Allen into the contentious fray of Civil War ballooning. In learning his profession, Wise endured crashes, hydrogen fires, and bankruptcy, but persisted with his art. He approached his calling with the point of view of a scientist, conducting various meteorological experiments and publishing two books on his profession. In the process he developed better materials for balloons and experimented with parachutes, using them to drop animals safely to the ground. Even more miraculous, he made a living by flying balloons. Wise had proposed sending war balloons to bomb into surrender the Castle of San Juan de Ulua at Vera Cruz in 1846, before the start of General Winfield Scott's ultimately successful land campaign that ended the Mexican war in victory in 1848.

Ambition seemed to be an occupational hazard of balloonists, and Wise was consumed by it, for he wished to use the prevailing west-to-east winds to fly across the Atlantic Ocean. It was a daunting task, one that would not be accomplished until the flight of the *Double Eagle II* in 1978. The challenge also fascinated one of his former students and future rival, John La Mountain.

La Mountain had attracted sufficient capital from a wealthy investor, O. A. Gager, to make a transatlantic balloon of 120,000-cubic-foot capacity and able to lift 25,000 pounds. Some 2,200 yards of Chinese silk were used in its construction, and a lifeboat was prudently slung beneath the conventional basket. The Trans-Atlantic Balloon Corporation was formed, with La Mountain, Gager, Wise, and two investors as principals.

A preliminary test of the *Atlantic,* as it was optimistically named, took place on July 1, 1859, lifting off from St. Louis with La Mountain, Wise, Gager, and William Hyde, a newspaperman, on board. It was an epic voyage, filled with storms, danger, and finally a risky landing at Henderson, New York. In an unparalleled flight, they had traveled 809 miles in twenty-hours and forty minutes. The stage was set for further great adventures—but arguments intervened that left Wise and La Mountain enemies and substantially affected ballooning in the Civil War. There was no questioning the patriotism of these men; the problem was their ego, which demanded primacy of place in the ballooning world.

Wise at fifty-three was widely recognized as the premier balloonist in the United States, and could easily have avoided military service. Instead he volunteered to raise a company of expert riflemen in his native Lancaster, Pennsylvania, and lead it into battle. His reputation preceded him, however, and he was asked by Captain Amiel W. Whipple, the Deputy Chief of the Bureau of Topographical Engineers, how much it would cost to prepare a balloon capable of lifting five hundred pounds and provide an aeronaut to operate it.

Wise responded immediately that the balloon would cost $300, and that he would volunteer to be the balloonist at no cost to the government. When the balloon specifications were changed, he responded with a second estimate of $850. By July 1, 1861, Wise was officially appointed a military balloonist, unaware that another archrival, Thaddeus S. C. Lowe, was actively competing for that role.

In retrospect, the interpersonal competition was ludicrous. The Union would soon be spending millions of dollars a day on the cruelest war in American history, and could well have afforded to have dozens of balloonists assigned to each of its far-flung armies. But in the confusion and the haste of preparing for war, the United States military leadership was too engrossed in day-to-day events to pay the attention that military ballooning required to be a success, and the bickering of balloonists did nothing to solve this essential problem.

Whipple was a conscientious officer of limited vision who did not understand that so innovative a weapon as the balloon would require trained personnel and special wagons for handling equipment and the generation of hydrogen. The times were stressful, and Whipple lacked the patience to ensure that the inflated balloons were assigned to the custody of officers who would transport them with the care they required. He also failed to understand that the balloons were subject to wind and weather restrictions that did not affect more familiar weaponry.

The end result was that Wise, despite his best efforts, was not given the assistance needed to use the balloons effectively, and as a result, failed in his attempts to support Union troops. It is a shame, for had he been able to control events, it is probable that he could have been in position at the infamous Battle of Bull Run on July 21, 1861. Instead, a combination of a delay in orders and inadequate transport resulted in the destruction of the balloon before it reached the front and after the Confederates had scored a victory.

It is difficult to resist the temptation to play "what if" with great battles, and the influence of air power might have been established for all time if Wise had been available on the twenty-first at 3:00 P.M. It was then that victory seemed within the grasp of Union Brigadier

General Irvin McDowell, who was roughly handling the outnumbered troops of his opponent, General Pierre Beauregard. McDowell had, with great foresight, posted troops to prevent Beauregard's being reinforced by eight thousand troops from the Shenandoah Valley, under the command of Brigadier General Joseph Johnston. Johnston was one of the best of the Confederate generals, and he infiltrated his troops past McDowell's blockade. If Wise had been airborne, he might have observed Johnston's troops bypassing the Union holding force, and warned McDowell. The Union commander could then have changed his dispositions enough to hold off the combined Beauregard/Johnston attack and win the day. If he had, he might have brought the Civil War to an end in its first summer, saving the country much suffering and avoiding his own subsequent dismal military career.

But it was not to be. Wise not only failed at Manassas, but suffered a continuing series of humiliations, including the loss of a balloon that he was attempting to move, inflated, across the Georgetown aqueduct bridge. This balloon became a notable air-power first when it was brought down by friendly musket fire from the ground—the world's first aerial victory, scored by unnamed riflemen of the Union Army. Sadly, neither of the failures was Wise's fault, but were caused by a general lack of understanding of the use of balloons and the kind of expert support that they required.

The misuses of resources would be a continuing problem in military aviation, from the way in which Royal Air Force fighters were squandered in ground attack missions during World War II to the manner in which the USAF was forced by rules of engagement to employ its bombers and fighters during the Vietnam War.

Wise's erstwhile partner in the *Atlantic* escapade, John La Mountain, had somewhat better luck in his operations, if not in his career. He too had volunteered early as a balloonist, but no one responded to the bombardment of letters he sent to everyone from the Secretary of War on down. Apparently by coincidence, and based on his well-established reputation as a balloonist, he received a letter from Major General Benjamin F. Butler, who was soon to earn the nickname "Beast Butler" from the ladies of New Orleans. Butler required his services as an aeronaut at Fortress Monroe, which was situated at the very point where the James River enters the Chesapeake Bay. The fort overlooked Hampton Roads, the Confederate batteries at Sewall's Point, and Norfolk.

After much effort, La Mountain was in place by July 25 at Fortress Monroe, where he made several uneventful ascensions. However, on the thirty-first, he made history with the first effective use of military air power in the United States, ascending to fourteen hundred feet and spotting several previously undetected Confederate encampments. Further, his observations made it clear that Butler was not opposed by nearly as large a force as he had thought, putting to rest, for a moment, his fears of being overwhelmed.

La Mountain followed up this exploit with further ascensions, including the first American use of what might be termed an "aircraft carrier." He stationed his balloon on the armed transport *Fanny,* from which La Mountain made an ascent to two thousand feet to study the Confederate encampments.

General Butler was entirely satisfied with La Mountain's services, and readily approved the invoice the balloonists had submitted for the costs he had incurred. La Mountain, however, was soon caught up in one of the typical wartime bureaucratic misunderstandings. Butler was ordered to another command, and his successor, Major General John E. Wool, had no knowledge of the personal arrangements Butler had made with La Mountain. As a result, La Mountain had to go, hat in hand, to Washington to seek further employment.

While there was no question of La Mountain's knowledge and daring—he would later undertake free-flight reconnaissance of Confederate lines, driven over the lines by winds in one direction, than rising to catch a different wind at high altitude for the return trip. He had exaggerated his ability to build hydrogen-generating equipment, so that at the crucial moment, he was unable to deliver the services he had promised.

Simultaneously, La Mountain found that his archrival, Thaddeus S. C. Lowe, was proving to be more adept politically. While La Mountain was on active service, conducting reconnaissance for Butler's forces, Lowe had maneuvered himself into a position of army aeronaut, with the assignment to operate balloons for the Army of the Potomac. There is no little irony in the fact that Lowe rose to political favor in Washington during the same period that both La Mountain and Wise were struggling against all odds to serve the Union cause in the air.

Lowe had become a balloonist in 1854, at the age of twenty-two, and, like Wise and La Mountain, had wished to create a balloon that would cross the Atlantic. He built a balloon, the *City of New York* (later the *Great Western*) of huge proportions. It was some 130 feet in diameter, with a gas capacity of 725,000 cubic feet and a lifting capacity of 45,000 pounds, but he never succeeded in getting it ready for the transatlantic attempt.

Yet his methods were deemed scientific, and he received the full support of the Secretary of the Smithsonian Institution, Joseph Henry. This would prove to be an invaluable relationship, one that would link him to President Abraham Lincoln and be a pathway to control of ballooning in the Union Army.

Like Wise, Lowe had demonstrated his airmanship with a long-distance flight, using a smaller balloon, the *Enterprise,* a popular name selected for use by ships of the line, balloons, aircraft carriers, a Space Shuttle, and television science fiction spaceships. On the morning of April 20, 1861, Lowe lifted off from Cincinnati, and landed nine hours later at the inappropriately named Unionville, South Carolina. There the locals were undecided whether he was a devil or a Yankee spy, but he was soon befriended by people of repute who knew his reputation and arranged for his rail transportation to Columbia. His timing was bad, however, for he had landed only eight days after the war had begun, and had been so imprudent as to carry a bundle of abolitionist newspapers in his basket. In Columbia his status changed from possible devil to certain spy, and he was arrested and briefly held in jail. Ultimately, he was released and given a safe-conduct pass back through Confederate lines.

In retrospect, Lowe was in fact a spy, for he noted the numerous Confederate troops on the train trip from Columbia to Louisville, Kentucky, and made up his mind on the spot to offer his services to the Union. Unlike Wise and La Mountain, however, Lowe was at heart a politician, and he sought a position through the auspices of his old friend, Murat Halstead, the editor of the *Cincinnati Commercial.* Halstead used his influence with the Secretary of the Treasury, Salmon P. Chase, to get Lowe a post as a Union balloonist. Lowe was presented as a scientist, and not a "showman" as Wise and La Mountain were, by implication.[7] Lowe then sought the blessing of Secretary Henry of the Smithsonian as backup. It was a formidable political combination, one that would result in Lowe's being interviewed personally both by Secretary of War Simon Cameron and President Lincoln himself. Lowe also differentiated himself from the efforts of Wise and La Mountain by proposing not just balloon flights, but also the creation of an aeronautic branch of the military service. The depth of his thinking should be noted; he understood that to be successful, a corps of well-trained, well-equipped troops had to support the balloonist and his balloons, and, further, that military commanders had to learn how to take advantage of what the balloon offered.

Lowe planned a demonstration in which he would make a balloon ascension near the Smithsonian Castle (on the site of the present National Air and Space Museum). On the ascension he carried field glasses, telescopes, and a telegraph transmitter and receiver. He made observations at various altitudes from his tethered balloon and transmitted reports of them to the ground, which further transmitted them directly to the White House. It was a public relations coup, grand in conception, and well executed on June 1, 1861.

George McDowell Burns, the Washington superintendent of the American Telegraph Corporation, and Herbert C. Robinson, an expert telegrapher, accompanied Lowe. At an altitude of five hundred feet, Lowe surveyed the area, and sent the following message to President Lincoln:

> Balloon *Enterprise*
> June 1, 1861
>
> To the President of the United States:
> Sir:
> This point of observation commands an area nearly fifty miles in diameter. The city, with its girdle of encampments, presents a superb scene. I have pleasure in sending you this first dispatch ever telegraphed from an aerial station, and in acknowledging indebtedness for your encouragement for the opportunity of demonstrating the science of aeronautics in the military service of the country.
>
> T. S .C. Lowe

It is reported, but not confirmed, that Lincoln dictated a telegraphed reply to Lowe, which, if true, would be the first presidential aerial command and control action.

Mindful of senior military sensitivities, Lowe also sent messages to Philadelphia and Alexandria and to members of the Department of War including the corpulent General Winfield Scott. It would be interesting to know if Scott was aware that balloons had been proposed for use during his famous Mexican campaign fifteen years earlier.

Lincoln personally inspected Lowe's equipment, which had been towed to the White House, and to his bright mind the experiment was highly successful; he intuitively believed that the balloon could be very useful.

There followed a brilliant sales effort by Lowe, giving demonstrations on the south lawn of the White House, carrying dignitaries, and actually making observations of enemy activity in the Confederate-held towns of Vienna and Fairfax, Virginia. Lowe understood how effective it was to take up a senior staff person on the combined adventure of a first balloon ascent and the direct observation of enemy troops. Nor did he neglect reporters, who reciprocated with favorable stories in many newspapers. Lowe then backed up his demonstrations with approving scientific appreciations from his Smithsonian friend, Secretary Henry.

In short, Lowe had done with his balloon what all successful military contractors do with their products today: differentiate them from the competition (which Lowe had done by combining the balloon and the telegraph), then take them to the hottest market (Washington, then and now), and sell them at the highest level possible (starting with the president, if possible). The next step was to attend carefully to the interests of everyone in the procurement hierarchy, from the public to the contracting officer, generating the maximum amount of publicity possible. Lowe took care of all of this promotion.

Although still lacking any formal association with the government, Lowe was pressed into service on June 22, 1861, by General McDowell, still a month away from his debacle at Bull Run. The general was concerned about reports of a strong Confederate presence in Virginia.

Lowe made several ascents during which Major Leyard Colburn drew remarkably accurate maps of the surrounding territory and the enemy dispositions. Despite these successes, in the next weeks, Lowe would be confronted with a bureaucratic problem that has haunted procurement in aviation from that day to this. He was asked by Whipple to make a proposal for a balloon and its equipment to the Topographical Bureau, unaware that John Wise had also been asked to propose.

Lowe made a carefully thought out bid, assuming that he had the inside track, and was dismayed to find that Wise had been the low bidder by two hundred dollars. All of Lowe's careful preparations seem to have been in vain, and he was insulted when Whipple suggested that as an alternative Lowe might consider piloting one of Wise's balloons.

The struggle at Bull Run was drawing near, and, as noted, Wise, for reasons beyond his control, was unable to be at the battle. Seeing an opportunity, Lowe made an effort on his own to take his balloon to the front, but was overwhelmed by the hordes of routed Federal troops streaming back toward Washington. Instead, he made a daring free ascension at Fort Corcoran, in Arlington, that yielded information on the movement of enemy troops. The flight itself was dangerous, and when he returned to Federal lines by means of wind at an upper level, he was fired on by Union forces.

The flight, however, was the solution to his problems, for on the following day he was invited to the White House to meet with President Lincoln. Though there were many difficulties ahead, from General Scott's lack of interest in balloons to yet another argument with the unfortunate Whipple, Lowe was finally employed by the government.

Once given official status, Lowe launched into action, supervising the construction of a balloon, the *Union*, within sixteen days. Getting a ground crew authorized took another two weeks, but the new balloon was in action at Fort Corcoran by August 29.

There followed a period of sustained mobile operations by Lowe, proving that the balloon could be moved from point to point, and valuable observations made whenever weather permitted. More important, he took such important persons as Generals George McClellan, Fitz-John Porter, and Irvin McDowell aloft, where they could see for themselves the advantage that height gave an observer.

Lowe's plans for a Balloon Corps were at last given substance, and by March 1862, he had created a force of seven balloons and no less than twelve portable hydrogen generators. A former coal barge *George Washington Parke Custis* was equipped to carry a balloon, a portable generator, and its crew on the waters served by the Potomac and other rivers.

Lowe's backers also saw to it that each balloon company was adequately manned. The observations were to be undertaken by an aeronaut, but the work was to be done in military fashion by a captain and fifty enlisted personnel.[8] Normally four balloons were attached, and a train of ten wagons were required, including the three needed for the generation of hydrogen. Somewhat surprisingly, the pool of available balloonists was large enough that Lowe could be selective, and he recruited eight experienced men to assist him as aeronauts. Perhaps more important than anything else, there had been five months of solid training during the winter.

The concept of a Balloon Corps was so radical that no one in the Union Army seemed to wish to assume responsibility for it. As a consequence, its administrative governance was shifted from organization to organization so that, ultimately, Lowe functioned almost with autonomy. He himself was paid at the approximate rate of a colonel in the Union Army, but was not commissioned in that rank.

The next thirteen months of Lowe's career can be called a complete success if viewed solely from the perspective of the effective operation of balloons in combat on several fronts. On one of these ascents there occurred the first incident of a joint aerial operation, when a United States Navy commodore, Andrew H. Looe, provided one of Lowe's aeronauts, John Steiner, with a flatboat to use as a launch platform. In exchange, Steiner provided Lowe with information on the advance of General John Pope's troops as well as information on where to aim his mortars.

Lowe himself was ordered to support General McClellan, an ardent balloon supporter, in the ill-fated Peninsular Campaign. Using the *Custis* as transport, Lowe brought four balloons and equipment to Fort Monroe, and then took them to the front lines in front of Yorktown. Generals Fitz-John Porter and Daniel Butterfield made several tethered ascensions to gather information. Lowe had to return to Fort Monroe, and, feeling that things were well established, left an old rival, James Allen, in charge of operations.

Porter had made so many ascents that he felt qualified to go aloft without an aeronaut. On April 11, 1862, he rode into the balloon camp at five o'clock in the morning, and jumped in a waiting balloon basket and demanded to be raised.

Unfortunately for Porter, instead of the customary three restraining ropes, only one was attached, and it had been weakened earlier when corrosive fluid from the hydrogen generator had been spilled on it. At about fifty feet up, the rope parted, and Porter was on his way to the first free-flight reconnaissance by a general officer over enemy territory.

As the balloon rose, air currents drifted it west over Confederate lines. The valve cord to release gas, normally at hand, was tucked up in the balloon netting, and could not be reached. Porter coolly made the best of a bad situation, and, using his telescope, reconnoitered the Confederate lines. He then climbed up the netting that surrounded the balloon envelope, reaching the valve cord and releasing gas—a dangerous but necessary task if he was not to be taken prisoner.

The descending balloon fell into air currents that carried him back into Federal lines, but he had misjudged the amount of gas to be released, and the balloon collapsed—into an impromptu parachute. Porter hit the ground, stepped out of the basket, and immediately began sketching enemy positions that he described as having been recorded as "instantaneous impressions like a photographic instrument." (The next general officer to fly over enemy lines would be Billy Mitchell in 1918.)

The Federal balloon operations had great psychological effect upon the Confederates, causing them to waste a great deal of time in avoiding being seen, doing their construction under cover of trees, and in general posing an uncomfortable sense of inferiority. Their natural response was to fire artillery shells at the balloon. None ever hit, but the errant shells did a great deal of damage to all of the Federal positions around the balloon sites.

Lowe was aware of the psychological effect, and when Union troops moved up the Peninsula, he flew his balloon as often as possible, knowing that it would be seen in Richmond and be regarded there as an ominous sign of the Federal presence.

On the Peninsula, Lowe and his balloon proved to be of tremendous value. The hesitant McClellan had become bogged down near Fair Oaks, with his forces split by a swollen Chickahominy River. Canny Joe Johnston saw an opportunity, and launched a massive attack on the smaller section of McClellan's army. The vigilant Lowe saw the attack coming, and sent warning to McClellan, who had time to order additional troops to face Johnston. The resulting bloody two-day battle ended in a draw, but would certainly have been an overwhelming Confederate victory had it not been for Lowe's timely intelligence.

Here the influence of air power on history is clear. Had the Union Army been destroyed on the Peninsula, Lincoln would almost certainly have had to come to an accommodation with the South.

The Union generals were by now generally convinced of the utility—some said necessity—of the Balloon Corps. This belief was not translated to an effective command system. Lowe fell under the authority of officers who were more interested in auditing his accounts than assessing the information he provided. This approach proved to be disastrous to Lowe, who had largely ignored paperwork, channels, and common sense in his determination to get balloons into action. It was easy for the auditors to find discrepancies, and Lowe was suddenly on the skids.

In the meantime, the military balloon proved its use in two great battles. No balloon was present at the Battle of Antietam on September 19, 1862, and its absence was deeply felt by McClellan, who declared to Lowe that it would have been invaluable to him. Then on December 13, 1862, at Fredericksburg, Virginia, Lowe personally flew in a tethered balloon throughout the day, providing invaluable information to the staff of the self-proclaimed inadequate General Ambrose E. Burnside. Had Burnside correctly interpreted the information Lowe was giving him, he would have recognized that the Confederates occupied an impregnable position, and that his troops would inevitably be slaughtered if they attacked. Living up to his own image of himself, he did not make the correct interpretation, and his troops were slaughtered.

Despite this bravura performance, Lowe's star was setting. He came under personal attack for his bad paperwork, and his pay was cut from ten dollars to six dollars per day—the wage of one of his aeronauts. It was too much, and Lowe resigned—but offered to serve without pay. It was a hopeless ploy. The Federal Army continued to use balloons, with Lowe's former assistants operating them, and they provided invaluable intelligence at the Battle of Chancellorsville. Once again, however, the commanding general, in this case General Joseph Hooker, was already so demoralized by the almost magic movements of Robert E. Lee and Stonewall Jackson that he did not make intelligent use of the information he had.

The bumbling by Burnside and Hooker in regard to air intelligence would be repeated down through the years, from General Hugh Trenchard's miscalculations about offensive operations in

World War I to Saddam Hussein's underestimation of the effects of air superiority in the Persian Gulf War. In every major war, and in most of the minor ones, gross miscalculations were made by one side or the other (and sometimes both) in interpreting air intelligence. In fairness, however, it must be noted that as the air weapon became more familiar to military leaders, air intelligence was used in an exceedingly capable manner, as typified by the British pinpointing Peneemünde, the site of the German experimental base for V-2 weapons, as a target in World War II, the American discovery of missile sites in Cuba, and the later intelligent achievements of the Persian Gulf War.

Even as the Civil War balloon operations dwindled because of lack of interest, Lowe continued to make efforts to be reinstated, but it was a lost cause. The Balloon Corps simply collapsed, and would not be revived in the United States until thirty years later.

The Union Balloon Corps experience was not unlike the experience of the French Aérostiers. Despite giving good service, and being appreciated by some general officers, others did not have the ability to analyze and interpret the reports of the balloonists, even when those reports were furnished by qualified military officers. In both cases, the "others" outnumbered those who believed in the balloon as a weapon of war, and in both cases these "others" abandoned the concept as soon as possible.

In closing the subject of Civil War ballooning, it should be noted that the South made periodic use of both hot-air balloons and balloons filled with gas from the Richmond city gas mains. There were very few hot-air balloons, and only two gas-filled balloons. One of the hot-air balloons, manned by young Captain John Randolph Bryan, made several ascensions. The most important of these was an inadvertent but significant free-flight reconnaissance in mid April 1862, which provided valuable information on advancing Federal forces to General Johnston. The gas-filled balloons used silk in their construction, leading to the myth that they had been built from the dresses of patriotic Confederate women. Neither of the gas balloons was used in a significant way.

Balloons would continue to see limited use by various military units, but there were no further attempts to use them on the scale achieved by either the French Aérostiers or the querulous American Civil War balloonists. The British Army used balloons in the Boer

War. The Italians had rather less success with balloons in Ethiopia in 1890 than it would have with aircraft forty-five years later. The French used them in what would become French Indo-china in 1894 and in Madagascar in 1895. The United States made limited but successful use of the balloon in Cuba during the Spanish-American War of 1898.[9]

It was not until World War I that the dictates of trench warfare made balloon observation indispensable. The intensive use that all warring factions made of balloons was covered earlier.

Development of lighter-than-air vehicles continued, however, with great advances made in powered airships. Henri Giffard had created the first airship in 1852, and over the next fifty years many more would follow. The Brazilian *bon vivant*, Alberto Santos-Dumont, had success, as did Thomas Scott Baldwin, who demonstrated his airship the *California Arrow* at the St. Louis World's Fair of 1904.

And there was another thread in this story, one that directly links the ballooning efforts of the Civil War and the Siege of Paris with the air campaigns of both World War I and World War II. The custodian of that thread is Count Ferdinand von Zeppelin.

As a young man of excellent family, von Zeppelin was treated royally on his visit to the United States in 1863, during which he observed a balloon ascension. Then, in his capacity as a dashing cavalry officer in the Wurttemburg Cavalry Brigade in 1871, he witnessed the French use of balloons. These early experiences would lead him, late in life, to the career in which he became world famous, and which would inaugurate a totally new phase in air power, that of strategic bombardment. The fleet of Zeppelins that bombed England during World War I had an influence on military thinking out of all proportion to the damage they caused. More important, they had great effect upon German and British planning before World War II.

Notes

Chapter 1

1. Lee Payne, *Lighter than Air, An Illustrated History of the Airship* (New York: Orion Books, 1991), 28.

2. Charles H. Gibbs-Smith, *The Rebirth of European Aviation* (London: Her Majesty's Stationery Office, 1974), 182.

3. Lee Kennett, *The First Air War, 1914-1918* (New York: The Free Press, 1991), 13.

4. Pietor Maravigna, *The First War Flights in the World, Libia MCMXI* (Rome: Historical Division of the Italian Air Force, 1953), 53.

5. Ibid.

6. Robert K. Massie, *Dreadnought: Britain, Germany and the Coming of the Great War* (New York: Random House, 1991), 178.

7. Robert K. Massie, *Nicholas and Alexandra* (New York: Dell, 1967), 388.

8. John H. Morrow Jr., *The Great War in the Air* (Washington, D.C.: Smithsonian Institution Press, 1993), 24.

9. Charles Christienne and Pierre Lissarrague, *A History of French Military Aviation* (Washington, D.C.: Smithsonian Institution Press, 1986), 39.

10. J. M. Bruce, *The Aeroplanes of the Royal Flying Corps (Military Wing)* (London: Putnam, 1982), 57.

11. Peter Gray and Owen Thetford, *German Aircraft of the First World War* (London: Putnam, 1962), ix.

Chapter 2

1. Walter J. Boyne, *Silver Wings: A History of the United States Air Force* (New York: Simon and Schuster, 1993), 29.

2. Morrow, 35.

3. Hilary St. George Saunders, *Per Ardua: The Rise of British Air Power 1911-1939* (London: Oxford University Press, 1944), 29.

4. Alan Durkota, Thomas Darcey, and Victor Kulikov, *The Imperial Russian Air Service: Famous Pilots and Aircraft of World War I* (Mountain View, Calif.: Flying Machines Press, 1995), 4.

5. Morrow, 46.

6. Bruce, 471.

7. Harald Penrose, *British Aviation: The Pioneer Years* (London: Putnam, 1967), 360.

8. J. M. Spaight, *The Beginnings of Organized Air Power* (London: Longmans, Green and Co., 1927), 293.

9. Christienne and Lissarrague, 119.

10. Spaight, 293.

11. Sue Fischer, "Thomsen, Hermann von der Lieth," *Air Warfare: An International Encyclopedia,* Walter J. Boyne, ed. (Denver, Santa Barbara, Oxford, U.K.: ABC-Clio, 2002), 626.

12. Spaight, 293.

13. Durkota, 5.

14. Peter M. Grosz, George Haddow, and Peter Scheimer, *Austro-Hungarian Army Aircraft of World War One* (Mountain View, Calif.: Flying Machines Press, 1993), 1.

15. Ibid.

16. Walter Raleigh, *The War in the Air, Vol. I* (Nashville, Tenn.: The Battery Press, 1998), 234.

17. W. M. Lamberton and E. F. Cheesman, *Reconnaissance and Bomber Aircraft of the 1914-1918 War* (Letchworth, Herts, U.K.: Harleyford Publications, Ltd., 1962), 70.

18. Bruce, 378.

19. Walter Bloem, *The Advance from Mons* (London: Peter Davies, Ltd., 1930), 138.

20. Saunders, 39.

21. August G. Blume, in a letter to the author dated January 10, 2002.

22. John R. Cuneo, *Winged Mars, Vol. II* (Harrisburg, Pa.: The Military Publishing Services Co., 1947), 38.

23. Peter Mead, *The Eye in the Air* (London: Her Majesty's Stationery Office, 1983), 17.

24. George P. Neumann, *The German Air Force in the Great War* (London: Hodder & Stoughton, Ltd., 1921), 6.

25. Christienne and Lissarrague, 69.

26. Ibid.

27. Saunders, 42.

28. Lamberton and Cheesman, 10.

29. Christienne and Lissarrague, 184.

30. Gray and Thetford, 202.

31. Saunders, 52.

32. Gray and Thetford, xxxvii.

33. C. H. Barnes, *Shorts Aircraft Since 1910* (London: Putnam, 1967), 60.

34. Ibid, 12.

35. Royal Air Force Air Historical Branch, *The Royal Air Force in the Great War* (London: The Imperial War Museum, 1936), 254.

36. Owen Thetford, *British Naval Aircraft Since 1912* (London: Putnam, 1977), 82.

Chapter 3

1. Walter J. Boyne, *Aces in Command: Fighter Pilots as Combat Leaders* (Dulles, Va.: Brasseys, 2001), 1.

2. Norman L. Franks, Frank W. Bailey, and Russell Guest, *Above the Lines: A Complete Record of the Fighter Aces of the German Air Service* (London: Grub Street, 1993), 76, 134.

3. Morrow, 92.

4. J. M. Winter, *The Experience of World War I* (New York: Oxford University Press, 1989), 124.

5. Christienne and Lissarrague, 96.

6. Kennett, 71.

7. Ibid, 72.

8. Norman L. Franks, Frank W. Bailey, and Russell Guest, *Bloody April . . . Black September* (London: Grub Street, 1995), 110.

9. Norman L. Franks, Frank W. Bailey, and Rick Duiven, *The Jasta Pilots* (London: Grub Street, 1996), 319.

10. Gray and Thetford, 154.

11. "The Infantry Aeroplane and the Infantry Balloon," British translation of a captured German document dated 1 September 1917 (Washington, D.C.: War Department, Army War College, 1918).

12. Bruce, 550.

13. *USAF Statistical Digest.* Washington, D.C.: SAF/FMC, USAF, 2000.

14. Christienne and Lissarrague, 83.

15. Morrow, 128.

16. Ibid, 335.

17. James J. Sloan Jr., *Wings of Honor: American Airmen in World War I* (Atglen, Pa.: Schiffer Publishing Company, 1994), 313.

18. Walter J. Boyne, "The St. Mihiel Salient," *Air Force Magazine,* February 2000, 74.

19. David Wragg, *The Offensive Weapon: The Strategy of Bombing* (London: Robert Hale, 1986), 34.

20. Lee Kennett, *A History of Strategic Bombing* (New York: Charles Scribner's Sons, 1982), 20.

21. Douglas H. Robinson, *The Zeppelin in Combat* (Atglen, Pa.: Schiffer Publishing Company, 1994), 355.

22. Peter Kilduff, *Germany's First Air Force 1914-1918* (Osceola, Wis.: Motorbooks International Publishers, 1991), 26.

23. Raymond Fredette, *The Sky on Fire: The First Battle of Britain, 1917-1918* (New York: Harcourt, Brace Jovanovich, 1966), 39.

24. Ibid, 40.

25. Christopher Cole and E. F. Cheesman, *The Air Defense of Great Britain, 1914-1918* (London: Putnam, 1984), 242.

26. Ernst von Hoeppner, *Germany's War in the Air* (Nashville, Tenn.: The Battery Press, 1994), 133-37.

27. Royal Air Force Air Historical Branch, 237.

28. G. W. Haddow and Peter M. Grosz, *The German Giants: The Story of the R-Planes, 1914-1919* (London: Putnam, 1962), 3-4.

29. H. A. Jones, *The War in the Air, Vol. II* (Nashville, Tenn.: The Battery Press, 1999), Appendix I.

30. Ibid.

31. Jones, Vol. VI, 366, 367.

32. Jones, Vol. II, 182.

33. Ibid, 270-71.

34. Royal Air Force Air Historical Branch, 294.

35. Ibid, 382.

36. Sir John Slessor, *The Central Blue* (New York: Frederick A. Praeger, 1957), 46.

37. Royal Air Force Air Historical Branch, 321.

38. Jones, Vol. VI, 145.

39. Ibid, 153.

Chapter 4

1. Harald J. Penrose, *British Aviation: The Adventuring Years, 1919-1929* (London: Putnam, 1973), 19.

2. Martin Gilbert, *Churchill: A Life* (New York: Henry Holt & Co., 1991), 405.

3. Andrew Boyle, *Trenchard, Man of Vision* (New York: W. W. Norton & Company, 1962), 331.

4. Ibid, 349.

5. H. A. Jones, *The War in the Air, Vol. VI* (Nashville, Tenn.: The Battery Press, 1999), 136.

6. John A. Terraine, *A Time for Courage: The Royal Air Force in the European War 1939-1945* (New York: McMillan, 1985), 20.

7. Gilbert, 485.

8. Ian Kershaw, *Hitler 1889-1936: Hubris* (New York: W. W. Norton & Company, 1999), 444.

9. Slessor, 54.

10. Terraine, 54.

11. Terry C. Treadwell and Alan C. Wood, *Airships of the First World War* (Stroud, Gloucestershire, U.K.: Tempus Publishing Limited, 1999), 123.

12. Philip S. Meilinger, "Giulio Douhet and the Origins of Airpower Theory," *The Paths of Heaven, the Evolution of Airpower Theory,* Col. Philip Meilinger, ed. (Maxwell Air Force Base, Ala.: Air University Press, 1997), 3.

13. Ibid, 4.

14. Giulo Douhet, *The Command of the Air,* 1927 edition translated by Dino Ferarri in 1942 (Washington, D.C.: Office of Air Force History, 1983), 23.

15. Dr. James S. Corum, "Airpower Thought in Continental Europe between the Wars," *The Paths of Heaven,* 160.

16. Walter J. Boyne, "The Spirit of Billy Mitchell," *Air Force Magazine,* June 1996, 66.

17. Mark A. Clodfelter, "Molding Airpower Convictions: Development and Legacy of William Mitchell's Strategic Thought," *The Paths of Heaven,* 83.

18. Maurer Maurer, ed., *The U.S. Air Service in World War I, Vol. II* (Washington, D.C.: Office of Air Force History, 1978), 145.

19. Boyne, "The Spirit of Billy Mitchell," 70.

20. Maurer Maurer, *Aviation in the U.S. Army, 1919-1939* (Washington, D.C.: Office of Air Force History, 1987), 120.

21. Ibid.

22. Richard Suchenwirth, *USAF Historical Studies No. 160: The Development of the German Air Force, 1919-1939.* Harry R. Fletcher, ed. (New York: Arno Press, 1970), iii.

23. Corum, 169.

24. Suchenwirth, 2.

25. Ibid, 13.

26. Hans Bauer, *Hitler at My Side* (Houston: Eichler Publishing, 1986), 50.

27. E. R. Hooton, *Phoenix Triumphant: The Rise and Rise of the Luftwaffe* (London: Arms and Armour Press, 1994), 96.

28. Samuel W. Mitcham, *Men of the Luftwaffe* (Novato, Calif.: Presidio Press, 1988), 9.

29. Anthony C. Cain, *The Forgotten Air Force: French Air Doctrine in the 1930s* (Washington, D.C.: Smithsonian Institution Press, 2002), 2.

30. Christienne and Lissarrague, 259.

31. Ibid, 241.

32. William Shirer, *The Collapse of the Third Republic* (New York: Simon and Schuster, 1969), 254.

33. Ibid, 272.

34. Christienne and Lissarraque, 260.

35. Ibid, 276.

36. Corum, 163.

37. George Mellinger, excerpted from material sent to the author in preparation of *Air Warfare: An International Encyclopedia*.

38. Mark R. Peattie, *Sunburst, the Rise of Japanese Naval Air Power, 1909-1941* (Annapolis, Md.: Naval Institute Press, 2001), 151.

Chapter 5

1. Paul Schmidt, *Hitler's Interpreter* (London: William Heinemann, 1951), 41.

2. David Irving, *Goering: A Biography* (New York: William Morrow & Co., 1989), 163.

3. Wayne S. Cole, *Charles A. Lindbergh and the Battle Against American Intervention in World War II* (New York: Harcourt Brace Jovanovich, 1974), 34.

4. Al Williams, *Airpower* (New York: Coward-McCann, 1940), 198.

5. David Irving, *The Rise and Fall of the Luftwaffe: the Life of Field Marshal Erhard Milch* (Boston: Little, Brown and Company, 1973), 64; Williamson Murray, *Luftwaffe* (Baltimore: The Nautical and Aviation Publishing Company of America, 1985), 20.

6. Christienne and Lissarrague, 300.

7. Ian Kershaw, *Hitler 1936-1945: Nemesis* (New York: W. W. Norton & Company, 2000), 121.

8. Ibid, 173.

9. Slessor, 62.

10. George Mellinger, "Stepan Suprun," *Air Warfare: An International Encyclopedia,* 608.

11. V. S. Shumikhin, *Sovetskaia voennaia aviatsiia 1917-1941* (Moscow: Izdatel'stvo Nauka, Institute voennoi istorii Ministerstva oborony SSR,1996), 252-53. (Translated and provided by George Mellinger.)

12. Robert Jackson, *The Red Falcons: The Soviet Air Force in Action, 1919-1969* (London: Clifton House, 1970), 59.

13. Richard C. DeAngelis with D. Y. Louie, "Sinking of the USS Panay," *Air Warfare: An International Encyclopedia.* (Information provided electronically to the author by Mr. DeAngelis.)

14. Alan Bullock, *Hitler and Stalin: Parallel Lives* (New York: Alfred A. Knopf, 1992), 735.

15. Airpower Research Institute (CADRE/AR), *Italo-Ethiopian War, 1935-36.* Expeditionary Warfare: The World Wars http://www.airpower.maxwell.af.mil/airchronicles/ct/research/ May, 2002.

16. Kershaw, *Nemesis,* 16.

17. Raymond L. Proctor, *Hitler's Luftwaffe in the Spanish Civil War* (Westport, Conn.: Greenwood Press, 1983), 31.

18. Spencer Tucker, "Spanish Civil War, Air Aspects of," *Air Warfare: An International Encyclopedia,* 590.

19. Gerald Howson, *Aircraft of the Spanish Civil War, 1936-1939* (London: Putnam, 1990), 137.

20. Edward F. Homze, *Arming the Luftwaffe* (Lincoln: University of Nebraska Press, 1976), 182.

Chapter 6

1. Homze, 222.

2. Ibid, 232.

3. Cyril March, ed., *The Rise and Fall of the German Air Force, 1933-1945* (London: Her Majesty's Stationery Office, 1983), 33.

4. Jerzy B. Cynk, *History of the Polish Air Force, 1918-1969* (Berkshire, U.K.: Osprey Publishing Company, 1972), 121.

5. Ibid, 100.

6. Hooton, 188.

7. Walter J. Boyne, *Clash of Wings: World War II in the Air* (New York: Simon and Schuster, 1994), 39.

8. Cain, 2.

9. Christienne and Lissarrague, 325.

10. Boyne, *Clash of Wings,* 50.

11. Christienne and Lissarrague, 327.

12. Terraine, 123.

13. Boyne, *Clash of Wings,* 47.

14. March, 66.

15. Christienne and Lissarrague, 345.

16. Sholto Douglas, Marshal of the Royal Air Force, Lord Douglas of Kirtleside, with Robert Wright. *Sholto Douglas, Combat and Command: The Story of an Airman in Two World Wars* (New York: Simon and Schuster, 1963), 393.

17. Hooton, 240.

18. Faris R. Kirkland, *The French Air Force in 1940.* Aerospace Power Chronicles. www.airpower.maxwell.af.mil/airchronicles/aureview/1985/Sep-Oct/Kirkland.html, 1.

19. Kershaw, *Nemesis,* 297.

20. Boyne, *Clash of Wings,* 66.

21. Ibid, 67.

22. Ibid, 84.

Chapter 7

1. March, 165.

2. Franz Halder, *The Halder War Diary, 1939-1942* (Novato, Calif.: Presidio Press, 1988), 446.

3. Von Hardesty, *Red Phoenix: The Rise of Soviet Airpower 1941-1945* (London: Arms and Armour Press, 1982), 31.

4. Bill Gunston, *Aircraft of the Soviet Union* (London: Osprey Publishing Company, 1983), 109.

5. Boyne, *Clash of Wings,* 161.

6. Agawa Hiroyuki, *The Reluctant Admiral: Yamamoto and the Imperial Navy* (Tokyo: Kodansha International, Ltd., 1982), 189.

7. Walter J. Boyne, *Clash of Titans: World War II at Sea* (New York: Simon and Schuster, 1995), 193.

8. E. B. Potter, *Nimitz* (Annapolis, Md.: Naval Institute Press, 1976), 83.

9. Robert T. Finney, *History of the Air Corps Tactical School, 1920-1940* (Washington, D.C.: Center for Air Force History, 1992), 63.

10. Ibid, 76.

11. Stephen L. McFarland and Wesley Phillips Newton, *To Command the Sky: The Battle for Air Superiority over Germany, 1942-1944* (Washington, D. C.: Smithsonian Institution Press, 1991), 105.

12. Richard C. DeAngelis, "AWPD/1 and AWPD-42," *Air Warfare: An International Encyclopedia,* 59.

13. Robert Frank Futrell, *Ideas, Concepts, Doctrine: Basic Thinking in the United States Air Force, 1907-1960* (Maxwell Air Force Base, Ala.: Air University Press, 1989), 131.

14. McFarland, 109.

15. Terraine, 295.

16. Boyne, *Clash of Wings,* 284.

17. E. B. Potter and Chester W. Nimitz eds., *The Great Sea War* (New York: Bramhall House, 1960), 227.

Chapter 8

1. Boyne, *Clash of Wings,* 330.

2. W. A. Jacobs, "Operation Overlord," *Case Studies in the Achievement of Air Superiority,* Benjamin F. Cooling, ed. (Washington, D.C.: Center for Air Force History, 1994), 292.

3. Boyne, *Clash of Wings,* 296.

4. Walter J. Boyne, *Beyond the Horizons: The Lockheed Story* (New York: St. Martin's Press, 1998), 112.

5. Max Hastings, *Bomber Command* (New York: Dial Press, 1979), 295.

6. John Searby, *The Bomber Battle for Berlin* (Shrewsbury, U.K.: Airlife, 1991), 157.

7. Henry Probert, *Bomber Harris: His Life and Times* (London: Greenhill Books, 2001), 318.

8. James H. Doolittle with Carroll V. Glines, *I Could Never Be So Lucky Again* (New York: Bantam Books, 1991), 380.

9. Ray Wagner, *Mustang Designer* (New York: Orion Books, 1990), 64.

10. March, 322.

11. Jacobs, 297.

12. March, 302.

13. McFarland, 170.

14. Boyne, *Clash of Wings,* 337.

15. Walter J. Boyne, *Messerschmitt Me 262: Arrow to the Future* (London: Janes, 1980), 38.

16. John Ellis, *World War II, A Statistical Survey* (New York: Facts on File, 1993), 233.

17. R. J. Overy, *The Air War 1939-1945* (New York: Stein and Day Pub., 1981), 120.

18. W. A. Jacobs, "Battle for France," *Case Studies in the Development of Close Air Support,* Benjamin F. Cooling, ed. (Washington, D.C.: Office of Air Force History, 1990), 283.

19. Thomas A. Hughes, *OVERLORD, General Pete Quesada and the Triumph of Tactical Air Power in World War II* (New York: Free Press, 1995), 19.

20. Kenneth P. Werrell, *Blankets of Fire* (Washington, D.C.: Smithsonian Institution Press, 1996), 140.

21. Wesley F. Craven and James L. Cate, *The Army Air Forces in World War Two, Vol. V: The Pacific: Matterhorn to Nagasaki, June 1944 to August 1946* (Washington, D.C.: Office of Air Force History, 1983), 613.

22. Boyne, *Clash of Wings,* 373.

23. Thomas B. Allen and Norman Polmar, *Code-Name Downfall: The Secret Plan to Invade Japan and Why Truman Dropped the Bomb* (New York: Simon and Schuster, 1995), 296.

Chapter 9

1. Thomas Parrish, *The Cold War Encyclopedia* (New York: Henry Holt, 1996), 149.

2. Jeffrey G. Barlow, *Revolt of the Admirals: The Fight for Naval Aviation, 1949-1950* (Washington, D.C.: Brassey's, 1998), 248.

3. Walter J. Boyne, *Beyond the Wild Blue: A History of the USAF* (New York: St. Martin's Press, 1997), 41.

4. Bill Gunston, *Aircraft of the Soviet Union* (London: Osprey Publishing Company, 1983), 323.

5. Carl H. Builder, *The Icarus Syndrome* (New Brunswick, N.J.: Transaction Publishers, 1994), 35.

6. Norman Polmar and Timothy Laur, *Strategic Air Command, 2nd ed.* (Baltimore: The Nautical and Aviation Publishing Company of America, 1990), 185.

7. Jacob Neufeld, *The Development of Ballistic Missiles in the United States Air Force 1945-1960* (Washington, D.C.: Office of Air Force History, 1990), 242.

8. Jackson, *The Red Falcons: The Soviet Air Force in Action, 1919-1969,* 160.

9. George Mellinger, email communication to author of July 19, 2002, based on his research in Soviet archives.

10. David Rezelman, "CORONA Spy Satellites (Discoverer)," *Air Warfare: An International Encyclopedia,* 154.

11. Walter J. Boyne, *Beyond the Wild Blue,* 140.

12. Ibid.

Chapter 10

1. *The Military Balance, 1970-1971* (London: Institute for Strategic Studies, 1970), 1-12.

2. Robert F. Futrell, *The United States Air Force in Korea, 1950-1953* (Washington, D.C.: Office of Air Force History, 1983), 372.

3. Jerry Miller, *Nuclear Weapons and Aircraft Carriers* (Washington, D.C.: Smithsonian Institution Press, 2001), 93.

4. Earl H. Tilford Jr., *Setup: What the Air Force Did in Vietnam and Why* (Maxwell Air Force Base, Ala.: Air University Press, 1991), 34.

5. Ibid, 35.

6. Clodfelter, 27.

7. Edwin E. Moise, "Pierce Arrow Operation," *Encyclopedia of the Vietnam War,* Spencer C. Tucker, ed. (Santa Barbara, Calif.: ABC-Clio, 1998), 573.

8. Tilford, 1.

9. Ibid, 103.

10. Boyne, *Beyond the Wild Blue,* 155.

11. Charles D. Bright, ed., *Historical Dictionary of the U.S. Air Force* (New York: Greenwood Press, 1992), 286.

12. John Robert Greene, "Nixon Doctrine," *Encyclopedia of the Vietnam War,* 504.

13. Lewis Sorley, "Vietnamization," *Encyclopedia of the Vietnam War,* 799.

14. Dale Andrade, "Easter Offensive" *Encyclopedia of the Vietnam War,* 187.

15. Henry A. Kissinger, *The White House Years* (Boston: Little, Brown, and Company, 1979), 1180.

16. Earl H. Tilford Jr., "Linebacker II," *Encyclopedia of the Vietnam War,* 379.

17. Phillip S. Meilinger, "More Bogus Charges Against Airpower," *Air Force Magazine,* October 2002, Vol. 85, No. 10, 53.

18. Walter J. Boyne, "Linebacker II," *Air Force Magazine*, November 1997, Vol. 80, No. 11, 50.

Chapter 11
1. Walter J. Boyne, *The Two O'Clock War: The 1973 Yom Kippur Conflict and the Airlift that Saved Israel* (New York: St. Martins Press, 2002), 283.
2. Ibid, 11.
3. Ibid, 253.
4. Lon O. Nordeen Jr., *Air Warfare in the Missile Age* (Washington, D.C.: Smithsonian Institution Press, 1985), 184.
5. Ibid, 186.
6. Ronald E. Bergquist, *The Role of Airpower in the Iran-Iraq War* (Maxwell Air Force Base, Ala.: Air University Press, 1988), 78.
7. Boyne, *Beyond the Wild Blue*, 217.
8. Lt. Col. David S. Fadok, "John Boyd and John Warden: Airpower's Quest for Strategic Paralysis," *The Paths of Heaven*, 373.
9. Williamson Murray, *Air War in the Persian Gulf* (Baltimore: The Nautical and Aviation Publishing Company of America, 1995), 19.
10. Richard P. Hallion, *Storm Over Iraq* (Washington, D.C.: Smithsonian Institution Press, 1992), 188.
11. Benjamin S. Lambeth, *The Transformation of American Air Power* (Ithaca, N.Y.: Cornell University Press, 2000), 160.
12. Air Vice Marshal Tony Mason, *Air Power: A Centennial Appraisal* (London: Brassey's, 1994), 236.
13. Edward J. Felker, "Soviet Military Doctrine and Air Theory: Change Through the Light of a Storm," *The Paths of Heaven*, 509.
14. Ibid, 520.
15. Mark D. Witzel, "Deliberate Force," *Air Warfare: An International Encyclopedia*, 173.
16. Mark D. Witzel, "Allied Force," *Air Warfare: An International Encyclopedia*, 33.

Chapter 12
1. According to a definition in the June 5 Congressional Research Service Report "Iraq: Defense Program Implications for Congress", network centric warfare refers to using networking technology—computers, data links, and networking software—to link U.S. military personnel, ground vehicles, aircraft and ships into a series of

highly integrated local- and wide-area networks capable of sharing critical tactical information on a rapid and continuous basis, (CRS-46).

2. At the time of the Iraq War, about 220,000 reservists were on active duty. By April 25, 2003, 286,000 reservists were activated for federal service, while another 47,000 were tasked for other situations, e.g. to serve as members of the National Guard. Since World War II, only the Korean War mobilization of 858,000 reservists was larger. (CSR: Iraq War: Defense Program Implications for Congress).

3. Congressional Research Service Report "Iraq War: Defense Program Implications for Congress", June 5, 2003, p41.

4. This is to the extent that Arab opinion of the United States and its policies can be affected positively by short-term actions. It is the author's belief that the decision to pursue the policy of minimizing collateral damage does not secure the "hearts and minds" of the Arab world, but certainly must have an effect upon other nations. Securing genuine and wide-spread Arab friendship will not occur for many decades, if ever.

5. Boyd described a decision-making cycle as an OODA loop, in which an observation is made, orientation is achieved, a decision is made, and action is taken in a process that involves the continuous feedback of information to modify and shape each of the steps. The person who exercises his OODA loop activities faster than an opponent will win; the goal is to get "inside" the enemy OODA loop and stay there. For an excellent discussion of Boyd's theory see "John Boyd and John Warden: Airpower's Quest for Strategic Paralysis" in *Pathways to Heaven, the Evolution of Air Power Theory*, edited by Philip Meilinger.

6. Mark Ayton, "War Diary", Air Forces Monthly, May, 2003, p58.

7. Bruce Rolfsen, "Air power unleashed", Armed Forces Journal, June, 2003, p30.

Appendix
1. Payne, 2.

2. Donald D. Jackson, *The Aeronauts* (Alexandria, Va.: Time/Life Books, 1981), 14.

3. F. Stansbury Haydon, *Military Ballooning during the Early Civil War* (Baltimore: John Hopkins University Press, 2000), 2.

4. Ibid, 8.

5. Ibid, 10.

6. Lee Kennett, *A History of Strategic Bombing* (New York: Charles Scribner's Sons, 1982), 10.

7. Haydon, 169.

8. Tom D. Crouch, *The Eagle Aloft* (Washington, D.C.: Smithsonian Institution Press, 1983), 358.

9. Kennett, *A History of Strategic Bombing,* 10.

Bibliography

Agawa, Hirouki. *The Reluctant Admiral: Yamamoto and the Imperial Navy.* Tokyo: Kodansha International, Ltd., 1982.

Airpower Research Institute (CADRE/AR). *Italo-Ethiopian War, 1935-36.* Expeditionary Warfare: The World Wars http://www.airpower.maxwell.af.mil/airchronicles/ct/research/ May, 2002.

Allen, H. R. *The Legacy of Lord Trenchard.* London: Cassell, 1972.

Allen, Thomas B. and Norman Polmar. *Code-Name Downfall: The Secret Plan to Invade Japan and Why Truman Dropped the Bomb.* New York: Simon & Schuster, 1995.

Andrews, Allen. *The Air Marshals: The Air War in Western Europe.* New York: Morrow, 1970.

Andrews, William F. *Airpower Against An Army: Challenge and Response in CENTAF's Duel with the Republican Guards.* Maxwell Air Force Base, Ala.: Air University Press, 1998.

Appleman, Roy, James M. Burns, Russell E. Guegeler, and John Stevens. *United States Army in World War II. Okinawa, the Last Battle.* Washington, D.C.: Center for Military History, 1993.

Arnold, Henry H. *Global Mission.* New York: Harper & Brothers, 1949.

————"First Report of the Commanding General of the Army Air Forces to the Secretary of War." (Also Second Report and Third Report.) *The War Reports of General of the Army George C. Marshall, Chief of Staff; General of the Army H. H. Arnold, Commanding General, Army Air Forces; and Fleet Admiral Ernest J. King, Commander in Chief, United States Fleet and Chief of Naval Operations.* Philadelphia: Lippincott, 1947.

Ball, Desmond and Jeffrey Richelson. *Strategic Nuclear Targeting.* Ithaca, N.Y.: Cornell University Press, 1986.

Ballard, Jack S., Ray L. Bowers, et al. *The United States Air Force in Southeast Asia, 1961-1973: An Illustrated Account.* Washington, D.C.: Office of Air Force History, 1984.

431

Barlow, Jeffrey G. *Revolt of the Admirals: The Fight for Naval Aviation, 1949-1950*. Washington, D.C.: Brassey's, 1998.

Barnes, C. H. *Shorts Aircraft Since 1910*. London: Putnam, 1967.

Bauer, Hans. *Hitler at My Side*. Houston: Eichler Publishing, 1986.

Belote, James H. and William. *Titans of the Seas: The Development of the Japanese and American Carrier Task Forces During World War II*. New York: Harper & Row, 1975.

Bergquist, Ronald E., Maj. *The Role of Airpower in the Iran-Iraq War*. Maxwell Air Force Base, Ala: Air University Press, 1988.

Bloem, Walter. *The Advance from Mons*. London: Peter Davies, Ltd., 1930.

Boggs, Charles W. Jr. *Marine Aviation in the Philippines*. Washington, D.C.: Historical Division, Headquarters, U.S. Marine Corps, 1951.

Bowers, Peter and Gordon Swanborough. *U.S. Military Aircraft Since 1909*. Washington, D.C.: Smithsonian Institution Press, 1989.

Bowers, Ray L. *The United States Air Force in Southeast Asia: Tactical Airlift*. Washington, D.C.: Office of Air Force History, 1983.

Boyle, Andrew. *Trenchard, Man of Vision*. New York: W. W. Norton & Co., 1962.

Boyne, Walter J. *Clash of Wings: World War II in the Air*. New York: Simon & Schuster, 1994.

———*The Two O'Clock War: The 1973 Yom Kippur Conflict and the Airlift that Saved Israel*. New York: St. Martins Press, 2002.

———*Clash of Titans: World War II at Sea*. New York: Simon & Schuster, 1995.

———*Beyond the Wild Blue: A History of the USAF, 1947-1997*. New York: St. Martins Press, 1997.

———*The Smithsonian Book of Flight*. Washington, D.C.: Smithsonian Institution Press, 1986.

———ed. *Air Warfare: An International Encyclopedia*. Denver, Santa Barbara, Oxford, U.K.: ABC-Clio, 2002.

———*Silver Wings: A History of the United States Air Force*. New York: Simon and Schuster, 1993.

———*Aces in Command: Fighter Pilots as Combat Leaders*. Dulles, Va.: Brasseys, 2001.

———*Beyond the Horizons: The Lockheed Story*. New York: St. Martin's Press, 1998.

———*Messerschmitt Me 262: Arrow to the Future*. London, Janes, 1980.

Bradin, James W. *From Hot Air to Hellfire: The History of Army Attack Aviation.* Novato, Calif.: Presidio Press, 1994.

Bright, Charles D., ed. *Historical Dictionary of the U.S. Air Force.* New York: Greenwood Press, 1992.

Brodie, Bernard, ed. *The Absolute Weapon: Atomic Power and World Order.* Freeport, R.I.: Books for Library Press, 1972.

Broughton, Jack. *Going Downtown: The War Against Hanoi and Washington.* New York: Orion Books, 1988.

Bruce, J. M. *British Aeroplanes 1914-1918.* London: Putnam, 1957.

——————*The Aeroplanes of the Royal Flying Corps (Military Wing).* London: Putnam, 1982.

Builder, Carl H. *The Icarus Syndrome.* New Brunswick, N.J.: Transaction Publishers, 1994.

Bullock, Alan. *Hitler and Stalin: Parallel Lives* New York. Alfred A. Knopf, 1992.

Cain, Anthony C. *The Forgotten Air Force: French Air Doctrine in the 1930s.* Washington, D.C.: Smithsonian Institution Press, 2002.

Cannon, M. Hamlin. *U.S. Army in World War II: Leyte, The Return to the Philippines.* Washington, D.C.: Office of the Chief of Military History, 1954.

Carter, Kit. C. and Robert Mueller, eds. *The Army Air Forces in World War II: Combat Chronology, 1941-1945.* Washington, D.C.: Office of Air Force History, 1991.

Chandler, Charles DeForest and Frank Lahm. *How Our Army Grew Wings: Airmen and Aircraft Before 1914.* New York: Arno Press, 1979

Chang, Gordon H. *Friends and Enemies: The United States, China and the Soviet Union, 1948-1972.* Stanford, Calif.: Stanford University Press, 1990.

Chant, Christopher. *A Compendium of Armaments and Military Hardware.* London and New York: Routledge & Kegan Paul, 1987.

Chesnau, Roger. *Aircraft Carriers of the World, 1914 to the Present: An Illustrated Encyclopedia,* 2nd edition. London: Arms and Armour Press, 1992.

Chinnery, Philip D. *Vietnam: The Helicopter War.* Annapolis, Md.: Naval Institute Press, 1991.

Christienne, Charles and Pierre Lissarrague. *A History of French Military Aviation.* Washington, D.C.: Smithsonian Institution Press, 1986.

Churchill, Winston S. *The Second World War* (six volumes). Boston: Houghton Mifflin, 1948-1953.

Clark, Alan. *The Fall of Crete*. New York: Wm. Morrow and Co., 1962.

————*Barbarossa: The Russian-German Conflict, 1941-1945*. New York: Wm. Morrow and Co., 1965.

Clodfelter, Mark. *The Limits of Airpower: The American Bombing of North Vietnam*. New York: Free Press, 1989.

Coffey, Thomas M. *Iron Eagle: The Turbulent Life of General Curtis LeMay*. New York: Crown Publishers, 1986.

Cole, Jean Hascall. *Women Pilots of World War II*. Salt Lake City: University of Utah Press, 1992.

Cole, Wayne S. *Charles A. Lindbergh and the Battle Against American Intervention in World War II*. New York: Harcourt Brace Jovanovich, 1974.

Cooksley, Peter G. *Flying Bomb*. New York: Charles Scribner's Sons, 1979.

Cooling, Benjamin Franklin, ed. *Case Studies in the Development of Close Air Support*. Washington, D.C.: Office of Air Force History, 1990.

————*Case Studies in the Achievement of Air Superiority*. Washington, D.C.: Center for Air Force History, 1994.

Cooper, Malcolm. *The Birth of Independent Airpower: British Air Policy in The First World War*. London: Allen and Unwin, 1986.

Copp, DeWitt S. *Forged in Fire*. Garden City, N.Y.: Doubleday, 1982.

Corbett, Julian S. *Some Principles of Maritime Strategy*. Annapolis, Md.: Naval Institute Press, 1988.

Corum, James S. and Richard R. Mueller. *The Luftwaffe's Way of War: German Air Force Doctrine 1911-1945*. Baltimore: The Nautical & Aviation Publishing Company of America, 1998.

Coyne, James P. *Airpower in the Gulf*. Arlington, Va.: Air Force Association, 1992.

Crane, Conrad C. *Bombs, Cities and Civilians: American Airpower Strategy in World War II*. Lawrence: University Press of Kansas, 1993.

————*American Airpower Strategy in Korea, 1950-1953*. Lawrence: University Press of Kansas, 2000.

Craven, Wesley Frank and James Lea Cate, eds. *The Army Air Forces in World War Two* (seven volumes). Washington, D.C.: Office of Air Force History, 1983.

Crouch, Tom D. *The Eagle Aloft*. Washington, D.C.: Smithsonian Institution Press, 1983.

Cuneo, John R. *Winged Mars* (two volumes). Harrisburg, Pa.: Military Services Publishing Co., 1945-47.

Cynk, Jerzy B. *History of the Polish Air Force, 1918-1969.* Berkshire, U.K.: Osprey Publishing Company, 1972.

Davies, R. E. G. *A History of the World's Airlines.* London: Oxford University Press, 1964.

Davis, Benjamin O. Jr. *Benjamin O. Davis, Jr. American: An Autobiography.* New York: Plume, 1992.

Davis, Richard G. *Carl A. Spaatz and the Air War in Europe.* Washington: Center for Air Force History, 1993.

Day, George E. *Return With Honor.* Mesa, Ariz.: Champlin Museum Press, 1989.

Deichmann, Paul. *Spearhead for Blitzkrieg: Luftwaffe Operations in Support of the Army, 1939-1945.* London: Greenhill Books, 1996.

De Seversky, Alexander P. *Victory Through Air Power.* New York: Simon & Schuster, 1962.

Donald, David, ed. *US Air Force, Air Power Directory.* London: Aerospace Publishing, 1992. Ridgefield, Conn.: Airtime Publishing, 1992.

Donnelly, Thomas, Margaret Roth, and Caleb Baker. *Operation Just Cause.* New York: Lexington Books, 1991.

Doolittle, James H. with Carroll V. Glines. *I Could Never Be So Lucky Again: An Autobiography.* Atglen, Pa.: Schiffer Military/Aviation History, 1995.

———*I Could Never Be So Lucky Again.* New York: Bantam Books, 1991.

Dorr, Robert F. *Air War Hanoi.* London, New York, Sydney: Blandford Press, 1988

Dorr, Robert F. and Warren Thompson. *The Korean Air War.* Osceola, Wis.: Motorbooks International Publishers, 1994.

Douglas, Sholto with Robert Wright. *Sholto Douglas, Combat and Command: The Story of an Airman in Two World Wars.* New York: Simon & Schuster, 1966.

Douhet, Giulo. *The Command of the Air* (1927 edition translated by Dino Ferarri in 1942). Washington, D.C.: Office of Air Force History, 1983.

Dunmore, Spencer. *Wings for Victory: the Remarkable Story of the British Commonwealth Air Training Plan in Canada.* Toronto: McClelland and Stewart, 1994.

Durkota, Alan, Thomas Darcey, and Victor Kulikov. *The Imperial Russian Air Service: Famous Pilots and Aircraft of World War I.* Mountain View, Calif.: Flying Machines Press, 1995.

Edmonds, Walter D. *They Fought with What They Had: The Story of the Army Air Forces in the Southwest Pacific, 1941-1942*. Washington, D.C.: Center for Air Force History, 1992.

Ellis, John. *World War II, A Statistical Survey*. New York: Facts on File, 1993.

Emme, Eugene M., ed. *The Impact of Air Power*. Princeton, N.J.: D. Van Nostrand Co., 1959.

Eschmann, Karl J. *Linebacker: The Untold Story of the Air Raids Over North Vietnam*. New York: Ballantine Books, 1989.

Finney, Robert T. *History of the Air Corps Tactical School, 1920-1940*. Washington, D.C.: Center for Air Force History, 1992.

Flanagan, John F. *Vietnam Above the Treetops*. New York: Praeger, 1992.

Flintham, Victor. *Air Wars and Aircraft: A Detailed Record of Air Combat 1945 To Present*. New York: Facts on File, 1990.

Foulois, Benjamin D., Gen. with Carroll V. Glines. *From the Wright Brothers to the Astronauts: The Memoirs of Major General Benjamin D. Foulois*. New York: McGraw Hill, 1968.

Francillon, Rene J. *Japanese Aircraft of the Pacific War*. Annapolis, Md.: Naval Institute Press, 1979.

Frank, Benis M. and Henry I. Shaw Jr. *History of U.S. Marine Corps Operations in World War II, Vol. V. Victory And Occupation*. Washington, D.C.: Historical Branch, Headquarters, U.S. Marine Corps, 1968.

Frankland, Noble Dr. *The Bombing Offensive Against Germany*. London: Faber & Faber, 1965.

———gen. ed. *The Encyclopedia of Twentieth Century Warfare*. New York: Crown Publishing, 1989.

Franks, Norman L., Frank W. Bailey, and Russell Guest. *Above the Lines: A Complete Record of the Fighter Aces of the German Air Service*. London: Grub Street, 1993.

———*Bloody April . . . Black September*. London: Grub Street, 1995.

Franks, Norman L., Frank W. Bailey, and Rick Duiven. *The Jasta Pilots*. London: Grub Street, 1996.

Fredette, Raymond H. *The Sky on Fire: The First Battle of Britain, 1917-1918*. New York: Harcourt, Brace Jovanovich, 1966.

Freeman, Roger A. *The Mighty Eighth: A History of Units, Men and Machines of the U.S. 8th Air Force*. Osceola, Wis.: Motorbooks International Publishers, 1991.

Friedman, Norman. *U.S. Aircraft Carriers: An Illustrated Design History*. Annapolis, Md.: Naval Institute Press, 1983.

Friedman, Norman. *British Carrier Aviation: The Evolution of the Ships and Their Aircraft.* Annapolis, Md.: Naval Institute Press, 1988.

Fuchida, Mitsuo and Masatake Okumiya. *Midway: The Battle that Doomed Japan.* Annapolis, Md.: Naval Institute Press, 1955.

Futrell, Robert Frank. *Ideas, Concepts, Doctrine: A History of Basic Thinking in the United States Air Force, 1907-1964.* Maxwell Air Force Base, Ala.: Air University Press, 1971.

————*Ideas, Concepts, Doctrine: Basic Thinking in the United States Air Force, 1907-1960, Vol. I.* Maxwell Air Force Base, Ala.: Air University Press, 1989.

————*Ideas, Concepts, Doctrine: Basic Thinking in the United States Air Force, 1961-1984, Vol. II.* Maxwell Air Force Base, Ala.: Air University Press, 1989.

————*The United States Air Force in Korea, 1950-1953.* Washington, D.C.: Office of Air Force History, 1983.

Galland, Adolf. *The First and the Last.* New York: Holt, 1954.

Gantz, Kenneth F., Lt. Col., ed. *The United States Air Force Report on the Ballistic Missile.* New York: Doubleday & Company, 1958.

Gaston, James C. *Planning the American Air War: Four Men and Nine Days in 1941.* Washington, D.C.: National Defense University Press, 1982.

Geust, Carl-Fredrik. *Under the Red Star: Luftwaffe Aircraft in the Soviet Air Force.* Shrewsbury, U.K.: Airlife, 1993.

Gibbs-Smith, Charles. *The Rebirth of European Aviation.* London: Her Majesty's Stationery Office, 1974.

Gilbert, Martin. *Churchill: A Life.* New York: Henry Holt & Co., 1991.

Goldrick, James and John B. Hattendorf, eds. *Mahan Is Not Enough: The Proceedings of a Conference on the Works of Sir Julian Corbett and Admiral Sir Henry Richmond.* Newport, R.I.: Naval War College Press, 1993.

Gorn, Michael H. *Harnessing the Genie: Science and Technology Forecasting for the Air Force, 1944-1986.* Washington, D.C.: Office of Air Force History, 1988.

Gorrell, Edgar S. *The Measure of America's World War Aeronautical Effort.* Northfield, Vt.: Norwich University Press, 1940.

Gray, Peter and Owen Thetford. *German Aircraft of the First World War.* London: Putnam, 1962.

Green, William. *Warplanes of the Third Reich.* New York: Galahad Books, 1990.

Greer, Thomas A. USAF Historical Studies: No. 89. *The*

Development of Air Doctrine in the Army Air Arm, 1917-1941. Maxwell, Air Force Base, Ala.: USAF Historical Division, 1955.

Gross, Charles Joseph. *Prelude to the Total Force: The Air National Guard, 1943-1969.* Washington, D.C.: Office of Air Force History, 1985.

Grosz, Peter M., George Haddow, and Peter Scheimer. *Austro-Hungarian Army Aircraft of World War One.* Mountain View, Calif.: Flying Machines Press, 1993.

Groves, Leslie R. *Now It Can Be Told: The Story of the Manhattan Project.* New York: Harper & Brothers, 1962.

Gunston, Bill. *World Encyclopedia of Aircraft Manufacturers.* Northamptonshire, U.K.: Patrick Stephens, 1993.

———*Aircraft of the Soviet Union.* London: Osprey Publishing Company, 1983.

Gurney, Gene, Col. *Vietnam: The War in the Air, A Pictorial History of the U.S. Air Forces in the Vietnam War: Air Force, Army, Navy, and Marines.* New York: Crown Publishers, Inc., 1985.

Haddow, G. W. and Peter M. Grosz. *The German Giants: The Story of the R-Planes, 1914-1919.* London: Putnam, 1962.

Halberstadt, Hans. *The Wild Weasels: History of US Air Force SAM Killers, 1965-Today.* Osceola, Wis.: Motorbooks International Publishers, 1992.

Halder, Franz. *The Halder War Diary, 1939-1942.* Novato, Calif.: Presidio Press, 1988.

Hall, George M. *The Fifth Star.* New York: Praeger, 1994.

Hall, R. Cargill. *Missile Defense Alarm: The Genesis of Space-Based Infrared Early Warning.* Chantilly, Va.: NRO History Office, July 1988.

Hallion, Richard P. *Storm over Iraq.* Washington, D.C.: Smithsonian Institution Press, 1992.

———*Strike from the Sky: The History of Battlefield Air Attack, 1911-1945.* Washington, D.C.: Smithsonian Institution Press, 1989.

Halsey, William F. and Bryan J. *Admiral Halsey's Story.* New York: McGraw Hill, 1947.

Hammel, Eric. *Air War Europa: America's Air War Against Germany in Europe and North Africa, Chronology 1942-1945.* Pacifica, Calif.: Pacifica Press, 1994.

———*Air War Pacific: America's Air War Against Japan in East Asia and the Pacific, Chronology 1941-1945.* Pacifica, Calif.: Pacifica Press, 1998.

Hardesty, Von. *Red Phoenix: The Rise of Soviet Airpower 1941-1945.* London: Arms and Armour Press, 1982.

Harris, Arthur. *Bomber Offensive.* London: Collins, 1947.

Harrison, Marshall. *A Lonely Kind of War: Forward Air Controller, Vietnam.* Novato, Calif.: Presidio Press, 1989.

Hastings, Max. *Bomber Command.* New York: Dial Press, 1979.

Haydon, F. Sterling. *Military Ballooning During the Early Civil War.* Baltimore: John Hopkins University Press, 2000.

Higham, Robin. *Air Power, a Concise History.* New York: St. Martin's Press, 1972.

Hoeppner, Ernst von. *Germany's War in the Air.* Nashville, Tenn.: The Battery Press, 1994.

Holley, I. B. Jr. *Ideas and Weapons* Washington, D.C.: Office of Air Force History, 1983.

Homze, Edward F. *Arming the Luftwaffe.* Lincoln: University of Nebraska Press, 1976.

Hooton, E. R. *Phoenix Triumphant: The Rise and Rise of the Luftwaffe.* London: Brockhampton Press, 1994.

Howson, Gerald. *Aircraft of the Spanish Civil War, 1936-1939.* London: Putnam, 1990.

Hudson, James J. *Hostile Skies: A Combat History of the American Air Service in World War I.* Syracuse, N.Y.: Syracuse University Press, 1968.

Hughes, Thomas A. *OVERLORD, General Pete Quesada and the Triumph of Tactical Air Power in World War II.* New York: Free Press, 1995.

Hunsaker, Jerome C. *Aeronautics at the Mid-Century.* New Haven, Conn.: Yale University Press, 1952.

Hurley, Alfred F. *Billy Mitchell, Crusader for Air Power.* New York: Franklin Watts, 1964.

Hurley, Alfred F., Col., and Robert C. Ehrhart, Maj., eds. *Air Power and Warfare.* Washington, D.C.: Office of Air Force History, 1979.

"The Infantry Aeroplane and the Infantry Balloon." British translation of a captured German document dated 1 September 1917. Washington, D.C.: War Department, Army War College, 1918.

Irving, David. *Goering: A Biography.* New York: Wm. Morrow & Co., 1989.

——*The Rise and Fall of the Luftwaffe: the Life of Field Marshal Erhard Milch.* Boston: Little, Brown and Company, 1973.

Jackson, Donald D. *The Aeronauts.* Alexandria, Va.: Time/Life Books, 1981.

Jackson, Robert. *The Red Falcons: The Soviet Air Force in Action, 1919-1969*. Brighton, U.K.: Clifton House, 1970.

Jentschura, Hansgeorg, Dieter Jung, and Peter Mickel. *Warships of the Imperial Japanese Navy, 1869-1945*. London: Arms and Armour Press, 1977.

Jones, R. V. *Most Secret War*. London: Hamish Hamilton, 1978.

Kennett, Lee. *A History of Strategic Bombing*. New York: Charles Scribner's Sons, 1982.

————*The First Air War, 1914-1918*. New York: The Free Press, 1991.

Kerr, E. Bartlett. *Flames over Tokyo: The U.S. Army Air Forces' Incendiary Campaign Against Japan, 1944-1945*. New York: Donald I. Fine, 1991.

Kershaw, Ian. *Hitler 1889-1936: Hubris*. New York: W. W. Norton & Company, 1999.

————*Hitler 1936-1945: Nemesis*. New York: W. W. Norton & Company, 2000.

Kilduff, Peter. *Germany's First Air Force 1914-1918*. Osceola, Wis.: Motorbooks International Publishers, 1991.

King, Ernest J. and Walter Muir Whitehill. *Fleet Admiral King: A Naval Record*. New York: W. W. Norton & Company, 1952.

Kingston-McLoughry, E. J. *War in Three Dimensions: The Impact of Air Power upon the Classical Principles of War*. London: Jonathan Cape, 1949.

Kirkland, Faris R. *The French Air Force in 1940*. Aerospace Power Chronicles. www.airpower.maxwell.af.mil/airchronicles/aureview/1985/Sep-Oct/Kirkland.html.

Kissinger, Henry A. *The White House Years*. Boston: Little, Brown, and Company, 1979.

Lamberton, W. M. and E. F. Cheesman. *Reconnaissance and Bomber Aircraft of the 1914-1918 War*. Letchworth, Herts, U.K.: Harleyford Publications, Ltd., 1962.

Lambeth, Benjamin S. *The Transformation of American Air Power*. Ithaca, N.Y.: Cornell University Press, 2000.

Lauer, Timothy M., Col., and Steven L. Llanso. *Encyclopedia of Modern U.S. Military Weapons*. New York: Berkley Books, 1995.

LeMay, Curtis E. with Mackinlay Kantor. *Mission with LeMay*. New York: Doubleday, 1965.

Littauer, Raphael and Norman Uphoff, eds. *The Air War in Indochina*. Boston: Beacon Press, 1972.

Lloyd, Alwyn T. *A COLD WAR LEGACY—A Tribute to Strategic Air Command 1946-1992.* Missoula, Mont.: Pictorial Histories, 2000.

Loftin, Laurence K. Jr. *Quest for Performance: The Evolution of Modern Aircraft.* Washington, D.C.: National Aeronautics and Space Administration, 1985.

Lundstrom, John B. *The First Team: Pacific Naval Air Combat from Pearl Harbor to Midway.* Annapolis, Md.: Naval Institute Press, 1984.

———*The First Team and the Guadalcanal Campaign.* Annapolis, Md.: Naval Institute Press, 1994.

Mahan, Alfred Thayer. *The Influence of Sea Power upon History, 1660-1783.* New York: Hill and Wang, 1957.

Maravigna, Pietor. *The First War Flights in the World, Libia MCMXI* Rome: Historical Division of the Italian Air Force, 1953.

March, Cyril, ed. *The Rise and Fall of the German Air Force, 1933-1945.* London: Her Majesty's Stationery Office, 1983.

Mark, Eduard. *Aerial Interdiction in Three Wars.* Washington, D.C.: Center for Air Force History, 1994.

Massie, Robert K. *Dreadnought: Britain, Germany and the Coming of the Great War.* New York: Random House, 1991.

———*Nicholas and Alexandra.* New York: Dell, 1967.

Mason, Tony, Air Vice Marshal. *Air Power: A Centennial Appraisal.* London: Brassey's, 1994.

Maurer, Maurer, ed. *Aviation in the U.S. Army, 1919-1939.* Washington, D.C.; Office of Air Force History, 1987.

———*The U.S. Air Service in World War I* (four volumes). Washington, D.C: Office of Air Force History, 1978

McCarthy, James R , Brig. Gen., and George B. Allison, Lt. Col. *Linebacker II: A View from the Rock.* Maxwell Air Force Base, Ala.: Airpower Research Institute, 1979.

McDonald, Robert A. *Corona Between the Sun and the Earth: The First NRO Reconnaissance Eye in Space.* Bethesda, Md.: American Society for Photogrammetry and Remote Sensing, 1997.

McFarland, Stephen L. and Wesley Phillips Newton. *To Command the Sky: The Battle for Air Superiority over German, 1942-1944.* Washington, D.C.: Smithsonian Institution Press, 1991.

Mead, Peter. *The Eye in the Air.* London: Her Majesty's Stationery Office, 1983.

Meilinger, Phillip S. *Hoyt Vandenberg: The Life of a General.* Bloomington: Indiana University Press, 1989.

————ed., *The Paths of Heaven, the Evolution of Airpower Theory.* Maxwell Air Force Base, Ala.: Air University Press, 1997.

Mersky, Peter and Norman Polmar. *The Naval Air War in Vietnam.* Annapolis, Md.: The Nautical and Aviation Publishing Company of America, 1981.

Mesko, Jim. *Airmobile: The Helicopter War in Vietnam.* Carrollton, Tex.: Squadron/Signal Publication, Inc., 1984.

Mets, David R. *Master of Airpower: General Carl A. Spaatz.* Novato, Calif.: Presidio Press, 1988.

The Military Balance, 1970-1971. London: Institute for Strategic Studies, 1970.

Miller, Jerry. *Nuclear Weapons and Aircraft Carriers.* Washington, D.C.: Smithsonian Institution Press, 2001.

Miller, Ronald and David Sawers. *The Technical Development of Modern Aviation.* New York: Praeger, 1970.

Momyer, William W., Gen. *Air Power in Three Wars: WWII, Korea, Vietnam.* Washington, D.C.: Department of the Air Force, 1978.

Moody, Walton S. *Building a Strategic Air Force.* Washington, D.C.: Air Force History and Museums Program, 1996.

Morison, Samuel Eliot. *History of United States Naval Operations in the Second World War* (fifteen volumes). Boston: Atlantic-Little Brown, 1947-1962.

Morrocco, John. *Thunder From Above: Air War, 1941-1968.* Boston: Boston Publishing Company, 1984.

Morrow, John H. Jr. *The Great War in the Air: Military Aviation from 1909 to 1921.* Washington, D.C.: Smithsonian Institution Press, 1993.

Morse, Stan, ed. *Gulf Air War Debrief: Described by the Pilots That Fought.* London: Aerospace Publishing, 1991.

Mrozek, Donald J. *The US Air Force After Vietnam (Postwar Challenges and Potential for Responses).* Maxwell Air Force Base, Ala.: Air University Press, 1988.

Murphy, Paul, ed. *The Soviet Air Forces.* Jefferson, N.C.: McFarland & Co., 1984.

Murray, Williamson. *Luftwaffe.* Baltimore: The Nautical and Aviation Publishing Company of America, 1985.

————*Air War in the Persian Gulf.* Baltimore: The Nautical and Aviation Publishing Company of America, 1995.

Nalty, Bernard C., ed. *War in the Pacific: Pearl Harbor to Tokyo Bay.* London: Salamander, 1991.

Neufeld, Jacob. *The Development of Ballistic Missiles in the United States Air Force, 1945-1960.* Washington, D.C.: Office of Air Force History, 1990.

———*Reflections on Research and Development in the United States Air Force.* Washington, D.C.: Center for Air Force History, 1993.

Neumann, George P. *The German Air Force in the Great War.* London: Hodder & Stoughton, Ltd., 1921.

New World Vistas: Air and Space Power for the 21st Century (Summary Volume). Department of the Air Force, 1995.

Nordeen, Lon O. Jr. *Air Warfare in the Missile Age.* Washington, D.C.: Smithsonian Institution Press, 1985.

Overy, R. J., Dr. *The Air War 1939-1945.* New York: Stein and Day Pub., 1981.

Parrish, Thomas. *The Ultra Americans: The U.S. Role in Breaking the Nazi Codes.* Briarcliff Manor, N.Y.: Stein & Day, 1986.

———*The Cold War Encyclopedia.* New York: Henry Holt, 1996.

Parton, James. *Air Force Spoken Here: General Ira Eaker and the Command of The Air.* Bethesda, Md.: Adler & Adler, 1986.

Payne, Lee. *Lighter than Air, An Illustrated History of the Airship.* New York: Orion Books, 1991.

Peattie, Mark R. *Sunburst, the Rise of Japanese Naval Air Power, 1909-1941.* Annapolis, Md.: Naval Institute Press, 2001.

Penrose, Harald. *British Aviation: The Great War and Armistice.* New York: Funk & Wagnalls, 1969.

———*British Aviation: The Pioneer Years.* London: Putnam, 1967.

———*British Aviation: The Adventurous Years.* London: Putnam, 1973.

Pocock, Rowland F. *German Guided Missiles of the Second World War.* New York: Arco Publishing Co., 1967.

Pogue, Forrest C. *George C. Marshall: Ordeal and Hope, 1939-1942, Vol. 1* (three volumes). New York: Viking Press, 1966.

Polmar, Norman and Timothy Laurer. *Strategic Air Command.* Baltimore: The Nautical and Aviation Publishing Company of America, 1970.

Potter, E. B. *Nimitz.* Annapolis, Md.: Naval Institute Press, 1976.

Potter, E. B. and Chester W. Nimitz, eds. *The Great Sea War.* New York: Bramhall House, 1960.

Powaski, Ronald E. *Return to Armageddon: The United States and the Nuclear Arms Race, 1981-1999.* New York: Oxford University Press, 2000.

Price, Alfred. *Instruments of Darkness.* London: Janes, 1982.

Probert, Henry. *Bomber Harris: His Life and Times.* London: Greenhill Books, 2001.

Proctor, Raymond L. *Hitler's Luftwaffe in the Spanish Civil War.* Westport, Conn.: Greenwood Press, 1983.

Raleigh, Walter and H. A. Jones. *The War in the Air* (six volumes). Oxford: Clarendon, 1922-37.

Ravenstein, Charles A. *The Organization and Lineage of the United States Air Force.* Washington, D.C.: Office of Air Force History, 1986.

Reynolds, Clark G. *The Fast Carrier: The Forging of the Air Navy.* Annapolis, Md: Naval Institute Press, 1992.

Richards, Denis. *Portal of Hungerford.* London: Heineman, 1978.

Richards, Denis and Hilary St. George Saunders. *Royal Air Force 1939-45* (three volumes). London: Her Majesty's Stationery Office, 1953, 1954, 1955.

Robinson, Douglas H. *The Zeppelin in Combat.* Atglen, Pa.: Schiffer Publishing Company, 1994.

Roskill, S. W. *The War at Sea 1939-1945.* London: Her Majesty's Stationery Office, 1954.

Royal Air Force Air Historical Branch. *The Royal Air Force in the Great War.* London: The Imperial War Museum, 1936.

Saunders, Hilary St. George. *Per Ardua: The Rise of British Air Power, 1911-1939.* New York: Arno Press, 1972.

Schaffel, Kenneth. *The Emerging Shield: The Air Force and Continental Air Defense, 1945-1960.* Washington, D.C.: Office of Air Force History, 1998.

Schaller, Michael. *Douglas MacArthur: The Far Eastern General.* New York: Oxford University Press, 1989.

Scharr, Adela Rick. *Sisters in the Sky: The WAFS.* Gerald, Mo.: Patrice Press, 1986.

Schlight, John. *The War in South Vietnam: The Years of the Offensive, 1965-1968.* Washington, D.C.: Office of Air Force History, 1988.

Schmidt, Paul. *Hitler's Interpreter.* London: William Heinemann, 1951.

Searby, John. *The Bomber Battle for Berlin.* Shrewsbury, U.K.: Airlife, 1991.

Sherrod, Robert. *History of Marine Corps Aviation in World War II.* Washington, D.C.: Combat Force Press, 1952.

Shumikhin, V. S. *Sovetskaia voennaia aviatsiia 1917-1941.* Moscow:

Izdatel'stvo Nauka, Institute voennoi istorii Ministerstva oborony SSR, 1996.

Slessor, Sir John, Marshal of the Royal Air Force. *The Central Blue.* London: Cassell, 1956.

Sloan, James J. Jr. *Wings of Honor: American Airmen in World War I.* Atglen, Pa.: Schiffer Publishing Company, 1994.

Spaight, J. M. *The Beginnings of Organized Air Power.* London: Longmans, Green and Co., 1927.

Speer, Albert. *Inside the Third Reich.* New York: Macmilllan, 1970.

Strategic Air Command History Office. *From Snark to Peacekeeper: A Pictorial History of Strategic Air Command Missiles.* Offutt Air Force Base, Nebr.: Office of the Historian, Headquarters Strategic Air Command, 1990.

Sturm, Thomas A. *The USAF Scientific Advisory Board: Its First Twenty Years, 1944-1964.* Washington, D.C.: Office of Air Force History, New Imprint, 1986.

Suchenwirth, Richard. *USAF Historical Studies No. 160: The Development of the German Air Force, 1919-1939.* New York: Arno Press, 1970.

Swanborough, Gordon and Peter M. Bowers. *United States Military Aircraft Since 1909.* Washington, D.C.: Smithsonian Institution Press, 1989.

————*United States Navy Aircraft Since 1911.* New York: Funk & Wagnalls, 1968.

Sweetman, Bill and Bill Gunston. *Soviet Air Power.* London: Leisure Books, 1978.

Taylor, Theodore. *The Magnificent Mitscher.* New York: W. W. Norton Co., 1954.

Tedder, Marshal of the Royal Air Force Arthur, Lord. *With Prejudice.* London: Cassell, 1966.

Termena, Bernard J., Layne B. Peiffer, and H. P. Carlin. *Logistics: An Illustrated History of AFLC and its Antecedents, 1921-1981.* Wright-Patterson Air Force Base, Ohio: Headquarters, Air Force Logistics Command.

Terraine, John A. *A Time For Courage: The Royal Air Force in the European War, 1939-1945.* New York: Macmillan, 1985.

Thetford, Owen. *British Naval Aircraft Since 1912.* London: Putnam, 1977.

Thompson, Jonathan. *Italian Civil and Military Aircraft, 1930-1945.* Los Angeles: Aero Publishers, 1963.

Tilford, Earl H. Jr. *Search and Rescue in Southeast Asia, 1961-1975*. Washington, D.C.: Office of Air Force History, 1980.

————*Setup: What the Air Force Did in Vietnam and Why*. Maxwell Air Force Base, Ala.: Air University Press, 1991.

Tolson, John J., Lt. Gen. *Vietnam Studies: Airmobility, 1961-1971*. Washington, D.C.: Department of the Army, 1973.

Treadwell, Terry C. and Alan C. Wood. *Airships of the First World War*. Stroud, Gloucestershire, U.K.: Tempus Publishing Limited, 1999.

Tucker, Spencer, ed. *Encyclopedia of the Vietnam War*. Santa Barbara, Calif.: ABC-Clio, 1998.

Van Staaveren, Jacob. *Interdiction in Southern Laos, 1960-1968*. Washington, D.C.: Center for Air Force History, 1993.

Wagner, Ray, ed. *The Soviet Air Force in World War II: The Official History*. Translated by Leland Fetzer. Garden City, N.Y.: Doubleday, 1973.

————*Mustang Designer*. New York: Orion Books, 1990.

Warden, John A., III. *The Air Campaign (Planning for Combat)*. Washington, D.C.: National Defense University Press, 1988.

Watson, George M. Jr. *The Office of the Secretary of the Air Force, 1947-1965*. Washington, D.C.: Center for Air Force History, 1993.

Webster, C. and Noble Frankland. *The Strategic Air Offensive Against Germany, 1939-1945*. London: Her Majesty's Stationery Office, 1961.

Weisgall, Jonathan M. *Operation Crossroads, the Atomic Tests at Bikini Atoll*. Annapolis, Md.: Naval Institute Press, 1994.

Werrell, Kenneth P. *The Evolution of the Cruise Missile*. Maxwell Air Force Base, Ala.: Air University Press, 1985.

————*Archie, Flak, AAA, and SAM: A Short Operational History of Ground-Based Air Defense*. Maxwell Air Force Base, Ala.: Air University Press, 1988.

————*Blankets of Fire*. Washington, D.C.: Smithsonian Institution Press, 1996.

Williams, Al. *Airpower*. New York: Coward-McCann, 1940.

Winter, J. M. *The Experience of World War I*. New York: Oxford University Press, 1989.

Wolf, Richard I. *United States Air Force Basic Documents on Roles and Missions*. Washington, D.C.: Office of Air Force History, 1987.

Wolk, Herman S. *Planning and Organizing the Postwar Air Force, 1943-1947*. Washington, D.C.: Office of Air Force History, 1984.

Wood, Derek with Derek Dempster. *The Narrow Margin*. London: Arrow Books, 1969.

Wragg, David. *The Offensive Weapon: The Strategy of Bombing*. London: Robert Hale, 1986.

Y'Blood, William T. *The Little Giants: U.S. Escort Carriers Against Japan*. Annapolis, Md.: U.S. Naval Institute, 1987.

Yonay, Ehud. *No Margin for Error: The Making of the Israeli Air Force*. New York: Pantheon Books, 1993.

Index